CW01025022

BEYOND DISPUTE

Dedicated to
THE OPEN MIND

Qui prius respondet quam audiat stultum se esse demonstrat et confusione dignum
—Proverbiorum Liben 18:13 (*Vulgate*)

He that answereth a matter before he heareth it, it is a folly and shame unto him.
—Book of Proverbs 18:13 (*King James*)

The Managerial Cybernetics of Organization

BEYOND DISPUTE
The Invention of
Team Syntegrity

Stafford Beer

JOHN WILEY & SONS
Chichester • New York • Brisbane • Toronto • Singapore

Published 1994 by John Wiley & Sons Ltd,
Baffins Lane, Chichester,
West Sussex PO19 1UD, England

Telephone (+44) 243 779777

Other Wiley Editorial Offices

John Wiley & Sons, Inc., 605 Third Avenue,
New York, NY 10158-0012, USA

Jacaranda Wiley Ltd, 33 Park Road, Milton,
Queensland 4064, Australia

John Wiley & Sons (Canada) Ltd, 22 Worcester Road,
Rexdale, Ontario M9W 1L1, Canada

John Wiley & Sons (SEA) Pte Ltd, 37 Jalan Pemimpin #05-04,
Block B, Union Industrial Building, Singapore 2057

Library of Congress Cataloging-in-Publication Data

Beer, Stafford.
    Beyond dispute: the invention of team syntegrity / Stafford Beer.
        p. cm. — (The Managerial cybernetics of organization)
    Includes bibliographical references and index.
    ISBN 0-471-94451-3
    1. Organization. 2. Organizational behavior. 3. Cybernetics.
    4. Work groups I. Title. II. Series.
    HD38.B3627 1994   94–2439
    658.4′02—dc20   CIP

British Library Cataloguing in Publication Data

A catalogue record for this book is available from the British Library

ISBN 0-471-94451-3

Typeset in 10/12pt Times by
Mathematical Compositions Setters Ltd., Salisbury, Wiltshire.
Printed and bound in Great Britain by Bookcraft (Bath) Ltd.

CONTENTS

PREFACE

This book is new in every sense, although it is issued under the usual generic heading of my books: *The Managerial Cybernetics of Organization*. Why do I persist in using a word that has finally penetrated the wall of public unknowing in the grotesque shapes of cybermen and cyborgs, and whose original and inspirational meaning wanders like a lost shade through the groves of an uncomprehending academe? It is because a reductionist world badly needs its holistic message: a science of the regulation of large, complex probabilistic systems actually exists that is interdisciplinary in approach and consequently inclusive in its world view.

Society today is wracked with difficulties throughout the world that have been engendered by tunnel visions of a fragmented whole. Perceptions of the bits and pieces are fixed in a mosaic that is set in a matrix of dogma. Then the epistemology of cybernetics is needed to discern a different pattern, and humanity cannot afford to ignore its discoveries indefinitely. Of course, those discoveries are hard to communicate to people entrenched in the battlefield between outmoded paradigms: they have to lift their eyes to see a new horizon. Meanwhile there is a duty to preserve and develop insights and techniques in which so much investment has been made over half a century. This is one such contribution: the theory of team syntegrity, and the social technique of syntegration.

Warren McCulloch (1898–1969) was one of the founders of cybernetics. The final piece that he wrote was published posthumously (McCulloch, 1974). He said of cybernetics: 'It was born in 1943, christened in 1948, and came of age ... in the early 1960s. In its short majority it has certainly done best for those fields where it was conceived. It has been a challenge to logic and to mathematics, an inspiration to neurophysiology and to the theory of automata, including artificial intelligence, and bionics or robotology. To the social sciences it is still mere suspiration.' But McCulloch believed managerial cybernetics to be possible even so. This is why he gave it his attention, and why we became friends, and why he used the word suspire—which means 'to sigh, to breathe, to utter with sighing breaths.'

Another founder, Norbert Wiener, held similar views. He wrote in the introduction to his seminal book *Cybernetics* (Wiener, 1948) that McCulloch had 'rightly seen the psychological and sociological implications of the subject, and had co-opted into the group a number of leading psychologists, sociologists, and anthropologists.' He himself went on to write *The Human Use of Human Beings* (Wiener, 1954), a noted work of social humanism.

The next question that might be asked is: if interdisciplinary cybernetics has been hard at work for half a century, and has such value, why are its achievements not generally acknowledged? The answer is that they *are* acknowledged, but are unrecognized to be what they are. Once essentially interdisciplinary discoveries are made, but only then, can they be categorized to fit academic taxonomy that could not even have conceived of them beforehand. McCulloch's collaborator Walter Pitts was credited with the remark that problems are either trivial or insoluble—and an insoluble problem is trivial once it has been solved.

Another of the pioneers, Heinz von Foerster, wrote the Preface to McCulloch's *Collected Works* (McCulloch, 1989). He says there: 'For the pursuit of one of his (McCulloch's) ideas alone, neural-nets-as-parallel-computers, the government of the United States has set aside no less than $300 million for research on this topic over the next six years.' The current beneficiaries of this grant, aided by computer search procedures, are probably aware of those early papers, but it seems unlikely that they realize how astonishing it was in 1943 to have someone writing about a logical calculus of the ideas immanent in nervous activity (McCulloch and Pitts, 1943). Neurophysiologists did not talk much about logic at that time (when I myself was an undergraduate student of both neurophysiology and logic) and logicians were completely indifferent to the way brains work. As to computers and neural nets ... the world's first stored-program electronic computer ran at Manchester University five years *later* (21st June 1948) for the first time.

The arguments in this book are interdisciplinary: they derive from biology as well as physics ('the animal and the machine', in Wiener's phrase), from psychology as well as engineering, and pervasively, from mathematics and philosophy. Whether this whole is greater than the sum of these parts depends largely on the reader and his or her interests—since we shall be discussing relevancies as far apart, ostensibly, as company management and the nature of consciousness. This is sufficient indication that much remains to be done. In fact, potential graduate projects seem to jump out of every paragraph, and the arms grow numb to contemplate the weight of all those dissertations. But on the evidence adduced above, all this could take a long, long time to mature.

All I can do now is to launch a new idea. I hope that it will be seized upon and used, because it works in practice, and offers a potent management tool for developmental planning.

I have put matters forward in narrative form in the hope that the offerings will be palatable, and at a level of explanation that I hope will also make them digestible. But I am in no doubt that my cybernetic aims are ambitious; the dedication of this book was chosen with that in mind, and with a cheerful heart, and with particular reference to Part Four.

Above all, I propose a theory and a technique which McCulloch might regard as advancing into the social sciences a little beyond 'mere suspiration.' Sigh no more, Warren, sigh no more ... He at least knows the rest of that quotation, and is smiling.

Stafford Beer
Toronto
5th October 1993

ACKNOWLEDGEMENTS

There have been times when the efforts surrounding the developments recorded here seemed to have the dimensions of a cottage industry, and I am greatly indebted to a host of collaborators. Invidious as it may be, I wish to mention some by name.

First comes the group who have provided the fascinating Part Five of the book, Collaborators' Surplus. Outstandingly, Dr. Assad Jalali of the European Business Management School at University College, Swansea, Wales, undertook the careful mathematical investigation published here; and Joe Truss, President of Team Syntegrity, Inc., whose name is often but probably insufficiently mentioned, has probed into the spatial geometrics of the icosahedron (and many more polyhedra) with both vigour and rigour ever since the happy day when we first met and the project attracted his instant enthusiasm. Alan Pearson and Dr David Beatty, both of Toronto, are old friends and collaborators in projects antedating syntegrity by many years and I am most grateful for their steady friendship and their current contributions. Josephine Hancock, who is also in Wales at University College, Swansea, is building her doctoral thesis around her work reported here: thank you, Jo, for both the algorithms reported. This leaves my partner, Dr Allenna Leonard, who teaches managerial cybernetics and has written some here. My debt to her goes far beyond the debt already evident to others.

Next I want to thank my collaborators 'in the field:' Dr Marcus Schwaninger of St. Gallen University in Switzerland; Denis Adams at the Business School and Dr Roger Harnden in the Multimedia Centre of Liverpool John Moores University, and David Sutton of System Six, all in England; David Schecter at Pacific Bell near San Francisco, USA; all of these have been responsible for running pioneering syntegrations. Roger Golten, in England, has made many elaborately handpainted models, while William Perk, in Illinois, has a kit with edges five feet long in which participants may learn the 'inside story' of the icosahedron. Then come those, mentioned in the text, who played major roles in the Toronto syntegrations: Amanda Brown, Boris Freesman QC, and Wendy Walsh, plus Mike Mussington—who has also done other (electronic) things.

Four other people in particular have provided most valuable comments and suggestions about this book: Dr Donald Burrill and Susan Francis in Toronto, Professor Robert Vallée in Paris, and Diane Bowling in England. I thank them for making such an effort on my behalf and hope they will excuse me for not adopting their every proposal. If inadequacies remain, it is likely to be because I ignored some of their good advice.

There are sponsoring organizations for whose support I have been grateful. Three academic bases in Britain have all been active in these developments: the Business School at Manchester University, where I have been Visiting Professor for 25 years and which housed the first two syntegrations; at Liverpool John Moores University, which houses the Stafford Beer Collection; and at the University of Wales in Swansea, where most of my teaching is done, and where Professor Bryn Gravenor and his faculty have shown much interest in these ideas. The Ontario Institute for Studies in Education also provided a home for syntegrations in Toronto. I thank them all, as also Garry Davis, President of the World Service Authority based in Washington, DC, for the initial stimulus and subsequent contract that metabolized theory into action. Finally under this heading comes my dear friend David Whittaker, who as a bookseller in Oxford may not exactly think of himself as a sponsor of anything. His knowledge of books, and their rapid acquisition is, however, making him indispensible to a growing cluster of interdisciplinarians.

Finally, there are two friends from whose knowledge, insight, and care I benefit, and this work has benefited as well through many conversations. They are Dr Charles Gregory of Vancouver, psychiatrist extraordinary, and Jerry Meek of Northumberland, extraordinary.

THE STORY OF AN ORGANIZATIONAL IDEA

Chapter One

A LONG GESTATION

Master and slave, squire and servant, boss and employee, ruling classes and proletariat ... the notion of hierarchy is endemic to the human experience of social system. And yet it seems never to suffice as an organizing principle. Ways are always found to supplement, indeed to enrich, the simply autocratic 'chain of command.'

As a young staff officer at the end of World War 2, I was startled to find the extent to which I carried the Area Commander's clout, although I soon discovered that the purview was limited in rather precise ways ... Then there are examples from long-lived institutions other than armies. The management of the Roman Catholic Church is actually known as 'the hierarchy'; and yet so strong and inflexible an organization is interpenetrated by the influence of monastic orders to major effect—as the history of the Second Vatican Council testifies. So much in this vein is known to social anthropology that it is sad to be given the typical organization chart put out by business or a government department. There stands the usual 'family tree' in all its unsubtlely: a mere instrument for discovering who is to blame. The most sophisticated addendum that we are likely to find is a pattern of dotted lines in the horizontal plane indicating mysterious liaisons—committees of cousins, maybe.

informal networks

And yet serious work has been going on for many years in examining non-hierarchic solutions to the general problem of regulatory systems, which has resulted in practical spin-off: outcomes range from the creation of presidential offices to neighbourhood cooperatives. These are real, and effective, but perhaps fairly pragmatic in design. It might be advantageous to have a more rigorous theory. At any rate, there seems to be a steadily increasing need to offer a new focus for discussion and possible development.

The main reasons are the international trend away from centralization; a growing repugnance towards the very concept of hierarchy detectable in public debate; and the increasing elimination of what used to be called middle-management activity by automation. This has led to the phenomenon of 'plateauing,' or 'flat management' structure, in which few positions are senior to any other. The social consequences outside the organization may well be dire; but the more immediate consequences have to do with creating new ways of working, that I shall call protocols, for operating the new kinds of organizational structure. And how indeed shall they themselves be described?

The purpose here is to recount and to record a process that began nearly 40 years ago, flared into considerable activity 20 years ago, and occupied me throughout 1990 in a series of five major experiments. It is not a comparative study. I am well aware of many other approaches, and reference notably Kelly's Personal Construct Theory and Repertory Grid Technique (Kelly, 1955), which seems to me most valuable, and the various forms of matrix organization, which do not. The reasons that led me down the routes actually followed had to do with the place occupied by these matters in the context of all my other work, as both manager and consultant, rather than in academic appraisal.

THE START

At the time of my first civilian appointment in the steel industry in 1950 (heading operational research) we had no computers. But we also had little in the way of scientific process control. Pyrometry, for example, was no more than an experimental science in dealing with temperature control on the shop floor. With the help of expert workers, I had learned how to control a Bessemer converter by watching the colour and shape of the sparks blown off as the iron was purified into steel. In the rail mill, the experts judged the rolling temperature by throwing little bundles of twigs onto the steel and watching them ignite; in the billet mill they simply spat on the hot slabs instead. They were all very accurate and they had not a single qualification between them. They were the workforce. Their managers could not do these jobs ... Hierarchy?

Trying to model this kind of situation was not easy. The new science of cybernetics had recently been officially born: in the Proceedings of the Eighth Conference on Cybernetics appeared an attempt to describe various kinds of social structure as networks in a Euclidean plane space—it was the work of Alex Bavelas (Bavelas, 1952). It looks mathematically simplistic in these days of graph-theoretic insight, but it was the first time that I had seen any proposal of a rigorous kind, and so made much use of it.

Bavelas devised three measures for quantifying the organizational pattern. The first is Group Dispersion. Take each member of a network, and count the minimal number of steps it takes (according to the protocol established) to reach every other member. Some will be one step away. To reach others, one might need to ascend and descend various hierarchical ladders. That count for one member is his/her minimal connectivity. Having made the count for every person, add up the results. This is now an unequivocal measure of the extent to which the group is dispersed.

Each member now has a personal Relative Centrality. To calculate this, divide the Group Dispersion by the minimal connectivity of the individual.

Third, the measure of Peripherality for member Fred Bloggs is the Relative Centrality of the most central member, minus Bloggs's own.

Using these three measures made possible the theoretical investigation of paradoxes that seem to underlie attempts to adjust protocol, and as many empirical checks as could be made were made (recall that this was done in a real-life OR context and not under laboratory research conditions). In particular, the impact of protocol on morale is important. The central paradox resides in this: morale is improved by diminishing Peripheral isolation, but adjustments to Relative Centrality to achieve this lack efficiency and inhibit the emergence of leadership. And here we are, 40 years on, observing exactly this phenomenon in cooperatives under observation in Britain—not to mention the inverse effect in the Baltic States.

The original considerations and conclusions were presented to the First International Conference on Cybernetics, held in Namur, Belgium, in 1956 (Beer, 1956). Four embryonic models of a non-hierarchic kind were then put forward.

One of these models was drawn from servomechanics. 'Most progressive action in industry is driven forward by the organization using the positive feedbacks of formal [supportive] sanctions and informal encouragement,' I wrote. 'Most catastrophes in the field of industrial development, as well as in the sphere of routine production, are averted by the organization using the negative feedbacks of criticism and inspection respectively.' Ratios were developed that isolated technical factors in the productivity equation from the interplay of all the other personal and social considerations that generate shop-floor reality. Let us call the latter 'systemic' factors, insofar as they are outputs of the system-we-have. A simple model distinguishing between technical and systemic unit step functions of displacement in a steady-state system enabled a study of transient behaviour to be made.

In particular, I had examined the impact of incentive schemes as a means of raising productivity, considered as triggering servo-systems: there was a negative correlation between the technical and residual systemic components. In this lay an explanation as to why 'some incentive schemes "freeze," while others "run away".' The transient behaviour of the mixed technical/systemic stability was such that crude technically based incentives either confirmed inefficiency in setting up a barrier to the change of state, or caused production to increase in an uncontrolled way by destabilizing the system itself.

Another model proposed on these 'network' bases at the 1956 Namur Conference was drawn from entropy. After all, in a fully connected organiz-ational network, Relative Centralities tend to equality. Entropy rises, and less energy is available to work the system. But if the organization be centralized, in order to liberate that energy, Group Dispersion increases, and a terrible loss of morale will be associated with the ensuing Peripheral Ignorance. Over 35 years after Namur, the Soviet Union finally acknowledged that point. In the meantime, this work was the origin of the theory of autonomy eventually advanced in *The Heart of Enterprise* (Beer, 1979). But I had already been profoundly influenced by Wiener's demonstration (Wiener, 1948) that infor-mation is formally equivalent to negative entropy, as the Namur paper states. Western bloc countries and their financial institutions are taking even longer to acknowledge *that* point and to grapple with its consequences for the Third World.

Some space was devoted at Namur to yet a third model: it sought to quantify the networks under discussion by propagating stochastic processes (and in particular messages considered as Markovian self-avoiding random walks) through organizations depicted as transitional probability matrices. The main lessons learned at that time (which were recognized later as manifestations of Ashby's Law of Requisite Variety) had to do with the nature of organizational structure as a variety inhibitor. If N people are engaged in a network, and the passage of some form of message involves any unspecified number of them, then the number of ways in which the group could behave is approximately $eN!$. If the network has only ten people, that number of possible arrangements reaches nearly ten million. Constraints were imposed on this preposterous proliferation of messages by inserting barriers representing organizational rules, depicted in the simulations (pre-computer, recall) as Boolean functions. Even so, we could not stop the messages from reverberating (rumour, gossip, folklore?) until a 'dead man' was installed in the system. He did not pass any message to anyone, and came to be recognized as a familiar bureaucratic persona. I mention with affection that this uncoffined corpse was the invention of Michael Aczel.

Some years later, and based on these experiments, an analysis was developed of the standard hierarchic protocol in which senior people may reach *any* junior person in one step, whereas a junior person must appeal to *each* more senior level in turn in order to reach an eventual boss. Trying to adjust the organizational design to optimize centrality for everyone resulted in a theorem proving that half the people (plus one) are in the bottom echelon. It has never been clear to me whether this result offered a powerful insight, or whether it is a trivial mathematical artifact of the protocol itself. It was for safety's sake never published.

All of these models greatly influenced the development of a cybernetic approach to management (Beer, 1959). But the fourth of the models, which was presented first, was based on neurophysiology and the nature of synaptic transmission. It was this which developed into a set-theoretic model of the brain as an exemplar of management (Beer, 1962), and eventually became the first of the books (Beer, 1972) dealing with the Viable System Model (Beer, 1972, 1979, 1981, 1985; Espejo and Harnden, 1989). It is germane to the work described here as Team Syntegrity to note that these models are all based on interlocking homeostatic subsystems, and are non-hierarchic in character for that reason—contrary to the critiques of some rather casual readers. The essential idea was that the brain is engaged in balancing the reports it has in the sensory and motor cortices, so that action will be continuously appropriate to appearance. This approach belongs to the philosophies of subjective idealism, in that it contemplates internal rather than external 'realities.'

The 1956 paper, having proposed this normative theory of management, was led to a final set of reflections on its psychopathology in overwork, shock, trauma, and neurosis. All of these presenting symptoms have been apparent in these cybernetic enquiries ever since, not least in the five 1990 experiments in Team Syntegrity to be described later.

CATEGORIES AND PRIORITIES

Throughout the 1960s and 1970s of my experience, it became more and more clear that whatever one might do to undermine hierarchy and autocracy in structural terms, in political protocol, or in social rubric, powerful influences tended to maintain the *status quo ante*. It has to be accepted as a cynosure of the human condition that the pursuit of power is ubiquitous and prevailing. Well and good: utopia is indeed, as says its name, the nowhere place. But it pays to reflect on the extent to which our very way of speaking—never mind cupidity—underwrites the system that needs reform.

If people gather to discuss the existing state of affairs, with a view to creating a new vision of the future, they begin by acknowledging the accepted categories by which those affairs are discussed. They speak of health, education, and welfare—just as if it were not the same person who is well or ill, literate or not, nurtured or abandoned. In each profession, the same reductionism applies. It is possible to be attended by various doctors, or lawyers, or accountants, or teachers, to each of whom one is separately accountable—just as if it were not the same person who had gout and epilepsy, malfeasance and tort, cash flows and taxes, syntax and simultaneous equations ... never mind the same person who suffers from all of these things at once. Each of us is stretched out on a Procrustean bed of society's devising. Small wonder that sages universally point out that spiritual freedom lies only in abnegating the whole structure, and wandering away. The sages are right. Meanwhile, business affairs and government must be conducted.

Then we should ask ourselves this question:

how shall we ever conceive
however express
a new idea
if we are bound by the categorization
that delivered our problem to us
in the first place
?

There is a supplementary issue to this denial of fixed agenda. Even if we were to agree that agenda actually exist—that there are topics to be named that ought to be discussed—in what order should they be taken?

Pliny the Younger wrote a letter (Book VIII, letter xiv) to fellow Senator Titius Aristo about the fate of a prisoner not yet judged. If he were guilty, he could be sentenced either to death or to exile. Pliny elucidated the fact that it made a difference if one first decided on guilt or innocence, and then on the sentence—or vice versa. The argument is a treasure of subtle reason. Crude manipulators of agenda in politics, academia, and business today are not nearly so clever, but may be twice as corrupting. 'Let us get our priorities right' is a common cry. Yet in a holistic account of an interactive system, the cry makes no sense. Shall we build roads to converge on a hospital, and then, having run out of money, fail to build the hospital itself; or shall we first build a hospital in the desert, and run out of money trying to make it accessible? The dilemma merely illustrates the point, but actual incidents as bizarre as this are commonplace in the developing world.

Then a technique is needed that recognizes that if a meeting sets out with agenda, it has structured the whole outcome in advance. Anything truly novel has two minutes as Any Other Business. Second, the meeting is merely a series of platforms for those who determined the agenda on which to ride their familiar hobby horses. Third, the requirement to put the agenda in order says something (perhaps complicated) about the priorities of the organizers rather than the exigencies of the problem. These arrangements work well enough for purposes of routine management; but we have been talking about directional planning. In that case, they do not work at all.

The technique proposed is called the Problem Jostle.

THE PROBLEM JOSTLE: PROVENANCE

Meetings with no agenda must generate their own; and they must generate their own categories too—amid much exhortation not to fall back on established ways of talking. A recent protocol for doing this, emerging from the 1990 experiments, is given in detail later. Here are its origins.

Problem Jostling was invented for 'Marlow Seventy,' whereby the 1970 Council of the Operational Research Society redesigned its Constitution under my presidency. Note: small group; definite purpose; open-ended list of outcomes; highly successful (for an account, see Beer, 1979; pp. 490–498). After some more experimental plays, during which it became obvious that the size of the group was critical, the approach was used at the Silver Jubilee Meeting (1979) of the Society for General Systems Research (now the International Society for Systems Sciences) as a means of capturing the informal talk 'Later in the Bar.' The keynote address (Beer, 1980) outlined the plan, and Anthony Judge subsequently made a thoroughgoing analysis of what happened—contributing some potent thoughts of his own about future possibilities (Judge, 1980). Note: group of several hundreds; no definite purpose; open-ended list of outcomes; successful enough to be copied in various conferences around the world.

We had overcome the problem of numbers by the use of facilitators, the continuous public posting of results with further signatories invited, and by a first attempt at statistical cluster analysis. Naturally ('nothing works'), the London University computer broke down and data had to be rerouted around the country, imposing damaging delays, but the experience fired the imagination of many as a liberating agent in the context of the orthodox formality of a prestigious international conference.

In 1984 during my Residency at the McLuhan Centre in the University of Toronto, a major new experiment was attempted, varying various parameters, and deliberately relaxing all constraints. Note: smallish group; hopelessly indefinite purpose such as 'what shall we do?'; totally open ended; whole development of cluster analysis which was intended to pull these very loose threads together had to be abandoned because the computer team failed to deliver (or even appear); not at all successful.

In 1987 I designed a meeting for Premier David Peterson of Ontario, at which some 120 delegates of the Liberal Party, including the parliamentary caucus, met over a long weekend to discuss the future of the Province. Of course, there were no agenda. There were ten facilitators, posting with signatories plus continuous voting; cluster analysis worked (and went on all night). Note: large group in five subgroups interacting; definite purpose; open-ended—47 outcomes were agreed. Cybernetically, this was highly successful. It was marred in its effect. I discovered on my return from a trip that the Friday night launch had been cancelled in favour of political speechmaking, leaving the process to start from cold after breakfast. Despite all cajoling, the delegates from ridings brought their own agenda in their saddlebags ... Finally, the results were not vigorously injected into the government programme: it can never be known if the government would have gone beyond its second term had it acted on its own projected vision. It did not.

The question of critical size, which had haunted this work since the 1950s, was evidenced in the Ontario meeting—and accounted for the division of the total group into interacting subgroups ...

THE INFOSET: PROVENANCE

What makes 'a group' out of a random assortment of people? It surely has to do with motivation, and with what I had earlier been calling morale. I proposed that what brought people into cohesive groups was the shared information that had changed them into purposive individuals. Data themselves do not supply this cohesion: it is the *interpretation* of data that procures purpose, and it is the *shared* interpretation between individuals that procures group cohesion. Thus groups of this kind were nominated as infosets.

The origin of the term INFOSET (Information Set) is found in an unpublished text called *Status Quo* which I wrote in Chile, June–August 1973, while working for President Salvador Allende. The President, working through his Minister Fernando Flores, had invited me to design a regulatory system for the social economy of the country. The story of what we accomplished, with Dr Raul Espejo as the Chief of Staff, is recounted in the last five chapters of *Brain of the Firm* (Beer, 1981). The plot to 'destabilize' Chile is well documented

(US Congress, 1975) and led to the coup of 11th September 1973, during which the President was murdered and many Chileans suffered torture and death.

Now President Allende was a Marxist–Leninist who did not accept the model in use in the USSR. In particular, we were (20 years ago) busily engaged in a decentralizing system of regulation that would use Peripheral knowledge (as defined here) through a whole series of interlocking 'operations rooms,' or management centres. It was indeed by that means that the notorious CIA-financed 'gremio' strike of October 1972 was defeated.

Meanwhile, I had been asked to reconsider the tenets of the government's political philosophy in cybernetic terms. For example, Allende was well aware that the Hegelian concept of the dialectic, used by Marx, was paralleled in the ubiquitous biological mechanism of homeostasis—and the cybernetician Ross Ashby had already evolved a mathematical theory to elucidate this (Ashby, 1952). (It is interesting that both Allende and Ashby, who never met, were originally trained as physicians.)

My idea was to replace the Marxist 'classes' (where the ruling class exploits the proletariat) with a richer and less tendentious categorization based on shared information. 'Exploitation' then becomes the deprivation of information; and the text points out that what are (laughably) called 'the mass media' very often carry

> 'not zero, but *negative* information—insofar as they take away the opportunity to acquire positive information. (The concept is the same as 'opportunity cost' in capitalist economics.)
>
> Now information, in cybernetic terms, is negative entropy; the infosets operate in terms of selection entropy, which absorbs information. If the information is not there, the selections are not possible—that is obvious. What is less obvious is that to feed the people what is effectively negative information, is to feed them *negative negative entropy*, which is to say 'pure' entropy.
>
> It follows that the exploited and alienated classes, with which we began, will lose any sense of revolutionary ferment—because their entropy as a class is rising to the limit of unity ... The new sets, however, identified as they are by their informational characteristics, are negentropy *pumps*—which is to say, by cybernetic definition, potentially revolutionary forces in society.'

I worked sporadically on these ideas for the next 10 years, undertaking a few experiments with people and many more with 'paper machines.' But it was not until I started working with Garry Davis and the notion of world government that the political drive to do something returned. World Government: we required 'potentially revolutionary forces in society' indeed. Davis is the

World War 2 bomber pilot who renounced American citizenship very publicly in 1945, and has ever since worked tirelessly towards his ideal of One World.

No man is an island, maybe. But Garry Davis is not only his own man but also his own Infoset! The rest of us would need structure, but it had to be non-hierarchical; and we would need a procedural protocol, but it had to be non-hieratic. In short, we needed a perfect democracy.

In the *Monadology* of Leibniz, as also in much Eastern teaching, all parts *are* identical because all parts *are* the whole. The notion is wonderful, but difficult to make rigorous. I started with an attempted model through holography, in which the whole picture is reformulated in any broken piece of glass, but could not get a hold via Denis Gabor's mathematics—and he was by then dead. Then I stumbled on an old gift from Buckminster Fuller—an inscribed time map of his own life—and started to think more about his geodesics. I also read again the materials that Anthony Judge had been sending since we met at the Silver Jubilee mentioned above: Tony was pioneering applications of Fuller's work to social science as long ago as 1977, and has special interest in computer environments. And I heard again in my own head Bucky's dictum: all systems are polyhedra. It is an amazing insight.

SYNTEGRITY: PROVENANCE

Fuller formulated the idea that nature exists in an equilibrial balance between the forces of compression and tension. Obviously the existence of both forces was already known, but their collaborative coexistence in all physical systems had not been emphasized. For example, an architectural column is essentially a compressive structure—but vertical pressure creates unnoticed surface tension around the girth. A stressed rope is in tension: it twangs. But if it is not clear that the tension induces compression at right-angles to the pull, stick a finger between the twisted strands of the rope—and then pull ...

Overwhelmingly, architecture has recognized compressive force in obtaining structural stability: the triumph of the arch was to hold the span *up* by pressing the keystone *down*, for example. But the result was that nature set a limit to the clear span of a compressive roofing dome—because of its ever-increasing weight. That limit is about 150 feet. Even then, the forces bearing down are so great that both St Peter's in Rome and St Paul's in London are reinforced by massive iron chains around their circumferences.

In 1948, Buckminster Fuller began by building domes—of which many thousands now exist, and may exceed the 150-foot compression barrier to arbitrary limits—that incorporated his own principle of structural relationship. According to this, the wholeness, the INTEGRITY, of the structure is guaranteed not by the local compressive stresses where structural members are joined together, but by the overall tensile stresses of the entire system. Hence came the portmanteau term for Tensile Integrity: TENSEGRITY.

Now in considering an Infoset and its behaviour, we might well contemplate its tensegrity. After all, Buckminster Fuller argues that it is an omnipresent aspect of nature, and makes a very good case for this indeed (Fuller, 1979). One matter in which (I argue) holistic thinkers ought to agree is that, when a good case for a natural invariant is presented, we are entitled to be excited by a possible advance in human understanding of the natural world and to seek out further examples. On the contrary, say the inherent reductionists (and of course these include many academic specialists), we have no reason whatsoever to compare architectural systems with social systems; and phrases such as 'false analogy' abound.

To these I say, please suspend disbelief. After all, a new carbon molecule was recently discovered—a polyhedron named buckminsterfullerene by gratified chemists. Consider what we know of group behaviour in the sense of an Infoset. Then such a group is consciously struggling to express its integrity, its wholeness; it looks for the *compression* of its shared idea into a cohesive statement, let us say. But it well knows that the popular term 'consensus' is likely to represent merely a lowest common denominator that robs the group of its whole *raison d'être*. It is also aware of *tension*: what else but tension generates discussion, never mind argument? Is this not indeed an exemplar of a Fullerian tensegrity balance?

These considerations led me straight to the notion of logical closure. Tensile integrity suggests that the Infoset already defined by its membership as a closed system (give or take the loss/gain of occasional members), probably *behaves* as a closed system—and gains its tensegrity from that fact. After all, a small group of friends who often discuss (say) politics among themselves, come to know positions—and watch them modify, to a greater or lesser extent! Of course the Infoset is not closed to information: new outside developments are pumped in as the lifeblood of the group's body-politic. But the views that we hear consolidate, gain or lose adherents, subtly change ... these views are REVERBERATING around the closed system. To put the point dramatically: some node within the system propagates an idea, which then bounces round other nodes—and returns (somewhat modified) to hit its progenitors on the back of the neck.

This concept of Reverberation came to mean to me the instrumentality of tensegrity within the Infoset: it generates *synergy*. So when it happened that collaborators discovered Fuller's term tensegrity had been expropriated for commercial use by architects, Boris Freesman suggested that my own emphasis on the synergy attributable to reverberation should be acknowledged. He coined the word syntegrity, which draws together synergistic tensegrity, and Team Syntegrity has been the name for this technique ever since. Of course, it depends on structural closure. So how is an Infoset network to be structurally closed? The Bavelas nets were structurally closed in a Euclidean plane space; but Fullerian domes are essentially three-dimensional. The answer may be found in any convex polyhedron.

The structure that we seek must reflect the notion of a perfect democracy, as was argued before. It surely means that no individual, and initially no cause, should have ascendance over any other. Then in looking for polyhedra on which to construct democratic tensegrity models, we must consider only *regular* polyhedra: figures which have no top, no bottom, no sides—indeed no feature by which they may be specially oriented at all. These regular polyhedra may be distinguished by the number of their faces: the tetrahedron (four), the cube (six), the octahedron (eight), the dodecahedron (twelve), and the icosahedron (twenty). The cube's faces are squares, and the dodecahedron's are pentagons; otherwise, the faces are all equilateral triangles.

THE CONVEX POLYHEDRON AND ITS CLOSURE

According to Euler's law, there is a fixed relationship between the numbers of faces, the number of vertices that the faces define (that is, points where they join), and the number of edges that define the faces. Euler says that the number of faces plus the number of vertices is equal to the number of edges plus two. Then take a look at the models on offer:

Faces + vertices = edges + 2. Totals: No. of edges per vertex

Tetrahedron	4 + 4 = 6 + 2 = 8 : 3
Cube	6 + 8 = 12 + 2 = 14 : 3
Octahedron	8 + 6 = 12 + 2 = 14 : 4
Dodecahedron	12 + 20 = 30 + 2 = 32 : 3
Icosahedron	20 + 12 = 30 + 2 = 32 : 5

Without pursuing all the relevant arguments here, I decided to base my major experiments on the icosahedron, and to consider the edges as representing Infoset members (namely 30) and the vertices as representing topics or key issues (namely 12), with the result that the edges conjoining at each vertex (namely 5) would be protagonists for each topic. There is an indefinite number of ways of doing this modelling, but once these conventions were adopted, the attraction of the icosahedron above the other polyhedra becomes fairly evident. There are no proofs to offer, but there is accumulated knowledge about interpersonal systems.

In the first place, five discussants per topic is a 'good' number whereas three is certainly low. In the tensegrity team, or Infoset, each person has a *responsibility* in the two teams (vertices) that define the ends of his/her edge, which means that one third of the Infoset has direct responsibility in topic formulation and development for any two topics. This is a high Centrality ratio, whilst not being stressful for the member concerned. Next, the fact of 30 members in an Infoset chimes well with experience: 30 guarantees a reasonably high variety of viewpoints, without reproducing too many clones or lookalikes. Moreover, and perhaps for just that reason, 30 people are often, though roughly speaking (a personal observation), the key number of influential members of a management group. A government may have 80–100 ministers, and a 'kitchen cabinet' of 8–10. Perhaps 30 offers a balance of power that has to be seriously considered in order to maintain it.

We are left with the residual fact that in such a scheme there will be 12, exactly 12, topics ... This sounds like imposing a straitjacket. The more this was reviewed via the experiments the more obvious it became that the number is arbitrary. Any number of topics may be contracted or expanded to 12 by sensible drafting. What matters is whether 12 topics are sufficiently discriminatory—neither swamping us with 'the world is a mess' on the one hand, or boring us for a lifetime with 'the 793rd item is the drainage system in the Priscelli Mountains.' It was a clear judgment of experience by many, the participants in the 1990 experiments, that 12 topics made for rich discrimination but were not by their mere numbers overwhelming.

Thus it is that physical icosahedral models have been springing up in many contexts and sizes in many parts of the world just recently. And since every edge represents a person belonging to two teams, many of these models are coloured in 12 hues. There is a Ms Red–Yellow, who belongs to both the red and the yellow topics, and a Mr Silver–Gold whose 'edge' lands in both the silver and gold vertices. Many people have newly begun to study the works of the great R. Buckminster Fuller; and this is the time to mention a wonderful synopsis for those daunted by the massive and difficult volumes of his already referenced. 'The Synergetic Geometry of R. Buckminster Fuller' is the subtitle of this slim volume. Please consult the references (Edmondson, 1987) for the title itself, which I find it hard to write down ...

The icosahedron already exhibits tensegrity: it is a remarkably strong structure. In his never-ending search for 'more with less' improvements, however, Bucky elaborated its shell with sets of triangles implanted within the triangles of the icosahedral faces, and thereby created a kind of extra skin to reinforce his domes. He wanted to keep the internal space inviolate: because the idea was to live, exhibit, or otherwise operate *inside* the geodesic dome. No such inhibition is exerted on the designer of a Team Syntegrity, for whom the internal icosahedral space is purely notional. This space is fascinating in itself: again, then, beyond its architectural embodiment. It fascinated Plato, Leonardo da Vinci, and Kepler before Buckminster Fuller, and may fascinate the designer of social systems further yet.

QUANTIFICATIONS OF THE ICOSAHEDRON

There are, astonishingly enough, only three quantities that measure the physical extension of the icosahedron. The first is the length of an edge—the distance between a pair of vertices. The second is the distance between opposite poles, which is the longest length in evidence. There are six axes to the icosahedron, which can be made to spin serenely between each pair of poles. Buckminster Fuller referred to 'spinnability' and considered that the need to neutralize (as it were) a pair of poles in order to effect the spin accounted for the invariant factor two in Euler's equation. It is a surprising idea: but never take a genius too lightly.

The third stable quantity is the distance, through the internal space, of next-but-one neighbours. Five vertices depend from each vertex that are neither neighbours nor polar opposites. That makes 60 internal *tensile* relationships, represented by 30 internal struts, that can be conceived as pulling all the vertices in toward each other. The strength of the whole edifice is now spectacular. What we need to know is what these tensegrity components could possibly represent in human terms.

And yet it is obvious. Insofar as an Infoset member (an edge, recall) 'belongs' to the two teams that are the vertices of *this* edge, the teams represent the compressive strength of their members—although it is true, because of *reverberation*, that the icosahedral whole will exercise tension at each vertex. If however, each team of five at each vertex appoints one member each as a CRITIC to the next-but-one neighbour team, then the whole icosahedral space is interlaced with tensile componentry. The consequence for each individual is that not only is s/he a *member* of two teams, but also a *critic* of two near-neighbour teams. There are now 120 roles being played out in the Infoset. Consider the strength, the cohesion ... the tensegrity that deserves its new name of *syntegrity*. And yet no-one is overwhelmed with variety, as so easily happens (for example in the Matrix organization mentioned before).

The fact is that in a group of n members, there are $n(n - 1)$ relationships—allowing for the undeniable fact that these relationships are directional. (That is to say that an uncle is not the same thing as a nephew.) So the total connectivity of a 30-Infoset is 870. An Infoset meeting that tried to accommodate this number of direct personal interactions would take forever. But if each person has only four roles, we reduce proliferating variety to 120—and this, it seems, can be handled. But (as we shall see) it still takes time.

It is interesting to apply the Bavelas measures with which we began to the three-dimensional closure of the icosahedron. Even though he did not envisage the extension from a plane space to three-dimensional space, he had already—all those years ago—offered closure in the shape of the Ring Net. Well, if a Team Syntegrity player is directly a member of two teams, and also a direct critic of two other teams, he may contact 20 people (including his *nodal* self) in ONE step. This leaves the 10 people comprising the teams at his two polar opposites, each of whom may be reached in THREE STEPS around the polyhedron, making 30 steps. Thus each person has full connectivity in 50 steps, and Group Dispersion enumerates to 1500. Each person's Relative Centrality is 1500 divided by 50, which is 30. But since the Centrality of the most central player is 30, and all players are alike, Peripherality is $30 - 30 = $ zero. This is exactly what our presuppositions about democracy and symmetry led us to expect from adopting such a model as this: zero marginalization of any one person.

Anyone who finds these crude attempts to quantify the complexity of interpersonal relations sufficiently interesting to embark on a detailed examination is likely to realize how unfamiliar three-dimensional spaces are, and how difficult otherwise ordinary processes of counting. Donald Burrill is one friend who arrives at different numbers from those given—but the details are not so important as the insight into their numerical irrelevance. As Dr Burrill writes: 'Syntegrity requires each person to have identical values for Group Dispersion and for Centrality, so that Peripherality for each member is identically zero whatever the value of Relative Centrality.' This is the result that matters: the invariant. Those who worry about the arbitrary nature of cybernetic measures of variety (and many scientists do) might take the point.

Similar calculations can be satisfactorily repeated for other polyhedra, of course. But it is worth reverting to the choice of the icosahedron in terms of the tensile role of critic. In a tetrahedron, all vertices are already connected by edges, so there is no internal tensility to play with unless the protocol is changed. Dr Robert Pisani of Pacific Bell has reported success by doing so. A pyramid on a square base has eight people discussing five topics, and only two tensile components. A double pyramid on a square base (octahedron) has eight uniform triangular sides; three tensile components could be inserted across the apices. In the model as conceived (edges = people) this would involve twelve people in discussing six topics. The cube is an interesting case: we have twelve people discussing eight topics; but in the tensiles, if we want to maintain perfect symmetry, we have no less than sixteen critical functions—four body-centred and twelve face-centred, to use crystallographic nomenclature. Playing with all these alternatives is a fascinating pursuit, and perhaps it is clearer now why the chosen polyhedron was selected.

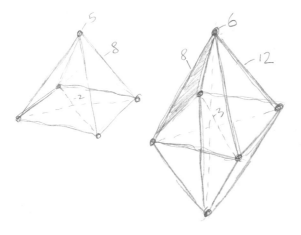

A preliminary version if this chapter appeared in Schwaninger and Espejo (1993).

Chapter Two

ON PROTOCOLS

At the start of the first chapter I said that 'ways of working' would be called protocols. There is some support for this usage in the Oxford English Dictionary, where (under the heading of diplomatics) a distinction is drawn between the 'official formulas' of some charter or instrument and 'the text which contains its subject-matter.' This is precisely the distinction it seems helpful to draw, so long as it includes behaviour in its formulas. The term 'rubric' covers behaviour; it might be preferred, were it not for its specifically ecclesiastical connotation.

We are not very good at protocol, perhaps because it is inherited: 'this is the way that things are done around here,' and that way is rarely questioned. For example, I have made a good many attempts to vary the protocol of various kinds of Board Meeting (from business, through the military to academia) on which I sat as a member, with little success. The item 'any other business' sounds innocuous. What happens is that anyone planning skulduggery waits until most people have left, making their apologies, and slides a minute into the record right under the Chairman's sleepy eye and inattentive nose. But try budging A.O.B.: you have to be Chairman yourself to get away with it.

Here are two hilarious examples of protocols that do not work. The Korean Armistice Commission sat through eleven hours at its (12th April 1969) 289th meeting. As if these two numbers were not enough as a critique of the protocol involved, please note that the meeting ended in four hours of total silence.

In British Whitehall, we could not possibly be so uncouth. When a British civil servant is called to give evidence to a Royal Commission, he certainly does so. Listen to Sir Thomas Padmore, giving evidence to the Royal Commission on the civil service itself, a few years ago:

> 'What I have said has demonstrated that it is very difficult to find an answer to that question, but if I were pressed for an answer I would say that, so far as we can see,

taking it rather by and large, taking one with the other, and taking the average of Departments, it is probable that there would not be found to be very much in it either way.'

The distinction between the official formula and text containing subject matter is perfectly clear in each case.

The protocol proposed for a Team Syntegrity session must provide both a procedure and the means for making that procedure effective. Effectiveness specifically includes the criterion that people are not to be bored. What follows was intended as such a protocol, meant to implement the Problem Jostle and the reverberative resolution that should follow it, yet—even so—to release rather than delimit or suppress creativity.

The reader is asked to take special note that, within the five experiments to be discussed in the next four chapters, this protocol was formulated specifically for the *third* experiment. The reason why it is presented here is twofold:

First, the first two experiments were conducted (see next chapter) on an informal basis—precisely to examine the need for formal protocol. Thus many hypotheses were being examined in this regard, and trouble will be spared if the reader knows in advance where these tests led in setting up the third experiment. It will make more sense of the first two to be let in on the secret in advance.

Second, the critique of the third experiment is expressed in terms of a commentary on this protocol, which must therefore be presented before Chapter Four, where it historically belongs.

The major advantage of this not-quite-historical presentation is also twofold. First, the reader of Chapter One will surely be wondering what 'all this' comes down to in practice—so here is one possible answer. Second, some terms are now introduced which were actually generated by the Manchester Tensegrities, or Syntegrations as we should now call them, and with hindsight they perhaps became more accessible. Obviously, there will be some redundancy between what follows as protocol and what was presented in Chapter One as argument, but the facility to have such a protocol that stands on its own, and can be reproduced as such, seems a good bargain.

PROTOCOL FOR A TEAM SYNTEGRITY INFOSET

An Infoset consists of 30 people who share information and interest in some area of mutual enthusiasm, and who wish to investigate it further, form a plan, or otherwise generate advance. Let us suppose the process is one of planning.

Tensegrity, a crucial aspect of the concept of syntegrity, means tensile integrity, and refers to arrangements (called a protocol) for conducting proceedings within the group to maintain its productivity and creativity.

An arch stands up because of its *compressive* strength: it binds together. In like manner, an Infoset consists of people bound together by a common bond. But suppose that the arch threatens to collapse outwards. It is supported by a rod fixed between the tops of the two supporting pillars: then this is *tensile* strength. Similarly, the tension that exists within an Infoset is seen as conducive to keeping it together. This is not just psychological tension, but structural tension. The objectives that emerge in planning are not contradictory —but they are often antinomies: more food may be grown, perhaps at the expense of woodlands that the atmosphere needs; people want the products of industries that probably pollute that atmosphere as well ...

The protocol, used in the sense of a prescribed ritual, is based on mathematical principles, and is designed to exploit both the compressive and tensile attributes of the Infoset. It creates an investigative *structure* within which the group may freely move. If it sounds restrictive, that is because it must make clear how it needs to work. The Rules of the Game do not inhibit players once they agree to go on to the field; the design of a cathedral, and decorous conduct inside it, do not set limits to praise and prayer ...

There are three parts to the Protocol: the Problem Jostle, which is the initial phase, the Topic Auction, which allocates roles, and the syntegrity iterations, called the Outcome Resolve, which follow. The Protocol has the same basic design however the Infoset decides to work in terms of time and place.

The Programme that follows is probably the minimum: it uses four periods of four hours each, and takes three syntegrity iterations to reach its conclusions, with all players in one location.

The 'long weekend in the mountains' is favoured, and even longer meetings are envisaged. A programme might be conducted around sporadic meetings; but beware of losing the tensile integrity if the players lose track of the dynamic interaction they generate. This warning might also apply to a tele-tensegrity protocol: obviously communications could be made by electronic media, with players scattered all over the world, but there have been no experiments yet to vouch for the cohesion of such an Infoset.

THE PROBLEM JOSTLE

MINIMAL REQUIREMENTS

- 30 players.

- 4 facilitators.

- A few helpers, who also act as reserve players.

- A large room, able to contain all these people *in motion*.

- 40 movable chairs.

- A continuous buffet, serving coffee, tea, minerals and small snacks.

- *Extensive* wall space or large screens to which documents may be affixed.

- A highly visible clock, that can be set to time a period. It has to be obvious how much time has been consumed or is left in each period.

- 50 large cards and supply of broad felt-tip markers, together with some means of propping up the cards (call them stands) to make them visible all round the room. Poles with thumb tacks are ideal. (Flip charts could be used but it is difficult to muster 16; flip chart paper requires support if the signs are to be visible to all.)

- 2 large whiteboards, preferably with print-out facilities.

- 30 packets of 12 adhesive markers, such as circles or stars, one packet for each player.

- A supply of small, plain file cards.

- Pads of paper and pens.

BEFOREHAND

Briefing

Players are briefed according to the intentions of the organizers, but:

- Players must understand that the purpose of the Problem Jostle is to generate Agenda for their own meeting, which will require 12 topics, and

- Each player must now submit to the facilitators at least one Statement of Importance (SI)—there is no limit on numbers, but each SI must be written on a separate plain card.

An SI is a brief (one- or two-sentence) assertion that the player considers crucial to the planning to be undertaken. Try to be original: no banalities, no hobby horses.

Test for detecting motherhood statements: negate the statement, which must still be debatable. 'God exists' becomes 'There is no God': keep it in (men have died over less). 'We should do all within our power, and take every step that is legal ...' Throw it out: the negatives cannot be argued. Possible exceptions are extremely potent bits of rhetoric ('Freedom!'—although people do not often march shouting 'slavery!'), and telling jokes ('oxymorons for limited nuclear war'—the negation of which kills the joke).

The Room

The 12 tables should be set casually around three walls in a ring, with a few chairs at each table. On the tables are the stands and several of the large white cards, together with paper and pens.

On the end wall, a large circle is inscribed, with 12 positions marked on the circumference, exactly like a clock. Call, therefore, these positions the HOURS.

Write the exact title of the Infoset's task in the centre of the ring.

The SIs

The facilitators must scrutinize the SIs. Let us say there are 50 of them. Some of them will say almost exactly the same thing, and these should be elided. But facilitators must be ultra-sensitive about this stage. It is all too easy to push SIs into standard categories ('Oh, this is something to do with education')—

and then the Infoset will be plunged into the orthodox discussions that we seek to avoid. It is also easy to let the slip of one's own value system show. Facilitators: please be alert to novel ideas, however embryonic or ineptly expressed. This may be the very gold that we are panning for.

A list of SIs, suitably elided, should be typed and made available to the players in advance if at all possible. Otherwise this has to happen at the first Problem Jostle session. We guessed that there were 50 SIs submitted; maybe the list has come down to (say) 32.

THE PROBLEM JOSTLE, SESSION ONE, 90 MINUTES

Each player, having surveyed the list of SIs, now has a choice. S/he may recognize an SI in the list as having extreme importance, whether s/he placed it there or only wishes s/he had, and decide to pursue it at all costs. Then s/he should stride to a table, write a short name for the topic on a large card, and display it on the stand provided.

The alternative is to do nothing, and move around the room sipping coffee. The informality cannot be overemphasized. We are used to our own brands of politeness, and these will not apply ...

Anyone may go and sit at any table, and join in the discussion. But it is crucial to these dynamics that anyone may simply walk away, and go somewhere else, without explanation. Why should s/he do that?

This is a self-organizing system that depends upon complete information. There are at least three reasons why the player moves. A discussion is developing somewhere else, and the topic written up is sensational. Second, a group of Infoset friends, known to me, is huddled around an innocuous-looking sign, but they are getting excited. Third, I have suddenly thought of a great new idea—so I am going to take myself a table, put up a sign, and hope for business.

Please note that anyone who is bored at a Problem Jostle has only him/herself to blame. We are not sitting through 80 agenda items for the 20 of (marginal) interest ... Note secondly that reaching for novelty, and seeking to abandon the crutch of established comfortable formularies, can lead to feelings of embarrassment that only banalities or fantasies are emerging. Keep at it!

Action

As soon, at a given table, as there is agreement on some kind of topic definition, and enthusiasm for its propagation, those present write it on a standard sheet of paper, and those who wish sign it. There is a qualifying threshold of five signatories. These may be canvassed from someone who was in the group, said 'obviously' and left, or from some 'John/Sue: read this, I know you'll agree.'

What we have here is a well discussed, refined and somewhat elaborated SI. It could run to a paragraph—but only say eight lines. The signed sheet is delivered to the facilitators, who post it as one of the HOURS on the end wall.

The facilitators have to consider the developing process all the time. We may encounter something similar to the individual SIs that needed elision. This time, the facilitators will not take too many liberties: they will post the two statements side by side on the same HOUR and they will draw the attention of the signatories to the similarity. With any luck, the two groups will get together, and all members will sign a joint statement.

As to the HOUR selected, the facilitators will start to take cognizance of the antinomies referred to earlier, and will seek to position any pair of 'polar opposites' at polar opposite HOURS (12 and 6, 2 and 8 HOURS, for example).

All the topic tables do as they please throughout. They may abandon topics and rewrite large card displays. (Facilitators: watch that this is done. People get carried away, change the topic, and forget to say so—then other players are getting false information.) Topics and tables may be abandoned altogether, all the players may move elsewhere.

People should watch the clock. At the end of 90 minutes, the bell rings, and topic groups who wish to move fast will have only 5 minutes grace to get their statements in.

THE PROBLEM JOSTLE, SESSION TWO, 45 MINUTES

It is time for a general break. It is assumed that players have been taking occasional moments to look at progress, and to add signatures to the lists on display. Probably, thanks to the enthusiasm of topic protagonists, all twelve HOURS have statements beside them. Players will now have 15 minutes or so to sign themselves on, and should have no hesitation in supporting somewhat similar statements if they agree with each.

The facilitators now have the task (since they have had a synoptic view of the total development) of leading a discussion on the emergence of topics. Everyone knows that the final goal is to define 12 topics, but many more than that may be in evidence. It has to be expected that a constellation of refined SIs is competing for each of the HOURS. Volunteers will be sought to form tables to meld together convergent statements into Composite Statements of Importance (CSIs). These groups should naturally be formed out of the signatories to compatible SIs. But there is still no limit on numbers; and even now inspiration or ingenuity might lead to reformulations. What matters is not to lose the work already put into refinement just because a superficially attractive but unexplored notion suddenly surfaces.

THE PROBLEM JOSTLE, SESSION THREE, 45 MINUTES

This session is devoted to the creation and polishing of CSIs which by now might be two paragraphs long (maximum 20 lines).

Organizers should give thought to the earlier staff work implied at this stage. The SIs posted against the HOURS should have been copied. Ideally, those who wished, or now (Session Three) wish, to develop ideas on a whiteboard with print-out, should have been running the reiterations as their work progressed. Probably the facilitating team should have secretarial help (and 'helpers' were mentioned earlier for this reason among others). Anyone wishing to have a copy of anything posted should have been given it. And so forth. None of this has been proposed as obligatory: it needs thinking through in the local context.

CSIs should be submitted as soon as completed, with the appropriate signatures. The facilitators now have the task of replacing SIs with CSIs around the HOURS, but there will still be constellations, even of CSIs, competing for the 12 positions. IMPORTANT: the alternative CSIs may be competing for the 'wrong' HOUR. It was the facilitators' decision to site them where they are. However, Session Four will resolve this dilemma. Staff people need to note that the CSI sheets have to have an empty half-sheet added at the foot (see below).

THE PROBLEM JOSTLE, SESSION FOUR, 15 MINUTES

Each player has 12 adhesive stars or circles. S/he now *votes* for the twelve 'best' CSIs by sticking a symbol on the foot of the relevant sheet. One symbol may be added to each of 12 sheets; symbols do not have to be used up; all 12 symbols may be added to one sheet, or any combination of sheets.

Reflection will confirm that this process is far more complicated than it looks. People are still interacting, watching each other's moves. If a CSI is a runaway, whereas I had expected to put all my stickers on it, I shall feel free to vote elsewhere ...

THE PROBLEM JOSTLE, SESSION FIVE, 45 MINUTES

This session is in the hands of the whole Infoset, led by its facilitators.

It will by now be fairly obvious what has happened but there will undoubtedly be loose ends. For example, if the voting disrupts the facilitators' (continuing) attempts to create polarity among issues, what then?

By the end of this session, 4 hours in total, we should have agreement on the 12 agenda topics, 12 rather well defined CSIs, and a polarity basis indicating six lines on the wall that cross each other at the centre.

And everyone should go home feeling fulfilled and satisfied.

THE TOPIC AUCTION

This is the most complicated transaction of the whole exercise. It should take only about 30 minutes, but players need time to prepare for it.

A player already knows that s/he will be a member of two teams, and must be asking him/herself: of *which* two teams? All possible combinations are by no means available. S/he has five alternatives left out of eleven. The constraints are given in the diagram called Team Syntegrity One.

Thus (for example), once a player is a member of the Red Team, s/he may also be a member of Purple, Yellow, Light Blue, Gold, or Orange—but no other.

Next, as we see from the diagram called Team Syntegrity Two, s/he will be appointed as a CRITIC of two other teams: one in a Red Capacity, and another in the alternative capacity as above—which is not yet settled.

Finally, s/he may wish to note that his/her membership of two teams involves becoming an 'observer' (defined later) of the two polar opposite teams.

In order to decide what to do at the Topic Auction, each player needs to consider

- Which two topics most concern me—and is one more important than the other?

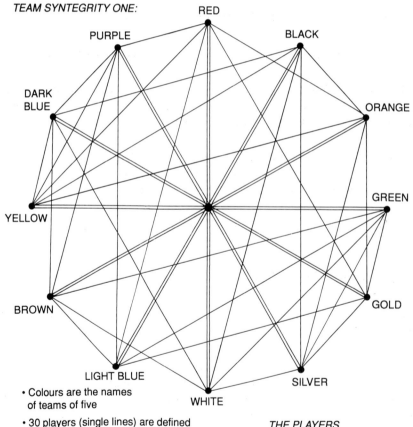

TEAM SYNTEGRITY ONE:

RED

PURPLE

BLACK

DARK
BLUE

ORANGE

GREEN

YELLOW

BROWN

GOLD

LIGHT BLUE

SILVER

WHITE

- Colours are the names
  of teams of five

- 30 players (single lines) are defined
  by membership of two teams each

THE PLAYERS

- Teams connected by double lines
  are polar opposites

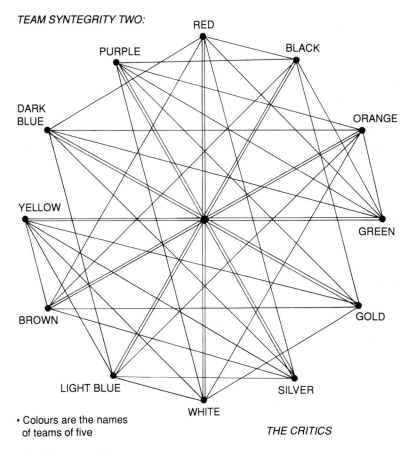

TEAM SYNTEGRITY TWO:

- Colours are the names
  of teams of five

- Each team appoints one
  member as a critic of another
  team as shown

- Teams connected by double lines
  are polar opposites

THE CRITICS

● Given that I resolve this question, what priorities do I entertain as to the 10 topics of which I might end up as a critic? Or does it matter?

● What interest or not do I have in the polar opposite teams of those of my potential choice?

Then s/he needs to take account of the following protocols for the Topic Auction, and to simulate in advance the consequences of taking the decisions that must now be taken, while watching the actions of his/her fellow players. As with all auctions, timing and bluffing are of the essence.

PRELIMINARY

The facilitators arrange the room in a ring of 12 tables. They reduplicate the HOURS on the wall by writing the short topic titles of the CSIs on large cards exhibited on stands at the tables.

ROUND ONE

After the facilitators have asked players who are happy to be members of any team to stand aside, the following question is put:

- Will anyone who opts for an over-riding preference for playing in a single team go and stand at the relevant table?

So far so good, unless more than five people try to stand at any one table. Facilitators must negotiate with them, reminding them that this decision pre-empts various alternatives down the line.

ROUND TWO

The following question is put:

- Will anyone who opts for a dual role (that is colour 1–colour 2) that determines both of his/her playing teams go to the centre of the ring and point to his/her two choices?

It is up to facilitators to resolve any clash that is now manifested, or to allocate the players. Since a player can stand at only one table, a small card bearing the player's name will be exhibited on the other table, registering him/her as a team member.

ROUND THREE

The following question is put:

- In view of what has happened, is there a remaining player who wishes to take a first choice option?

Note that this question can result only in a satisfactory outcome, unless two players make for one remaining team place. Facilitators forward.

ROUND FOUR

Remaining players must obviously be persuaded to adopt a role.

Everyone now has a dual-role identity as a player, such as Red–Gold or White–Brown. S/he should take his/her Identity (ID) Card from the pack provided and make sure that s/he is registered as a team member on both teams.

ROUND FIVE

Each team needs to consult together (realizing that at any moment it may be non-existent—since each of its members may be somewhere else!) in order to appoint on its behalf one of its members to act as a critic of one of the five teams indicated in Syntegrity Two.

Each player, who already holds an ID card, adds to it (in equivalently large letters, but in another colour) the two teams of which s/he is an appointed critic.

Facilitators should ensure that the large card at each table exhibits the names of five members, five appointed critics, and five RECEIVED critics from other teams.

PROGRAMMING NOTE

Not only is it uncertain that the 30 minutes proposed for the Topic Auction will be adequate, but in any case the time taken is not included in the schedule given here.

The Auction has to happen either at the end of the Problem Jostle, or just prior to the first session of the Outcome Resolve, or in a special session in between. If the overall time of $4 \times 4 = 16$ hours cannot be compromised, then the time must be stolen from the schedule as the organizers think best.

However it is handled, the Topic Auction is vital to success. Organizers are urged to allow the self-organizing propensities of this whole approach to determine the allocation of roles. If not, they might as well sit in their offices and appoint task forces, inter-departmental committees, and so forth, as they have always done—and with the same turgid results ...

THE OUTCOME RESOLVE

A Total Session, in this case of 4 hours, consists of six 40 minute Meetings on the part of two teams each time. Since this Total Session involves ten players and ten critics at each Meeting, there will always be ten other players 'on the move,' looking at new draft CSIs which they may sign, and noting in particular the activities of their two 'polar opposite' teams.

Antithetic Management has two manifestations. As we now know, critics are appointed to each team. Their role is to listen, and then to bring to bear the understanding they possess—generated primarily from their playing roles in other teams. The protocol is given below.

The role of 'polar opposite' is more subtle. A team player is supposed to note his/her polar opposite team (s/he will have two), as a MONITOR. There is no *formal* interaction, although people are encouraged to make themselves known. As issues dynamically reverberate round and round the Infoset, the 'most distant' team, that least directly connected, has special call on *tensile integrity*. The role has not yet been fully articulated, but look at the implied power in the tramlines of the two Syntegrity diagrams. Maybe the role is something like a godparent ...

A Meeting, 40 minutes: a Meeting consists of five team members and the team's five critics, who are considering the CSI to which the team is dedicated. How can this be developed and expressed? We are aiming for a single page result, which is a draft FSI (Final Statement of Importance).

The team works for 30 minutes, in which time the critics must be silent. They then have 10 minutes in which to say something helpful and germane. Or a critic might be so satisfied that s/he simply signs the draft FSI.

During the Meeting, and particularly at its close, facilitators will take care to obtain fresh drafts to post on the wall. Remember that now there are always ten players waiting to peruse them ...

The Total Session of 6 × 40 minutes = 4 hours is over when the draft FSIs have all been posted at their HOURS.

Members of the Infoset should now consider which they will sign, and which they will seek to alter. The role of facilitator has never been more important. *Ad hoc* discussions as relevant to all parties are the order of the day.

Iterations are a succession of Total Sessions, just as they are themselves a succession of meetings.

There should be at least (as provided for in this example) three iterations of the Outcome Resolve.

Two comments on WHY and HOW:

- WHY? It is time to say that the strange diagrams in the figures Syntegrity One and Two are mathematical projections on the plane (meaning flat space) of a complicated three-dimensional model meant to represent a pure democracy. That is, no player can be distinguished from any other player as to rank and role.

- HOW? When the Meetings of teams add up to Total Sessions, and when they enter into Iterations, the Infoset experiences a REVERBERATIVE effect.

This means that what everyone is saying to everyone else, within the team, within the critical apparatus, and having regard to polar opposites, in terms of statements and restatements (SIs), composite statements (CSIs), and eventually final statements (FSIs), is constantly rebounding around the group. Everything is endlessly reflecting and reacting to everything else—like a (three-dimensional!) snake eating its own tail.

The Conclusion is meant to be a convergence on twelve FSIs, with the whole Infoset in agreement.

It is impossible to specify rubrics for iterations of Total Sessions that are already collections of meetings, because we cannot predict the particular evolutionary trajectory that any one occasion will follow.

We have to rely upon the goodwill of players and the wisdom of facilitators.

This might be a reasonable expectation for an Infoset. Would that it were for the whole of mankind.

Chapter Three

PATH-FINDING EXPERIMENTS

The Infoset that met (at the players' own expense) at the Manchester Business School on 26–29th January 1990 began on the Friday night, with a convivial cocktail hour, dinner, and an introductory explanation. What identified the Information Set was that they were all friends, or friends of friends. This (see later) led to a certain loss of tension (cf. tensile integrity), but it did mean that a lot of new friends were made. It also meant:

Q. Did you enjoy yourself?

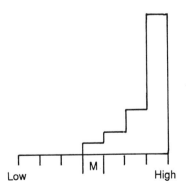

We find this graph to be readily reproducible. It can certainly be said for Team Syntegrity that it meets its first design criterion in not boring people.

The Infoset as now defined was a small group prepared to believe that it had a common purpose in identifying issues of concern to the concept of world governance. Its purpose then was definite although wide ranging. In those respects it recapitulated Marlow Seventy. We had two full-time and two part-time facilitators; and the elaborate business of scoring and cluster analysis by computer could well be irrelevant, especially among so informal a group. At any rate, the Manchester experiments deliberately relaxed most of the procedural constraints that had been used before.

It was obvious that we confronted a major new issue, however. All the experience of Problem Jostling, over 20 years, had sought an open-ended list of outcomes. But the icosahedral tensegrity model would seek closure on exactly 12. Could this be done without massive manipulation? Yet, why not, if players understood the need for it?

A PRIOR TRIAL RUN

It was primarily this issue that led to a prior experiment with 30 graduate students of MBS, scheduled for 8th, 9th and 10th January 1990. Day One was an introduction to cybernetic thinking, which was new to them. The Problem Jostle was run on Day Two without constraints, other than the focus on 12 needed outcomes, and without aids other than facilitation. It worked very well indeed as a procedure. Moreover, the statements were all interesting in the sense that each is debatable. The test whereby a proposition that cannot be seriously challenged when negated is not worth saying, had been emphasized.

Here are the twelve initial statements from the one-day event:

TWELVE STATEMENTS FROM THE GRADUATE STUDENTS'
PROBLEM JOSTLE

Manchester Business School, 9th January 1990

1. Community survival is dependent upon the agreement and obedience to ethical common standards.

2. Everyone should do as they wish so long as they do not disturb others.

3. Human society will not behave optimally while gender is used as a means of discrimination.

4. Materialism and environmentalism are mutually incompatible.

5. Dominance/hierarchies are inescapable. Materialism is an example.

6. The development of a cohesive community requires a common enemy.

7. Materialism is the corruption of our desire to fulfil basic human needs.

8. Terrorism: individuals must have complete control over their own destinies.

9. Increased self-actualization leads to creative global solutions.

10. There is a role for a global community based on common values and understanding. These values include environment and health.

11. Cultural differences should be maintained.

12. Polarization of wealth is an inescapable component of human society.

Some commentators have found this list banal. Given the unexpected nature and vast scope of the call made on them, I consider that the students did well. At the least we were spared the familiar list of topics that would map existing world agencies. And we were also spared the usual comment that what is needed is *education* to propagate existing solutions that conspicuously have failed.

The process itself had flowed smoothly, and had converged (with little help from facilitators) on the required numbers of topics. This gave confidence; thus two and a half weeks later (27th January 1990) we embarked on the Problem Jostle with the Manchester Infoset itself in the same format—that is, without any scoring or voting procedures. It was a mistake.

THE MANCHESTER INFOSET

As already mentioned, the Infoset was a set of friends rather than a set of political allies. It was a high-level group intellectually, mostly academic but with worldly experience, including two Professors Emeriti. Having used the first evening as described, the Infoset pitched into the Problem Jostle on Saturday morning with a will.

The homogeneity and amiability of the group was such that having engendered about 17 topics around the room, and knowing that only 12 were needed, the players began a vigorous process of condensing them. As a facilitator, I observed with alarm that the process was runaway: the total had been reduced to about ten, and from this synoptic vantage point I predicted that we should end up with only four. Suppose indeed that the Infoset came up with only one statement!

This would have been a triumph for the group, but it would have killed the second stage of the experiment. Perhaps I should have let the process occur and unravelled it backwards to 12 statements later. However, there was not much time; besides, the issues meant for 'antithetic management' discussion would have been already aired. So I made a second mistake. I moved among the condensing four or five groups and explained the dilemma. The result was disastrous: there was an explosion of variety, and 37 statements appeared at the closure.

Having provoked a violent oscillation, I had no choice but to call in the central command function (me again, as experimenter) and engage in 'resource bargaining.' The Infoset was most helpful, and duly underwrote 12 state-ments. This saved the day for the icosahedral stage of the experiment, but at a huge price—heavily underlined in both oral and written statements later. The converging process had been working well, refining concepts and statements alike until I intervened, creating the variety explosion, the fresh statements being not at all refined. There were thus 37 statements on the whiteboard with varying status in terms of refinement, and this variation was statistically confounded during the variety attenuation from 37 to 12. Moreover, the process caused a delay of 3–4 hours in the intended schedule.

The conclusion drawn from this experience in terms of a reliable protocol had to be that the constraining and facilitating procedures that the experiment abandoned on the 'advice' of the graduate trial must be reintroduced. They were, as readers have already seen in Chapter Two. Thus, in incorporating the Infoset's Problem Jostle outcomes, as follows, and in fairness to those participating, it is emphasized that the unevenness in drafting was due to uncouthness in the experiment. None the less, the lack of overlap with the student's statements is noteworthy, although the absence of banality is yet more encouraging.

TWELVE STATEMENTS (WITH AGREED SHORT TITLES IN PARENTHESES) FROM THE MANCHESTER INFOSET PROBLEM JOSTLE

Manchester Business School, 27th January 1990.

1. There are no rights, only power to impose, or concern to propose moral codes. There are no rights without obligations. Dependency and interdependency are issues. Individual freedom is an illusion which proposes a non-integral theory of organization. (FREEDOM AND OBLIGATIONS)

2. We should make beneficial change by planting biological and conceptual acorns. [This was taken from a story of a peasant who single-handedly transformed a rural area by planting acorns and other trees every day. He did not tell anyone what he was doing for many years.] (ACORNS)

3. Language leads to knowledge leads to use and application leads to understanding. (EPISTEMOLOGY AND PRACTICE)

4. World Citizenship needs an extraterrestrial motivating force [such as God]. (EXTRATERRESTRIAL PROPHETS/CREATING MOTIVATION TO ADAPT)

5. How do we integrate conditions for sustainability? (SUSTAINABILITY)

6. Get agreement on states of the world to avoid. Look at ideals, goals and strategies. (STATES TO AVOID)

7. Western civilization sacrifices innovation for security. (INNOVATION)

8. Ideals are all very well, but how can they be put into practice? (PRAXIS)

9. There must be a balance between Reason and Emotion. (INNER HARMONY)

10. Gaian hypothesis: respect for other created things is needed. Traditional values cannot be revalued without the identification of a higher recursion. (HIGHER RECURSION)

11. Conflict resolution will always be required. Love and hate are continuous factors. (CONFLICT RESOLUTION)

12. Identity is vital. Its pursuit will dominate behaviour. This is not well recognized in discussion of group and individual selfishness. (IDENTITY)

Note that this account of the Manchester Experiments has dealt only with the Problem Jostle event. We shall soon see what happened in the Outcome Resolve stage of triple reverberative iterations. In between, however, comes the Topic Auction—which has subsequently become the most difficult procedural problem in Team Syntegrity. It was not clearly identified as a difficulty with the Manchester Infoset, doubtless because of the confusion mentioned before and the loss of time. People wanted to get on with the experiment, and had no deep investment in the topics: they therefore accepted roles as was expedient. This complaisance was very misleading.

PROTOCOL FOR THE OUTCOME RESOLVE

What should be the *programme protocol* for conducting the Outcome Resolve? If the reverberative effect is crucial, then meetings ought not to be spread out in linear fashion like so many episodes of a weekly TV series wherein one cannot remember what is going on. The closure must be evident: a three-dimensional ouroboros (the snake that eats its own tail) in action. And the reverberations must be sensed: otherwise a strut has been effectively broken. Even so, many configurations are possible. These experiments were designed for maximum condensation of time, and that requires simultaneous meetings it would seem.

The programming problem was investigated independently by myself and a Canadian colleague, Alan Pearson. We came to identical conclusions—which were too complicated for comfort. The fundamental problem is this.

Three teams of five players may sit down simultaneously under the observation of another three teams—who are the critics. This uses up all the players—30. On the elapse of one time epoch, the two sets of teams may change roles for a second epoch, since the selections can be made whereby each set of teams includes and exhausts the polar opposites of the other set. On the face of it, since the icosahedron is regular, it would seem possible to 'rotate' the groupings, so as to consider the other two issues in epochs three and four. But this is not possible.

The reason is clear enough. There is no central plane that divides the icosahedron in half (without 'snapping' the struts).

There is a *twist* imparted to the progression of equilateral triangles as they move around the 'globe.' This is most easily seen in the Euclidean plane space version (see diagram) where there are 'leftover' triangles at both ends. Thus, having once selected the two sets of three teams, one cannot recombine them under the same set of rules.

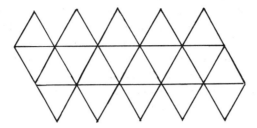

The protocol devised for Manchester saw this as a remediable defect in the 3 × 3 procedure outlined above. I wanted compactness, and tried to achieve it by having people playing more than one critical role simultaneously. The mistake was to 'over compact' the players: there were only 30 present after all and, as it turned out, some were supposed to be in two places at once.

Returning to 10th January, then, and the preliminary experiment with the graduate group, I had intended to try out the (flawed) protocol. Unfortunately, many of the group had been double-booked with their academic programmes. However, there were sufficient enthusiasts present to *simulate* the protocol. The mathematical root of the problem was made much clearer; and I reflect that it constitutes a coenetic variable generating robustness in a geodesic polyhedron, and confusion in the visualization of three-dimensional spaces ...

Hence the second mistake. Reaching the unreachable star is a fine ambition, but I patched the unpatchable flaw—between the Graduate and Infoset meetings. It did not work.

THE HARNDEN SCHEDULE

In the event, it soon became evident that the patching would not hold. Dr Roger Harnden perceived the likely effectiveness of holding simultaneous meetings of polar opposite teams. The triple threesome approach, on the other hand, had tried to creep sequentially round the twisting periphery of the icosahedron. Meetings of polar opposite teams plus critics obviously account for 20 people per session. They form 'polar caps,' as it were, which do not programmatically interact. The 'trouble' with this solution is that 10 people per session have 'nothing to do'—a situation that we had assiduously tried to avoid from the start for reasons of economy of time.

But the Harnden Schedule works sedately round the 'spinnable' globe, pole to pole, enhancing reverberative effects. It is essentially Fullerian. As to the unemployment factor: it has become clear that spare time (to read emerging outcomes, to consult, to relax) is essential. Elasticity in the procedure has turned out to be a great help towards group metabolism. Moreover, a degree of stress develops which has to be offset. There was a General who was taken out of a (British) simulated computer war game on a stretcher suffering from battle fatigue: I was often reminded of him during these experiments, which are more than 'not boring'—they are exciting. In every experiment there was friction, and in two cases it almost came to blows ...

However, the Harnden Schedule does use time. A good way to look at the Outcome Resolve process is to think of the six time epochs that it takes to exhaust the meetings of 12 teams—in pairs of polar opposites. If each meeting lasts for an hour, then one iteration uses a day, that is, six work sessions plus breaks and turn-around time. The experience is that three iterations are required to 'Resolve.' So that means three days, to be added to a day's worth of the Problem Jostle. There has to be an introductory session, and there is the vexed question of the topic auction (which we shall revisit). It is easy to see why the majority opinion has favoured an activity lasting a week. Condensing sessions to 30 minutes is exhausting. In any case, many far less fruitful management 'courses' take a week—this one has a potent outcome.

THE OUTCOME RESOLVE

The Manchester Infoset did not recast its findings into gradually more polished Consolidated Statements of Importance, culminating in a Final Statement of Importance as was intended; instead, the teams mostly added further observations to their first efforts. Thus it becomes a question as to whether the Syntegrity structure had added much to an orthodox succession of meetings. Here is the Infoset's own opinion:

Q. Did the syntegrity approach work?

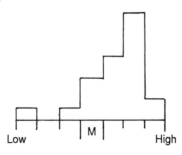

Here are some highlights drawn from a scrutiny of the records.

- It was the Orange Team that developed the 'seeding' idea of planting *Acorns* (item 2 in the Problem Jostle). By the third iteration, the Light Blue Team, dealing with *Freedom and Obligations* (item 1), had adopted this idea—and the acorn nomenclature. There is a 'critic' connection between the two teams.

- The *Extraterrestrial* (item 4) was first clarified by the Brown Team to mean a global vision of the planet, metasystemic to its management. The second iteration warned that global visions could, however, lead to oppression and even world domination, while the third contemplated replacing 'global vision' with cosmology. (The reference to God was a personal commentary added by someone unknown.)

- The Green Team, considering *States to Avoid* (item 6), had already set out the Brown point about oppression in its first iteration, and had put it strongly: 'Positive goals for a world government will lead to tyranny.' There is a common membership of the Brown and Green Teams—in the shape of Ms/Mr Brown–Green ...

- The matter of *Inner Harmony* (item 9) made an advance at the second iteration when the Silver Team wrote that 'Fallacious inference might enter into a positive feedback loop with emotion.' At the first iteration the point was simply to contend that explicitly Western thinking denies the validity of emotional reactions, and the second began by noting that reasoning often flows from false premises. Note that there exists a Ms/Mr Silver–Gold.

- The Gold Team discussing *Conflict Resolution* (item 11) began by noting that 'Love can be as destructive as hate.' Conflicts are about different perceptions of identity (the Yellow Team's topic) and therefore had to be solved at a meta level. But, said the second iteration, 'At what level?' And is the activity done by authority or as a service? The third iteration advanced to the notion that conflict is a symptom, which might be a solution to the problems of another system—and therefore perhaps not necessarily bad.

- Significantly, in light of this, the Yellow Team's work on *Identity* spent the whole of its second iteration deleting the phrase that an individual 'has chosen' to align with various groups that determine his/her identity —in the recognition that alignment might be imposed. There is a 'critic' connection between Gold and Yellow.

A full-scale post-mortem on exactly what happened is not possible, because no detailed scoring system was in use, but the colour connections referenced are perhaps relevant. In any case, of course, there is full disclosure (as near to real time as possible) of the proceedings; and polar opposite groups were asked as a matter of 'antithetic management' to check each other's progress. The scrutiny reveals no evidence that this had effect—or even happened. We are left with the question, answered positively in subjective terms by the Infoset as we know, whether *syntegrity reverberation* is a fact. The scoring techniques used in later experiments attempted to amass data that would provide an answer. But, as we shall later see, an effective statistical test remains to be invented.

Again, then, we have only the Infoset's own evaluation as to how well the experiment succeeded. Here are the group's answers to two important questions.

Q. Did you gain insight into TOPICS?

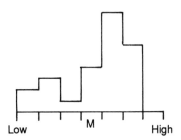

Low   M   High

This certainly counts as success, given that the meeting concerned the future of the world. The question is very encompassing, and the group was sophisticated. It is noted that even the four malcontents on this score still enjoyed the whole process, as the histogram produced earlier shows. What seems even more surprising is that the Infoset, many of whose members have personal expertise in the matter, were so positive in answer to the following question.

Q. Did you gain insight into GROUP PROCESSES?

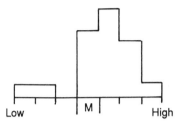

Low   M   High

Arising out of these observations by the Infoset, its judgement on another question is particularly interesting.

Q. How dependent is the model on correct numbers?

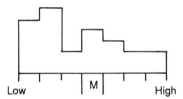

Low   M   High

In reporting back to the Infoset on the experiment, and referring to this histogram and the final discussion we had held, I wrote the following:

'There seemed to be a lack of appreciation of two key notions in this approach. Symmetric closure is one; reverberation round the system under repeated iterations is the other. Remember that these two concepts support the geodesic dome, and that they are the reason why the orthodox mathematics of mechanics could not be applied by Fuller. I have tried snapping struts on physical models, but cannot discover what is the formula for the threshold of collapse. Note that without tensile components, a jointed icosahedron such as mine collapses with the failure of a single strut; it is catastrophic collapse at that. These physical experiments provoke doubts about maintaining correct (i.e. model-determined numbers) in team syntegrity. The Manchester Infoset did not share my doubts! But I am not yet convinced.'

Three experiments later, I am now convinced. It seems that there is enormous redundancy in the team syntegrity process, and that my colleagues in Manchester had understood this. I continued to take the line that we could not relax the constraint on numbers ('the 30') until we had first understood how the process worked in its formally correct structure. After that, it would be scientifically appropriate to study what happens when numbers are varied according to some systematic statistical experiment. It would make a fine piece of research, but it is beyond my resources. Meanwhile, I have acquired a lot more confidence in the technique's capacity to adapt to the exigencies of real life.

As has already been shown, the experiment achieved high scores for enjoyment, and for the success of the Team Syntegrity approach in general. But what of the particular components of the protocol? The only component that had been named at Manchester was the Problem Jostle, and there had been problems with that—as already mentioned. Proceeding without restraints (as had worked well so often in the generation of an unconstrained list of topics) was unsatisfactory when it was necessary to condense proliferating variety on to 12 stations. It seemed that the Infoset's members were lenient in producing the following judgement.

Q. Did the Problem Jostle work?

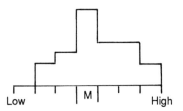

Low   M   High

It seemed that the general satisfaction must have been engendered during the triple iteration *after* the Problem Jostle. Hence that part of the protocol acquired its own identity as the Outcome Resolve. Significantly, the questionnaire did not refer at all to what is now called the Topic Auction: it had seemed to be a straightforward piece of logistical planning! In fact (as was made clear in Chapter Two) it is a difficult component of the protocol to manage effectively, and is still open to a variety of interpretations. Again, systematic research would increase understanding, and thereby help users to choose the

Auction protocol that most suited their needs. I no longer believe in an optimal method of allocation at this critical phase: see Chapter Two's remarks on Pliny's letter, and further comment later in Part Five.

All of this bears on, and I hope finally answers, the question of why Chapter Two—the *product* of the Manchester experiment—has already been introduced out of chronological order. An explanation was indeed given at the time; but having by now shared something of the experience the reader may see that Manchester was needed as a means of assessing the amount of structure and the degree of protocol that smooth-running syntegrities are likely to need. Meanwhile the reader needed some advance notice of how the idea and the nomenclature would be developing, in order to save time.

A few more questions were asked of the Manchester Infoset. Let us conclude with a particularly interesting and perhaps perplexing one, which was based on experiences with the icosahedron that I had been unable to interpret.

Some management people are enraptured by the icosahedron: the verb is not too strong. It seems to open new vistas for them. Others are left completely cold: the phrase 'silly toy' seems to be visible in the balloon above their heads. Well, of course, it is not necessary to explain the geodesic foundations of Team Syntegrity at all. Once a firm protocol is established, the geometry is self-generating. Indeed, the protocol could be embodied in a software package. An Infoset could then put itself through the programme, just as a clerk may press a key to read out a standard deviation without defining variance, or a person may drive a car without knowing how internal combustion actually works.

The innocuous examples are given in juxtaposition to the Infoset as a 'human machine.' Everyone is uncomfortable with such a notion, and with good reason for suspicion: people can rather easily be manipulated by protocols they do not understand, and the rubrics of cults offer sufficient instances. On the other hand, people are content, in many cases, as with religions they count as benign, or with the whole industry of sport, to become parts of a 'human machine' whose functioning is not fully understood. This is not a treatise on ethics: the idea is simply to alert potential users to an issue which demands a policy input, and to present the fascinating disagreement among the Manchester Infoset in answer to a practical version of the following question.

Q. If introducing this to a management group as a tool of DIRECTIONAL PLANNING, would you explain the underlying model BEFOREHAND, AFTERWARDS, OR NOT AT ALL?

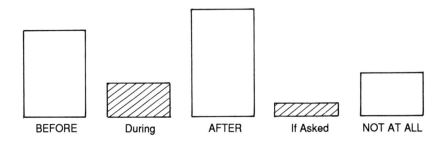

The two hatched categories were invented by the respondents.

Chapter Four

THE ACADEMIC MILIEU

The experiments held during January 1990 were studied in February and April in Toronto. March was largely consumed by work in Mexico. Thus a report went out to all concerned early in May, and this contained an Appendix on protocol which has been presented already in Chapter Two.

Readers may wish to refresh their recollections of this, and to reflect on the extent to which history (Chapter One), and Manchester (Chapter Three) in particular, affected the genesis of this design. And at this juncture, it is appropriate to mention the first publication on Organizational Tensegrity, also in 1990. It happened in this way.

The greatly distinguished philosopher and scientist in the management field, Russell L. Ackoff, retired from his Chair at the Busch Center of the Wharton School in the University of Pennsylvania in April 1984, and I was at the surprise (it really was a surprise) party thrown in his honour. Associated with the celebration of Russ's career to that date was a further surprise: a *Festschrift* volume was to be published for him. Therefore, I wrote (Beer, 1990) a piece known as 'Suicidal Rabbits.' Section 3 of that writing is called 'Organizational Tensegrity' (the term syntegrity had not yet replaced it) and gives a short statement of the idea, together with the model already elucidated here. It does not offer an operating protocol, saying simply that experiments 'are easy to envisage.' As we now know, there is a gap between envisaging and effecting!

The next surprise was that the *Festschrift* did not materialize as planned: it emerged years later as a special edition of *Systems Practice* (Beer, 1990). All this is recorded because the journal says that 'Suicidal Rabbits' was received in May 1989—true, of course, but the Syntegrity argument had been circulating widely in typescript during the intervening 5 years. People have mentioned this to me as confusing. Let it be so no longer, any more than the discovery that Dr Ackoff is just as active professionally today as he was before he 'retired' ...

Now the first test of the (Chapter Two) protocol was to be at the Graduate School of Economics, Law, Business, and Public Administration (known as the Hochschule) at St Gallen in Switzerland, where I was a visiting professor during June and July 1990. Dr Markus Schwaninger was my host, and it was he who co-directed the Team Syntegrity experiment there. The Hochschule is an outstanding institution; the environs are incredibly beautiful; the people are kindness itself; and the facilities for the experiment were greatly superior to those available at any of the other sites mentioned here.

The Infoset at St Gallen was provided by students in their final (fourth) year. The Hochschule elected to use the Syntegrity approach to discuss 'The Future of Management Education,' and the Infoset came up with no less than 52 Statements of Importance in the first place. We shall consider their conclusions later. First let us see what happened to the protocol, and especially to the problems generated by the CLOCK and its HOURS. The technique was first mentioned early on in Chapter Two's protocol, under the heading 'Beforehand,' and it is used continually thereafter in the sorting of data.

Consulting the section dealing with the Topic Auction, we find the use of the clock and its hours to define the *composition* of the 12 teams in terms of players and critics, rather than the topics under development by the 12 teams that are to be voted upon as events progress. In either case, however, we are seeking to delineate the 12 vertices of the icosahedron in a plane. The relevant diagrams are presented in Chapter Two.

On setting out to St Gallen, I viewed these planar figures with satisfaction as solving an outstanding practical problem. The icosahedron-with-tensegrity is a difficult (and therefore, one way or another, expensive) artefact to fabricate—especially in 12 colours. By squashing the three-dimensional entity flat, I could show all the player–critic relationships without ambiguity, and merely write down the colours as names. And this certainly works. It is noteworthy that team syntegrity participants often consult these flat figures to check on their formal relationships. But it is even more noteworthy that there is hardly a moment during the entire exercise when the big, commanding, three-dimensional model is not being brooded over by several people. What are they doing? They must be assimilating something more than the formal connectivity demonstrated by the planar nets.

Although at the time we did not know that this behaviour is ubiquitous, as seems to be the case, the organizers ourselves noticed that we were unsatisfied with the planar representations. Markus Schwaninger and his two assistants, Joachim Hirt and Andreas Schimpf, and I spent hours going over the protocol. We constantly reverted to the full-scale model: why was that? Joachim Hirt in particular was emphatic that the 'clock' would not do. The two-dimensional projection of the icosahedron did not convey all the information, and yet it should.

Although I had invented the clock, it was obvious that it was defective. It seemed banal to say that 'of course, it is not closed,' because we knew that already. But what gradually came out of our discussions was the fact that we did not have too little information, but too much—and the 'too much' was denying us closure.

Thanks to the closure of the particular polyhedron that we were handling (and that is meant literally, to say 'hands on'), there are only three distances involved in the entire icosahedral tensegrity. The point was made explicitly in Chapter One. Yet inspection of the planar projection indicates *six* distances. The 'length' of the individual participant as player is always the same in three dimensions; the 'length' of a critic is the same throughout; and the 'length' of polar opposition is the axis of the icosahedron. But the *perception of distance* in the planar dimension is wholly distorted. This seems to account for the preoccupation of participants with the physical object—which was evident everywhere, but most marked during the fifth experiment in Toronto. Of course, it has implications for the applicability of this technique. I should not embark on a Team Syntegrity exercise *with explanation* (see the end of Chapter Three) without a three-dimensional model, expensive though it be.

THE SCHWANINGER PRINCIPLE

When this cognitive dissonance between the three-space and two-space models was finally clear, a clarity that I attributed to Markus Schwaninger himself, I proposed that we name the Perception after him. After all, many people had studied the projections, and no-one until this moment had properly identified the problem—never mind its solution. But the 'solution' was so far half-baked. Markus kept saying that we should focus on the fact that in three dimensions distances (that are disparate in two dimensions) are actually the same.

Finally, he propounded this Principle:

'The assumption that distances between the SIs or CSIs or Topics are randomly distributed is useful. It leads to the abstract idea of equidistance, which means that, in principle, any one of the 12 CSIs or Topics could be taken and put into the imaginary central (focal) point, from where distances to all the topics (vertices) would be the same. In holographic terms, this focal point would contain a representation of the whole icosahedron.'

This is important, because it reflects the original intention in choosing the icosahedron—which had somehow been lost in the process of flattening it out. Moreover, the Schwaninger Principle suggests an excellent way of focusing the thinking of a given team meeting. Maybe if this scheme were adopted people would not, after all, be so beholden to the three-dimensional model. Consider the prior preparation of 12 large boards, which we will call the FOCUS BOARDS. Each depicts a clock having 11 'hours' arranged around the perimeter of a circle, and a central hub.

Each board has a single colour named at the centre, and the 11 other colours are named around the periphery. The spokes of this wheel are then of three kinds. Take the case where Silver is in the hub location, which means that the board is to be exhibited whenever the Silver Team meets. Its five members are Silver–Gold, Silver–Orange, Silver–Black, Silver–White, and Silver–Green. Then the spokes from the Silver Hub terminating at Gold, Red, Black, White, and Green are distinctively marked. A second class of spokes represents the five members of the Silver team in their roles as critics, namely Silver–Blue, Silver–Red, Silver–Yellow, Silver–Dark Blue, and Silver–Brown, and these spokes are also distinctively marked. The remaining class of spokes, marked in turn, lead from the hub to the five teams with which the Silver Team has no formal connection. Unique among these is the polar opposite team, Purple, requiring a special designation for its role in antithetic management.

It would seem that this planar depiction of the icosahedron, which reverts to three distances as designated by marking the spokes, would satisfy the difficulty discussed at St Gallen. In practice, the Focus Board would require devices by which to assign the roles of the actual people (Bill, Jane, and so on) to the diagram. Hence there would need to be a space at the hub under 'Silver' to write the short title of the Silver Topic. Bill and Jane and the others would be marked against the spokes that made them each a member of two teams and a critic of two teams. All colours noted on the periphery would need spokes in which to write the short titles of their current topics. Would not their Focus Board now tell the team as much as the three-dimensional model itself?

Even if it does, and no experimental work has yet been done on the idea, an icosahedron as such still needs to be present. To this kit we may now be adding a set of Focus Boards, together (perhaps) with computer software. And even the equipment specified in Chapter Two is not inconsiderable. It remains to be seen whether individuals and organizations are content to 'muddle through' a Syntegrity exercise extemporizing, and lashing-up equipment as they go, or whether they would prefer to buy a complete kit—or use consultants who are previously prepared. Requirements and opportunities are being investigated now. In the meantime, the initial experiments have been inadequately serviced with these kinds of equipment. But of them all, St Gallen was the best— because two computers were made available to edit evolving Statements (and to process them for general consumption). Even more, there was a knowledge-able support staff. Martin van Kempen, Erich Olgivie and Maarten Willemsen joined the Director and his two Associates as facilitators.

As we are already steeped in the technology of Team Syntegrity, let us reserve a discussion of content until later, and continue to learn whatever we can from the St Gallen experiment as it occurred. I hand over here to my Co-Director. He wrote these notes in the form of an Amendment to the protocol with which we started, and without hearing of the subsequent putative invention of the Focus Board. Thus his clocks are the original TWELVE-HOUR clocks.

INFOSETS AND TEAM SYNTEGRITY

Markus Schwaninger writes:

The order follows the order of the original protocol.

1. Layout for a Syntegrity Workshop

1.1. Protocol

1. Dealing with a rather complex issue, a duration of 1 week would be desirable. Three iterations should usually be enough for effective work and reverberation. Yet, if possible, in further experiments the protocol should permit one or even more additional iterations for those teams which desire them as an option.

2. Scheme for a programme schedule as suggested:

- First day: Problem Jostle and Topic Auction.

- Second to fourth days: Each for one iteration (one day = 6 sessions of 1.5 hours each).

- Fifth day: Time for an additional iteration (optional), and final Plenary Session.

3. Plenary sessions are an important device to handle the variety inherent in a syntegrity workshop. Therefore, they should be mentioned explicitly in the protocol. These sessions are used to initiate and finalize the workshop and to introduce each module of the protocol. Additional plenary sessions between the iterations of the Outcome Resolve may turn out to be useful. See also Sections 2 onwards.

1.2. Room Requirements

Two rooms are necessary. A large one is used for plenary sessions, Problem Jostle and Topic Auction. During the Outcome Resolve, this room is also used for one group discussion at a time. For the parallel session a separate room, located close to the first one, should be available.

2. Preparation of Participants

Before engaging in any step of a syntegrity programme, the participants must understand its purpose, the precise procedure, and the specific ideas underlying it. At this point, a desirable solution for this issue seems to be a combination of a preparatory session with the purpose of a general introduction, and thorough explanation while coaching the process.

Preparatory Session

This session should be devoted to

a. establishing and naming the general goals of the experiment;

b. explaining the ideas (tensile integrity) and structural model (icosahedron, team structure) inherent in the syntegrity approach;

c. outlining the purposes of the main parts of the protocol: Problem Jostle/ Topic Auction, Outcome Resolve, Final Plenary;

d. initiating the formulation and collection of the first Statements of Importance (SI). Do not forget to explain the test for motherhood statements (Method: Negation of the Statement).

Plenary Sessions

1. Plenary sessions are vital for transmitting thorough understanding of the purposes and procedures of each step of the programme. They should be held at least at the beginning of each major module—Problem Jostle, Topic Auction, Outcome Resolve—or at the end of the previous one.

2. When preparing the Problem Jostle, facilitators should have the right not only to elide SIs, but also to formulate their own. This would meet the concept of 'participant observer.' Availability of the complete list of SIs for each participant, at the latest at the beginning of the Problem Jostle, or better some time before, is very important.

3. The Problem Jostle

3.1. Physical Requirements

Alternatively, the 12 tables can be set along three walls or along two opposite walls. (The original instruction '...tables should be set... *around* three walls...' was difficult to understand.) The walls should permit the attachment of enough flip charts with titles, statements, and drawings above each table. Fixation devices (for example, easily removable adhesive tape) must be available.

3.2. Plenary Session Initiating the Problem Jostle

Of critical importance: Explain the main ideas expounded already in the protocol, stressing the main principles and practices such as:

- Principles of work: Free Choice, Individual Initiative, Self-organization, Openness, Creativity, etc.

- Role of facilitators (support, help).

- Formal requirements for 'topics' (five signatures).

3.3. Sessions of the Problem Jostle

A visible repartition of the Problem Jostle into the five sessions, as outlined analytically in the Protocol, may not be necessary. Often, several statements are merged to Composite Statements of Importance (CSIs) before they are attached to the clock.

The 12 statements which emerge as 'Topics' are not necessarily six pairs of polar opposites. There may only be very few statements, which are in clear opposition to others. Anyway, topics which are clearly antithetical will be positioned as polar opposites, while those which are clearly similar will be positioned as neighbours.

Henceforth, in this text, the term 'polar opposite' will designate the formal positions on the icosahedron, as well as on the 'twelve-hour clock,' which determine the nature of discussions. However, it does not necessarily indicate a polar opposition with regard to the contents.

3.4. Plenary Session at the End of the Problem Jostle

In a plenary session towards the end of the Problem Jostle the participants must be confronted with the 12 Agenda Topics. To facilitate communication, the topics will already be related to the colours at this stage. The titles and their corresponding colours should already be listed on a big board.

In this plenary, two questions have to be treated:

Q1. Have all the important statements of the initial list been considered, nothing important lost; or would someone like to add anything to the statements?

This may lead to a prolongation of the Problem Jostle.

Q2. Does everybody agree about the 12 Topics as a whole, in the sense that they set the agenda for the 12 teams? To continue the workshop, the plenary must come to an agreement about this.

At this stage, the voting process with stickers will take place. Before it, an additional voting process can be inserted, which is part of the test of Stafford Beer's 'convergence hypothesis' (see Section 7).

A fairly large interval should be provided between the Problem Jostle and the Topic Auction (it could, for example, be combined with lunch). The plenary session before the interval should already be used as an introduction to the Topic Auction (see Section 4.1).

4. Topic Auction

4.1. Preparing the Topic Auction

At the end of the plenary session which finalizes the Problem Jostle, participants should be sensitized for the crucial role of the Topic Auction and understand the complexity of the choice of roles. The following messages have to be communicated:

1. During the interval, each participant has to reflect thoroughly on the question, in which two teams s/he would like to be a player. There is one restriction to the free choice of roles: s/he cannot chose two colours which are polar opposites on the icosahedron. (Reason: the Outcome Resolve will proceed in parallel sessions of the 'polar opposites'.)

2. Further, s/he must take into account the considerations (listed in the Protocol) that deal with the combinations of roles—player/critic—in each team of which s/he is a member.

4.2. Handling the Topic Auction

1. The restriction against the choice of polar opposites mentioned under Section 4.1 would be eliminated if colours were not assigned prior to this session. In such a case, two consequences would have to be considered:

a. The Topic Auction as planned in the Protocol may become very complicated, cumbersome, and time consuming, or even unmanageable.

b. The result of the Topic Auction will most probably lead to new positions of the Topics on the icosahedron. Therefore the positions on the 'clock' will also have to be rearranged.

2. In case a Topic Auction as described in the Protocol should turn out to be unmanageable, the facilitator must resort to an abbreviated procedure. The version tested in the St Gallen experiment proved to be viable:

a. The 30-role combinations are announced in the plenary, one by one, and distributed to those who show interest first. The few conflicts that arise are negotiated *ad hoc*.

b. When all roles have been distributed, a written opinion survey is held on the question, 'Are you satisfied with your roles (Player/Critic/Combination)?

—Please answer only with "yes" or "no"!.' If more than a given number (suggestion: 20 of the participants) give a positive answer, the process is continued; if not, the Topic Auction should be done again.

4.3. Finalizing the Topic Auction

The Topic Auction must not be closed before a card or flip chart at each table exhibits the names of five members, five appointed critics, and five received critics. Facilitators should have structured and posted these 12 forms beforehand.

The distribution of critic roles demands a basically sequential procedure. Facilitators must call the teams one by one to make that decision together. In practice, self-organization leads to some abbreviation of that phase.

5. Outcome Resolve

5.1. Physical Set-up

1. To support the communication processes within the groups, the parallel discussions must take place in two separate rooms. One of them can be the room which is also used for the plenary session.

2. The evolving statement must be continuously transparent to all participants and observers. The best audiovisual support would be whiteboards with integrated copiers, which copy the text on the board on to a small format. Alternative solutions would be overhead projectors or, best of all, computers linked to overhead projectors. PC networks with advanced 'groupware' would open up a new range of possibilities.

3. To support overarching communication and observation processes, at the end of the plenary room or somewhere between the two team discussion rooms, big boards should exhibit a permanently displayed body of all statements produced during the workshop.

4. To facilitate individual orientation, at the end of each iteration, an individual selection (or a complete set) of the statements produced during that iteration should be available to each participant.

5.2. Meetings

1. The rule of partitioning the discussion into a phase of team discussion and a phase of the critics' statements makes sense. Anyhow, the experience of the St Gallen workshop suggests that an active participation of critics in the discussion, at an earlier stage, fosters reverberation.

Whichever of these two modes be chosen, enough time should be reserved, in advance, to sort out the arguments, integrate them, and attain a sensible statement, within the time budget available.

2. The idea of assigning one facilitator to each discussion, as a 'coach,' seems attractive. Another option would be to offer facilitators' support on demand, without assigning them. In these cases, facilitators would have to be highly skilled, or else the self-organizing process could be seriously prejudiced.

3. Observers should have the right to inject critical questions into any one of the discussions from outside, and be encouraged to do so. This principle should be abided by, as long as it does not lead to serious obstructions of the process.

6. Conclusion

The conclusion should be embodied by (at least) one final plenary session. The minimal program for this session is a projection of all statements on to a screen, one by one, for all participants to read. This should be accompanied by two voting procedures, first to assess the acceptance of the statements elaborated one by one, and second to compare the relative importance attached by each individual to the different statements (see Section 7). These voting procedures are important for methodological purposes, namely to improve the syntegrity method. The same applies to the distribution and filling in of a brief questionnaire to assess the workshop.

A more extensive version of a concluding plenary session would then focus on a joint effort to consolidate the final statements.

7. Convergence Test and Voting Procedures

7.1. Votes to Test Acceptance

The hypothesis that a syntegrity workshop should lead to a convergence of the views of participants can be examined by surveys in the process. 'Growth of acceptance of statements' could be used as a descriptor for 'convergence of views'. For the next experiments, the following procedure is recommended.

A voting procedure is held in the plenary session following the Problem Jostle (compare Section 3.3) and repeated in the final plenary session:

- Participants are confronted with the Topics (first occasion), and the Final Statements of Importance (last occasion), which are projected on a screen, one by one.

- After each projection, each participant has to answer the question, 'Can you accept this statement?' (Yes/No/Indifferent). The voting procedure can be open (headcount) or secret (questionnaire).

The convergence hypothesis would be corroborated if a growing rate of acceptance between the first and second voting results were identified.

Statistical exploration of a more differentiated questionnaire, which could also refer to subject matters of the workshop, and require scaled assessments, could lead to more profound answers to the convergence issue in the future.

7.2. Preference Votes

The other voting procedure—distribution of a finite number of stickers to the 12 subjects—may open new insights into the process that occurred, if repeated and compared, as the first one (see Section 7.1). The St Gallen experiment showed that four topics of enhanced interest had emerged in the process. This voting procedure is probably of little use in relation to the convergence hypothesis.

Schwaninger concludes his notes at this point.

THE PROBLEM JOSTLE

As already mentioned, the students produced 52 Statements of Importance to initiate their Team Syntegrity discussion on the future of the St Gallen University. The Problem Jostle duly reduced this variety to 12, and seemed to work well. However, the experience was evidently not as enthralling for the students as might have been hoped.

Q. Did the Problem Jostle work?

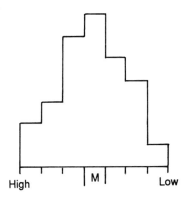

High   M   Low

The mean and mode share the central position and there are 11 players registered on each side.

Here are the twelve initial statements:

TWELVE STATEMENTS FROM THE STUDENTS' PROBLEM JOSTLE

St Gallen University, 22nd June 1990

1. More female characteristics needed in management.

2. Interdisciplinarity: *No* specialities: problem solving approach.

3. Work for Third World ecology mandatory: social competence.

4. Market-oriented Business School—Do we want it?

5. Training for fitness in a comprehensive sense: cf. Darwin—'the fittest' vs mass education.

6. Management *cannot* be learnt.

7. The Hochschule as a laboratory for a new society.

8. New forms of learning.

9. Tools (to be taught by PC) vs Essentials (to be taught differently).

10. The business of business is business.

11. More international orientation.

12. Emphasis on personal development.

As usual, it is not the current purpose to trace through all the iterations, or to print the whole text of the Final Statements. But it is surely of interest to learn from the new scoring procedure how support for these 12 motions moved between the first and last sessions.

The items on Female Characteristics (No. 1), Interdisciplinarity (No. 2), International Orientation (No. 11) and a Market-oriented Business School (No. 4) all gained substantial support during the Syntegrity Meeting, at the expense of all the other eight topics. It needs to be noted that the 'market' advocated in item 4 is not, as might be supposed, the commercial world that offers jobs to students: the student is taken to be the market for management education, which is the product of the university!

A graph of this overall movement is shown in Figure 4.1. It was kindly provided by Andreas Schimpf, who undertook the statistical analysis. He performed chi-squared tests on the changes observed, and found as follows:

- Votes were not distributed evenly at the first session (95% level of significance).

- Votes were not distributed equally at the last session (even at a 99.9% level of significance).

- The distribution of votes in the last session compared with that in the first session is unequal (99.9% again).

The original hypothesis that Team Syntegrity would lead to a convergence of views was clearly ill-formulated, because it is ambiguous. If it meant (and this was my original expectation) that we should conclude with 12 balanced statements that had equivalent support and therefore equivalent 'importance' (if FSIs), then this experiment clearly falsifies that hypothesis. But if the hypothesis refers simply to a coagulation of views around certain topics, then it is vindicated. The Infoset drew support to those four key topics from all other sources.

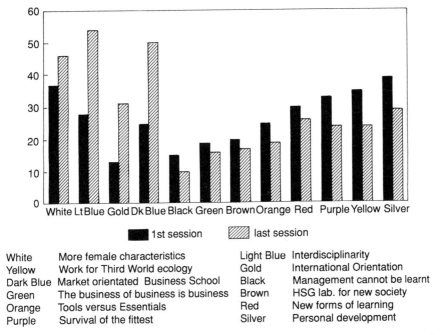

White   More female characteristics   Light Blue Interdisciplinarity
Yellow   Work for Third World ecology   Gold   International Orientation
Dark Blue   Market orientated Business School   Black   Management cannot be learnt
Green   The business of business is business   Brown   HSG lab. for new society
Orange   Tools versus Essentials   Red   New forms of learning
Purple   Survival of the fittest   Silver   Personal development

Figure 4.1 Syntegrity Workshop, Hochschule St Gallen, June–July 1990. Votes on topics/
statements

REVERBERATION

There was much evidence in favour of the reverberation hypothesis at St
Gallen, which might well be analysed in detail in a separate paper by
protagonists concerned. Of course, it would have to be hermeneutic rather
than statistical—the record of iterative statements being the only readily
verifiable information available. That is to say, we have the written
proceedings, plus any investigative addenda that might be available. What
follows is an analysis of the White Team's development of the FSI, where I
am able to quote the iterative statements—and to draw on my own enquiries,
made at the time, into how some remarkable reverberations actually occurred.

The topic of the White Team concerned a perceived need to introduce more
'female characteristics' into management. At the Problem Jostle, which
produced the one-sentence statement already recorded, I noticed a marked
feminist discussion, and determined to chart its progress in particular. The
reason was that I knew St Gallen to have less than 20% of its students female
(in marked contrast to much of the western world, where closer to 50% would

by now be a reasonable expectation), and to have only two women members of the entire faculty.

Here is the First Iteration of the White Team:

Chinese philosophy of yin and yang:

yin	yang
contractive	expansive
conceptive	aggressive
cooperative	competitive
altrocentric	egocentric

oriented towards

the environment	the ego
compassion	rationality
holistic and	linear, focused
non-linear thinking	analytical thinking
synthesis	disintegration

How are we going to enforce gender quota regulations? Should we have a, say, 50% quota of female professors?

Are mathematics male?

Hard factors dominate over soft factors in management education.

We demand a strengthening of yin factors in management education and education in general in order to reach an equilibrium between yin and yang factors.

Methods will be explored in the next iteration.

This is exciting material as put forth in a male-dominated ethos. Let us note in particular the intention to *enforce* 'gender quota regulations,' suggested as 50%, as also the *demand* to strengthen yin.

Let us note what happened in the Second Iteration, and especially its opening statement:

We are talking about yin and yang factors and *not* about men and women!

Chinese philosophy of yin and yang:

yin	yang
contractive	expansive
conceptive	aggressive
cooperative	competitive
altrocentric	egocentric

oriented towards

the environment	the ego
compassion	rationality
holistic and	linear, focused
non-linear thinking	analytical thinking
synthesis	disintegration

Hard factors dominate over soft factors in management education.

We demand a strengthening of yin factors in management education and education in general in order to reach an equilibrium between yin and yang factors.

AIM: More quality-growth than quantity-growth.
Better global chances to survive.
Ameloriation of management techniques, social backgrounds.
Better motivation, etc.
Process orientation better than results orientation.

Important are not new tools but new methods.

General method:

Foundation of an organization that promotes the 'yin way.'

Methods in education:

1. Change way of thinking by:

  ● intensive group dynamic excerises

    — learning about interaction, reaction, compromises, ...

- longer and more intensive teamwork:

  — handling of interpersonal processes ...

    2. Research (e.g. 'yin' cost accounting and strategies).

Not only is there no longer a move to *enforce* gender quotas, we are talking of yin–yang factors, and '*not* about men and women.' The Third Iteration repeats this statement but now puts it in parentheses. There is no longer any demand. Here it is:

(We are talking about yin and yang factors and *not* about men and women.)

The 'yin' values have to be considered too.

AIM: More quality-growth than quantity-growth.
       Better global chances to survive.
       Ameloriation of management techniques, social backgrounds.
       Better motivation, etc.
       Process orientation better than result orientation.

Important are not new tools but rather new methods

Methods:

1. Change way of thinking by:

- intensive group dynamic exercises

  — learning about interaction, reactions, compromises, ...

- longer and more intensive teamwork:

  — handling of interpersonal processes ...

    2. Research (e.g. 'yin' cost accounting and strategies).

This seemed to me at the time a remarkable progression—which (note again) increased support for the basic idea during the Outcome Resolve. I therefore interrogated several members of the White Team, but especially the manifest leader of the group. Why, I asked her, did the White Team quickly abandon the demand for gender equality that was so forceful in the First Iteration? She replied that 'it became clear' (surely we may put this down to Reverberation) that any such aggressive statement would be instantly repudiated by the Establishment and therefore should not be put forward as a matter of tactics.

Personally, I was sorry to see that 'Are mathematics male?' was also expunged: it is such an interesting question.

Perhaps it was an over-reaction (Second Iteration) explicitly to *deny* that the gender factor existed. At any rate, the idea was furthered that the 'yin way' required attention and development. My questions now were answered by the ingenious argument that if the 'yin way' (non-gender specific) proved acceptable, then the University would automatically come to appoint more women to the faculty, and thereby to attract more women students. This degree of subtlety was (surely, again) the product of Reverberation.

The Third Iteration, by its still lower key and its general appeal to contemporary liberal ways of thinking, seemed to have abandoned the original intentions altogether—although it leaves a mysterious afterglow in conjuring 'yin cost accounting,' whatever that may mean. Well, the group had already decided that a non-gender 'yin' approach would inevitably and satisfactorily lead to more female appointments among the staff and students alike. Why, then, an even further retreat in the expressed message? What Reverberation was now at work?

The answer to this was startling indeed. It might become obvious, I was told, that the manoeuvre towards the more feminine was happening. The masculine Establishment could well recognize the tactical approach, and come to see the trend as irresistible. In that case they would proclaim the new doctrine *themselves*—and set about appointing those women to their male enclave who could be relied upon to endorse it and its values! (There are women, including stateswomen, whom I have often called 'bogus men'—much as I understand the double bind in which they find themselves.) Thus a new faculty, even with 50% women, (so argued the team) would endorse the established profile for 'successful managers,' 'leaders,' and so on. Instead of 'fresh air' being blown along the corridors of corporations, second-class copies of traditional managers would set up offices there.

It appears to me that this extraordinary set of Reverberations around the icosahedron offers a major example of Syntegrity at work. The obvious question is: would a succession of White Team meetings have uncovered these levels of subtlety if the group had been merely an orthodox 'Committee of White'? As a long-serving member of similar committees, I cannot believe it. The reader will take his/her own stance on the importance of icosahedral Reverberation: but what is to be made of this particular example? Apart from tactical subtlety, the group came a long way from their initial 'demands' and 'enforcements.' They came to realize that the prerequisite for the development of new-style female management talent is a change of the kind of selection criteria and the weights attached to them.

REACTIONS

Answers to the questionnaire are not presented here as histograms, although the actual measurements are appended (the Problem Jostle histogram has already been shown).

Let Dr Schwaninger introduce the figures, again prepared by Andreas Schimpf. He writes:

'According to the answers to the questionnaire filled in by the participants at the end of the experiment, most of them had enjoyed the workshop, and gained new insights.

However, the enthusiasm is less spectacular than with the participants in the Manchester experiments. The two samples of participants differ, in so far as the students in St Gallen were not pure volunteers, but participants in a seminar of their obligatory study programme. They were in the last month of their four years' studies. These students had to submit themselves to the rigid regimen of being present at all four sessions of the experiment, to obtain the credit for participation. This is quite unusual an obligation for a seminar at this University, all the more demanding in the context of students being overloaded with commitments from teaching and excursion programmes within their specializations, as well as the preparation of their final exams.'

Here are the numbers, evidently skewed to the right although the PROCESS result is bimodal. Attention is drawn to the last result, indicating the ambivalence that many of the organizers themselves have felt.

	Low	-3	-2	-1	0	1	2	3	High
Did you enjoy yourself?		3	0	3	3	9	8	1	
Did you gain insight into group topics?		0	2	4	7	5	8	3	
Did you gain insight into group process?		1	0	2	9	4	9	4	
Did the Syntegrity approach work?		1	3	1	7	9	6	2	
How dependent is the model on correct numbers?		5	5	4	1	2	5	8	

Chapter Five

THE CORPORATE SCENE

THE SURVIVAL OF IDENTITY

The notion of the Infoset is intended to have intrinsic power: there is an identifiable set of people who share information about a topic that excites them. At Manchester, the sharing was a deutero-learning experience, and therefore somewhat remote from the tussle of existence. For although we all shared an interest in the future of humankind (as who does not?), the Infoset had rallied around interest in the technique of Team Syntegrity itself. That aroused more passion than might have been expected; but it is not a matter of intense commitment or dedication. Similarly, the St Gallen students constituted an Infoset simply because they shared the same university course and the intention to gain credit for attendance that was in any event mandatory. Their topic, the University's own future, certainly interested them strongly; but they were leaving that institution, and had yet more serious matters on their minds.

The corporation is a different matter altogether. Writing as a quondam manager and perennial consultant, I know the Corporate Infoset rather well. Senior managers explain with gusto how their organization is unique. They are wrong. They explain that one manufacturing industry has no resemblance to any other, that financial services corporations are as different from construction companies as chalk is different from cheese, that profit and non-profit institutions have nothing in common even if both are making a loss, and that government and business have fundamentally dissimilar motives and roles. All are wrong, because they distinguish between superficialities. In other books I have explained that viability, which is survival-worthiness, is basic to all human organizations, and that there are laws or precepts of viability that underlie them all invariantly. I do not disclaim a word. And I call the protesters wrong because they are not drawing their comparisons at an appropriate level to discover whether or not *survival* is assured or not. It is a deep matter: it concerns the preservation of *identity*. After all, in certain conditions both chalk and cheese will crumble, and neither will be fit for its purpose any more.

In this book, however, we are examining what I take to be another invariant among all kinds of human organization that are already taken to be viable. It is the Infoset that drives the whole show. A group of people in command *share the intention to survive*. Chapter One argued that this group, possibly (or often) comprising about 30 individuals, work from the same information base, which they interpret from the same values, and the same determination that the organization they command should indeed survive—even though it may have to change radically in the process. The value set they use entails judgements about others: that s/he is/is not 'one of us.' And the intensity of that identification in turn determines what actually is the Infoset in command. We have all witnessed *coups d'état*, at the national level; many of us have lived through the palace *coup*—whether in government or in corporations. The shift of power may ostensibly revolve around a charismatic individual or a potent idea: neither will carry the day unless embodied in an Infoset.

Of course, this is because of mass effect. It is strange that the idea of 'critical mass' is deeply embedded in and understood and exploited by the physical sciences, whereas it has not been systematically investigated by the social sciences. Elias Canetti, in *Crowds and Power* (Canetti, 1962), has much of interest to say, but he does not deal with the political power of the caucus, the 'inner wheel,' the Infoset that consists of 'us.' *That* is our current concern. Obviously it has been the concern of much social history, from the machinations of august families in Imperial Rome, to the Medici, and on to the Mafia, to refer to Italy alone. Modern 'democratic' politics, which has in fact to do with elective dictatorships, is concerned with little else. But accounts are descriptive, hypothetical, anecdotal, and imbued with the cult of personality. Perhaps the nearest thing we have to a sociological *text* about power is Machiavelli's *Prince*.

Once the Infoset notion has been accepted as a plausible invention, though yet to be investigated fully even within the confines of these covers, we are suddenly concerned with *structural* relationships between unnamed players in a 'game,' rather than with particular people who have interacted historically or who might be observed interacting now—although the latter observation is the empirical method of our enquiry as recorded in this Part of the book. The concept of Team Syntegrity, in short, is about structure, and the protocols that activate that structure. And, as with all scientific inquiry, it is about the *invariance* in performance that might be predicted from undertaking teamwork in well defined structural ways.

The howls of academic protest that these preliminary paragraphs will provoke are perfectly audible to me already: and no-one has read them yet. It is familiar stuff. Is this not positivistic phenomenalism? (I should not think so.) Is this perhaps neo-Kantian determinism? (I deny it.) Has this fellow considered the positions of Habermas and Foucault? (Never heard of them: I just invented these names to confuse you.) If I can hear the howls of protest, why do I not express myself more tactfully, more insightfully, with less bravado and panache? Oh, now, that's an easy one. If I did, readers might never understand the sheer power of the Infoset. The howls are what attest to its existence. That is the point. Accreditation on the one hand and exclusivity on the other are the marks of what I shall call Power Infosets, and I have just tried to give the flavour of their preposterous acerbity as lightheartedly as I can. I hope to show that we can replace Power Infosets by Synergistic Infosets, but that comes later.

THE POWER INFOSET

Even if the point about power is (however reluctantly) taken, the question of individual freewill is left hanging in the balance—just as if Darwin and Bishop Wilberforce had not exhausted the whole argument over a century and a half ago. If you take me by the heels and drop me over a cliff, you will probably kill me. I think that you should know that. My freewill is not, as it happens, in dispute. Nor in dispute is the 'so-called' (what valid skepticism we have here) Law of Gravity. It is not relevant to me that you are not Isaac Newton or that I am not an apple. You will probably kill me. Please be careful.

So: let us by all means acknowledge that the individual who operates within a human organization will do 'whatever s/he likes.' But, s/he will be constrained in various ways, and it is silly not to take note of those ways. We *normative behaviour?* are persuaded that people should wear clothes to work; we may even be persuaded that they should answer the telephone with phatic utterances: 'How are you today?'; 'Take care'; 'Have a nice day.' In a similar way, in most of the organizations that we know, we take account of hierarchy, with the result that its existence must be ritually denied. (I find that in Canada you have to know people for years before you can use, or maybe even discover, their surnames.) But always and anon, the individual who operates within these constraints is not only exercising free will. S/he is pursuing personal ambition: what is of interest is only the point on the overt/covert scale of self-aggrandizement at which s/he operates.

This is not cynicism, it is patently observable fact. And it is nowhere more patent than in the performance of Team Syntegrity, wherein (of course, and thank heaven for our humanity) people try to exploit the rules of the protocol. In none of the experiments recounted here did some one (or two, or three) fail to do so. Is this not revealing? It is just what people do in real life. And that applied in Manchester, in St Gallen, and in Toronto (yet to be discussed); and we are still no more than creeping up on the *corporate* scenario. Here the 'players in the game' have real stakes to play for ...

The Theory of Games flourished for a while in the 1950s and 1960s, as a first and exciting attempt to uncover the strategies of power, and to make formal analysis of such aspects of strategy as coalition and (here comes the synergistic notion) what was called 'Collaborators' Surplus.' The lessons have not been learned in the political, juridical, or managerial arenas, where strategy seems to be based on confrontation and adversarial modes of conduct to this day. Perhaps the difficulty was that there was no realistic dynamic in the Theory of Games. Static positions were investigated as in an incomplete game of chess; and although the supposition was made that the play would continue to unfold over time, analytic power was focused on a succession of frozen frames. By contrast, Team Syntegrity makes Collaborators' Surplus an evident process as the experience unfolds: it is a manifestation not so much of strategy as of *stratagem*. There is a pejorative connotation of trickery or cunning attached to that word which precludes my setting out a Theory of Stratagems in this work; but there is a meaning (O.E.D.) of stratagem as 'skill in devising expedients' which perfectly expresses what happens.

There expedients are about compromise, and the stuff of them is tension—as represented by the model. The outcomes, the FSIs, are supposedly higher syntheses in the Hegelian mould—and not the lowest common multiples of consensus. It seems to follow that if the corporate Infoset were arranged to juxtapose conflicting interests or ideas, then the adversarial stance ought to be eclipsed by synergistic reverberation. Nowhere ought this to be more productive than in management–union 'negotiations' (the inverted commas denote the euphemism). Suppose that we reject the 'them–us' confrontational model, and instead consider all the stakeholders. Certainly these include the management and the unions; but they may also include non-union workers: part-timers and temporaries, for example, whose status is often germane to the dispute these days. Next come the customers or clients; and maybe we need to include disgruntled non-clients who do not use a service (for instance the post office or the law to which they supposedly have a right of recourse) because it does not fit their needs. Shareholders are stakeholders, obviously; and it has even been suggested that crooks, computer hackers and other opponents of the system be considered as stakeholders too—as a means of examining security provisions and of defeating fraud. Well, the icosahedral Infoset has 30 members ... It is a fascinating exercise to consider which stakeholders, and how many of each, should be offered positions in a Team Syntegrity 'negotiation,' or on a Team Syntegrity Planning Commission. It seems evident that such a group, although it might become heated, is unlikely to polarize into a typical 'them–us' configuration.

Syntegrity arrangements of this kind are prefigured by widely reported experience with action learning and other role-switching techniques. In my own case, the opportunity arose soon after the arrival of a Ferranti Pegasus computer in 1956 at United Steel, UK. As far as could be traced, this was the first computer anywhere in the world to be installed by a management science department exclusively for its own purposes. We had begun with large-scale process simulations, and quickly realized that we could simulate business itself. ('Business Games' were already known, but they were not run on computers, and had no stochastic element—which was central to our own simulation concept.) Role-switching was an early experiment, and had hilarious results, reported elsewhere. The point for us now is that an Infoset of multiple stakeholders would be exchanging roles without assuming artificial bogus appointments—because that always happens in the Infoset as Reverberation operates. People 'forget themselves' in more ways than one.

THE CALIFORNIA EXPERIENCE

In our experimental year of 1990, the corporate milieu was represented by Pacific Bell Telephones, based at San Ramon, near San Francisco. The application did not involve a labour dispute (happily), nor even, as it turned out, an icosahedral Infoset. It came about as a result of long-standing discussions between myself and David Schecter, the in-house cybernetician, who has published (Shecter, 1993) his own account of the matter, from which I shall with his permission quote as we go on. Schecter was early enraptured with the work of Buckminster Fuller, and had been experimenting with physical models of all kinds of polyhedra. And it was he who introduced Dr Robert Pisani, Curriculum Director of Pacific Bell's own School of Management, to the organizational potential that I proposed. Pisani headed a group of six training managers, so that is why (as reported here in the last paragraph of Chapter One) he came to use the tetrahedral model, under a special protocol devised for the purpose.

Of course, the tetrahedron has six edges: no problem there for the group of six managers. There are four vertices: that meant consolidating the list of the team's projects and condensing them into four topics. This process is equivalent to the Problem Jostle in the 30-strong Infoset, but presumably it did not require an elaborate procedure. The Topic Auction, too, must have been more

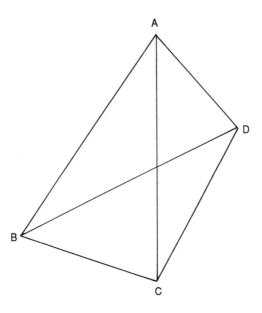

easily handled than in the larger case: each member 'chose' the two topics in which s/he was most interested—the constraints on each individual are evident, since each edge must be uniquely determined. As to the critics: Chapter One says that no *internal* tensility is available for them, since each player already has direct connection with all vertices. Thus the change in protocol is simply to say that each player is a critic of the two topic groups of which s/he is not a member. Thus the six occupy 24 roles, four each. There is evident strength in this, although it has a certain incestuous quality about it. For Mr AB must be a critic of topics C and D, so that his critical roles are defined as AD and BC; but Ms DA and Ms CB already exist as player members ...

Now each topic has three player members (the edges that meet at each vertex), and these teams each chose a team leader as chairperson. S/he was first among equals, without supervisory responsibility. Strangely enough, three different levels of official corporate status were involved; even more strangely, perhaps, the highest ranking person in any team did not necessarily become its leader. In one case, the group staff clerk became leader of a group that included supervisory managers. It seems that the democratic impetus in Team Syntegrity is strong ... How did it all work out? Schecter writes:

'For Bob Pisani, the tetrahedron structure meant a tremendous amount of delegation, of pushing responsibility downward. Whereas he had been the chief decision maker on all his group's projects, he was now chief decision maker on none of them. His people began taking much more initiative than they had in the past. Sometimes this was uncomfortable for him, but it was also very liberating. His group members ended up with more interesting jobs and responsibilities, as well as better communication between them. The main difficulties were two: first, the critic role was not well understood; second, one of the group members was located 500 miles away from the rest of the group, which made participation difficult. Also, this new way of doing things did not always blend well with the larger Bell culture—for example, some of Bob's peers resented having to interact with a lower ranking team leader on a project when they used to talk directly to Bob. Nevertheless, the group was enthusiastic about the tetrahedron structure.'

This was the first time that the tetrahedron had been used, and is especially interesting in that it is the lowliest member of the set of three-dimensional polyhedra. (Mathematically, the plane hexagon belongs to the same set of graphs, but I have not used it.)

There is another point. All the emphasis in the development of this approach had been on *process*: ways of resolving conflict, ways of planning, and so on. From the start on the West Coast, Schecter had been interested in using the whole set of concepts to define or design a *structure*. Here then, historically, was the Pisani group—presumably the first ever to adopt Team Syntegrity as an organizational design. But Dr Pisani himself had become interested because of his prior collaboration with Schecter in the case of the company's systems engineering group of some 20 engineers, headed by Louis Hureston. And Hureston and Schecter were looking for structure rather than process. So when they turned to Team Syntegrity, their use of my original working papers [which included the MS of *Suicidal Rabbits* (Beer, 1990)] was based on a misunderstanding ... This is how Schecter recounts the story:

'Louis had already abolished the first level of management in his group, and all the team members reported directly to him. Although his span of control had doubled, his job had become easier, because his team was now more autonomous. Louis came to me with a very unusual request. He did not have a problem for me to solve. He wanted me to help him understand why things were going so well, so he could make them better. Specifically, he was hoping to increase empowerment and organizational effectiveness, and free himself from supervisory activities to concentrate on higher level issues. One of his concerns was to find some viable form of non-hierarchical organizational structure for his team.'

He then goes on to describe the process/structure misunderstanding, and the establishment of a project to investigate further. This was when Dr Pisani was asked to join in as an advisor, because he is well known for his work on participatory research. He would 'help keep the project from degenerating into yet one more case of "democracy imposed from the top down",' says Schecter. As an earnest of this, too, a relatively junior member of the group,

Dave Melendez, was appointed project manager. I had been in telephone touch, but was soon to be present in California. Schecter writes:

'We started with the plan of re-organizing Louis's group in an icosahedral structure. After a while we abandoned this idea because it was too difficult to make the numbers come out right and still have a viable organization (at the beginning Louis had planned to expand his group to 30 people—later this became impossible). Instead, we decided to conduct a two day offsite planning meeting using Beer's protocol, in order to deal with the contentious issues facing his group. We invited Beer to help us do this. He came to Pacific Bell twice—first for an exploratory planning meeting with the group, and then to facilitate the conference.

In preparation for the conference, I interviewed each of the members of Louis's unit for an hour, asking them: (1) What is going well with the group? (2) What is going badly in the group? (3) What would you like to see changed? (4) What outcomes do you want from the offsite planning meeting? In several cases I held additional face to face meetings or continued the conversations by telephone. What emerged was a very mixed picture. The new structure had provided more freedom, more and better communication with peers, and more feeling of equality. Everyone agreed that Louis cared a lot about developing team members. On the other hand, people felt that Louis could not adequately develop and evaluate everybody. There was not enough accountability and there was confusion about roles. Several team members thought the group had too many managers and not enough workers. There were also some bitter interpersonal conflicts.'

THE STEERING TEAM

The first meeting that I attended was of a steering team still devoted to the idea of structural change. The Hureston group had already made use of the Viable System Model in the first reorganization, and were familiar with its shape and nomenclature. We spent a fascinating two days, sitting on the floor of Hurestons's house, discussing the relevance of the syntegrity model in the context of the VSM. For the last half-day the steering team expanded to include the whole group. The outcome was that we did not know whether syntegrity should be used structurally, as it had been misapprehended, or procedurally, as it had been intended—and therefore it was resolved to *use the procedure* to find out how the group could best be organized. Meanwhile, the conflicts that Schecter had detected were certainly surfacing; but they were handled by the group with good humour, and it was especially heartening to note the skill and sheer decency with which Hureston (a lion in a den of Daniels) responded.

Earlier in this chapter the matter of conflict between stakeholders was discussed. The meeting just described, however, was not ostensibly dealing with interpersonal conflicts, but with organizational matters—and a conflict of *issues* emerged. Which is the more important: the content or the quality of the work undertaken by the group? These are days of Total Quality Management (TQM), and the group had held seminars to discuss excellence in the performance of their work. They had highlighted the criteria by which they wished to judge themselves—listed their desiderata, if you will. Amid a good deal of hilarity, it was revealed that (no doubt by serendipity) 12 such issues added up to quality assurance for this group. There are 12 vertices in the icosahedron on which they expected to model the expected group of 30 people. Why not go the whole fashionable way with TQM, and organize the group around its own permanent criteria of excellence, rather than the shifting happenstance of project content?

Such a proposal is surely novel. At any rate, it generated a truly remarkable discussion. All manner of scenarios were contemplated, and they became more and more removed from the job as they became more and more ambitious for excellence *per se*. Individuals were happy to propose themselves and each other as monitors of quality. After emotional exhaustion had supervened, I asked, 'Louis, who is going to do the actual work?'

During the considerable uproar which followed this intervention, the following thought evolved. Direct the Problem Jostle to devise

- six wealth-producing (System One) topics that exhaust the mission; that is to provide categories into which job-content must necessarily fall;

- six activities—for example monitoring, auditing, invigilating—that will guarantee excellence (System Three Star).

Then every one of the 30 participants would be an edge (or 'rod') with membership in two teams, as usual. But now s/he would belong to one wealth-producing project team and one quality assurance team. The systems convention in parentheses above is drawn from the VSM: anyone who is familiar with that may think of this proposal as creating a characteristic repetitive loop: Three–One–Three Star–Three. The meeting found the suggestion interesting, but it has not been tried. It belongs to an immense list of variants on the fundamental notion of Team Syntegrity which any group considering its use will develop, and is most welcome to explore. The fecundity of this invention is perhaps its greatest attraction: despite the practical need at some point to determine protocol before a meeting, the model is not at all a conceptual straightjacket.

In the 4-month interval between this steering meeting and its upshot, the numbers to be catered for changed several times; in the end only 18 people appeared. Because of the arguments above about stakeholders, and given the size of Pacific Bell, not to mention its market, it was a great pity that we could not augment the size of the group with both internal and external clients (at the least) and run the icosahedral game with 30 players. It would have been highly productive to do that. However, the 'political' exigencies of the situation demanded that the exercise be kept in-house. The constraint had one merit: it compelled reconsideration of alternative or truncated polyhedra as models. Recall that we already had the Pisani tetrahedron as a guide.

All my discretionary time went into these explorations. For example, the Problem Jostle could still generate the (preferred) 12 topics, which could then be considered in groups of four by three Pisani Tetrahedra. But how to regain the synergy lost by the fission of the 18? Various possibilities, involving a kind of inter-subset barn-dance, were elaborated; but the interweaving would take time, and the two days available were already too short. Next came a whole gamut of truncations of the icosahedron. For example, what would happen if there were only 29 players? No-one knew. Using the physical model, I experimented with the removal of struts. The endeavour was disquieting: I never had (nor do I now have) any confidence in the engineering *analogy*—we needed mathematical isomorphisms. According to my epistemology of cybernetics (Beer, 1989, Chapter One, for instance), models can be scientifically underwritten only when mathematical invariances that link domains and experience (such as the physical and social realms) have been shown to exist. At the time in question, no demonstration was in sight.

For a while, I favoured breaking apart two 'polar caps' of the icosahedron. That is to say: by taking two vertices joined by Fuller's spinnability axis, one creates two poles that nominate two groups of five players. Each of these groups is in direct touch with five other players, who join the free ends of the polar-supported edges. Then 10 people are involved at each polar cap, using 20 players in all. The 10 missing players are the edges that spiral round the icosahedron linking the two polar caps. Suppose that 20 people are available (and there were 20 in Hureston's group), maybe a protocol could be devised to link the new inventions, the polar caps, in the absence of 10 missing edges (rods, struts). This might have been accomplished by defining a set of 'critic' roles that would have the effect of holding the polar caps apart. Wrestling with the problems of this initiative lost all attraction when the news came: there would actually be only 18 players.

When the 1990 experiments were completed, and the post-mortem was also done, I gained confidence from empirical evidence that the model is in fact very robust, and would probably 'hold up' under impoverishment of players to a large extent. But the extent was not specifiable, nor was the least dangerous pattern of impoverishment. It was at this time, then, that I introduced Team Syntegrity to a Faculty Seminar at my base in the European Business Management School in the University of Wales at Swansea. The help of mathematicians especially was invoked. For surely, if the Syntegrity concept could be freed from physical, three-dimensional space, and dependency on the Platonic solids, then a protocol-generating procedure might be developed that would cope with an arbitrary number of players as input. Dr Assad Jalali at once volunteered to help, proposing that Graph Theory could simplify the methodology. But this was for the future: we must needs return to California 1990.

OCTAHEDRAL SYNTEGRITY

Eighteen players and two days to go: I fell back on another alternative that had been fairly thoroughly explored—the octahedron. This has six vertices (equals topics) and twelve edges (players). The only way to instal *internal* tensility is by linking the three pairs of polar opposite vertices. Then instead of nominating *players* to be critics, as usual, we should nominate other people to perform the tensile role alone.

$18 - 12 = 6$: when twelve members take on player status, six are left to perform the tensile function. There are three tensile connections; but for A to pull on B is not the same as for B to pull on A. Thus six members could be appointed—two to share each polar cross-connection in opposite directions— and they would automatically find themselves to be members of the polar opposite team to the team they observed. This schema coalesces the antithetic (polar opposite) and the critical connections with which we are so far familiar: here I shall call them cross-polar members. The whole exercise is much diminished in variety compared with the icosahedron; and yet to squash the procedures into two days still proved very stressful.

The Problem Jostle, as noted, had to generate six topics of vital concern to the organization of the group. The titles were:

- organization itself

- clients

- communication

- decision making

- evaluation, reward and recognition

- resource allocation

This identification of topics was not too difficult to winnow out of the Jostle. Forty SIs were reduced to fourteen SIs by Jostling in 2.5 hours, thus saving 1 hour on the programme. However, three facilitators took 2 hours to isolate six topics as CSIs, and to arrange them in polar opposite pairs. Changes were made in the content of the six topics, by switching contained SIs, but the identities were not changed (although the name of one was amended). Players perceived this process as an administrative chore, and wandered off to chat. The list of titles shows rather well how separable issues within a team syntegrity can be brought into focus one at a time, while still and quite consciously constituting an interrelated whole.

The Topic Auction was remarkably easy to arrange, and took only 30 minutes. People were asked to go to the station of first option, and then to negotiate among themselves for the secondary roles—as both players and tensilities. The Auction was over in 30 minutes, after some uneventful shuffling.

OCTAHEDRAL TEAM SYNTEGRITY

Twelve compression players demarcate the boundaries of the octahedron, and Red–Yellow (for example) is the same person as Yellow–Red.

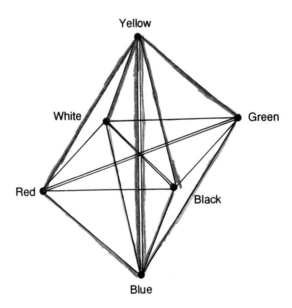

There are six tension players; but White–Black, Red–Green, and Yellow–Blue are different people from Black–White, Green–Red, and Blue–Yellow.

The team accommodates 18 players in all. Because the antithetic and critic roles are coalesced, the syntegrity player in each team has to operate in private collusion with his/her tensility pair (for example, Yellow–Blue with Blue–Yellow).

Sample of a Simultaneous Meeting of Polar Opposites:

YELLOW TEAM	BLUE TEAM
Players:	Players:
Yellow–White	Blue–Red
Yellow–Green	Blue–White
Yellow–Red	Blue–Black
Yellow–Black	Blue–Green
Tensility:	Tensility:
Yellow–Blue	Blue–Yellow

But once again the protocols for tensility were faulty, and for some bad reason now forgotten, three tensilities were expected at each meeting. Thus the six people cast in that role were engaged in every session and became exhausted. Moreover, the effect of massive interaction across the Infoset domain is easy to underestimate. Experiencing it in unpredicted ways is frustrating to facilitators, even though it reinforces the intuitions they might have about valuable reverberation in the system. The next chapter will show how the structural implications of the model for the critical role finally became clear in the case of the icosahedron. Mistakes about the allocation of critical roles in California had the lame excuse that this was the first use of the octahedral model, but they became clear as soon as the Outcome Resolve was under way. 'Excuse me,' someone says to a facilitator on all such occasions, 'but I am supposed to be in two places at once.' It is humbling to have to resolve such confusions *ad hoc*, but that was what had to be done.

Speaking of reverberations, however, and recalling the example about 'feminine management' encountered in St Gallen, let us note a productive example from San Ramon. Remember that the senior manager in charge of this group is called Louis Hureston. Remember also the basic provision that tables and chairs are provided, with some to spare, so that anyone may seize one as a platform by announcing a chosen topic on a flag or poster for all to see. Here is Schecter again, writing as a facilitator. He begins with an incident at the Problem Jostle, and follows the results into the Outcome Resolve.

'One of the initial Statements of Importance was "Lou needs mentoring" (English translation—"Lou needs to get a lot better at his job!"). From my preparatory interviews I knew that some of the group members were very unhappy about Lou's performance as a manager, while others had the opposite opinion—a difficult issue for sure. I wondered who, if anyone, would start a table to discuss this topic.

It did not take long to find out. At the very beginning of the Problem Jostle, Louis himself walked up to one of the stations and wrote "Lou needs mentoring" on the sign. At first nobody came to talk with him. Then he took me aside and asked "Is it okay for me to pull somebody into this discussion?" I told him to go ahead. He picked one of his most vocal critics. Then someone else joined, and pretty soon they had a lively discussion going. At first I was pleased at how cordial the discussion was, considering the difficulty of the subject. After a while I began to think the discussion was *too* cordial, and something was missing.

A little later, one of the team members took me aside, pointed to the "Lou needs mentoring" table and said "You know, Lou shouldn't be in that discussion." "Why not?," I asked. "Because his presence is discouraging other people from participating." I told her I thought Louis had the right to be in the discussion, but suggested that she should start a separate discussion on the same topic. So she went to another table, picked up a marking pen, and wrote "Lou needs mentoring (without Lou!)" on the sign. Soon a whole new group gathered around this table and began to talk.

The people in the second group had strong complaints, and did not feel comfortable about expressing them directly to their boss. During the first session they were mainly complaining, letting off steam, and happily discovering that they were not alone in their concerns about Louis's leadership. I was a little worried about a major confrontation. However, as the sessions progressed and the groups rotated, I saw a definite change in the content of both discussions. In the second session, one of the team members said, "You know, we can't put this all on Louis. We have some responsibility in this too." Later both discussions started producing specific recommendations that Louis could act on. By the third session, the suggestions were for the whole group, not just Louis. I am convinced that if we had been following an ordinary meeting protocol, many people would not have voiced their complaints, or else there would have been an angry confrontation that made things worse for everyone concerned.'

Bob Pisani and I, as the other two facilitators, were exceptionally interested in the development of this reverberation. He was the expert in participatory research, after all, and this was participation writ large. For my part, details of the reverberatory process proved fascinating. It is noted that they prove to be extremely difficult to record—on this occasion as in all others. Formal CSIs (the increasingly Consolidated Statements of Importance) embody the state of reverberation at the moment of compilation, certainly. But the effect of individual utterances in the team syntegrity context sometimes has the social impact of a dropped bead of mercury splattering on a table. And because the mini-beads then bounce off the concave polyhedral surface ... Another metaphor would be the generation of interference patterns of coherent light within that surface—and we are back to the holographic analogy with which these ideas began in Chapter One. Suffice it to say that proper research into these social phenomena needs the tools of a subtle choreography, to try a third metaphor, because the variety of the Infoset-in-action is so very high.

Because this occasion was not merely an experiment in social cybernetics but an important corporate meeting, the full documentation of the SIs, CSIs, and FSIs is reserved. But the company had been most forthcoming otherwise in permitting publication, as witness this quotation from the Schecter reference:

> 'In the outcome resolve we went through three rounds of discussion on the topics. By the end of the second day, the groups had generated a lot of insight and purposeful conclusions, but not all of them had adequately specified action steps to implement the conclusions. This was a source of great frustration for some of the team members at the very end of the meeting. Nevertheless, various team members volunteered to continue the work in sub-committee meetings over the next several weeks, and I saw significant progress during that time (Louis recently informed me that his group has continued to make progress on these issues).'

Two comments on this question of frustration are perhaps in order. As this record has gradually demonstrated, and as was just now argued in principle, the high variety generated by the team syntegrity process is inevitable—and is indeed a valued product of the approach. Then by Ashby's Law (that only variety can absorb variety), the requirement for sufficient time to work through the combinatorial interactions of the topic teams is absolute, and its likely measure has been emerging as a whole week of 5 days. Only 2 days were available in California, and owing to various administrative delays even this working time was eroded. At the end of the meeting, the duration of topic sessions had to be restricted to 20 minutes each. It might be guessed that this would be inadequate, and so it proved. This was surely a factor in the failure to complete all the FSIs to include action modalities. All this was the case despite the greatly reduced size of the Infoset, and the relative simplicity of the octahedral model compared with the icosahedral.

The second comment reverts to the discussion with which this chapter began. When we are dealing with the political reality of a corporate group, power clashes and power plays have to be expected. On two occasions during this short meeting a pair of antagonists (not the same pair on each occasion) came almost to blows, and each time one of the pair stormed out. This poses a challenge to the facilitators, and it can be a difficult task to win the disgruntled player back. We met the same problem in Manchester; we shall meet it again in Toronto in Chapter Six, even though the meeting there was not held under any corporate aegis with its likely tensions. So the question arises of whether a highlighting of dissent is likely to exacerbate it, or whether its evolution in a supportive environment might not clear up bad feeling that might otherwise fester within the Infoset for years.

David Schecter (Schecter, 1993) had views and speculations about team syntegrity of his own. Here it is appropriate to record that section of his observations wherein he reflects on the San Ramon meeting itself:

'Perhaps the most important advantage of the team syntegrity process is that it is very democratic. First, the whole group sets the agenda in an open process. No amount of democratic process is sufficient if the agenda is set behind closed doors by a powerful few. Second, everyone has close to complete information. Third, the roles of each individual and each group are the same. Fourth, in the Topic Auction each person gets to choose what topics they want to work on. Fifth, the self-organizing format of the Problem Jostle helps reduce the possible domination of the discussions by the most powerful personalities—people who feel intimidated in one discussion are free to leave and join (or initiate) another.

In addition to being democratic, the team syntegrity process is very conducive to the development of dialogue and community. Primarily this is a result of the multiple membership protocol during the Outcome Resolve. It is common practice in my experience to have large group meetings break up into sub-groups for discussion, then report their conclusions back to the larger group. While this gives each group member the opportunity for discussion, the members of each small group get no information about what goes on in the other small groups except for the attenuated version that gets reported back to the larger group. In addition, it is very difficult to achieve synergy from the results of the small groups, because there is no connection between them.

By having each person be a member of two groups and a critic of two others, much more lateral connection is achieved. Everyone knows a great deal about what everyone else thinks. The compressive force of sub-groups coming to agreement among themselves is balanced by the tension between the different sub-groups. This protocol is very conducive to dialogue. In the Pacific Bell example, I observed people changing their minds about issues much more easily than they would have under a traditional meeting protocol (some of the participants confirmed this).

The third major advantage of the syntegrity process is that it seems likely to improve the output of decision making processes (I have deliberately placed this last, because I believe that the output of decision making processes is usually less significant than the extent to which the decision process helped or hindered the development of the democratization of the group). The Problem Jostle encourages innovation by not setting the agenda in advance and allowing unusual ideas to develop. The result should be that some surprising and stimulating ideas get onto the table. This was certainly true in the Pacific Bell case. Because the team syntegrity process encourages lots of interaction at every stage, it helps to achieve synergy among the ideas generated by the individuals and the sub-groups. Through the concept of antithetical management (the special roles of critics and polar opposite teams), Beer's process seems to make productive use of conflict rather than trying to stifle it or smooth it over. Like all good group decision making processes this one increases the possibility of an output that is supported by the group, which means that the plans produced have some chance of successful implementation. And, last but not least, the process is enjoyable.'

HISTOGRAMS OF SCORES: CALIFORNIA MEETING

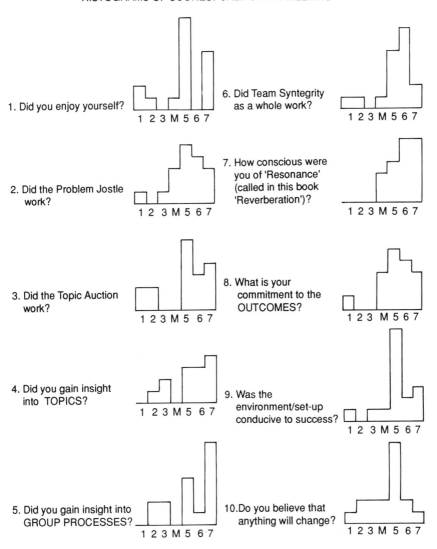

NOTE: There were 17 respondents out of 18 participants.
Not every question was answered.

THE FIRST CORPORATE INTERVENTION: REACTION

Yes, the process does seem to be enjoyable, as witness the first of the histograms appended (p. 85). Thirteen people rated the experience as better than average, one played safe at the median score, and there were three malcontents. It is tempting to interpret such results, especially because of the statistically strange discontinuity at score 6. It could be that the malcontents are change-resistant by nature, that the sevens are euphoric for novelty, while nearly half the participants wish to be seen as positive though prudent. To say so would be pure invention were the people concerned not under close observation ... But it is hoped that all users of this developing technique will collect data of this kind from participants, so that a properly scientific perspective may be gained.

The 'six effect' occurs in no less than four of the ten results, but so does the overriding bias towards favourable judgements. The malcontents are at least consistent, and they tend to isolate themselves from the rest: note that eight out of ten histograms show a malcontented discontinuity. Since the question of reverberation (referred to at this epoch as 'resonance') has been a matter of research importance from the very beginning, and will gain in importance as we proceed, attention is drawn especially to the answer to Question 7. Not only is the reaction strongly positive: even the malcontents were silent— perhaps because they generated a significant part of it. Finally, the reaction to Question 10, which epitomizes cautious optimism, might raise a smile.

Chapter Six

IN THE COMMUNITY

Having used the Team Syntegrity technique with two groups of students (Manchester and St Gallen), a group of professional friends (Manchester), and a corporate department (California), it was time to involve a more general public. In Toronto there is published a free 'alternative' weekly called *NOW* magazine, which was confidently expected to show editorial interest in a new approach to the causes of community which it espouses: we needed to capture the attention and ultimately the time of 30 readers—so we told the Editor. The magazine did not respond: new ideas are always anathema—in this case to, ironically, a repository of new ideas ...

The group who came were recruited mainly by word of mouth. But the numbers would not have been made up without the help of the public library on the corner of our street. The Ontario Institute for Studies in Education kindly, and appropriately enough, provided the venue. Secretarial and commissarial expenses were supported by the World Service Authority, because of their interest in the validation of the Team Syntegrity technique. But the main donation came from the participants: four days of their holidays between Christmas and New Year's Day.

Thus the Infoset was assembled in an unusually arbitrary way: we may call it such a unity only because of its members' all being drawn to the heading on the poster: 'What Kind of Future Do You Want?' It was surprising, then, to find so statistically good-looking a group. The following occupations were listed: academic, artist, businessman, cybernetician, economist, engineer, futurologist, landlord, lawyer, pensioner, personnel, physical chemist, software, student, teacher, world government, writer. The gender split was two thirds male, one third female. Here is the age distribution:

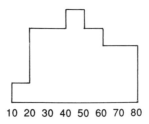

10 20 30 40 50 60 70 80

Toronto syntegrity: age distribution

It is likely that (on this occasion) the reactions to the meeting also reflected the characteristics of the Infoset, in that the people attending must have been highly motivated. On the other hand, that fact also argues that they might easily have felt disappointed. This will be more readily assessed after reading the Commentator's observations: but, however interpreted, the responses surely support the syntegrity experience as highly positive. Please compare the two relevant histograms below, drawn to the same scale, because the bunching towards satisfaction in the second case is particularly encouraging.

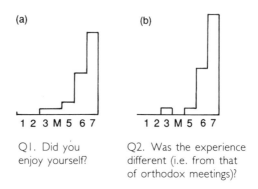

(a)

(b)

1 2 3 M 5 6 7   1 2 3 M 5 6 7

QI. Did you   Q2. Was the experience
enjoy yourself?   different (i.e. from that
                    of orthodox meetings)?

According to the original plan, there should have been four facilitators: two were out of town, and the two who came were press-ganged into service as participants—to make up the numbers. The role of rapporteur was supposed to be that of independent observer; but again had to double with that of participant. There were no extra helpers, as really are required. It should be noted that the full-scale icosahedral team syntegrity is a big undertaking: it is clear (as argued already) that it should last for 5 days, and ideally it needs four facilitators and four support staff competent to handle both paperwork and refreshments. That adds up to a considerable investment: the benefits are, however, overwhelming.

THE ACTUAL START

The following account of what happened is illuminated throughout by direct quotations from our official commentator, Amanda Brown. As was said, she was hampered by playing a dual role as a player, but the cybernetic status of *participant observer* is high in methodological repute, and it seems to have been most effective in practice. The meeting began 'from cold' by formulating the initial Statements of Importance which in normal circumstances would have been sought in advance as inputs to the Problem Jostle. It is best to ask for them before bedtime after an introductory dinner, so that the facilitators can work over them during the night. In Toronto, we did not have the luxury of a prior evening: no dinner. But it could be that our commentator's candid statement says more about what actually transpired.

Amanda Brown writes:

'I noticed that some people sat and formulated statements, deliberating their relevance to the focus and process of this meeting. Others wrote one or two statements and posted them. They read others that were posted and then sat and wrote a few more. Some people read, jostled and grouped these statements being posted, where they felt themes were evident. Reverberations led some to write statements in a deliberate attempt to make links between the statements posted.

I tended to sit and ponder so it was impossible for me to get around the room and participate fully in this process in the time allotted. My friend, on the other hand, was highly mobile through this phase and told me that he had gained a sense of who the other players were through the issues, ideas, and points of view found in the statements. They also fed his thought process and introduced the issues which led to his topic group choice.

In this experiment there were 137 SIs produced. These were not made available to the players, in raw, ungrouped, unelided form until the third day of this meeting.

When I read these statements two days after the topic statements had been established, I was surprised to see how many related to the topic areas I was involved in. I feel that their inclusion in our original statement development deliberations would have provided an added dimension.'

Note that the terms 'jostled' and 'reverberation' are already figuring (though with hindsight, of course) in this description, and that the number of SIs is very high—consistently with high motivation, no doubt. The criticism in the last paragraph is justified: here the need for support staff is well demonstrated. Even so, it is interesting that the SIs, although lost sight of in their original form, did in some sense survive—in that they related to the final topics.

THE TORONTO PROBLEM JOSTLE

The Problem Jostle proceeded in the usual way, exhibiting the usual toing-and-froing that the protocol is designed to promote. It should be noted that anyone who takes on 'ownership' of a potential project enjoys restricted access to this process, simply because the owner dedication takes most of the time. Amanda Brown was trapped in this way, and felt excluded from whatever else was happening in the room while she held court under her own topic statement. She not only did not discuss the meaning of other topic headings with their adherents, she did not even read them—although the room is purposely designed to ensure that reading titles at the least is possible. Her comment is valuable: 'The discussion generated around the topic that I originated was interesting, complex, and thought-provoking, and I chose not to break my focus and move out to integrate something completely new.' Well, she did *choose*; and every choice is valid in this arena. Very often people in this situation will obtain the mandatory five signatures, or perhaps push for a significant ten (a third of the Infoset, note), and feel confident that the topic is a runner. Then it is common to find an empty topic stand, whence the signatories have departed to catch up with progress on other topics. A delightful photograph of a deserted stand at St Gallen, for example, shows five empty chairs under the topic heading TWO YEARS OF INTENSIVE STUDIES ARE ENOUGH. The absentees had taken their own opinion seriously, it seemed. In fact, they were content, and busily reading other statements.

Not only is the option to choose vital to this design, but also the option to adopt a tactic that will sway votes in just the same way that tactical voting is often suspected in by-elections. When people are casting their votes by sticking markers on a tally clock, in particular, it is clear that a vast amount of tactical information is flowing: people eye each other and the distribution of each other's votes, plunging in or holding back in an attempt to secure the 12 topics they consider the most important for the final resolution. Individual behaviour at the Problem Jostle too is not just a matter of choosing to focus one's attention or to disperse it widely, but of implementing a tactic that supports this decision.

Once more, the Toronto experience was to suffer from the shortage of staff, and especially the lack of facilitation. The situation that Amanda Brown now describes should never have happened. Indeed, it has not happened elsewhere, because facilitators were guiding the process of defining the required number of topics continuously to converge. Here is the scene:

'When time was called there were seven topic statements displayed, five short of the twelve required to begin the Topic Auction. At this point I took a quick look around the room and noticed that a number of issues which could have some bearing on the conference, were missing from any statements. I then posted another statement. I discussed this briefly with one other person and suggested that she write a paragraph defining the focus.

The statement that she wrote diverged from our original discussion significantly and attracted no adherents. There was no insistence that a topic acquire validation by attracting five signatories. Lack of time and the shortage of alternative topic options resulted in this statement defining a discussion topic group.'

Instead of a topic's arriving in the final list by default, as happened here, proper facilitation should have helped the Infoset to tease the seven topics apart. It would also have drawn attention to SIs that were relevant and had become lost—or to insinuate new ones if those relevant notions had never achieved expression as SIs.

The more that I work with team syntegrity, the more robust the process seems to be. In this case, and despite the defect in the procedure just noted, the participants seemed reasonably satisfied with the outcome. The 12 statements that had emerged were exhibited for scrutiny, and to collect further signatures. Opinion (with hindsight) is represented by the histogram below. This result is not a triumph: however, only three people registered a score below the median.

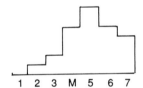

Q5. Did the Problem Jostle work?

THE TORONTO TOPIC AUCTION

As can at once be seen from the following histogram, the Topic Auction was much less satisfactory.

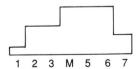

Q6. Did the Topic Auction work?

Throughout this account, it has had to be admitted that the designation of topics and the allocation of players and critics between them were not working properly. We have to remember that each player has to find four roles out of 120 roles in total, and that this is a complicated matter: each role carries the entailment of dealing with a specific quarter of the topics, and thereby of losing direct—although not indirect—involvement in three-quarters of the work. This is a deliberate part of the design, and I do not regret it. It is idle to pretend that everyone is equally interested in every aspect of the task, and we set out to obviate boredom. On the other hand, people can and do have a marked influence on the remaining three quarters—through formal procedures, through transparent voting activity, and through informal discussion. Next comes the split of activity for each person between the player and the critic roles. In practical terms: people want to know with whom they will be working, and the designating process (as so far practiced) is a happening in which this very information is changing continuously as people swap places. This does not have to be the case, of course. Complicated transferable voting systems could be implemented on a computer, and participants informed of 'who they are.' So far, the human auction has seemed preferable, precisely because it *is* human, and interactive, and withal transparent.

One way or another, at any rate, quadripartite identity cards (QIDs) have to be issued. A two-stage process is involved. First the *player* identity, in two colours (e.g. Mr Green–Blue) must be fixed. The player identity cards (IDs) of which there are 30, can be preprinted. The possible combinations of two colours are fixed by the icosahedron itself. Then we require a means of distributing them. But the acceptance of an ID has serious implications. It delimits the alternatives for exercising the two critical roles, but it does not actually select them. Therefore, the two critic roles needed to convert the ID into a QID remain blank on the card. They depend on the Topic Auction.

Mention was made earlier of the idea that polar opposite vertices should denote opposing ideas, in so far as this has meaning. To go back to the Negation Test, there could easily be two topics resting respectively on theistic and atheistic premises. Then (we had been saying) these topics should be set up as polar opposites. By the time the experiment reached Toronto, the obviously analogical thinking behind this ruse looked superficial. Each polar topic involves five players and five critics ... it means that 20 people are tied into two simultaneous meetings which can never interact at all and therefore theists and atheists never confront each other directly. Moreover, the concept of opposing 'polar caps' that emerged in California takes account of the five topics contiguously associated with each polar cap. If this contiguity is allowed into the analysis, then all 12 topics and all 30 players are accounted for in one grand dichotomy. And so on for each meeting period: the syntegrity could be described as delineating six grand dichotomies in the sense defined.

To avoid this, the assignment of topics (with the consequential colour code for polar opposites dictated by the coloured icosahedron) at Toronto took *similar* rather than dissimilar contentions as polar opposite topics. This intended to allow individuals holding conflicting views to clash, face to face; and now there would be a chance to see how polar-separate groups would separately develop cognate ideas. But this experimental design changed a fundamental parameter of the Topic Auction. Although I knew why the change had been made, I had no means of assessing its likely impact on the Auction, and wanted to find out what it would be. As usual, and as the histogram has already indicated, there was a general sense of dissatisfaction with the process, and a great deal of difficulty in determining exactly what was wrong and exactly how to put whatever it was right. This was not just a confusion in algorithmic logic. What topic contentions are similar or dissimilar is an arbitrary distinction; whether people understand what they are supposed to do is unpredictable ...

Let us examine the actual experience of finding an ID (the two-colour player's card) in Toronto. Amanda Brown was joined by four other players standing beside the first statement that she had originated. So far, so good: a ready-made team of five were indicating (as invited) an over-riding preference to address this topic. But, she notes, it was not clear to her what options she had to join a second group as player. The topic colours had only just been assigned (because of the polarity issues discussed above), and so each of the group had to study the icosahedral model itself to determine the set of five possible linkages. This should not have been necessary: the five ID cards Yellow 1–5, for instance, were supposed to be at the yellow stand for the five first-choice Yellows to split between them. But, of course, the Yellow–Purple ID, for instance, would be found in the group of ID cards available at the *Purple* station! Having recognized this dilemma from the beginning, I had provided two sets of ID cards at Manchester. But this had resulted in two people's claiming each identity—Mr Yellow–Purple contesting with Ms Purple–Yellow for the honour of that single role. By Toronto, the ID selection was supposed to be done by stages of protocol, but people do not proceed with sufficient decorum; they get ahead of the game, of each other, and of themselves.

Amanda Brown wrestled with her options as revealed by the icosahedral model itself. She knew that she not only wanted interesting topics for her two full-scale memberships, but that some people were already recognized as being more empathetic than others. And it is clear that an identified two-colour player cannot arrive as a critic of either a contiguous or a polar opposite group on the icosahedral surface, because these are not designated critical pathways. Ostensibly she may compete for any designated critical pathway from either of her vertices; even then there is the question not only of topics to be critiqued but of the topic groups who are forming to represent them—empathies again. Hence the protracted wrestling with options. Meanwhile, the attempted protocol was proceeding. She writes with great clarity about the consequences:

> 'Before I was given a choice in obtaining a team identity card, people who had not allied themselves with any statement were asked to make their ID card choice. Two of these people chose membership in our group. Next, those teams with two or fewer members were asked to select their ID cards. By the time I and members of the group that I had originally chosen were asked to choose our cards, none were left which listed our group as either a first or second choice. This meant that none of our five original members would be players on the team we created. This was distressing to me and when brought to the attention of the Auction Facilitator he asked all persons who had cards for our group to give them back. These were then distributed among four of the original members of our group.
>
> In another group which had five original adherents, only one made it into the group as a player after the topic auction.
>
> With regard to the second topic statement that I had originated, this was a group of last resort. Of the five ID cards listing membership in the group, three were not claimed at all as there were 27 players in total for this experiment. The two players who were placed on this team had not chosen to be there deliberately and one expressed some anger with the process for having found himself there.'

Since this 'group of last resort' was based on her idea, Amanda Brown managed to become involved in it by using up an available critic role. That was the official position. However, as there were only two designated players in the group, all three supposed critics operated as players, and she was by now a player in three teams. It will be recalled that the Infoset was incomplete, and also that this original topic was illegitimate in that it had not been properly validated as to fivefold parentage from the start. It was not too surprising that the three missing icosahedral edges all terminated in holes in this vertex. And yet, despite such onerous disabilities in theory, the group worked excellently in practice. This was one of the happenings that increased my respect for the robustness of the design: it seems to carry a lot of structural (which translates into informational) redundancy. Whether that also implies that the full-scale design could be much simplified without loss is a possibility, but remains a conundrum.

Meanwhile, Amanda Brown battled on:

> 'I noticed that others who had received their topic choice colours were unclear of the procedure whereby you determine the groups in which you will attend meetings

in the role of critic, so after sorting things out with my first-choice group I visited three other groups and showed them how to make their critic group choices. There were no non-participant facilitators at this meeting and this was one of the points where their absence was felt.'

THE FREESMAN EXCLUSION

The complexity of the problem faced by the individual in working out critical options is considerable, even with the physical model to study. The first attempt at simplifying the matter was to provide a list at each station (named by its colour) of those groups (also colour coded) to whom representative critics should be dispatched, and a list of those groups from whom representatives should be received. These groups were left to negotiate which person took on each role—because (as was recently remarked) any person could *ostensibly* compete for any legitimate role. But if so, how did it happen that at each and every experiment a QID would determine that its owner had to be in two places at once?

The answer lies in the fact that the two groups making these appointments are not acting independently, but are linked by the one player who belongs to each of them. But the linkage is of no concern to either of them (and was therefore not noticed); it is vital to the single player concerned. And in the cases that kept cropping up, s/he was too preoccupied with quadripartite choices about topics and empathies to have noticed any other constraint. The facilitators made *ad hoc* rulings to escape the two-places-at-once dilemmas, and tended to assume that the victim was actually a culprit—someone who had not understood the rules. This was not so.

The rules, however, were not formulated until the muddle had occurred for the fifth time, in Toronto. Boris Freesman QC was a member of the Infoset who was instantly captivated by the properties of the syntegrity model: it was he (see Chapter One) who devised the name. He perceived what the problem was, solved it, and formulated the rules. To understand the point, it is essential to think from the individual's perspective as a unique player holding a QID, and not from a topic group perspective where only half of the QID is of any interest.

Then consider one player: Boris Freesman selected Mr Purple–Dark Blue for his example, and he listed the ostensible options for the critic role from each *group* in two columns, thus:

PURPLE GROUP SENDS CRITICS TO GROUPS	DARK BLUE GROUP SENDS CRITICS TO GROUPS
Gold	Silver
Orange	Orange
Green	Green
Black	Light Blue
White	Red

But now we must consider the situation confronting the unique *individual* Mr Purple–Dark Blue. You would need a coloured octahedral model in front of you to verify what follows, but the argument itself is sufficiently clear.

Four members of the purple-group might choose to become a critic of Gold— but *not* Mr Purple–DARK BLUE. That is because Gold is the polar opposite of Dark Blue, and those two teams meet simultaneously. So if Mr Purple–Dark Blue is attending a Purple meeting as a player, he cannot at the same time attend the Dark Blue meeting as a critic. The symmetrical case disqualifies him as a critic of the Silver group, as Silver is the polar opposite of Purple. So much is apparent to anyone who inspects his/her personal strut on the icosahedron, and of course players were warned by the organizers and facilitators to avoid committing this error in making their choices.

The lists as printed above next refer, in both cases, to the groups Orange and Green. This is because the Purple–Dark Blue strut subtends each of these vertices, and no problem arises for Mr PURPLE–Dark Blue or for Mr Purple–DARK BLUE in accepting the role of critic to either group.

The coupling that causes the problem experienced is concealed in the last pair of critical roles as listed: there is a hidden restriction of choice that no-one had noticed, or at least (if s/he had) had not made explicit. It is possible for Mr PURPLE–Dark Blue to choose the Black Group, or alternatively for Mr Purple–DARK BLUE to choose the Light Blue Group; but the integrated individual Mr Purple–Dark Blue cannot do both. Black and Light Blue are polar opposites, and will be meeting simultaneously. The symmetrical argument in this case says that Mr Purple–Dark Blue may accept a critical role in either the White or the Red groups, but not both—since White and Red are polar opposites.

This is the *Freesman Exclusion*. It says:

> 'A person may choose to play a critic role in only one of a pair of teams that are themselves polar opposites.'

Well, the fact is a second-order effect, and it was hidden within the ostensible choices; even so, given the trouble it was causing it should have been spotted sooner. Again we are forced to realize that we are unfamiliar with three-dimensional percepts, and to wonder whether a rigorous mathematical treatment would not give protection in the n-person case. In any event, the protocol for the Topic Auction (we could now see, after Toronto) had to be made more elaborate and thereby secure.

THE TORONTO OUTCOME RESOLVE

THE RESULTS

Among many others I have often claimed that in planning it is the process and not the product that counts. This was a demonstrated truth in Toronto. It could not be claimed that the FSIs that were composed embodied major new discoveries, although they may have done for some present. However, the process of getting there was richly enjoyed by almost everyone, and it is not possible to trace the extent to which individual insights became embodied in Infoset thinking. When we come further to explore recursivity in Part Two, there will be more to say about the likely emergence of true novelty from hyper-Infosets. If that ever happens, I have the conviction that it will derive from paradigm shifts in participants themselves working toward mass effects. In the Toronto experience we know that the absence of facilitation and the inadequacy of staffwork diminished the effectiveness of outcomes, and may well recall our Commentator's complaint that the list of SIs was not available for 3 days. Even so, reverberations of those statements could be felt: were not their progenitors saying them again in various formulations in various contexts?

Here are some of those thoughts, recorded in their original form as SIs. I do not know if they are 'original'; they are hardly banal.

- God is a verb not a noun.

- Each child spontaneously desires to develop responsibilities commensurate with its abilities.

- Censorship is a personal issue.

- Revolution must leave room for dancing.

- Gross National Satisfaction to replace GNP.

- Laughter is very important.

- The ultimate results achieved will be no better than the process of working towards them.

People *are* able to take seriously the prospect of reconsidering what they believe to matter, and to escape from their routine prejudices. All of these examples pass the Negation Test: their contradictions could all be argued— and doubtless would be. I have personally known revolutionaries who are too serious to dance, for example. The last of them well expresses the stated conviction behind this whole approach.

In the outcome, the following were the 12 topic areas chosen. I give a short title and a précis of the work because FSIs were sometimes verbose, and sometimes assumed (or not) the prior CSIs. There were sometimes dissenters, and comments recorded but not fully assimilated (staffwork again). But the general sense is preserved.

1. *Local Empowerment*: the need to push decision making downwards, especially in the case of abolishing nuclear war.

2. *Law and Government*: move from ownership to stewardship, control to guardianship, competition to cooperation, winners and losers to winners alone.

3. *How To Make World Peace*: sovereign individuals acknowledge and accept the responsibility of a (human) world social contract, towards environmental protection, security, and evolution of the planet.

4. *Universal Communication Networks*: for social involvement in individual spiritual, mental, emotional, and physical satisfaction.

5. *Mind Generates Reality*: in creating the world we want, and in taking responsibility for the world we create. A study in paradigm that did not use the word, closely related to:

6. *Paradigm Turbulence*: to reflect the current turbulence in 'reality,' cultivate informed optimism; value all opinions; use all sources of input—concrete or abstract, sensual or soulful.

7. *Strategies*: to approximate, rather than pursue, the ideal. Opposing perspectives to be encouraged: dissent is a catalyst for change.

8. *The Social Function of Philosophy*: to challenge ourselves in examination, evaluation, reflection, and contemplation of ideas and concepts —but also of visions and dreams.

9. *Tools Rule versus Rules for Tools*: to ensure democratic control of 'big science'; accepted that creativity, innovation, and exploration at the individual and small business level cannot be controlled by society.

10. *Power*: as an issue between the sexes, and related to individual and global violence. Condemns coercion, threats, and the exploitation of sexuality.

11. *All Sentient Beings of Equal Value*: realizing that the patriarchal world view of a hierarchy of values for sentient beings has led to imbalance.

12. *Runaway Technology*: emphasizes, as in topic 9, the need to control technology for safe and beneficial purposes, recognizing that nation-states and corporations dominate its development and use.

Topics 5 and 6 were similar in intent, and were therefore (on the argument given earlier) nominated as polar opposites. The startling differences in FSIs that were hoped for in using this device did not materialize. Could it be that despite the formal separation of Polar Caps, the informal network fostered reverberation and thereby resulted in homogeneous products? There was certainly reverberation between topics 9 and 12, in that they shared critics, and outcomes were similar. But my own feeling was that the SIs did not reflect the vigour of discussion at all well. In any case, there is more to be said about triumphant technology than that it has to be kept under control ...

Look at a much more punchy, not to say contentious, set of statements—an FSI complete in itself. It is a fine example of what can be expressed for all to read on what is called the Comment Wall. This is a large bulletin board consecrated to free expression. The messages there ranged from cries of distress to offers of accommodation in distant cities. This comment, on topics 9 and 12, was posted by an invited guest. She is Judith Merril, the writer, famed for her science fiction—into which preserve of male characters she introduced (Merril, 1969, for example) genuine women as distinct from lurex-clad princesses. She wrote:

'RE: "Overseeing" or "Controlling" Technology, Arts and Science:

   (i) All arts and sciences shall be communally (local, federal, global, university) funded, but no artists or scientists should be paid (no copyrights, no patents).

   Scientists/artists must earn access to studios, labs, computers, etc., by doing minimum hours of "essential" activities (garbage collecting, teaching, daycare, factories ...)

   (ii) *No* "regulation" or censorship for arts and sciences.

   Regulation of use of products of arts and sciences (environmental impact, religious bias, etc.) is tied up to community (local, federal, global ...)'

A final comment on the results of the Outcome Resolve bears further on the decision here to précis the FSIs. We are so conditioned to know 'the way it is said' that people who had understood and used to effect the Negation Test for significant utterance at the SI stage often became sententious after a few iterations. Here, for example, is an FSI, in its entirety, as agreed by one Topic group. Try the Negation Test on this. And if I am sounding harsh, can you even say for sure of which topic it is the Final Statement of Importance?

'We must continually define our guidelines and principles so that life on this planet can continue indefinitely in a state of well being, including humankind as a participant.

This requires that we be mindful of the consequences of the definition, pursuit and accomplishment of our goals.'

THE EXPERIENCE OF THE OUTCOME RESOLVE

As much importance (as we argue often) attaches to the process as to the outcome, and in the case of Team Syntegrity (as was said earlier too) it is probable that only those present can gain more than a glimpse of what the experience was really like. There are always participants who say afterwards that what happened actually changed their lives. This was the reasoning behind the appointment of a Commentator in Toronto. Despite the roles she assumed beyond the rapporteur role, or you may think because of them, she had a remarkable time during the Outcome Resolve. She is at her most lucid—and trenchant—in describing this. Here again is Amanda Brown:

'I Was a Member of Group "A"

At the first meeting we had two new members. One had not been present at the first day at all and she replaced an outspoken founding member of the group who would not be present for the rest of the experiment. The second new member had been watching us from the sidelines and had a keen interest in the topic. The discussions were open and wide in scope and involved everybody present. Some came with written statements, some spoke of ideas and meaning, others about methods of action, one person did not participate as much as place herself in the position of moderator and encouraged others to express themselves. At one particular meeting the "Moderator" was coaxing comments out of members and critics in a way that I thought indicated more concern that everyone speak out, than that the group develop and consolidate our statement iteration. I had no say in the statement that was produced by this method and when it was posted I indicated by writing on it that I did not support it. When asked, I told the group members what I felt was problematic in the statement and all agreed that it did not actually say what they thought it had. I also spoke with the "moderator" to encourage her to participate directly on the team, by sharing her own ideas with us all. The next day she did.

The topic of this group inspired and gripped me throughout the duration of the conference. I am still pondering the questions it raises.

I Was a Member of Group "B"

After the Topic Auction there was only one member of the original Group "B" which had five founding members. The founder of the group was present as a critic. This group began with everyone rejecting the original group statement paragraph and a restatement of the issues raised by the originating statement was submitted as the first iteration. This was a group of equals. Discussion was stormy and tempers flared between two of the team members at each meeting. At our second meeting someone suggested a protocol whereby we would each speak in sequence and without interruption for five minutes to begin the meeting. This calmed the atmosphere and that day all the critics commented on how well behaved we were.

I always felt a little detached from this group. This was partly due to the fact that our meetings took place directly after Group "A" where I was particularly focused and wilful.

Out of this group came one person with a commitment to determining how the Province of Ontario could institute a process which would include public input to political decision-making via a referendum procedure similar to those found in parts of Europe or California, but he did not actually follow through.

I Was Drafted into Being a Member of Group "X"

As mentioned above, a membership of two in this group necessitated full partici-pation of critics and observers who were present and willing. I became a full member of this group on the first day when one of the true members was late for the meeting and the other expressed lack of interest in the topic and anger at finding himself in the group. This member had been in a conflict with people in another group and brought that over into our first meeting. He expressed hostility to the group process, threatened not to come back the next day, vented anger about the topic, and was openly hostile to me and others present.

I had originated this topic heading and I explained to the group (of two), the purpose of my original statement and how this applied to the focus of this workshop. I dissociated myself from the descriptive paragraph which I had not written, which followed the statement. This made room for us to redefine the original topic and together we began an intense and dynamic process of investigation. Once we were all working together, this was a very open, creative, and fun group to be in.

I Was a Critic to Group "Y"

This was the only group in which I was a participant or witness, where one person was permitted to dominate the definition and discussion of the topic statement. One person stood .and spoke, described his vision, and originated a statement whose terms, we were told, did not require full clarification before people could pledge their adherence to it. He felt certain of the course required to achieve what he wanted, and the statement he had formulated provided a requisite part of that prescription. The three other members of this group were associates of the group leader. As critic I hoped that I could constructively aid in the elucidation of terms and concepts. I was interested in the scope and ramifications of the statement and attempted to probe for clarification, but I was obstructed. The process of implementation for the desired aims of this group did not open itself to reflection. Critical discussion of this subject was not welcome and the response to my queries was defensive. Other critics and observers remained silent. On the final day I spoke with three observers who I knew were interested yet unwilling to engage in discussion of the issues raised in this group. They told me that they perceived that the founder of this group wanted a soapbox to speak from and to "keep the peace" they chose to let that go unchallenged.'

How the other participants in the Outcome Resolve experienced the event is not known one by one, but their collective opinion is shown in the histogram below.

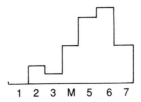

1 2 3 M 5 6 7

Q7. Did the Outcome Resolve work?

A NOTE ON VOTING

Four tally clocks were prepared, and used at the end of each day's work. Each was some 5 feet in diameter. Coloured circular stickers were used to register votes. All the players received 24 stickers each day, and were asked to write their team numbers on them—12 for one team membership and 12 for the other. The stickers were stuck to the clock, where each segment represented a topic.

It was deliberately left unclear as to the criteria to be used in voting: see the earlier remarks on choice of tactics. What surely should have been clear was that the tally would *rank* the topics. For whatever complex reasons, an order of priority would be established. There is a mean expectation that the number of votes registered in each clock segment will be twice the number of participants, since in a perfectly balanced Syntegrity all topics would be equally valued, and each person would enter two stickers in each clock segment. Naturally enough, in practice, people have a tendency to vote for their 'own' teams (Amanda Brown herself confessed to using 22 votes out of 24 to 'boost the profile' of the statement she most believed in during one iteration). But if this tendency is general—and there is evidence that it may be—then the biases so introduced would probably cancel out. It makes no difference (to simplify matters) if 12 people each put one vote in each of twelve segments on the clock, or if each person puts all 12 of his/her own votes in a single segment. All topics score 12 points in either case.

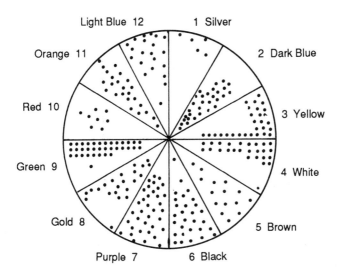

Impression of a clock during voting (polar opposites correctly shown)

In Toronto, there was considerable confusion, and the evident use of tactical voting. At the start, and until a convention was adopted to rectify this, the numbers (of topics) 6 and 9 were confused. Even then, totals did not always cross-check. But the data seem reliable on the whole. Topic 4 scored most votes at the conclusion, at 33 points above the mean expectation; topic 6 did worst, at 25 points below. Comparing the third iteration with the first, six topics improved their scores, and six others lost votes.

However, the protocols for voting need improving, particularly so that hypotheses about the way syntegrity at large, and especially reverberation as a feature, actually works may be more effectively tested. The whole topic will be revisited in Part Two.

REACTIONS OF THE TORONTO INFOSET

Histograms depicting the reactions of the Toronto Infoset, as provided by questionnaire at the conclusion, have already been given for various issues—where they seemed most appropriate to the text. (These covered the age distribution, and replies to questions 1, 2, 3, 5, 6, and 7.) The remainder of the reactions are shown below.

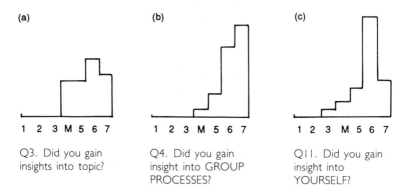

(a)

1 2 3 M 5 6 7

Q3. Did you gain insights into topic?

(b)

1 2 3 M 5 6 7

Q4. Did you gain insight into GROUP PROCESSES?

(c)

1 2 3 M 5 6 7

Q11. Did you gain insight into YOURSELF?

Amanda Brown states:

'The positive response to questions 3, 4, and 11 corresponds to my own experience. By the end of the second day I realized that I was being given an opportunity to see myself in group processes. I felt empowered and encouraged to express myself in the groups. I did not feel intimidated or pressured by other people present and I did not feel the need to censor myself. This is a real behavioural shift for me. The situations, surroundings, and people were all unfamiliar and instead of contracting

I felt expansive and vital. Seeing oneself drives the process of transformation; I have spoken to a number of people who feel that they have been changed by the process. This also supports why people voted high on question 2: "Was the experience *different*?" Not only was this a different way of meeting, but it made a difference to the people meeting.'

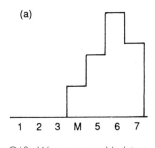

Q10. Were you enabled to contribute your skills?

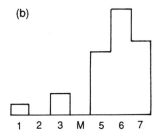

Q13. Did you FEEL the equality implied by the design?

Amanda Brown further comments:

'It is my sense that both questions 10 and 13 are addressing the group dynamic. In a group of five people the only way to withdraw is to engage the other four people present and state your intention not to contribute. This is a decision for which one must be accountable because if they remain physically present in the group their presence will be felt. A certain amount of attention is drawn in by their silence and other group members find themselves wondering "why isn't s/he saying anything?." Thus, this act becomes a statement and everyone in the group will be conscious of it. This same dynamic works to pull on the participants, to encourage their contribution. In this way cooperation is demanded and equity is established between group members.'

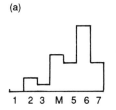

Q8. Did you experience the pull of syntegrity?

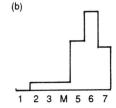

Q9. Did you experience REVERBERATION via iteration?

With only two or three people scoring these important questions below the median value, the positive answer seems to be unequivocal. But we still lack measures other than the poll of collective subjective impressions, and these must be sought.

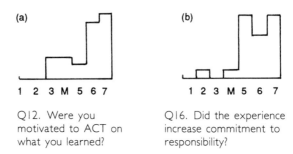

(a)

1 2 3 M 5 6 7

Q12. Were you
motivated to ACT on
what you learned?

(b)

1 2 3 M 5 6 7

Q16. Did the experience
increase commitment to
responsibility?

More positive reactions are revealed in the interesting pair of histograms shown below.

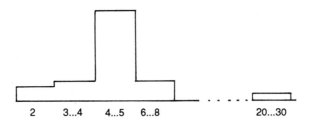

2   3...4   4...5   6...8   20...30

Q17. How many days ought this to take? (No guidance given: answers *ad liberandum*)

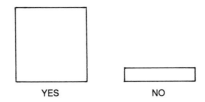

YES   NO

Q18. Would the Syntegrity dynamics be lost if there were breaks (e.g. if we used four weekends)?

The reply to question 18 is emphatic. Naturally it leads to speculation about the likely success of global electronic versions, which (like postal chess) would be subject to delays, and (unlike postal chess) are not very suitable for 'snapshot' examination in frozen frames.

Answers to questions 14 and 15 are not reported here as they concerned a 'little local incident.' Question 19 is included, just for fun. It was asked at the request of a dreamer (literally: REM sleep).

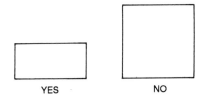

YES   NO

Q19. At night, have you dreamed of being in discussion groups?

But the final question was not whimsical at all:

Q20. Would you do it again?

YES: all remaining respondents.
NO: Zero respondents.

One can hardly say more than that.

ENHANCING PROCEDURES

Chapter Seven

PROTOCOLS REVISITED

There was much to think about after the year of experimentation, apart from the form of the model and the mathematical discoveries to which it gave rise. There were detailed records to study, including team members' responses, and the advice of facilitators was taken as well. This chapter reviews the situation for the first three of what are now nominated as the eight episodes of a 'meeting under syntegrity,' or (as it is now called) a SYNTEGRATION.

SYNTEGRATION EPISODE ONE

THE IMPORTANCE FILTER

The collection of Statements of Importance (SIs) comes after the general introduction, when the people of the Infoset are persuaded to let their imaginations soar, to be creative, and to generate new (and possibly wild) ideas. This is the first phase of an episode that will provide high-variety raw data for the syntegration. The picture evoked sounds like a description of the familiar technique of 'brain-storming'—and so it is—within a special format.

Some have argued that time could be saved if the SIs were provided in advance by the 30 members of the Infoset; that is surely true. But 'brain-storming' denotes a communal activity. It is a good and proven plan to start a syntegration in the evening with cocktails, so that members become at ease with each other, followed by the introductory talk, and then dinner. People are asked to provide SIs only at the coffee and liqueurs stage, when everyone is relaxed. They should be in the mood to feel like co-conspirators, or perhaps to outdo each other in the novelty of their SIs. Attempts to generate these data 'from cold' have been less than successful, because stereotypes will project themselves unless inhibitions are lifted at least a little. This is not a pharmacological comment: the Infoset has to gain the interpersonal confidence to give itself permission to be unorthodox.   It is the initiation of the group consciousness to which we hope to attain. (In North America the before and after terms are probably 'reception' and 'coffee and desert,' while the reference to pharmacology may be irrelevant.)

This having been said, it is both expected and permissible that some so-called Statements of Importance will instead be statements of protest, anarchy, bawdiness! That is part of the fun. The fact is, however, that the SIs constitute the raw data for the Syntegration—which need to be not only (as was said) of high variety, but also of high quality. There are criteria for this: not judgments to be exercised by facilitators so much as tests that they apply. For instance, the Negation Principle asserting that the contradictory must be arguable can be used to eliminate motherhood statements and those of little import. This raises the question of 'weightiness': people can be discouraged from including mere trivia—but beware the risk of eliminating a concealed profundity. At any rate, facilitators need to be in action during this phase to encourage the group and to moderate quality. Again, the whole procedure is conceived of as a group activity which is an integral part of the Syntegration itself. Therefore, it cannot be undertaken in advance without loss.

When the SIs have been written out on separate cards, essentially as single-sentence ideas, they should be shared. If the dinner party is invited to break up, members may fix their own SIs to the walls or a board. When they mill about, reading each other's statements, more variety generators go into action. Ideas spark further ideas; topics may begin to emerge. Folk should be invited to move the cards to reflect this: already a primal experience of Syntegration is happening. People depart at their own discretion, feeling happy and even liberated, eventually to retire to bed, and leaving the facilitation team with the debris ... But the debris also constitutes the high-variety, high-quality raw data of the Syntegration. There are likely to be upwards of 50 SIs exhibited, and might be three times that number.

Technically minded commentators usually want to mechanize the process just described. It can easily be done, of course. Cards may be typed (in a separate room, please) and will be the more legible in typescript when they appear. Better still, technically at least, the SIs would be projected on to the wall via a word processing computer and a liquid crystal. These manoeuvres cannot be conducted, however, without staff intervention in the human process—unless the Infoset itself happens to constitute a bunch of 'techies.' At this stage, the human mêlée is a preferable alternative, coupled with exhortations as to legibility. Remember that what is happening reflects a potential interplay of 30 people with each other, making a total of 870 possible interactions. The push-and-shove method of variety attenuation is more satisfying (again at this stage) than the intervention of machine processing, be it never so Ergonomically Correct.

The Infoset has retired to bed; the facilitator team must now set to work. The SIs must be presented, all of them, along with the fruit juice and cereals, at breakfast. We have heard Amanda Brown's scathing note about the failure in Toronto to publish the actual list of the 137 raw SIs until the third day. Such was the pressure (and in fairness, so inadequate the staffing) that the omission was not even noticed. If the evening's proceedings have led to the emergence of SI groupings, the facilitators may decide to present the list in those groups; it may be advisable, however, not to provide group headings, even if the topics are fairly obvious, as this may beg the questions intended to be resolved by the Problem Jostle.

The Importance Filter is the device Syntegration uses to capture raw data of high quality. Thus it is intended to filter out only the low-quality material put forward, and tentatively to begin the process of shaping a variety so high as to be inchoate. Much of that shaping will happen unexpressed within the members' minds. Under this timetable they will sleep on it ...

SYNTEGRATION EPISODE TWO

THE PROBLEM JOSTLE

The protocols governing the next phases of variety reduction revealed two major flaws.

It was glaringly obvious that the (various) arbitrary rules adopted in the experiments for the Topic Auction did not result in an optimal allocation of tasks. The attempt to handle complexity by an ordinal process of choice ('first decide on your most favoured topic for discussion') was defective, bearing in mind that each member has four interlocking roles.

A fresh approach to this problem was needed. But it gradually became clear that the origins of the difficulty lay within the Problem Jostle itself—which was supposed to discover the Consolidated Statements of Importance (CSIs) in one fell swoop. That is to say, exactly 12 items had to emerge from the process. Emphasis on this need suppressed some of the variety necessary to recognize the polar opposition that played so large a part in the Topic Auction. Before this *cybernetic* fact was recognized—that variety equations were directly involved—the issue of 'twelveness' was registered as a mere disquiet at the extent of the facilitators' intervention in determining them. People accepted the twelveness constraint as something required by the icosahedral theory; but the confusion caused by inept facilitation (mine) at Manchester in the convergence on 12 CSIs was haunting. Team Syntegrity should properly deploy skilled facilitation, but ought not to depend upon it absolutely.

The two problems were obviously related from the cybernetic standpoint of variety regulation. The Infoset has a mass of knowledge and experience which is supposed to explode creatively through the Importance Filter into a large number of SIs, and then to converge on outcomes, ultimately FSIs, shedding variety but gaining focus and potency on the way. The Syntegrity Protocols are meant to obtain these results with a minimum of interference in the inherently self-organizing properties of a system geared to a purpose—that is, an Infoset. Thus the two problems may be coalesced into one, by asking how the allocation of 30 people into 12 task forces where each person has four roles as defined, may be (so to speak) crystallized out of a supersaturated solution of SIs—using a single smooth protocol.

It was while thinking about this that the relevance of concurrent mathematical investigations became clearer. Outstandingly, the effect of polar opposition was pre-eminent in the syntegrity graph. As recorded earlier in Part One, the intuition that polarity mattered had been acknowledged from the start by referring to it as 'antithetic management.' In practice, no-one seemed to know how to discharge the duty of a team to keep its polar opposite team under surveillance, nor could most people see the point in so doing. The two teams never met, after all—but that was the whole reason for the surveillance rubric. To replace hierarchic and authoritarian notions of management with a polyhedral envelope that maintains its equilibrium through the geodesic principles of tensegrity was the very basis for adopting this model. Then strong internal connexions, pole to pole, were barred. Such arrangements would inevitably lead to centralization (see Chapter One, and compare the Star Net), and destroy the 'holographic' equality of perception and potency at the periphery that was sought.

Consideration of the two flaws discussed led to the recognition of a third (or underlying) flaw. It is that the meaning of polar opposition in terms of the propositional content of the CSIs at each pole had never been made clear. Facilitators had been asked to gauge which statements were most conflicting among the CSIs and place them 'on the clock' in polar opposition. Then, realizing that (even assuming it could be worked properly) this rule condemned participants to discuss one set of four poles and never their opposite contentions, the rule was varied so that facilitators judged which CSIs were most similar—and chose them as polar opposites instead. That was shallow thinking, and it did not help to correct the underlying flaw. These experimental manoeuvres were recorded in Part One, with insufficient emphasis perhaps on the feelings of inadequacy pervading the Facilitators' Room when debating these subjective judgments.

Facilitators' Room? *Their* subjective judgments? There is something quite wrong in all of this. Surely, the propositional meaning of the CSIs has been generated by the Infoset; so the semantic polarity of those statements must be somewhere implicit in the Syntegration debate. It is up to the Infoset itself to make it explicit, albeit with assistance. It certainly is not a judgmental characterization to be imposed by wiseacres sitting outside. But that is exactly what had been happening.

Thus the two problems that coalesced to one problem assimilated a third problem that had not been candidly acknowledged. The answer was to make an innovative change in the protocol procedure, and to replace the original practice of which Figure 7.1 is a schematic diagram. (The standard electrical sign for an attenuator is used to indicate a reduction of variety.)

The new approach recognizes that the Second Loop of facilitation shown above involves too much intervention in an organic process. The consolidation attenuator is still needed, because the SI list is too long and unfocused; but it should reach a new result that is natural to the Infoset, unfettered by the 'twelveness' criterion. The number of statements that the Infoset will publish after it has grouped and polished the list of SIs is not predictable. The facilitators simply encourage coherence, conciseness, and weightiness of content. Call the list thereby produced the Aggregated Statements of Importance (ASIs). The ASIs are now the output of the Problem Jostle. Then a fresh technique is needed within the Syntegrity to reduce the unknown number of ASIs to *six polar axes* (of an icosahedron). Thus the 12 CSIs needed will be condensations of the ASI list in locations of polar opposition—as determined by the insights of the Infoset itself.

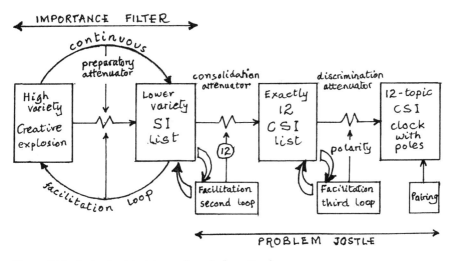

Figure 7.1   Basis of original (now discarded) protocol

SYNTEGRATION EPISODE THREE

THE HEXADIC REDUCTION

Strangely enough, the 'fresh' technique now described is an adaptation of George Kelly's *Theory of Personal Constructs* (Kelly, 1955). The strangeness lies first in that number one reference: this work had been in mind for many years but its relevance went unnoticed—except as precursive. Second, my partner Allenna Leonard has made use of the approach ever since the days of her doctoral research (Leonard, 1987); but it did not arise in the Syntegrity context until the dilemma just described had been formulated. At that point the new Episode Three was triggered into being by news that the Open University had described a Kelly application (originating in a collaboration between the Universities of Strathclyde and Arizona) in the context of management decision and strategic development. This was the third strangeness, adding up to serendipity indeed.

With these acknowledgements, and with no detailed account of the original work or its recent applications, here is the application that solves the problem stated, written simply as a set of instructions.

Having run the SI collection process and the Problem Jostle to result in a bundle of ASIs, whose number is not fixed in advance, write the titles of the ASIs as the columnar headings of a matrix, together with the identifying letters A, B, C, etc. Facilitators note that at least 12 columns are needed, but this is a lower bound and not an upper bound as well. Write the identifying letters naming the columns on cubes to be placed in a bag, or use alphabet blocks or Scrabble tiles. There now begins a process of random sampling of triplets without replacement.

The first three ASIs drawn are considered by the group. They are statements P, D, and Q. Which pair of the three pairs (PD, PQ, DQ) are most akin, compared with the third? Why is this? The job of the facilitator is to lead the discussion with the object of determining a dimension of perception underlying the Infoset's unity of purpose (that intention which identified these 30 as an Infoset in the first place), as prompted by the context of the ASIs, and as expressed on a polar axis. This deutero-discriminant of the ASI triplet is given a name that expresses not content, but the polarity disclosed by the group debate. Here is an example, considering the first-drawn triplet P, D and Q—three ASIs that have been nominated by drawing their letters randomly from the bag. We examine the three different ways in which the Infoset might discriminate between one statement and the remaining pair—although only one of these ways will actually happen.

The P, D, AND Q TRIPLET EXAMPLE

The three ASIs say the following:

- P   Do not squander our descendants' planetary resources.

- D   Show me the bottom line!

- Q   Feed the hungry.

One Infoset might decide that P is to be distinguished from the pair DQ, arguing that the intention of P is wholly altruistic (although it has ethical force) and refers to a distant future when humankind may be extinct, whereas both D and Q are severely practical and moreover urgent. Depending on the nature of the debate, as guided by the facilitator, the Infoset might decide to name this polarity 'ethical/pragmatic.' On another day, this same Infoset might call the polarity 'long term/short term.' It is up to them.

Another Infoset altogether might argue as follows: Q is the categorical imperative here. P ('squander resources') and D ('bottom line') are both economic criteria. So this second Infoset might call the polarity 'morality/profits.'

There is a third pairing of P and Q, which might be perceived by a third Infoset as underwriting human values—as compared with the money-grubbing of the D criterion. An Infoset seized with this thought might nominate the polarity 'compassion/greed.'

As mentioned in advance of the example, only one discrimination is actually drawn from the comparison of the P, D, Q triplet. The purpose of offering three alternative readings is to emphasize that the discriminatory authority *lies with the Infoset*, and cannot be either imposed or guessed at in advance. The same applies to the stance the Infoset takes if it insists on using pejorative words rather than merely descriptive ones, as those making the third pairing in the example are assumed to have done. Invective may be expected of a motivated Infoset, and there is little point in suppressing it until implementation tactics are considered. But that judgement comes afterwards. First we need to decide what we really think.

As the example emphasizes, the deutero-discriminant reflects the raw content of the ASI at a second level of abstraction that has only the compounded insights of the Infoset to underwrite it. It is a product of the self-organizing group process, and owes nothing to categories imported from any orthodoxy. Then the next question is obvious: if this particular polar antithesis has any utility in the syntegrity process, then it must be tested against each of the ASIs as being a helpful discriminator. We have already debated the ASIs marked P, D, and Q in these terms, so it should not be difficult to take the ASI called

P, and to score the statement on the polar scale just adopted. This polar scale becomes the first row of the scoring matrix, and the score is written into the first box under the heading P. The matrix needs to be inscribed on a large board, so that all may share in the process of development.

Here we depart from the usual technique for scoring which ascribes a '1' to one pole and a '3,' '5,' or '7' to the other, leaving the midpoint as an indeterminate outcome. The Kelly Grid, in this application, is invoked to facilitate the reduction of however many ASIs have evolved to the 12 CSIs required, and to help assign those CSIs to the six polar constructs that best capture their polarity. Then the application differs from many applications where the aim is to unfold a full picture, without special constraints, of the relationships between elements and constructs. If statistical techniques such as cluster analysis are to be used, then a numerical scoring system has to be devised. Syntegration, however, uses interpersonal adjustment and structural reverberation through three iterations of the Outcome Resolve to establish answers.

Far from inventing an arithmetic, then, the aim is to assign polar topics with as little added by comparative value assessment as possible. The construct 'ethical/pragmatic,' for example, is heavy with value judgements; and these may become associated with other polarities through numerical accident if scoring is by numbers. The risk to be avoided is that participants start to think of Ones as 'the good guys,' and Threes as 'the bad guys'—or vice versa. Nor should the possible inference that the measures are either precise or additive be allowed rein. Thus the scoring scale to be described indicates only strength and direction. In the Syntegration context, this is the only information that can actually be adduced, and it is all that is needed to assign topics to poles. Here is one way of doing this.

If we have selected P, D, Q as a triplet, this will define a pair of polar opposites, as we saw. Let us suppose that P defines one pole, and D/Q defines the other. All three statements score black (ideally this would consist in hanging a black card on the display board in the matrix element concerned: for convenience here we write B for black). Mark all three elemental Bs with two symbols. One is a ring—Ⓑ—to indicate that P,D, and Q were the original statements from which this particular polar distinction arose. The other symbol is an arrow, pointing either to the left or to the right, indicating to which pole (these having been labelled at the ends of the row) the statement was thought to veer.

Next, all the remaining ASIs are to be scored on this polar scale. If any such statement is very easily classified by this distiction, then it too will be scored black—and again an arrow will show to which pole the ASI veers. But the encircling ring will not be used: the statements now being considered did not contribute to drawing the distinction in the first place.

It is obviously unlikely that every remaining ASI will score heavily (equals Black) on this scale. Perhaps the scale will be seen as irrelevant; perhaps there is indifference in the group; or the case represents the traditional 'don't know.' In these cases, the matrix element score is grey: here we write G. But now the three point scale (pole–grey–pole) is enriched to five points, by permitting scores of Dark (D) Grey. Evidently, these scores still indicate uncertainty— they are not polar-committed. However, there is doubt in the mind of the Infoset, but a tendency to veer towards one pole rather than the other is noted. As before, arrows indicate to which pole this tendency points, while the Dark grade indicates that the greyness is not neutral. Then the scoring scale may be represented as shown below.

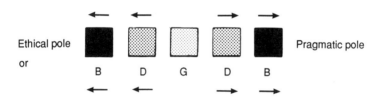

The cubes P, D, and Q are now set aside, and a second triplet is randomly chosen. Polarity is debated, and the deutero-discriminants are identified. This new polarity becomes the name of the second row, to be scored across the columns of ASIs. Then the programme of sampling without replacement will neatly generate the six determinants, if there happen to be just 18 ASIs.

But it is important that all ASIs are considered as generators of polar con-structs, and the process continues until the cubes are exhausted. (If the number of ASIs is not divisible by three, return all the cubes to the bag to draw the missing one or two letters.) In this case, more than six polar scales will emerge—unless indeed in some draws terms are chosen identical with those already selected, whereupon the new scales are redundant, having been scored already.

It is now a matter for the Infoset to decide which set of six polarities to choose. This is where the experience of debate and scoring comes into play. The Infoset has come to understand how it is using the words that denote the

12 poles, and which of those are the more powerful discriminants. This is not a matter of lexicography, but of usage in this particular context of these people and of their shared ideas. In practice, it is not difficult to make the hexadic reduction, because abstractions are themselves attenuators of the discrete particularities to be read in the ASIs. Besides, each row on the matrix has now been scored on the 'greyness' scale.

Consider how this helps. There are more than six polar discriminants, and some must go. The first to be eliminated is clearly the row where greyness predominates. In the limit, there are only three Black scores—the original triplet that suggested the scale. All the other squares are either Grey or Dark Grey, which proves that the proposed polar construct is not a good discriminant of the Infoset's outlook. As a group, it 'could not care less' as to how most ASIs register on that scale. But predominant Blackness, which is deepened by the dark greys, says that the Infoset holds strong views on this axis. Greyness might be assessed by eye, but a counting procedure helps. If Grey itself is awarded two points, and Dark just one point (as being more nearly black), it is easy to compare rows, and this does not involve inventing a structural arithmetic. Next count the arrows pointing to left and to right. If all but the original statement that points to the right (which must be there) are pointing towards the other pole on the left, then clearly this scale is not a good discriminator either. The most powerful axis is the one where the scores are preponderantly dark, and the arrows are evenly divided.

Using these criteria against the background of the Jostle debate, the Hexadic Reduction reaches its first target of proposing a sixfold division. It needs to be borne in mind that the decision space thereby nominated ought to exhaust the dimensionality of the purposes of the Infoset's syntegration. That is to say that, for example, if there is clearly an aesthetic dimension to the plenary issue addressed, then the hexadic set of discriminants must allow the possibility of expressing aesthetic values.

In the event that there are 12 (mandatory) or more but less than 16 ASIs to hand at the end of the Problem Jostle, the procedure is simple. Draw the triplets as before: four draws will generate four discriminants, and exhaust the bag of cubes. Replace all the cubes, and do the exercise again, discarding any replicated triplet. This will find six, seven, or eight polar discriminants in total. Any one or two in excess of the needed six are disposed of by the hexadic reduction as above.

The result is a scored matrix of six rows and at least twelve columns. If there are more than 12 ASIs, then they must be reduced to 12. Familiarity with both the procedure and the subject matter help by now to propose consolidations into the 12 CSIs. Once again, the scoring is indicative; and again a weighted count on the two greys is helpful. This time a column (rather than a row) that has a grey preponderance suggests that the ASI could readily be eliminated, or elided with another while a black preponderance invites inclusion in the final tabulation. The ASI that heads each column has, after all, been drawing votes—and the score called Black is high. Admittedly, the votes have been cast on a particular set of polar discriminants, but no limit was set on their number while the voting was in process. We know, however, that the final form of the Hexadic Reduction is not simply the nomination of axes, but the allocation of the 12 CSIs to their poles. It follows that the weight of the B and D arrows that point to particular poles on particular axes should be considered.

A computer program could be written to assess the net outcome of these directions and weights—but only if the selection of the six polar axes has been completed in advance. The fact is that the minds of the Infoset ought to be focused on the totality of the Hexadic Reduction while it is in progress. A skilful facilitator will not finally determine the six polar constructs to be used and then spring the surprise that each pole has to be associated with a CSI. What needs to be projected by the facilitator is the requirement to *squeeze* the matrix in both vertical and horizontal dimensions, until it is a 12 × 6 array with the actual CSIs already in place. As usual, the Infoset itself is involved as its

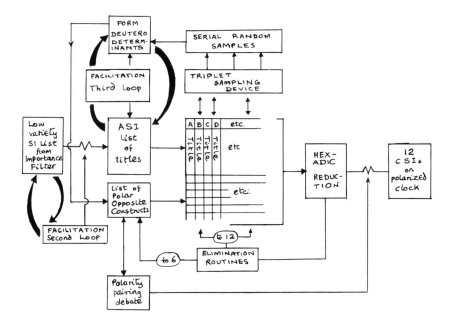

Figure 7.2 Basis of new protocol for Problem Jostle with hexadic reduction

own computer. A subtle and intricate communal process should be brought to bear to achieve the final result, despite the partitioned procedure described. The tonal scale of marking with its arrows was devised precisely as an aid to this end.

The Hexadic Reduction is completed when each CSI has been allocated to a colour on the model, in accordance with the protocol described. This may be done by making a 12-topic clock (for colour opposition see the diagrams in Chapter Two) and/or by hanging labels on a three-dimensional icosahedron ready painted in full colour. The new protocol is summarized in Figure 7.2.

Reflecting on her experiences with construct theory, and this application to Syntegrity, Allenna Leonard writes:

'George Kelly's Personal Construct Theory was introduced to me as a way to disentangle arguments when people were using the same words to mean different things. I was concerned especially with the disintegration of public debate where it seemed almost as if the protagonists were each taking to the ring in turn and boxing against an imaginary opponent. Naturally, the blows were neither blocked nor returned and the results contained more noise than information. Syntegration produces the opposite result and it seems natural, in retrospect, to turn to the Kelly Grid to help the group decide what it means by the use of its words.

The Kelly Grid is built on the premise that people construe their worlds by evaluating people, events, ideas, and objects (called elements) according to distinctions between their polar opposite characteristics. Each pole of each construct has meaning only when contrasted with its opposite. How can happy be understood without reference to unhappy or hot without reference to cold? Constructs may be fairly loose, like happy/unhappy, or much tighter, like hot/cold, when the physical context, e.g. a cup of coffee, is established.

Each construct or distinction has its focus of convenience in the elements to which it was originally applied and a wider range of convenience where the distinction remains helpful and informative or where creativity in interpretation may be exercised. Kelly noted that similarity among people did not depend on having had the same experiences but in interpreting their different experience according to the same criteria. Indeed, the group will often find the exercise of expanding and contracting the range of convenience a very illuminating experience. Constructs themselves may be "pre-emptive" when a single construct "says it all" about a particular element or constellatory when it immediately calls up other associations. The term "halo effect" has been used to describe these baggage laden constructs. Or it may be a propositional construct which does not carry a load of implications. The exercise of the Hexadic Reduction may be expected to reveal the sort of distinctions which are most central to the group and the halo effects, if any, surrounding them.

Kelly found that most individuals used only 20 or 30 basic distinctions to evaluate all the people and events in their lives. It is not surprising then, that a group, focused on a list of topics on a single theme, will usually begin to repeat themselves somewhere around "The Magical Number Seven, Plus or Minus Two" (Miller, 1967), and that the identification of twelve topics according to six distinctions is typical of grids used in many settings. This small number of constructs may also reveal some which appear to be core constructs or to imply other sub-constructs. It may be expected that these core constructs will prove to be most central to questions of identity and therefore most resistant to change.'

To install six Kelly-type polar constructs orthogonally within our icosahedral space creates a hypothesis at least that the proven potency of his technique will reinforce the power that Syntegrity itself has already demonstrated. Of course the whole of this geometry is full of interest—and full of surprises as well. To pick up the latest of these: a rectangle formed within the syntegrity graph by two icosahedral edges that are parallel and (therefore) distanced from each other at diameter 3, and the two critical tensiles that connect their ends, is proportioned as a golden section. That is, the ratio of the critical side to the edge side is (in integer terms of percentage) 62 : 38. Each of the corners of the rectangle described, moreover, is in polar opposition to its diagonal corner. (If this nomenclature is unfamiliar, a full account appears in Chapter Eleven.) Now Dr Leonard has pointed out that experimenters with Kelly's technique discovered (Benjafield and Adams-Webber, 1979) that when people were asked to identify such poles as 'like me' or 'not like me' the ratio turned out to be 63 : 37.

TAILPIECE

Mini-experiments with the Hexadic Reduction have revealed some interesting aspects that deserve mulling over.

In discussing the Importance Filter, which involves the initial collection of SIs, great emphasis was laid on the explosion of creativity. Stereotyped classifications were to be avoided, and the comparison with brain-storming techniques was drawn. There is a risk that stereotypes will spring to mind during the Hexadic Reduction, precisely because they are deutero-determinants: our abstract constructs are hard to dislodge. It will pay to consider novel constructs competent to embrace the novel ASIs we hope have emerged.

Here is an illustration to consider. The mini-experiment took as ASIs statements expressing overall preference for a series of restaurants well known to the experimenters. To this extent, there was nothing novel about the ASIs, and perhaps it would have been well to include statements about the characteristics of non-existent restaurants. It is evident, however, that these chimerical establishments would emerge as preferred to the rest: a sobering thought, *unless* you are planning to open a new restaurant ...

What is the first criterion that comes to mind when debating: Where shall we go to lunch? I suggest that it is the general ambience. Yet in the Hexadic Reduction, which looks for a polarity inside a triplet, this construct of ambience never emerged. This was a considerable surprise. But reflection soon found the answer, which lies precisely in the failure to incorporate novelty in the ASIs. It would never occur to the experimenters to go to a restaurant with a bad ambience; therefore, no such place appeared in the ASIs; therefore, this polar construct did not come up.

There are two lessons to be learned from this. Novelty is essential to Syntegration from the SI stage onward, and needs to be preserved at each phase of attenuation. Second, in so far as an important construct may become invisible because it is taken for granted, participants need to be sure that the fresh constructs chosen can bear the weight of innovative ASIs in its absence. It is a difficult issue for facilitators to keep in mind, because it could easily become the excuse for reverting to tradition or orthodoxy—thereby suppressing the discoveries of Syntegration. For example, cost did emerge as a factor in an 'expensive/cheap' polarity. But this construct was eliminated by the Reduction. However, the experimenters did not list restaurants outside their price range; so once again the reason was that costliness was taken for granted, even though it achieved expression.

It is also worth noting that the technique should be used to underwrite unlikely constructs which might easily never surface in a discussion—because of an embarrassing triviality—which nevertheless are actually influencing decisions. The fine example from this mini-experiment concerned chipped potatoes (US: French fries). In all the grand talk of haute cuisine and fine wines that is the familiar background for the choice of a restaurant, the excellence or otherwise of chips would hardly figure. Yet it proved to be a powerful determinant of decision in practice. A rapid review of some major business decisions in which I have been involved discloses many examples of hidden factors (the proximity of a trout stream to a possible plant location, for example) which were clearly influencing decisions to which they were not supposedly germane.

In various actual syntegrations to date, it has proven virtually impossible to apply this technique in the detail discussed: time is too short. It is easy, however, to think of circumstances (company mergers, constitutional wrangles) where even a long time so used would be well spent. But the hexadic reduction must be accomplished, however it is achieved, and the analysis is offered as a valid analysis of the difficulties involved. It is always worth bearing in mind that the techniques used to describe the high complexity of human affairs are responsible neither for that innate complexity nor for the difficulties it engenders.

Chapter Eight

VEXED QUESTIONS OF ALLOCATION

The geometry now developed, which will be fully explained in Part Three, imposes more constraints on people's choice of role than was at first assumed, as has been noted already in Chapter Six. The fact that no less than five internal braces, the tensiles, depend from each end of any one edge suggests that it would be easy 'somehow' to sort out the critic roles by players' preferences. As the story unfolded in Chapter Six, the attempt to organize the Topic Auction through the issue of Quadripartite Identity Cards, the QIDS, was a failure, but we had discovered why. I repeat the Freesman Exclusion that dealt with the problem:

> A person may choose to play a critic role in only one of a pair of teams that are themselves polar opposites.

This meant that only four of the tensiles remained available as legitimate roles at each end of the player's personal edge. But there are still choices to be made, and I retained faith in the negotiability of the lower quadrant colours shown on the QIDs. The spectrum of choice for the individual looking for a syntegration identity card could now be summed up like this.

S/he has two team member roles, but the choice of one team limits the second to five of the remaining eleven teams. This is a heavy constraint of which the members should be fully aware. In making choices, or rather bidding for them in the auction, the CSIs that now denote each vertex of the icosahedron have to be considered in pairs as determined by the edges that join adjacent vertices. These connections cannot be inferred from the clock representation on the wall, although they are made explicit in the 'clocks' of Chapter Two. Participants commonly say that it is most helpful to have a coloured three-dimensional model; but, as we shall see below, a tabular format is clear and might be considered adequate as a procedural tool. It cannot do much towards understanding the interpersonal space in which the Infoset subsists.

In the experiments, attempts were made to conduct the Topic Auction by choosing a first membership colour and then, after this was settled, choosing a second. This was unsatisfactory for most people, although there was usually a minority so dedicated to a single proposition that the second team membership was immaterial. The choice of an edge entails membership of two teams, and the 30 options should be considered (for the majority) as colour pairs. However, each of the colours chosen has something to say about the critical role. Each team of five members sponsors five critics who constitute the tensile mode of the syntegrity. In the case of any dual membership, XY, membership in X precludes that person from criticizing the polar opposite team Y, while membership of Y eliminates the critical tensile joining X to its polar opposite team. This constraint is the Freesman exclusion.

The next question for the individual is how to choose between these four options in each of his/her capacities X and Y. In the experiments (and especially pre-Toronto when the Freesman Exclusion was first recognized), there was nothing less than a scramble to register the critical roles for which people were competing. By now, however, and one might complain at long last, I was deeply suspicious of the apparent freedom to negotiate choices—because the scramble itself seemed to arouse such a high level of emotion. Studying the constraining effects of the model further, I discovered another exclusion principle, and one with startling effects.

THE ADJACENCY EXCLUSION

Consider a participant Green–Gold in his Green capacity. The critical options of the Green team are Dark Blue, Purple, Red, Black and Orange. Because this Green is also Gold, its polar opposite Dark Blue is debarred by the Freesman Exclusion. However, consider the Orange option. In his Gold capacity, Green–Gold is a member of a second team that includes Gold–Orange. We shall call the Orange team *adjacent*, to mean that it shares a member with the Gold team of which Green–Gold is in fact a member. Since Syntegration seeks to maximize its tensility componentry, it is best to strike out across the decision space defined by the icosahedron, and to criticize a team which is not adjacent as defined. Of the nominated teams, Orange is contraindicated, because of Gold–Orange. Gold–Green in his Green capacity could consider criticizing Purple, Red or Black. We must, however, consider Gold–Green in his Gold capacity too. In the Gold team we discover Gold–Red. This means that the

Red team is adjacent as defined. Then Red is eliminated from the critical options. It follows that by Adjacency Exclusion the critical roles of Green–Gold are fully determined as Purple and Black. These are the critical lines that maximize Green–Gold's tensility effect.

The Adjacency Exclusion, like the Freesman Exclusion, is effective on behalf of a Green–Gold, who is also a Gold–Green. To understand this, examine the following tabulations. Each depicts the situation affecting a *team* so that any relevant individual stands with a foot in both camps. First, consider the Green team (Table 8.1)

It has taken a long time to make explicit the rules under which the critical apparatus built into the syntegrity graph should optimally work. It may be of evolutionary interest to note that in the first publication (Beer, 1990), which was written in 1984, the perception of what constitutes the critical role was expressed thus:

> Each person is appointed a critic of that team of which s/he is not a member. The team to which s/he is thereby appointed a critic will appoint a critic to his/her right-hand team. Similarly, each person becomes a critic in that team of which s/he is not

Table 8.1 Critical options (with exclusions) of the Green team

| Critic to | Members | | | | |
	Green–Gold	Green–Silver	Green–White	Green–Light Blue	Green–Brown
Dark Blue	Freesman Exclusion	CRITIC	Adjacent Exclusion	CRITIC	Adjacent Exclusion
Purple	CRITIC	Freesman Exclusion	CRITIC	Adjacent Exclusion	Adjacent Exclusion
Red	Adjacent Exclusion	CRITIC	Freesman Exclusion	Adjacent Exclusion	CRITIC
Black	CRITIC	Adjacent Exclusion	Adjacent Exclusion	Freesman Exclusion	CRITIC
Orange	Adjacent Exclusion	Adjacent Exclusion	CRITIC	CRITIC	Freesman Exclusion

a member, but of which a right-hand team-mate is a member. And that team will appoint a critic to his/her left-hand team.

The use of 'handedness' and the dynamic of *returning* a critic to the other hand effectively prescribes the Adjacency Exclusion. For example, if Green were to dispatch a critic to the Red Team, Red would be obliged by this formulation to return a critic to Gold. But this is impossible: that connection is usurped in advance by the existence of a Red–Gold *person*. By the same token, a critic dispatched from Green to Orange would provoke a critical role Orange–Gold, and again such a person already exists.

The rules as originally given failed to discover the Freesman Exclusion, in this case due to the polar opposition of Green to Yellow and Gold to Dark Blue, because the original model did not have any construction along the polar axes, or acknowledge any organizational connection between the poles. The axes were not considered at all: the inspiration of tensegrity had been geodesic, and the polar balance was to be (as it still is) explicit in the geometry itself. So (in our example), the original rules would result in Green–Gold figuring as a critic to Black and to Purple, just as this analysis and tabulation has demonstrated.

It is a pity that the concepts of handedness and the return dynamic were lost sight of during the decade separating the formulation of the original rules and the experiments. The scrambles mentioned resulted from auctioning the quadripartite roles without stipulations. As we saw in Part One, this resulted in anomalous appointments to critical duties. But the original insight had clouded over, and the analytic machinery had not yet evolved. And no-one involved perceived what was wrong! The psychological difficulties of trying to visualize a three-dimensional geometry are enormous, and it is fascinating that although we inhabit a three-dimensional world we have sunk most of our perceptual investment in planar projections of it. The discovery of perspective as a device in art (a relatively recent invention) has much to answer for, and wrestling with syntegrity makes one more appreciative of the trials endured by Buckminster Fuller, whose critics did not comprehend him.

After this diversion, let us complete the new analysis by considering the critical options of Green–Gold's dual personality, Gold–Green. The Gold team's tabulation is shown in Table 8.2.

And so again we see that Gold–Green, the dual of Green–Gold, is required to be a critic of Purple and Black. These two people are, after all the same (no gender) person.

Table 8.2 Critical options (with exclusions) of the Gold team

	Members				
Critic to	Gold–Silver	Gold–Light Blue	Gold–Red	Gold–Orange	Gold–Green
White	Adjacent Exclusion	CRITIC	Freesman Exclusion	CRITIC	Adjacent Exclusion
Brown	CRITIC	Adjacent Exclusion	CRITIC	Freesman Exclusion	Adjacent Exclusion
Yellow	CRITIC	CRITIC	Adjacent Exclusion	Adjacent Exclusion	Freesman Exclusion
Purple	Freesman Exclusion	Adjacent Exclusion	Adjacent Exclusion	CRITIC	CRITIC
Black	Adjacent Exclusion	Freesman Exclusion	CRITIC	Adjacent Exclusion	CRITIC

A TEST OF PERCEPTION

It is well to have struggled through these arguments and tabulations, because the experience gives strength to the perception of the graphical space that the syntegrity graph delineates, and the extraordinary quality of cohesiveness that it exhibits. The reader may test his/her penetration of these mysteries at this point. Has s/he noticed anything of importance about the pair of tabulations that has not been mentioned in the text? If not, simply compare the left-hand columns that list critic availability in Tables 8.1 and 8.2, and discover the high-road to the original insight. As is now obvious, the critic availability of Green and of Gold intersect for Green–Gold and Gold–Green in purple and black alone. Everything else is eliminated. The convoluted personality of our example, that same person, is not even schizophrenic ...

Now it is clear that the critical roles are fully determined by the dual team membership; it is also clear that the Topic Auction cannot be undertaken in stages. What is on offer, 30 times over, is a discrete entity: it is a quadripartite indivisible role. This fact cuts down on the amount of scrambling, but much intensifies the qualitative competition. The first requirement is that everyone should have an extremely clear idea as to which four topics are associated with each quadripartite role. Procedures will be investigated shortly.

THE ENCOUNTER ASYMMETRY

Despite the constraints by now understood, which belong to the structural logic of the model, procedures for the outcome resolve guarantee a fizzling, bubbling interaction of all concerned. And because the model is symmetrical, and given that the processes follow identical cycles within and between each iteration, it seemed obvious that nothing would distinguish the interaction of any given player x with any other player y. Player x would meet with every other player, and all 29 of them would have the same status in his/her eyes. Jo Hancock, then a graduate student in Swansea, was investigating the topic of reverberation: she assured me that this was not the case. In fact, she reckoned that there would be players whom any given player would never meet at all! The exclamation mark stands for incredulity: how could this be the case? On careful examination, the full interplay perception relies on effective interaction *outside* the formal meetings—given that ten people are not in session in any given period. However, something in this was not properly understood, even so.

There was soon unveiled the output of a computer program, written by Jo Hancock in APL. It enshrined the formal protocols for running the Harnden Schedule, with its simultaneous meetings by polar pairs, in which the fully determined QIDs interacted according to the rules of the Outcome Resolve. It was used (in her words), 'to follow the pattern of a particular infoset member, highlighting those members s/he can never actually meet to speak to within the official protocol.' The aim of the program was declared to be 'To illuminate the possible pathways for reverberation.' The program could simulate the path followed by any player and count the number of meetings. The symmetry at last emerges: the count is the same for any player. But the relationships between any given player and the others are, as she had alleged, anything but symmetrical. Here is Jo's summary:

Any player x meets 4 people three times;
8 people twice;
8 people once.
That leaves: 9 people s/he never meets at all.

However, her analysis goes on to show that of these nine who do not actually interact, five may be met in other sessions when player x is not in session (two in one of the other iterations, two in the second of them, and one in either of these). That leaves four people whom player x cannot meet at all—within the confines of the official meeting programme, that is. As will be seen, this does not completely exhaust the possibilities.

Intuition remains gasping at this gross asymmetry of relationships. But I speak for myself: Allenna Leonard remembers that in the first experiments at Manchester, she had looked forward to encountering Professor Enid Mumford, whose work she had read, and failed to do so. She had recognized the encounter asymmetry. It is clear that I dismissed the wider asymmetry that she already perceived as part of the collapse of the schedule I had planned, which the Harnden Schedule had resolved, but which I assumed (wrongly) had teething troubles that would account for complaints. Obviously, the asymmetry introduces practical difficulties in maximizing reverberations between people, as distinct from the even spread of the information flow. However, the complication that is most disconcerting is the following. Suppose I were free to choose any role. I must trade off complicated alternatives as to content, and as to my functions in the game, as we know, to assume my quadripartite identity. But how about the actual people with whom I work? Should I take into account that my QID entails that I shall meet and not meet others according to the frequencies now laid bare? *Could* I do all of this, indeed, has anyone the mental grasp?

From Wales to Canada: in the meantime this disbalance had been discovered independently by Joe Truss. He had not used a computer algorithm, but had thought the matter through, and further, to a crucial point. It was to note that eight of the nine people who 'do not meet in the protocol could *arrange* to meet under various conditions, but that the ninth is totally inaccessible. S/he is the player who holds the edge role that is parallel to a given role, on the other side of the icosahedron. Joe called this the 'polar edge' by analogy with the polar vertex.

The only way in which the 15 pairs of polar edges thus defined can even see each other is outside the syntegration as such. They would need to recognize each other, and make a private deal to go off after closing time to a rendezvous at a nearby pub. Then this they ought to do, for the sake of cohesion. The trouble is, from my knowledge of syntegrations, closing time would have come after the pubs had closed ...) The following tabulation expresses the principle behind encounter asymmetry:

I am Silver–Green.

Those I can meet through direct contact are:

As a team of Silver: As a team of Green:

    Silver–White   Green–Gold
    Silver–Black   Green–Brown
    Silver–Orange   Green–White
    Silver–Gold   Green–Light Blue
    Silver–Green (*me*)   Green–Silver (*me*)

As a critic of Red: As a critic of Dark Blue:

    Red–Orange   Dark Blue–Purple
    Red–Gold   Dark Blue–Black
    Red–Light Blue   Dark Blue–White
    Red–Yellow   Dark Blue–Brown
    Red–Purple   Dark Blue–Yellow

As a *member* of Green topic team, I cannot attend Yellow topic meetings, but I meet:

Purple–Red	as	Critic of Dark Blue topic
Yellow–Red	as	Critic of Red topic
Yellow–Black	as	Observer at Black meeting
Yellow–Orange	as	Observer at Orange meeting
Yellow–Purple	as	?

As a *member* of Silver topic team, I cannot attend Purple topic meetings, but I meet:

Purple–Red	as	Critic of Red topic
Purple–Light Blue	as	Observer at Light Blue meeting
Purple–Brown	as	Observer at Brown meeting
Purple–Dark Blue	as	Critic of Dark Blue topic
Purple–Yellow	as	?

As a *critic* of Red topic, I cannot attend White topic meetings, but I meet:

White–Dark Blue	as	Critic of Dark Blue
White–Silver	as	Team member
White–Green	as	Team member

White–Brown	as	Observer at Brown meeting
White–Black	as	Observer at Black meeting

As a *critic* of Dark Blue topic, I cannot attend Gold topic meetings, but I meet:

Gold–Red	as	Critic of Red
Gold–Light Blue	as	Observer at Light Blue meeting
Gold–Silver	as	Team member
Gold–Orange	as	Observer at Orange meeting
Gold–Green	as	Team member

Next, accounting for more participants not so far eliminated:

I can OBSERVE at the following meetings

Black topic		*Light Blue topic*
Black–White	OR	Light Blue–Gold
Black–Yellow		Light Blue–Purple
Black–Orange		Light Blue–Brown

Orange topic		*Brown topic*
Orange–Gold	OR	Brown–White
Orange–Yellow		Brown–Purple

Note: Some of these are met in other capacities, too: for instances Light Blue–Brown and Black–Orange are critics of the Silver and Green topics, respectively.

Finally, I can in no circumstances see Yellow–Purple in action at all.

Here is a full tabulation for Silver–Green generated by the Hancock algorithm. Silver–Green meets all infoset members the following number of times per iteration:

1.	Red–Orange	3
2.	Red–Gold	1
3.	Red–Light Blue	3

4.	Red–Yellow	2
5.	Red–Purple	2
6.	Black–Orange	1
7.	Black–Silver	2
8.	Black–White	Observe at session 2 or meet privately at session 3
9.	Black–Yellow	Observe at session 2 or meet privately at session 3
10.	Black–Dark Blue	3
11.	Orange–Gold	Meet privately at session 2 or observe at session 3
12.	Orange–Silver	2
13.	Orange–Yellow	Observe at session 2 or session 3
14.	Dark Blue–Purple	2
15.	Green–Gold	1
16.	Green–Silver	Self
17.	Green–White	1
18.	Green–Light Blue	2
19.	Green–Brown	2
20.	Gold–Silver	1
21.	Gold–Light Blue	Observe at session 2 or meet privately at session 3
22.	Silver–White	1
23.	White–Brown	Meet privately at session 2 or observe at session 3
24.	White–Dark Blue	1
25.	Light Blue–Brown	1
26.	Light Blue–Purple	Observe at session 2 or session 3
27.	Brown–Dark Blue	3
28.	Brown–Purple	Observe at session 2 or session 3
29.	Yellow–Dark Blue	2
30.	Yellow–Purple	Cannot observe, can only meet privately

The Truss table of polar edges that cannot interact is shown in Table 8.3 and the Truss table of polar disjunctions in Table 8.4.

Both discoverers of the principles and details of the lopsided meeting arrangements that Allenna had remarked upon in the pathfinding experiments at Manchester deserve congratulation. It is tempting to dub this the Jo(e) Encounter Asymmetry.

Table 8.3   Truss table of polar edges that cannot interact

I AM SILVER–GREEN		
Meetings on left and right occur simultaneously		
Red–Orange		White–Brown
Red–Gold		White–Dark Blue
Red–Light Blue	CRITIC OF RED	White–Black
Red–Yellow		White–Green
Red–Purple		White–Silver
OBSERVER OF EITHER		
Black–Orange		Light Blue–Brown
Black–Silver		Light Blue–Purple
Black–White		Light Blue–Red
Black–Yellow		Light Blue–Gold
Black–Dark Blue		Light Blue–Green
OBSERVER OF EITHER		
Orange–Gold		Brown–Dark Blue
Orange–Silver		Brown–Purple
Orange–Yellow		Brown–Green
Orange–Red		Brown–White
Orange–Black		Brown–Light Blue
Green–Gold		Yellow–Dark Blue
Green–Silver	TEAM MEMBER	Yellow–Purple
Green–White	OF GREEN	Yellow–Red
Green–Light Blue		Yellow–Black
Green–Brown		Yellow Orange
Gold–Silver		Dark Blue–Purple
Gold–Light Blue		Dark Blue–Black	CRITIC OF
Gold–Red		Dark Blue–White	DARK BLUE
Gold–Orange		Dark Blue–Brown
Gold–Green		Dark Blue–Yellow
Silver–White		Purple–Red
Silver–Black	TEAM MEMBER	Purple–Light Blue
Silver–Orange	OF SILVER	Purple–Brown
Silver–Green		Purple–Yellow
Silver–Gold		Purple–Dark Blue
Left-hand and right-hand sides are polar opposites		

Table 8.4 Truss table of polar disjunctions

POLAR EDGES EXCLUSION

Red–Orange	↔	White–Brown
Red–Gold	↔	White–Dark Blue
Red–Light Blue	↔	White–Black
Red–Yellow	↔	White–Green
Red–Purple	↔	White–Silver
Black–Orange	↔	Light Blue–Brown
Black–Silver	↔	Light Blue–Purple
Black–White	↔	Light Blue–Red
Black–Yellow	↔	Light Blue–Gold
Black–Dark Blue	↔	Light Blue–Green
Orange–Gold	↔	Brown–Dark Blue
Orange–Silver	↔	Brown–Purple
Orange–Yellow	↔	Brown–Green
Orange–Red	↔	Brown–White
Orange–Black	↔	Brown–Light Blue
Green–Gold	↔	Yellow–Dark Blue
Green–Silver	↔	Yellow–Purple
Green–White	↔	Yellow–Red
Green–Light Blue	↔	Yellow–Black
Green–Brown	↔	Yellow–Orange
Gold–Silver	↔	Dark Blue–Purple
Gold–Light Blue	↔	Dark Blue–Black
Gold–Red	↔	Dark Blue–White
Gold–Orange	↔	Dark Blue–Brown
Gold–Green	↔	Dark Blue–Yellow
Silver–White	↔	Purple–Red
Silver–Black	↔	Purple–Light Blue
Silver–Orange	↔	Purple–Brown
Silver–Green	↔	Purple–Yellow
Silver–Gold	↔	Purple–Dark Blue

SYNTEGRATION EPISODE FOUR

THE TOPIC AUCTION

It is by now clear why the topic auction has presented so many practical problems to syntegration facilitators, and before the excursion into encounter asymmetry an investigation of procedures was promised. To facilitate the auction itself, the tabulation headed 'Topic Auction Data Sheet' (Table 8.5) has to be completed, and a copy distributed to each person. The short titles that emerged from the Problem Jostle as CSIs arranged in polar pairs should be entered in their proper places on each side of the sheet. Participants must be reminded that the opposite pole of the one allocated to them is the topic of their antithetic management: a special interest, therefore, but a matter in which they have no direct involvement. This is also the time to explain the need for each person to arrange a private meeting with his/her opposite polar edge, as just explained above. Next, they will be looking at the topics that attract them most, whilst bearing in mind that they must then select a pair topic from among the five listed. As they begin to focus on likely memberships, they will need to note the critical roles to which that section commits them.

The complicated cycle of computing that is needed to resolve the auction is now undertaken in the heads of individuals to a greater extent than before, but it is still a community task. People do after all hold expectations of each other, particularly after a day of Problem Jostling, and these expectations may be negative as well as positive. Importance is therefore attached to the information exchange given in the behaviour of people during the auction. However, if a scramble is to be avoided, the facilitator needs help. This is provided by the questionnaire headed 'Topic Auction of Thirty Quadripartite Lots,' shown below, p. 140.

Table 8.5 Topic Auction Data Sheet

←Polar Opposites→

TOPIC	MEMBER	CRITIC OF:		MEMBER	CRITIC OF:		TOPIC
RED TEAM TOPIC:	Red–Orange	Green	Dark Blue	White–Brown	Gold	Yellow	WHITE TEAM TOPIC:
	Red–Gold	Black	Brown	White–Dark Blue	Orange	Light Blue	
	Red–Light Blue	Silver	Dark Blue	White–Black	Gold	Purple	
	Red–Yellow	Silver	Brown	White–Green	Orange	Purple	
	Red–Purple	Black	Green	White–Silver	Light Blue	Yellow	
BLACK TEAM TOPIC:	Black–Orange	Green	Purple	Light Blue–Brown	Silver	Yellow	LIGHT BLUE TEAM TOPIC:
	Black–Silver	Red	Brown	Light Blue–Purple	Orange	White	
	Black–White	Gold	Purple	Light Blue–Red	Silver	Dark Blue	
	Black–Yellow	Gold	Brown	Light Blue–Gold	White	Yellow	
	Black–Dark Blue	Red	Green	Light Blue–Green	Orange	Dark Blue	
ORANGE TEAM TOPIC:	Orange–Gold	White	Purple	Brown–Dark Blue	Red	Silver	BROWN TEAM TOPIC:
	Orange–Silver	Light Blue	Dark Blue	Brown–Purple	Black	Gold	
	Orange–Yellow	White	Light Blue	Brown–Green	Red	Black	
	Orange–Red	Green	Dark Blue	Brown–White	Gold	Yellow	
	Orange–Black	Green	Purple	Brown–Light Blue	Silver	Yellow	

YELLOW TEAM TOPIC:

DARK BLUE TEAM TOPIC:

PURPLE TEAM TOPIC:

GREEN TEAM TOPIC:

Green–Gold	Black	Purple
Green–Silver	Red	Dark Blue
Green–White	Orange	Purple
Green–Light Blue	Orange	Dark Blue
Green–Brown	Red	Black

Yellow–Dark Blue	Silver	Light Blue
Yellow–Purple	Gold	White
Yellow–Red	Silver	Brown
Yellow–Black	Gold	Brown
Yellow–Orange	White	Light Blue

GOLD TEAM TOPIC:

Gold–Silver	Brown	Yellow
Gold–Light Blue	White	Yellow
Gold–Red	Black	Brown
Gold–Orange	White	Purple
Gold–Green	Black	Purple

Dark Blue–Purple	Orange	Green
Dark Blue–Black	Red	Green
Dark Blue–White	Orange	Light Blue
Dark Blue–Brown	Red	Silver
Dark Blue–Yellow	Silver	Light Blue

SILVER TEAM TOPIC:

Silver–White	Light Blue	Yellow
Silver–Black	Red	Brown
Silver–Orange	Light Blue	Dark Blue
Silver–Green	Red	Dark Blue
Silver–Gold	Brown	Yellow

Purple–Red	Black	Green
Purple–Light Blue	Orange	White
Purple–Brown	Black	Gold
Purple–Yellow	Gold	White
Purple–Dark Blue	Orange	Green

TOPIC AUCTION OF   Name or Pseudonym
THIRTY QUADRIPARTITE LOTS

                                                   ....

These are my bids in order of preference
(Write in up to seven colour combinations; strive for minimum)

Colour–Colour

7 6 5 4 3 2 1 .... – 1 2 3 4 5 6 7
7 6 5 4 3 2 1 .... – 1 2 3 4 5 6 7
7 6 5 4 3 2 1 .... – 1 2 3 4 5 6 7
7 6 5 4 3 2 1 .... – 1 2 3 4 5 6 7
7 6 5 4 3 2 1 .... – 1 2 3 4 5 6 7
7 6 5 4 3 2 1 .... – 1 2 3 4 5 6 7
7 6 5 4 3 2 1 .... – 1 2 3 4 5 6 7

PRICING OF BIDS:

Ring number for each colour to denote degree of enthusiasm to discuss:
7 is high.

If you (maybe with others) INITIATED a colour topic or STRONGLY
INFLUENCED its emergence in this form, ring a number twice—e.g. ⑦

I should like to AVOID colour topics

RED	WHITE	MARKING AGAINST COLOUR SHOWN:
BLACK	LIGHT BLUE	M (in capacity as Member)
ORANGE	BROWN	C (in capacity as Critic)
GREEN	YELLOW	MC (altogether)
GOLD	DARK BLUE	
SILVER	PURPLE	(Strive for minimum)

Each person is given a blank questionnaire to accompany his or her Data
Sheet, and is asked to complete it. In an ideal Infoset, it might be argued, it
would be a matter of indifference to anyone into which role s/he was cast,
because all 12 CSIs should be of vital interest to all participants. As a gesture
to this unreal optimum, people should now be urged to restrict their particular
desires as far as possible: all the questionnaires would be returned blank, and
the roles allocated at random in a 'perfect' Infoset, participants should be
told. Having made the point, the facilitator proceeds to accommodate the
human nature that the forms make manifest.

The room is set out as a horizontal 'clock' with 12 stations exhibiting the 12 CSIs, their colours stated. Anyone with a double-ringed 7 is invited to stand at the appropriate station. If any appear, they are asked about their *second* colour. For example, a colour pair ringed 7 and 5, say, is allocated to the form holder straight away, and s/he is given a badge to wear looking (for instance) as shown below.

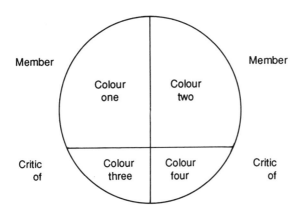

The facilitator works down the 'prices' list, calling for sixes after the sevens, and so on. Note that the completed questionnaires that people are holding are in use only as their own personal memoranda at this stage. Thus, as someone watches how a team is forming, s/he may suddenly opt to join it, regardless of what s/he originally thought and wrote down.

It may be possible to take the Topic Auction through to completion, issuing badges as the procedure unwinds, but facilitators are warned against generating frustrations in the group by forcing the issue beyond a gentle persuasion. If, as a result, the process comes to a halt, the facilitator collects the remaining forms, explaining that people will be allocated to remaining places, using their 'pricing' of the lots and their quasi-vetoes as far as possible. We are left with something akin to a preferential voting system.

The Topic Auction comes at the end of a long day (if the timetabling recommendations below are followed). This means that the facilitators have the discretionary time available to complete role allocation, minimizing the frustrations predicted by a study of the questionnaires. Difficult decisions should be acknowledged: a facilitator should take on the task of explaining to participants who are likely to be disgruntled how this has happened, and why the decision ought to be acceptable. This is frankly a sales pitch.

Evidently this process calls for an algorithmic treatment on the computer. The issues involved are probed in depth by Jo Hancock in her Surplus Three contribution to Part Five. She also explains her algorithm, and records its first test. This was to compare her procedure with a use of the Kelly approach already mentioned in Chapter Seven as having far too little time available to develop its proper potential. As can be seen, the Hancock algorithm doubled the mean score of Infoset satisfaction with the topic auction. The difficulty of the vexed question of allocation is reflected in the fact that this much improved mean score is itself no higher than the median score on the satisfaction scale. However, this provokes a question: in the face of all this complexity, is that outcome a good result? We are used to scoring euphoric levels of satisfaction for enjoyment, and that is fine; perhaps the median score is in some sense the optimum outcome for an allocation in which compromise is endemic.

Obviously other approaches to the allocation problem are possible. David Sutton has developed an heuristic version using a spreadsheet which, at the first experiment, took 3 hours to run. Now Alan Pearson, who has given much thought to the facilitation of syntegrations (see Surplus Four in Part Five) argues strongly that the assignment of topics to vertices is more important than the Topic Auction itself. If he is right, then David Sutton's approach is of particular interest. Taking tabulations of participants' preferences and indifference to topics, he finds correlations and anti-correlations between them. The anti-correlations are used to identify topics which would make good polar opposites. That is, he writes 'people who featured topic X in their list of preferences mentioned topic Y in their indifference list, or at least did not mention it at all.' Then 'the correlations between topics and the anti-correlations were used to decide a full arrangement of topics around the icosahedron.'

Sutton's scoring methods allow him to measure voter satisfaction with the outcome as a percentage of the ideal as expressed in the prior preferences. He obtained an overall fit of 71% for his heuristic solution, while the Hancock algorithm, which delivered in 30 min, gave a fit of 48%. This, of course, compares closely with the median score already mentioned, which was obtained *post facto* from questionnaires using a seven-point scale. Jo Hancock's first test, however, combined the hexadic reduction with the topic auction in a simple voting procedure. Thus only those votes cast for winning topics counted in the determination of preference. She concluded a two-stage procedure was clearly necessary.

Both approaches are in their infancy, and will doubtless be improved—maybe, as Sutton has been exploring, by making heuristic improvements to the automated algorithm. The whole matter is a research topic of considerable interest. Meanwhile, it is still perfectly possible to run syntegrations!

REVIEWING THE ROLES

Another potential set of frustrations may surface when it comes home (maybe much later) to participants that their speaking involvement in only four teams actually excludes them from speaking involvement in eight. Two of those are in polar opposition, and are the foci of antithetic management, a term used originally to apply to all tensile connections (that is, to include also teams criticized) but now restricted to polar opposites. More should be made of this antithetic role than was made in the first experiments, as has been argued before. People are told that their names are expected to appear on draft FSIs during the Outcome Resolve, whether in support of the statement, or denouncing it, or making a helpful written comment. The involvement, though indirect, should be real: it is *antithetic management*. And that means that each person is directly involved in six, that is half, of the outcomes.

Unless otherwise admonished, people tend to take too little interest in the remaining six activities. They should, first of all, be made alert to the reverberation aspect of syntegration. That means that they should *expect* the effects of their sixfold involvements to be felt in the other six debates. This entails observation, and also the freedom (though no longer the obligation) to comment on developing FSIs in the other six teams. This may certainly be done by writing on the drafts that are posted, but also in remarks made to colleagues during breaks. 'Haven't you noticed what the Silver team is saying? They're ahead of you! Their mode of analysis is more powerful than yours.' If made in writing, such remarks ought not to be anonymous, particularly as to team membership. [This is Archibald (writing)—(in his) Green (capacity): ARCHIE: GREEN.] Evidently, such interventions are likely to foster the reverberation phenomenon. We have known since Heisenberg that so-called observation is never neutral, and here we can see the effect in action.

In short, the role of Observer needs to be invested with a new dignity. Each person has four speaking roles, two analytical roles, and six observational roles—and twelve roles is quite enough within the icosahedral model. Notice that 360 roles in total are now involved. But if the role of observer is to be taken quite seriously, how is it to be discharged? The fact that when two teams are in session for the Outcome Resolve, and are thereby committing 20 people to meetings, 10 people have 'nothing to do.' They need to be encouraged to be active, primarily in their antithetical capacities, but also as participating Observers.

The tendency that people have to retreat into corners during what they perceive as free time in order to catch up with (or indeed thereby to generate) gossip with a friend is an incipient lapse of protocol. But the pressures are severe, it is necessary to catch one's breath and to unwind in various ways, and people ought not to be hounded. The fact remains that there *are* duties to be undertaken. Everyone has a third of sessional time to fulfil these non-speaking tasks, to which is added genuinely free time during breaks and in the evenings. A committed Infoset will use all of it. In this most participants surprise themselves; but the release of resources available to each person from the explosion of creativity in the group can be overwhelming.

THE SEQUESTRATION OF TIME

Nothing more needs to be said at this stage about the fifth to eighth episodes of a Syntegration: these consist of the three episodes that between them constitute the Outcome Resolve, and the Conclusion session. The Outcome Resolve presents no special problems, except perhaps in the voting procedure, which is discussed separately; and the Conclusion is very much a matter for the Infoset itself. What happens next? That is its theme. And the answer will depend on the sort of Infoset that it is, particularly as to context: a corporate Infoset considering the firm's future will have different criteria by which to judge its next steps from a group of citizen environmentalists who have been discussing the future of their river front.

One way in which the context of the Syntegration makes a great difference, and must always be considered, has to do with the time sequestered to unfold it. The advice of those who have so far undergone the experience has been strong: a five-day meeting held in isolation from the hurly-burly of ordinary activities would be ideal. Even corporate folk, who believe their time to be at a special premium, have judged this to be so; but it is significant that no company has taken itself up on the recommendation so far.

The main argument for the week-long meeting mixes the expectation of stress with the need for relaxation and reflection. It might, however, be biased by the deceptive simplicity of the timetable that it engenders. Recapitulating: the first three episodes take up a day. Six sessions per iteration of the Outcome Resolve at 1 hour each (giving an easy-going change-over allowance), plus an hour of voting on the results, invite us to contemplate a 7-hour working day, plus the wrap-up time that people find particularly useful. There will therefore be 3 days to complete the Outcome Resolve. The travel day uses up registration time, and an expanded period for introductions between participants and to the notion of Syntegrity. A final day allows for a full-scale discussion of What

Happens Next?—and a convivial departure. This adds up to 5 days in all. As a work-load it would be easy going, were it not for the problematic issues of peer group pressure, possible power-mongering, and whatever other forms of stress are implicit in the situation.

Consider the cases in which outstandingly people are likely to complain about this sequestration of their time: the corporation or the government. We need 'the' (however defined) 30 most influential managers/ministers and thinkers to consider the whole future of the company or nation. Suppose, as seems likely, that the prospect of devoting a whole week to issues of normative policy and directional planning appears outrageously indulgent and profligate with time. Then the problem of compression arises. Very well: but it must be recognized at once that the week-long timetable cannot simply be squeezed down into (say) 50- or 40-, or 30-min 'hours' and rewritten pro rata. The Episodes, as we have come to call them in this chapter, are integral wholes. If an iteration were to be broken in half by a night's sleep, it would lose its dynamics and therefore also its syntegrity. We must reconsider timing in terms of Episodes.

It seems that a session of 40 min is satisfactory for a team that has itself under control. That means its own control, although exigencies of time are likely to promote acquiescence in the seizure of initiative by a 'leader.' The changeover time will need regulation by the ringing of bells or the blowing of whistles, which may seem less than deferential to the top brass. But if the team then works hard for 25 min, if the critics prepare themselves as individuals and discipline themselves as a group to provide comments, necessarily pithy, in the space of the next 10 min, and if the team can metabolize this critique within the draft FSI in the final 5 min, then it can be done. This obviously reduces a 6-hour Episode to 4 hours. If the time for voting is halved, which again involves some regimentation, then it is possible to generate a day's work of 9 hours covering two iterations. It certainly seems impossible to work all three iterations of the Outcome Resolve into a single day: we can hardly propose to work for $13\frac{1}{2}$ hours. To cut the session length to half an hour which, with a 20-min vote at the end of the episode, results in a day of 10 hours work, reduces the critical protocol to a farce.

It seems that a two-iteration day is the irreducible maximum, and three iterations are needed. This cannot be cut without losing the reverberative quality: an induction from the experimental evidence at this point, but proven mathematically in Chapter Thirteen. It follows that the extra iteration has to be held either before or after the two-iteration day. To hold it before would mean compressing the Problem Jostle, Hexadic Reduction, and Topic Auction into $4\frac{1}{2}$ hours—if a 9-hour working day is acceptable. But this compression is literally impossible without prejudice to the principles underlying the procedures for specifying the 12 CSIs. If facilitation is to be exerted *against* a self-organizing Infoset with an open-ended mandate, instead of easing it towards acceptable conclusions, then the facilitators are effectively determining agenda, and the Syntegration is spurious thereafter. The extra iteration must be the *third* iteration, and it will take a morning to unfold.

These arguments determine the Syntegration of a minimum duration thus:

Day One
(evening):   Arrival; Reception; Cocktails; Dinner; Address of welcome and explanation; collection of SIs

        (Overnight: preparation of SI schedules; preparation of room)

Day Two: Problem Jostle to ASIs; Hexadic Reduction to CSIs; Topic Auction

        (Overnight: consolidation of topic and membership schedules; preparation of voting clocks)

Day Three: Outcome Resolve, Episodes One and Two, with voting

        (Overnight: analysis of votes, consolidation of draft FSIs)

Day Four
(morning)   Outcome Resolve Episode Three, with voting

        (Lunch: publication of FSIs to each member)

        Afternoon: Concluding Session

        Teatime: Depart

This timetable reduces the commitment to three full days, with three intervening nights. It is the best that can be done without betraying the Syntegration's basic efficacy. However, it is a more marketable proposition than 'a week,' albeit of 5 days, since it can readily be organized as a long weekend: Thursday (or Friday) evening to Sunday (or Monday) teatime. It sequesters only one working day. The future might be considered to be worth that investment.

POSTSCRIPT

Indeed it is. In January 1994, for example, a syntegration was held in Canada by a group called Open Futures. Jo Hancock ran her latest algorithm—involving some 16 000 tests within the hour available for lunch. Satisfaction is now measured by adding together the ordinal numbers assigned by individuals to their topic choices, where the score of 1 is the least favoured. The optimal result for each person is then 23 points scored (12 for the favourite, plus 11 for the next best choice). Thus the theoretical maximum score for a whole Infoset is $23 \times 30 = 690$, which would mean every person's representing his/her most favoured two topics. The ideal may not, of course, be attainable: preferences may well be disbalanced to overload some topics with competing protagonists. Despite that caveat, this most recent syntegration achieved 93% of the theoretical maximum satisfaction so scored.

Chapter Nine

DEVELOPMENTAL PLANNING

This part of the book is entitled 'Enhancing Procedures' and its first two chapters have been concerned with the enhanced procedures of syntegration itself. In this chapter and the next, the concern is with the use of syntegration to enhance other procedures that are central to the conduct of affairs, in enterprises and in government.

The model of enterprise called the Viable System Model and known as the VSM (Beer, 1972, 1981, 1985) cannot be recapitulated here at any length. For readers who have no knowledge of it, Allenna Leonard has written a general description in Chapter Twenty which should be consulted straight away. Her example emphasizes that the VSM is not a hierarchical but a circular model, exhibiting closure, because it includes its own environment in its organizational loops. Its five subsystems are profoundly interactive, so that notions such as 'top-down' and bottom-up' are as inappropriate as they are in the icosahedron. Even so, most if not all enterprises include notions of seniority, of leadership, and of responsibility as part of their organizational language and social ethos. It is striking, too, that enterprises that actually declare an intent to be wholly democratic and to avoid hierarchy are not, when observed in action, exempt from the outcomes of human nature. Thus communes, co-operatives and the like do in practice develop procedures which 'had better be' followed for the sake of smooth running, and 'allow' certain people to take the lead, even if they have to be 'compelled' to assume such a role. The quotation marks are obviously sardonic; one wonders how sincere the bishop-elect may have been when he cried *nolo episcopare* as he was dragged off to his enthronement ...

This being so, the VSM distinguishes sharply between the embedded viable systems that it contains (System One) and four other subsystems which are effectively ancillaries to the primary activities. Two of these four have very precise functions. System Two refers to that group of organizational behaviours that serve to damp oscillations inside System One, drawing its information from the synoptic picture available to System Three. System Five determines purposes for the enterprise, and in so doing cultivates its ethos. Thus it is often assumed to be a label for top management, who must surely by definition figure in such tasks. But recognizable bosses do not exhaust the role. All stakeholders are represented in System Five. In autocratic enterprises, the directors claim to represent the stakeholders but do not: even their representation of the stockholders may be no more than a legal fiction. What really happens in System Five is complicated and subtle; but sometimes a desire for democracy, or a more open style, leads to acknowledgement, as when student representatives appear on governing academic bodies. Again, such moves may be disingenuous.

It is, however, another sharp distinction that most concerns us here. This is the distinction, based originally on biological evidence, that viable systems have to respond almost instantaneously to some stimuli or situations, here and now, in real time, whilst some other reactions, together with the effecting of purposes, are long-range undertakings that require the simulation of alternatives, forecasting, and in one word *planning*. Management of the former kind is a function of System Three and of the latter kind a function of System Four. I have often used the terms Operations and Development to correspond to these two groups of functions. Often, as in the firm, the two functions have specific locations and specialized personnel: it is an organizational convenience, or so it seems. In fact, both activities permeate all the firm's activity, so that localization and specialization may become dysfunctional.

To take a common diagnosis: the general works manager and his considerable entourage of accountants, engineers, and so on perceive themselves as responsible (*qua* System Three) for directing the operations (System One) that create the company's wealth. They see the corporate planners, market researchers, R & D people, and so on, who deal with development (*qua* System Four) as organizational luxuries who frivol away the money that they, in System Three, are labouring to make. Conversely, the System Four folks perceive themselves as custodians of the company's future, in which they require the investment of monies actually being spent by System Three in doomed attempts to prop up decrepit plant serving a rapidly evaporating market. Since both System Three and Four functions are manifestly essential to viability, such attitudinizing is not productive. The situation is not ameliorated if the two functions are held professionally, socially, and structurally apart. They usually are, so that even when attitudes are kept sweet by skilled and responsible management, there is a total lack of synergy between the two vital forces.

The diagrammatic version of the VSM, which is complicated, has an eye-catching graphical feature meant to emphasize this problem, shown below.

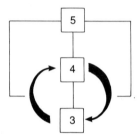

The heavy arrows are saying: Systems Four and Three must massively interact; the main job of System Five (any included bosses notwithstanding) is to see that this interaction happens—all the time. That is more important than issuing orders (*being* bossy) down the line. I call this symbol the Three–Four homeostat: its function is to maintain a balance between investment for the future and the maintenance required to keep the business going. In my opinion, the collapse of any enterprise (firms, of course, but also services and whole governments) turns out at the autopsy to be initiated by an imbalance here. It is the most vulnerable organ of the body politic. Very often the collapse will be attributed to some highly visible task that was a loser; very often a specialist diagnosis will describe the failure in the terms of its own system of filters: sales will see the situation primarily in terms of the sales policy, finance in terms of accounting, and so on. Often, especially in func-tionally organized companies, the information needed to integrate present and future activities is missing, to say nothing of the base that would be required to comprehend their appropriate balance. This advice says that it is well to look at the underlying Three–Four homeostasis. Incidentally, the emphasis here is on homeostasis as the maintenance of balance under a given set of criteria. Do not imagine that the emphasis is on absence of change—for the criteria of balance may themselves change as the viable system learns, adapts, and evolves within its environment. (A full discussion of the cybernetics involved in this question of emphasis may be consulted in Chapter Fourteen.)

PLANNING AS SEEN THROUGH THE VSM FILTER

It follows from this introduction that the developmental planning process on which viability depends cannot be isolated in System Four, although the VSM proposes that System Four be the concept of its focus. It has to do with internal homeostasis in which the day-to-day needs of the organism (of which System Three is the epitome) are balanced with the demands of an external environment and an unknown future, so that the process permeates the enterprise. Second, developmental planning is indeed a process and not a product. It is a continuous undertaking. In recognition of these two pre-requisites of viability, I put forward (Beer, 1969) the concept of the aborting corporate plan. Unless the enterprise's plan continuously aborts, that is to say, there is a real risk that someone will implement it, with unfortunate consequences inevitably, since by the implementation date a long lead time will have elapsed since the plan was carved in stone, and all manner of unforeseen factors will have entered into the equation. In considering these outrageously counter-cultural statements, please consider any plan of the kind scorned. The national economic plans of every political stripe are the glaring example from which to start.

Yet planning (and that means ahead) there must be. The answer has to be some type of adaptive planning, wherein the planning process is what is important, and not the plan; and what actually happens is the continuing spin-off of this process. Every event will take not only the purpose into account but also the very latest information pertaining to that purpose. No action will be taken without cognizance of the fruits of the action before. The whole argument of these two summary paragraphs entails that (however many staff are involved in the deliberations) only managers are authorized to plan, and that the act of planning is a commitment to action, with all that involves in cost, effort and consequences. People pay lip-service to some of these notions by now, but are often unable to live with those stern conclusions. It is more convenient for them to claim that high expertise was used to formulate the plan that failed, that expensive consultancy validated it and that (faceless) people are to blame.

Then how can we come to an understanding of adaptive planning, how visualize it, and how resolve its apparent contradictions? As usual, these puzzles are generated by the way it is customary, and professionally fashionable, to speak about things—by the accepted paradigm, in short. The puzzles are not the product of actual experience. The experience, however, is complicated, even though we live it, while the paradigm misleads by over-simplification just by trying to be clear. Here I risk an explanation that looks utterly daunting, because there is no paradigm to help the talk along, beyond the recently introduced and minimally explained VSM. But I claim that a little perseverence will pay off, just because this account of matters is what actually happens anyway.

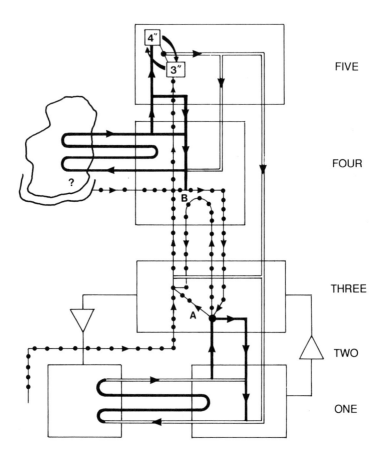

Start with System One: the very operations that are what the enterprise does. If it is in manufacturing, this is where the plant is. What we see is the management of the plant interrogating its own operational people about their needs. This dialogue goes on continuously, on a continual loop, drawn with heavy lines on the horizontal plane. There are two outside inputs to this dialogue. One (the double line) represents the 'ethos' of the enterprise, coming from System Five. The other comes from System Three, because Three has an overall view of Systems One (only one of which is shown). So the vertical loop of thick lines Three–One–Three is also continuous. Then the management of basic activity (One) is in dialogue with its own embedded operational people, and simultaneously with the operational management of the integrated enter-prise. It is easy to write script for this dialogue: the plant supervisors discussing their intentions, trying out ideas and trying on ambitions—some of which is routinely boring though necessary, and some of which One will itself try out at level Three. They all know each other; they know the current state of affairs and likely immediate future; the aspirations of all parties are familiar, although they gradually change.

Next look at the identical loop, also drawn with heavy lines, that characterizes System Four. Here the management is interrogating the outside world, providing a look-out post and seeking to evaluate the longer-term future (betokened by the question mark) on the vertical plane. It is interacting continuously with System Five in the vertical plane as well. Again, the people involved know each other well, and because of continuity the interaction is mostly free of surprises. Exceptions occur when the look-out post detects a major movement impending (for example, a new tax might be threatened) or when a major breakthrough arising from either in-house or outside research (for example, in technology or computing) is signalled. Then the evaluations have to be done and reports issued; but they are carried on the stream of dialogue as they arise. There is no hint here of the annual review type of catalogue.

The diagram is meant to convey continuity, connectivity, and the pervasive character of the information flow. But now that the two heavy-lined inter-actions have been identified, the eye may more easily focus on the actual Three–Four homeostat that the previous diagram depicted with such vigour. This is the dotted circuitry, in which the trombone-shaped loops that are never ending appear in the vertical plane. Continuous information circulating in the Three–One circuitry is sampled (or otherwise filtered) at connection A, and percolates System Three's own decision space into the System Four loop. At connection B, by a similar process, the Four–Five circuit feeds into the homeostatic loop. Further information flows from outside the system impinge on the homeostat too, but there is no need to examine them here. All that needs adding is the closure provided for the whole system by the double line. This derives from System Five as described earlier, and provides direct closure with the other systems, so that Three is not isolated from Five, for instance. The purpose of the double-line flow is, as indicated so clearly in the previous diagram, to monitor the activity of the Three–Four homeostat, rather as the heart has a pacemaker. The understanding that permits the ethos to flow is precisely System Five's awareness of the Three–Four homeostatic activity itself. This awareness is indicated on the diagram by the small replica of the homeostat inside the box that identifies System Five. System Three has representation there through the long vertical dotted line and System Four through the short vertical thick line.

This whole process *informs* action in the enterprise. It is the glue that keeps everything together and action coherent. It *is* planning insofar as informed, cohesive action occurs. What is normally called planning is the adumbration of that action. So when impending action is intended, the appropriate subsystem spins off the informational snapshot that its circuitry contains, and announces 'here is the plan.' This may happen at point A, when the One–Three loop spins off its content into System Four, or at point B, when System Four's interrogatory loop spins off its content into System Three. Action based on the Three–Four homeostatic outcome then happens inside System One. It is instantaneous, and there is no need to abort: the plan, the decision, the action are now one. This does not mean to say that planning refers to *results* that occur within the hour; it refers only to decisions to act, the planning decisions, which we said committed resources now so that the future may be different. The results may be well down the line: it is the commitment that is made now, and is irrevocable. It follows from this real-time concept of management that the aspects of a plan that continuously abort are those that are accessible to change at any snapshot moment in the information flow. Once that accessibility is lost, the plan is actual. (Much more detailed analysis of this whole planning model is available in Chapter Thirteen in *The Heart of Enterprise* (Beer, 1979).)

THE ANATOMY OF PLANNING

Obviously the contents of a complicated plan have different lifetimes in this action-oriented picture. Five-year plans always fail, because their myriad component plans abort at different times. Shorter epochal plans sometimes succeed in spite of this factor, because management techniques such as PERT and Critical Path Analysis are used to force events into line. However, epochal planning is basically misconceived. Whence came these artificial deadlines, the year, the quarter, the period? They come from accounting convenience (based on the now irrelevant constraints of pen and ledger technology) and the necessity to arrange meetings. They have no special magic of their own, as they do in the circadian rhythms of the body or the rotation of the seasons. There is a better way to view the basic requirement that needs to be accommodated in all this. It is not the lag between formulating a plan and deciding upon it, but the lag between the act of planning and the accrual of results. This lag is reflected in the calendar, but is determined by feasibility. I can decide now to catch the train that leaves in 1 hour, and be on it. But my decision now to catch the train that leaves next week will not have any quick results. It is feasibility that determines lags in natural fact, and this may be acknowledged without treating convenience as its proxy. No one can produce a child in a month by involving nine people of the opposite sex in today's procreative decision.

The following tabulation gives a view of planning that derives from the feasibility of intended action, rather than the purported time-scale for achieving results. The situation we are in at this moment is called *actuality*: planning is pure implementation, but is tactical to the extent that the implementation may be better or worse effected. In particular, the System Two role is to damp any oscillations that implementations might cause within System One. But we can always do better than we do: if it is currently feasible it is called *capability*, and it is the function of System Three's strategic planning to devise an implementation that exploits what can, after all, be done. By the same token, developmental planning seeks implementations of whatever benefits are latent in the situation, called *potentiality*. This potential cannot, however, be realized under present constraints: further investment of some sort will be needed. Thus implementation at this level includes the research, or the training, or the new money, so involved.

Brain of the Firm (Beer, 1972) gives detailed information on the use of the measures of feasibility, and the ratios between them, to form indices that can be monitored to regulate performance. They are also explained in that book as statistical tools that aid forecasting at each level of planning, which is the current topic. Then the types of planning are named after the levels of feasibility, and the table shows where responsibility for each is considered to reside. But these are all linguistic conventions that make discussion of managerial realities more fruitful: those realities themselves are aspects of the informational flux already examined.

Note that all these planning activities of the total enterprise achieve implementation in System One, which therefore has no planning to do for itself in this recursion. It simply receives the ancillary services of the other four subsystems. Even so, enquiries inside System One will uncover a spate of planning activities! For System One is the metasystem of the next embedded recursion: it contains all the ancillary subsystems just described, because it is a viable system in its own right. Finally, and to avoid possible confusion, it should be noted that in earlier writings (especially Beer, 1972) what are here called normative and developmental planning were sometimes elided under the label normative. It has since proved helpful to distinguish between them as shown. Normative planning deals with what should be done in the moral sense; and its imperative has been raised to what *must* be done, because here is the generation of the ethos of the enterprise that closes the loops of all the subsystems. What *should* be done under the developmental planning aegis is a desideratum, perhaps in a merely technological or economic sense, and so is not mandatory. Then the role of System Five in monitoring the Three–Four homeostat has the connotations both of ethicality and potentiality, which is why the elision happened in the first place, 25 years ago.

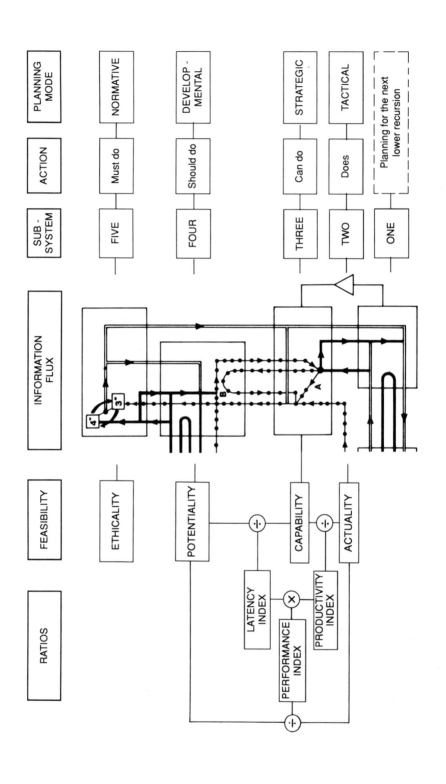

THE REDUNDANCY OF POTENTIAL COMMAND

It is against this extensive theoretical and descriptive background that the use of syntegration in the enterprise had better be considered if its true value is to be understood in the terms of managerial cybernetics. It is all too easy to say that this is a technique that is clearly relevant to planning. After which it is even easier to say that we cannot commit 30 people for 5 days to this nice idea—there are too many planning meetings scheduled ...

I offered to describe the situation as it actually happens, and I have done so. The description was complicated, but so are people, and even more complicated are the politics of every enterprise. (There are many psychologists in enterprises and too few anthropologists and ethologists.) So consideration of syntegration as a managerial technique is not just a matter of looking down the list for people who 'might be interested' and 'could be spared' for 'an exercise like this' ... the jargon is familiar enough. The first question worth posing, now that we have a fairly elaborate model to hand, is: how do people actually operate these homeostatic loops in practice? Managerial cybernetics knows very well that the organization chart with its neat boxes and organizational dependences is (as I always call it) a machine for apportioning blame. People in real life interact as they will, because social groups are self-selecting and societary units are self-organizing. What the chart says has influence as a set of constraints, and active people as distinct from name plates hasten to get around them.

The redundancy of potential command is another of McCulloch's terms, and its origin as usual in his work lies in neurophysiology. He described the brain without awe as a three pound electrochemical computer running on glucose at 25 watts. He already knew, however, that this machine is not organized hierarchically, is not single-valued, and does not work (as does the computer) with a binary logic, even though individual neurons are two-state devices when it comes to output: they fire or they do not. In many respects these brain cells have characteristics in common with people who comprise the enterprise. There are a great many, they are unreliable, and when they die they are replaced in their function by others. So the first thing is to say that neurons and people are organizationally redundant—highly redundant. This is not to disparage individual worth. It is only to say that graveyards are full of indispensable people. McCulloch reckoned that the brain is redundant in the order of 20 000 to 1. People are often heard to say that this means that there is a lot of unused brain that could be developed to exhibit extraordinary powers. It is not the point: we need redundancy to make up for unreliability, dysfunction, and demise; and society does too.

Although various regions of the brain normally deal with various recognizable functions, there is a lot of interchangeability that derives from redundancy. And in any case, brain functions are not totally localized and dedicated, as functions in the management hierarchy of the firm or the state are supposed to be according to the chart. So how are 'decisions taken,' if they do not follow a given pathway up a given chain of command? The answer is that a concatenation of neurons operates when and only when information collects that enables a reliable 'decision' to be made. Note that what I am calling a concatenation is defined from moment to moment by the presence of relevant information, and not by a pre-ordained structure hungry for facts. Now the number of possible subsets of 10 billion neurons is effectively infinite. This means that command is not prefigured, but is potential in any concatenation that shares the needful information. Well, this defines none other than an information set, an infoset. It is obvious that not only are individual neurons highly redundant, the infosets are too, since any infoset has the power of potential command.

It interested McCulloch, and me in turn, that the most successful human organizations, be they never so hierarchical in appearance, operate on an understanding of the redundancy of potential command. He analysed old battles, particularly those of Nelson, to demonstrate this. Sea mists and the smog of cannon fire made direct orders impossible to convey by signal flags, and Nelson's System One ship's captains took command of whatever local situation they could actually see and interpret in terms of the System Three strategic pre-battle briefing; of course, that had occurred the previous day in the context of System Four's war intelligence. Final System One implementation, attack, would obviously be undertaken within the System Five ethos of Royal Navy discipline plus the charisma of Nelson's leadership.

I soon discovered the same phenomenon in industry. Who is really taking the decisions about informational technology? It is not the bigwigs who have to sign the requisitions, but a subcultural infoset of junior young people, plus consultants who may not even belong to the organization, who know the latest technology. The Board pretends to understand, but is easily manipulated by those who know the facts. As to government, the manipulation of ministers and of policy itself is largely in the hands of infosets of civil service mandarins, lobby groups and *ad hoc* committees of experts. Potential command will be seized and made actual by fluid infosets of people who have the shared purpose and the shared information appropriate to the decisions involved.

THE DEVELOPMENT OF DEVELOPMENT

Enterprise of every kind is in a state of extreme uncertainty today, thanks to all manner of political, social, economic, and technological change. The cauldron seeths with unrest, fear, and cynicism. Leaders, so-called, in government and in society at large are held in a scorn that is close to contempt. There is much agreement that the situation does not yield to reductionist analysis and prescription according to a set of categories and a system of values that have been virtually discarded. Consider, then, the enterprise, of whatever kind, from small business to the social services to the nation state. How can the problems be addressed?—for there are seen to be many opportunities for change, and there is major new technology to back up whatever action is needed. What does management typically do?

Management pretends that nothing has changed while loudly protesting that everything has changed. It claims that it wants to mobilize new thinking, while zealously ordering its approaches to exclude it. It puts in place a vast and bureaucratic committee structure, with the same old people sparring with the same old motives, using the same old arguments deriving from the same old ideologies. After months, probably years, of serious labour, it will publish the same old plans, which will be packaged anew by the same old advertising and PR firms. The only new feature in the entire business is the fresh money paid out to do all of this, and the only thing to be said for all of this is that it is well intentioned.

Please consider carefully whether this is (as people would like to believe) a caricature, or the simple truth. Please consider the cost: the overt costs are breathtaking, the covert costs will exceed them many times, the opportunity costs are unfathomable—the enterprise may not even survive. Consider the chances of success. Review the last few years: from the failure of constitutional accords in many countries, through the failed redesign of health and education and economic systems, to the failure of whole regimes and innumerable firms. The list is long and too well known to need recapitulation. The situation is desperate.

The cybernetics expressed by the VSM is available to help. And if, as has been argued, the primary problem is the proper functioning of the Three–Four homeostat, then that would be a good place to start. We need to metabolize the creative and the synergetic resources of the enterprise. The directive management team of an enterprise is perhaps the most virile example of an infoset with which society is familiar. What is its constitution? Take, for example, the leading directors of a company board; add the most respected staff aides; include (possibly) representatives of workers, clients, and the community: here are 30 people strongly connected by a motive, a collegiate purpose. Can they afford to meet for an intensive 5-day exploration of the future of their enterprise, using the Team Syntegrity model and protocol? If not, they are probably condemning themselves to years of orthodox, strung-out committee work that ties up thinking time, exhausts patience, frustrates innovation—and may be too late.

However, I hope that the arguments in this chapter will lead a particular enterprise to consider how to encourage the self-selecting and self-organizing properties of infosets, and the redundancy of potential command in the particular circumstances that apply, rather than inventing a plausible check list, as the above example did. The special difficulty is easy to pin-point. Whereas infosets will always assemble themselves, and be motivated to meet over lunch or in each other's houses to plot and plan, a full-scale syntegration intended to make full use of the power of this technique is not at all easy to organize. It behoves the enterprise to think about its role as facilitator in this matter. Here is an indication of what might conceivably happen, based on an experience of 30 years ago.

At that time I advocated that business, industry, and government should purloin from academia the concept of the sabbatical year. As managing director of Sigma (Science in General management) Ltd, I adopted my own proposal. Each employee was credited with some paid leave in the sabbatical bank for each year of service. S/he did not have to wait 7 years to draw on this credit: I am opposed, after all, to epochal management. The idea was that at any time a staff member could propose to take the number of days of credit outstanding off work, in order to undertake a project near to his/her heart. The condition was that the project be not frivolous, and a panel constituted by System Five would be the judge of that. The project could not be to study probability theory in Monte Carlo, then. On the other hand, it did not have to be directly related to the professional work of the company. The invented example used in the company's regulations was of someone who wished to find out whether a particular moth had a habitat in the Himalayas—given that lepidoptery was a consuming side interest. The idea was, of course, that our people should not become workaholics, or so frustrated in pursuing matters of personal interest that they fled to academia itself. The scheme worked well, although credit was drawn upon for only a few days at a time. It was much appreciated by staff.

A variant on this scheme might be considered. Suppose it were made known by an enterprise that any self-organizing group of 30 staff could constitute itself an infoset, and apply for a week's leave to hold a syntegration. There would be no constraints on who might apply: above all, no requirement of seniority would be imposed. This time lepidoptery would not be respected: the group should undertake to discuss some aspect of the future of the enterprise, and to report its 12 findings to the management. Its concern for the enterprise could be open-ended or directed to a specific challenge such as quality improvement, multiculturalism or the impact of new technology. An enterprise adopting this idea would surely make facilities available, and costs would be minimal (one cannot hire consultants for the price of their wages ...). Such a scheme should not be attempted unless the management makes an undertaking to respond in some way that is not merely cosmetic. Who knows what degree of creativity might be released, or to what synergistic end? Many a lucrative idea has been adopted from the old-fashioned 'suggestion scheme' where brief recommendations, some of them polite, are dropped in a box. Voluntary syntegration raises the possible benefit by orders of magnitude.

There is no doubt that the need to recruit 30 people can be daunting, and it is at least possible that an infoset could be created out of smaller groups, which would quickly identify with each other through the basic characteristics of infosets: shared information and a unity of purpose. Among collapsing social services I usually quote the two that I have most investigated, education and health. But there is another that has fallen into serious disrepute in many countries: the system of justice. Might it be possible to constitute an infoset out of self-selecting teams of (say) five judges, five attorneys, five jurors, five criminals, five police officers, five probation officers and five members of the vulnerable public at large? The numbers are given only to set the scene, and I can add up; the point is that the numbers ought to be irrelevant, because these are not representative delegations; but it is difficult to express the idea in other terms. Self-selection should somehow be invoked at this level, as it was within the seven quoted groups. And who would sponsor such a syntegration? The same sort of scheme could be applied in many areas: the design of the constitution being an especially vexed example in many countries.

Chapter Ten

GOVERNANCE OR GOVERNMENT?

Recently it has become clear that the planet on which we all live is threatened with destruction. The wholesale realization of this could probably be dated to Hiroshima. Before that, ancient prophets and modern seers alike had sensed a likely doom for humankind; but in 1945 the instrumentality of nuclear destruction was demonstrated, and soon an escalating balance of terror dominated the international scene. The nuclear threat has by no means vanished. For even as the detente between the power blocs of the United States and the Soviet Union began well nigh miraculously to dissipate the East–West tension that had characterized nearly half a century, the likelihood that other countries have mastered—or soon will master—the problems of nuclear weaponry is very high. It does not matter that a country may be small: this capability bestows a wholly disproportionate significance. The same goes, the more potently because of the absence of sanctions, for any terrorist group that is properly organized—for there has been no mystery about the product itself for 40 years. Even so, everyone has learned to live with these risks; people under middle age grew up with them.

The risks of ecological disaster are a different matter. Writers who have been uttering warnings for decades to heedless governments and an uninformed populace have been amazed to see the explosion of concern. Green parties proliferate; young people are enthused. Even the media, perceiving the emotional and photogenic possibilities, have abandoned the scorn with which they treated 'prophets of doom,' as we were called, for so long. And the politicians have seen the votes on offer and at risk. The change is astounding. It is not long ago, when the extinction of species on the Earth reached the rate of one a day, that a British politician of cabinet rank to whom I pointed this out replied: 'Oh well, it's only evolution taking its course.'

This kind of response, blasé and irresponsible as it is, will no longer be accepted; therefore, it will no longer be offered. World governance will be high on humanity's agenda from now on. The trouble will predictably be that no-one knows *how* to achieve it. After all, the matter has been discussed by thoughtful philosophers and statesmen for a very long time. Apart from theorizing, well intentioned people were spurred into action by the awful experiences of two World Wars. The League of Nations, formed after the first of those wars, and the United Nations, formed after the second, both failed dismally to do anything at all about world *governance*. Arguably both had minor successes in a transnational coordinating role (although, given the cost and the bureaucratic confusion, I personally would not care to argue thus). By now the UN, once perceived as the cradle of Third World aspirations, is seen as another tool of rich world hegemony: corrupt, bureaucratic, and ineffectual.

Three of the five syntegrity experiments conducted in 1990 dealt with hopes and expectations for the future of the world, and these were succinct reasons advanced in the briefing sessions for the failures in world governance so far:

●   Organizations dedicated to the vision of One World conspicuously fail in their idealistic holism, because they are constructed in power blocs of nation states.

●   Some nations are 'more equal than others'—witness the veto system in the Security Council, and the economic clout exerted by the rich world against the poor.

●   The process of reaching consensus is supposedly based on the submission of resolutions or draft laws which must climb up hierarchical ladders within a nation state, via regional authorities and political parties, and must then enter the negotiating arena existing between regional and political power blocs on a global scale.

It is small wonder that such an ostensibly democratic process is short-circuited either by political manipulations or by practical exigencies, or by a mixture of both. It takes too long. It is too bureaucratic. It suffers from pressure to express a lowest common denominator, which inhibits all creative advance.

Here is an example. In 1982 I had an argument with (then) Prime Minister Menachem Begin of Israel in Jerusalem. I spoke of the nuclear risks in the Middle East and criticized his policies in that light. He asked if I had not heard of the Six Day War. Yes, I had. He assured me that there was no nuclear risk these days, because, 'you are in and out, and it's all over—before the Security

Council has moved to put an item on its Agenda. There were other wars to discuss before ours, meanwhile it was done.' Within days of that (semi-public) confrontation, Israel had invaded Lebanon—and became mired down, as everyone is all too aware. When commentators debated in mystified incomprehension why Mr Begin soon became an unkempt recluse in his own house, maintaining silence, it seemed he had explained everything in advance by his answer. (Fairness demands it be recorded that he scored heavily against me in this argument about the pacification of the world: the meeting happened two days after Mrs Thatcher ordered half the Royal Navy to the South Atlantic in preparation for her attack on Argentina over the Malvinas or Falkland Islands, which we both thought preposterous.)

A counter-argument to this depressing view of world governance will no doubt be mounted by those who saw the Resolutions about Iraq and Kuwait pass in the United Nations without the use of veto in 1990. It was certainly surprising at the time—less so with hindsight. And maybe it is not merely cynical to wonder whether the imposition of world order, discriminating as it was, self-serving as it was, is worth the near destruction of a country. The boast was made by the 'allied' generals that only a handful of people died. Those figures refer of course to 'allied' troops. By now the Iraqi dead, or doomed in the aftermath to die, seem to number at least a quarter of a million. Nor is this the only cost in a world that cannot afford to feed a third of its population, because dollars still count in these equations.

Halfway through Chapter One the fact is recorded that Garry Davis, the first self-proclaimed World Citizen, had asked me to work on his concepts. Under the banner of his World Service Authority he has 'worked tirelessly towards his ideal of One World,' we then said, since 1948—for a great many years, then, before he and I met a dozen years ago. In that period Davis has undertaken many courageous actions, and (like so many reformers) has seen the inside of many gaols—in his case, in many countries. It is hard to assimilate the fact that he has personally issued documents to a quarter of a million people, most of them stateless persons with no other resource than these papers in a world of bureaucrats and border guards. He has done all this in the name of the World Government that he heads.

Up to now, I have been careful to use the term World Governance, which I argued is a *sine qua non* of planetary survival—and is now seen to be so, because of ecological concern. The point is that governance is a concept that admits of many possible interpretations and instrumentalities, whereas a government is an entity, and one would expect it to have juridical status. Now Davis has claimed *de facto* status for his World Government in the very act of issuing documents—not to mention travelling the world on his own World Service Authority passport. His argument is simple. Everyone born on this planet is *ipso facto* a World Citizen, and ought to be recognized as such. Garry Davis, for his part, recognizes him and her, and issues papers to prove it. And, of course, he believes the nation-state to be (at the least) an irrelevance, and (at the worst) the source of all our troubles. It is not my purpose to argue all this further here. Davis has been denounced on too many grounds to cover here, as becomes a staunch opponent of the Established Order of Things, and is his own best explicator and defender (see, for instance, Davis, 1992).

However, I am cautious of any *entity* called world government. If everyone is in it, then it elects itself without knowing it, and that sounds harmless enough. But, as the Syntegrity experiments showed, many people regard the term 'World Government' as denoting something that must be intrinsically totalitarian, autocratic, and reprehensible. The syntegrity idea with its Infosets is something fundamentally different from what these people assume World Government to be. And if governance can be achieved only by 'law and order,' then their fears would be well grounded, in my view. That is because no-one would remain outside the compass of that government to question the validity or wisdom of its laws. Fortunately to a cybernetician, governance is a quality of self-organizing systems, and is not an imposition from outside.

This book tells a story, unfolds an experiment, and postulates a scientific theory about reaching group conclusions: it is not a political philosophy. I have drawn a distinction between governance and government here precisely because of this. For there has been a practical consequence of my involvement with Garry Davis and his cause—which I regard as the pursuit of universal brotherhood, having its legal basis in the Declaration of Human Rights. For Davis expected me, as a cybernetician, to evolve a protocol for the establishment of a World Convention. He saw this (at least at first) as a meeting, an occasion. Then who would attend, and by whom would they be nominated? Whom would they represent? I saw it instead as a *process*, a continuum of activity, in which *anyone* could take part.

What could a world convention mean?

The attempt to marry these cybernetic attitudes and postulates with Davis's intentions led to the following briefing for the organizing committee of the expected convention, and evolved into the 1990 Syntegrity experiments recorded here.

SINCE
the individual human being is

- a child of the cosmos;

- an inhabitant of this planet;

who claims empowerment as a World Citizen

THEN
a World Convention

- cannot acknowledge a nation-state format;

- cannot deal in any hierarchical formulation of the human condition;

- cannot accept 'delegations of negotiators' deriving authority from their history or geography, race, creed, or colour, wealth or poverty, high or low technology, power or impotence.

In a word, the World Convention could not 'happen'—it could only 'be.'

Here is an overwhelming statement of what constitutes a 'world convention' in my sense, and is certainly a potent denial of nation-statehood in the true Davis spirit. It was written (Cleveland, 1991) by Professor Harlan Cleveland, President of the World Academy of Art and Science, in 1991:

'What's most striking about these past two years is not, after all, the cascade of conversions to democracy. It's the cultural diversity that's busting out all over—the boiling over of resentments in the name of almost forgotten or newly discovered cultures.

Sociologist Elise Boulding speaks of "the 10 000 societies living inside 168 nation states." Even this arresting way of putting it understates a complexity in which so many of the "10 000 societies" are transnational, in no sense "inside" the familiar political lines on our conventional world maps.

There are multimillions of overseas Chinese and separatist Russians, millions of Hungarians and Romanians and Turks in other people's countries, millions of Catalonians and Basques and Kurds and Palestinians and Eritreans and Tamils and Ebos and Zulus and Tibetans, millions of Moslems and Hindus and Sikhs living in each other's laps in the Asian subcontinent, millions of Quebecois and North American Indians, who don't acknowledge as their "nation" the "State" in which they find themselves.

With most of Europe moving toward integration, the break-up of Yugoslavia heralds the Balkanization of the Balkans. In France there are now said to be more practising Moslems than practising Catholics—a slippery statistic, that depends a lot on what "practising" means. Mass migrations and differential rates of procreation are creating more and more societies where "everybody's a minority."

To me, the central paradox of our time is the tension between the outward "push" of modern science and technology and the inward "pull" of cultural identity.

New knowledge keeps making possible, and therefore necessary, wider forms of cooperation—common markets, arms control, worldwide trade and money bazaars, global environmental monitoring and weather forecasting.

Yet fierce loyalties to narrower cultural communities—bonded by ethnicity, religion, and ideology—are colliding everywhere with the homogenizing cultures of modernization.

Cultural diversity is enormously valuable. It is what we should be trying to make the world safe for. It is also troublesome to existing elites and authorities. What's unique cannot be universal. What's universal threatens, and is threatened by, what's unique.'

'Cultural diversity,' as Cleveland makes so clear, does not refer to a bunch of nation-states. It refers to a bunch of Infosets ... The whole question is: how might they be helped to self-organize? Could the protocol of Team Syntegrity help?

Taxonomy sets out the laws by which people make classifications. The nation-state classification results from historical processes which can variously be interpreted as accidental, as dialectical, or (in our current terms) as the inter-actions of Power Infosets. Whatever view one takes, the institution of the nation-states is a fact of international bureaucracy: their changing numbers may be counted as more and more achieve status at the UN congress. Taxonomically, we try to make sense of this anachronistic classification scheme by inventing new groupings, such as the First, Second and Third Worlds, or the North–South Divide. And if the classifications are too massive for particular purposes, then we might contemplate Cleveland's 10 000 ethnic societies, or the even greater number of Jane Jacobs' cities. For she regards the city as the natural societary unit (Jacobs, 1984), and what is a city but a very big Infoset? It has a unity of purpose that may well peter out in larger societary groupings.

When we turn, however, to the customary classifications of world problems, we find them to be based upon taxonomic 'principles' of a different sort. For example:

- health
- shelter
- food
- education
- security
- quality of life

- environment
- non-renewable resources
- sustainable growth
- wealth equity
- demographic shift (aged, etc.)
- posterity rights (the unborn)

are twelve items concerning the world and its future plucked from the air. They are in the air because they have been identified by the established professions, by the lobbies, by innumerable conferences—and broadcast wholesale by the media.

So what is the problem?

This kind of taxonomy is constructed in the first place by academia, which carves up the natural world to give each professor and each professional institution a chunk, and next by power brokers, who carve up the natural world for purposes of economic exploitation.

What has this division of resources to do with the World Citizen?

- The World Citizen is well or ill, fed or starving, literate or not, happy or miserable, as a single, integrated individual. S/he is not the sum of the bits handled by separate authorities and agencies.

- The desiderata of well being interact: they are functions of each other.

To express the thought once again in the World Convention briefing mode:

SINCE
the individual human being is

- an integral indivisible whole, who

- shares this humanity equally with all others ...

THEN
a World Convention

- cannot deal in a reductionist or exploitative taxonomy,

- cannot accept a divisive ideological basis for a world constitution.

Hence, just as the World Convention could not 'happen,' but only 'be'—on a continuous and universal basis, so it cannot afford to settle down to the exhausted debate of topics determined by an inappropriate taxonomy.

Summarizing the proposed solutions, the following notes on the Syntegrity approach to the organizational and taxonomic problems that have been presented were the basis for all the briefings—both to organizing groups and to the Infoset teams themselves.

ORGANIZING IN TEAMS OF GLOBAL INFOSETS

The One World of the World Citizen is a *Geosphere*, a planet of rock and water, enshrouded by its *Biosphere*, a seamless robe of life that permeates and inhabits both.

- Let us note that a more ancient view of life, as climbing into biological niches, has been outdated by microscopy and its perception of the living integument.

Similarly, and thanks also to technological advance, we may think of the World Citizen's One World as enrobed in a *Technosphere*.

- Instead of thinking about two people or two places being connected by a telephone line or a satellite link, recollect how the whole globe is now criss-crossed by innumerable fine lines that make a net—like a pumpkin held in a string bag.

- The holes in the net are as small as anyone wants to make them. S/he may call a friend on the other side of the globe, and have a message shouted to a neighbour—a message shouted by a neighbour at this end—across both garden walls. How fine a mesh is this.

Who are these people and these neighbours, and why are they in global touch? They constitute a global Infoset.

An Infoset is an information set of people who are focused on a common interest, however it is defined.

- The interest does not have to be an established area of concern. It is a sort of (maybe actual) family.

- Because there is a Technosphere, the people of the Infoset do not have to be located anywhere in particular.

- An Infoset is highly motivated in its focus of interest. That is why and how it comes to recognize itself—and to be self-organizing.

It is easy to visualize an Infoset that focused on our One World and its future. There could easily be thousands of them, each of manageable size, because no-one wants to wait for ever to speak, and each expressing its own idiosyncratic view.

Convention means 'coming together.' These days we may question whether this necessarily involves a lot of travel. A Convention of Infosets coming together (as each does itself) through the medium of the global technosphere would constitute a world convention.

CLASSIFYING IN TERMS OF NOVEL TAXONOMY

Using the Team Syntegrity process that is intended to generate Consolidated and ultimately Final Statements of Importance (CSIs and FSIs), we begin with a Problem Jostle of initial Statements of Importance (SIs). Here is the question that the team is asked to address.

- This group is united by shared information about the condition of the planet and its projected future. The task is to isolate twelve issues that are crucial to survival, to be embodied in a process designed to lead to effective survival.

Existing taxonomies are to be avoided. Topics such as education and health will necessarily arise; but the common issues of survival on which they bear are those to be discovered and elucidated freshly.

- For example, all are likely to agree that fundamental freedoms ought to be enunciated. But they have already been proclaimed by the General Assembly of the United Nations (1948) in the Universal Declaration of Human Rights. There is no point in trying to rewrite a fine document already subscribed to by the nations of the world.

The issue to be isolated must deal with the fact that not a single nation anywhere invariably honours the human rights it has acknowledged.

A Constitutional Statement has to be a commitment to a process leading to systemic change, rather than a statement of principle to be admired, but not containing the seeds of action. For instance:

- The will to abolish torture needs expression in terms of procedures that outlaw anyone manufacturing instruments of torture.

- Acts of state terrorism need modes of denunciation which instantly and automatically incur penalties imposed by the world community. Especially, it is vital to dispose of the filter that lets through 'our' acts of state terrorism as being ('obviously') in the interest of world peace, or (preposterously) in the best interests of the very people assaulted.

Both examples necessitate debate about the meaning of sanctions, methods of policing international affairs, and much else. If plausible answers were already known there would be no call on any Infoset to move into action. We are designing a system for generating new solutions that can win constitutional acclaim.

The issues sought are an order of discourse beyond the ethical principles on which they draw. They are statements about the proper unfolding of systemic affairs in an accelerating society.

'*Easier Done Than Said*' was the title under which these ideas and these experiments were launched. A totally new approach such as Team Syntegrity proposes is not at all easy to explain. It really *is* easier to collect the Infoset together, to teach rather than explain the protocol, and to embark on the process. But obviously that is not adequate, especially in the context of world governance. The misunderstandings that arise would be alarming to anyone not already familiar with the fact that novel ideas and procedures are typically perceived as threatening. On a global scale the threat is not only quantitatively overwhelming: it represents a qualitative change in the concept of governance, since it is all encompassing. A feeling somehow emerges that there are no checks to these balances.

STRUCTURE AS PROCESS

The foregoing arguments are a denial of organizational structure as we have known it in the arena of international affairs. Its hierarchical nature, its bureaucracy, its rigidity ... such properties seal its doom. Our arguments, on the contrary, progress toward self-organizing activities that define 'a constitution' as happening and a 'convention' as continuity. That sentence plays bewildering tricks with syntax for the sake of impact. Its point is to say that a global organization should not be thought of as a piece of architecture, in which the relationships between parts are fixed in stone; rather the parts are related according to the principles that underlie the practice of building, known as architectonics. The principles that underlie the practice of management are cybernetic principles, and a manager who has not studied them is in the role of someone who erects a dwelling without using architectonics: s/he simply looks around to see what works and what does not. (One can use the architectonics without necessarily hiring an architect, of course.) But the criteria 'what does and what does not work' are themselves virtually useless in the international arena, because everything on view there is merely a shambles. (Multinational corporations do not count in this context, because they are hegemonies.) Then it is now proposed that the appropriate cybernetic architectonic for the global problem discussed is the syntegral icosahedron.

To investigate the idea further, we need a few terms. The infoset as so far described in this book involves 30 people who are meeting according to the syntegration protocol—face to face. So what would the recently invoked concept of 'global infoset' mean in practice? It makes no sense to rely on appeals to 'our common humanity' to solve a practical problem. A major feature of common humanity is that too many people feel free to kill other people. The earlier reference did, however, mention the technosphere—and planted a seed of doubt about the necessity to travel—although it also alluded to *thousands* of infosets. Let us tease these notions apart.

The validity of syntegration as a valuable technique has been demonstrated only in face-to-face situations, and may turn out to depend on immediacy and contiguity. I have often wondered to what extent successful negotiations and relationships rely on atavistic response. The role of body posture is acknowledged, and in detail too: down to facial twitches in the work of Labin and eye movements in neuro-linguistic programming. But what is the role of pheronomes, of subliminal messages conveyed by muscles? Above all, does the evident possibility of actual physical assault—proscribed though it may be by convention or taboo by conditioning—influence matters, as I suggested many years ago when consulting on the future of the videophone and video conferencing? Given that there are no answers to these questions yet, let us note that all the work reported here dealt solely with face-to-face confrontation.

Then the terminology for the political sphere begins by labelling a *neighbourhood infoset*. According to the usage so far, this term is tautologous. Never mind: we may need to distinguish other possibilities later. The term is pleasing in the political context too, because it suggests *local action*. Then let it adhere to the rule-of-thirty as to membership. Again, this makes political sense in the light of the redundancy of potential command, already described at some length in Chapter Nine. Consider a demographic neighbourhood, such as a village, or the village-in-a-city that is now familiar worldwide. Why should the same 30 people do all the work, or take all the decisions? Organization by redundant infoset, considered as a process of course, should be effective by focusing infosettic awareness of some group of 30 onto a common purpose— and at the same time involving the whole community by the implications of potential command. Sooner rather than later, every motivated person in the village would be involved in some activity. And, as with any infoset, s/he would automatically be *not* involved in any agenda perceived as boring or irrelevant. There is no 'Catch 22,' then.

The collective noun for neighbourhoods is, naively, a town or a city, and I should happily replace its existing council with a collection of neighbourhood infosets, if that were allowed. However, as hinted earlier, the neighbourhoods might not be geographically contiguous. The 'neighbourhood' of fishmongers or playground-makers or diabetics in one town might recognize a collective of like-purposed neighbourhood infosets in other towns in the vicinity. In the absence of a collective noun for the wider connotation, let us divest the concept of its happenstance and call it a hyperset of neighbourhood infosets, or simply a hyperinfoset. By what means can such a collective be actually collected? Think once more of the redundancy of potential command, as applying to the vicinity this time. Would it be surprising to invoke an architectonic that identified 30 of them as pursuing a common purpose beyond the villages that provided the original constituency?

The architectonic of this hyperinfoset is obviously based on a syntegral hypericosahedron. We have to give substance to this highly abstract notion. Here, in a graphic image, is one possible protocol for generating results at what is actually a second level of recursive embedment. Each neighbourhood infoset has 12 propositions as output. Here are instructions for the final corporate act of each of their final meetings.

Consider the twelve propositions, and agree on the two most important (potent?; practical?; original?; convenient for the procedure?—select according to your own criteria of importance). Pull the icosahedron apart by these two vertices, so that the constructions begins to collapse. Catch hold of each of the remaining 10 propositions as they fall away from the cohesive whole, and seek to incorporate it in one of the two chosen statements.

The first-generation icosahedra are now struts (edges) of a new Staffordian graph, each carrying an enhanced proposition at each end. The ordinary infoset has a protocol for generating its initial statements out of the minds of its members; these second-generation inputs are expressions of the group minds of its founding infosets. One person who belonged to the primary infoset is to be an edge once more, and on arrival sheds the two complex propositions that s/he is carrying into the 'gene pool' of the hyperinfoset. This begins operations, then, with 60 SIs. At all levels of embedment above the primary level, where the SIs are taken 'out of the air' by participants, the set of SIs constitute a genome of 60 components inherited from the previous embedment stratum.

It is suggested that the human individuals who carry this through should be randomly selected, one each, from the original 30 infosets. It is vital, according to these principles, that they are not 'delegates,' but free spirits who have learned from their initial syntegration. Because they are in the vicinity, the collective of neighbourhoods, it is assumed that they can conveniently attend the second-level syntegration.

As happens with the generation of species, we should expect repeated generations of infosetters to form and to overlap in experience. But these are small societies, not individuals, and we should expect their membership to change according to the redundancy of potential command. The purpose of forming hyperinfosets is not to create a hierarchy of warriors or of logical propositions that have advanced status because they have 'risen to higher levels.' It is to make consolidated statements available that have been worked over by 900 people, 27 000 people, and so on. At the sixth generation of the process, nearly one billion people would in theory participate! Wary as anyone may be of the social fallacy that promotes chain letters or pyramid selling by like arguments, s/he may still recognize in these thoughts that there could be alternatives to representation that relies on hierarchical delegation.

My own expectation is that entropy in the language system and changing times will soon vitiate this 'hyper-hype' of the process. The expansion will fix its own limits by homeostasis. There is no prospect of gnarled ninth-level syntegrators formulating tenth-level propositions of unimaginable obscurity, emulating Hesse's Glass Bead Game. Potential command should see to that ... Alternatively, graph theoretic discoveries in the Staffordian Graph context may well result in an ability to formulate protocols that work n-dimensionally and therefore are not constrained to 30 infosetters at a time, as adumbrated in Chapter Thirteen. We shall see.

The structure as process idea has now been extended from neighbourhoods to vicinities, thereby preserving the principle of (approximate) contiguity—a vicinity being simply a neighbourhood in Latin—with the premise that the whole earth is a global vicinity. All we need are sponsors to pay people's fares, and to compensate them for loss of earnings, in order to generate many recursions of this self-organizing system. Then obviously we need to consider the facilities of the technosphere, and the possibility of an infoset of 'remote neighbours'—where the oxymoron is resolved by electronics. In terms of computer technology, it is hard to envisage the least difficulty in effecting the computer infoset. Machines equipped with modems abound, the protocols of bulletin boards are well known; millions of people, it is said, are already networking. And if the networking protocols are relatively crude, as they seem to be, there (again) seems to be no reason why they should not be enhanced for syntegrations through custom-built software. Team Syntegrity Inc. has indeed embarked on that job already.

The same cannot be said of the human componentry or the human networking as can be confidently said about their electronic counterparts. No research has yet been done, whereas the need for it was rehearsed sufficiently a few paragraphs ago. All that can be said here is to emphasize the distinction between the availability of the computer technology and the ignorance of the physiological, sociological, and anthropological integrity of syntegration in the absence of contiguity and interaction in real time. Any comparison with postal chess, for example, that may leap to mind is clearly invalid. We deal in euphoric reverberation, not desiccated gambitry ...

TAILPIECE

A large-scale experiment based on these ideas was planned in detail for the summer of 1993 on behalf of the World Service Authority. It featured in particular the creation of a syntegration manual that could be used by a highly motivated organizer to run a 3-day version of the technique, without prior knowledge, and without professional facilitators. The master plan called for 30 neighbourhood infosets to run simultaneously in various parts of the world, and for 30 electronic infosets to be run on prototype software connecting isolated individuals by keyboard and modem. The two groups of 30, obviously enough, were each to constitute hyperinfosets in due course, according to the protocols explained earlier. In the event, a scaled-down version of the neighbourhood plan alone proved possible; but its implementation continues, and it remains to be seen how it fares, and if sponsorship will be forthcoming to develop research along such ambitious lines.

In the meantime, and while the results so far accruing are being evaluated by the World Service Authority, it is fitting to echo the reported feelings of the hundreds of people who are involved worldwide with a paragraph written by the Project Director of this endeavour. She is Wendy Walsh, who, based in Toronto, was busy integrating the activities of syntegrations held everywhere during the last week of July, 1993.

She writes:

'As the Project Director of the World Syntegrity Project I had to resign myself to the fact that duties would prevent me from taking part in the local Syntegration in Toronto. I did have the incredible opportunity to observe, and by observing I was able to develop a whole new perspective of Syntegration. I saw that it was the structure of Syntegration, though it frustrated some players on the first day, that *protected the integrity of people and their ideas.* I believe it was that protection that allowed democracy to emerge. I saw, once again, that the process *does* allow group dynamics to solve problems and to sift differing viewpoints into a unified vision. Yet the most inspiring element of the Syntegration was the energy that could be felt physically and intellectually so that there was a sense of singleness. Now, as I receive the statements and responses from Organizers around the world, that sense of singleness is expanding. It encompasses more than I could imbibe from my former reality. Syntegration can not be viewed as a series of steps in a "workshop." Syntegration is a new dynamic, a vehicle. If we apply it wisely and well, we *can* create a new order. "May the whole earth be happy."'

Yes indeed: and it is surely a fact that there are people all over the world, sovereign individuals, who have ideas and purposes that they wish to share with others. They do not see themselves as bound by hierarchy (even to their own nation-states) or committed to the processes (even those called democratic) that demand the establishment of political parties, dedicated movements, delegations—or indeed high-profile leadership. These people are the material of infosets. The world needs an acknowledged procedure by which they may be recognized and integrated into whatever political framework is dominant at the time. Then they would exercise the freedom to formulate themselves, because they constitute potential command posts; they would spread themselves epidemically, demonstrating their redundancy; they would interact massively, as is the nature of shared commitment. It is not a commitment to some shared manifesto, but a commitment to circumvent folly, wherever it is found; it is a commitment to alleviate suffering; it is a commitment to brotherhood and peace.

Then it is not world government that these people seek, with all its overtones of duress and exploitation at the worst—or of patriarchy and submission at the best. In any case no feasible machinery exists or is yet envisioned that could supply such global surveillance and yet preserve true freedom. What is sought is not an architecture for world government, but the architectonics of world governance. And governance in its multifarious forms is the ultimate topic of this book.

THE FORM OF THE MODEL

Chapter Eleven

THE STRUCTURE OF
ICOSAHEDRAL SPACE

We are by now familiar with the model as a practical tool for syntegration. Let us recall that we alighted on the five regular convex polyhedra as suitable models of a fully 'democratic' organization, because each edge (a person) has exactly the same status in the geometry as every other edge. There is no top, bottom or sideways in any of the five structures. The selection of the icosahedron as the most useful of these structures for our purposes was discussed informally in Chapter One, 'without pursuing all the relevant arguments here' (it was said). The power of the model is, however, such that it will pay to probe its nature more deeply here in Part Three.

This task is daunting, as this is not a mathematical text—whereas it is a fundamentally mathematical potency with which we deal. Moreover, there is a vast literature in applied geometry that makes exciting reading. There is the range of biological manifestations: no wonder Plato called God a geometer. Then there are all the artifacts that imitate nature, in the proportions and shapes found in architecture and the design of furniture. In aesthetics, these proportions are discovered not only in space but also in time: we listen to proportional intervals and cadences, and call what we hear music. Much has been written and imagined about the mystical and speculative aspects of 'sacred geometry' of Gothic cathedrals, in the numerology of the Egyptian pyramids, in the mandalas of India and Tibet, in the monuments of the Maya, Aztec, and Inca civilizations, and going back to neolithic remains. Books have been written about each of these, wherein similar—often identical—geometries may be found.

The object of this chapter is to examine only those aspects of this geometry that are germane to syntegration, while restricting explanations to what is necessary. Please do not flick through the next pages only to become alienated by bursts of symbolism. The discussion works at the high-school level of difficulty; understanding everything is not easy, nevertheless—that much is acknowledged.

For example, high-school pupils know very well what pi refers to: it denotes the ratio of the circumference of a circle to its diameter. The number never varies; it is approximately 3.14159, but the decimal continues indefinitely. Pi denotes an infinite product. That is strange to contemplate. Pi is one of the transcendental numbers.

The important constant that we need to consider is not pi, but (another Greek letter) phi. This number never varies either, it also 'continues indefinitely,' but not because it is a transcendental number. It is an algebraic number. And it is not a ratio, like pi, but a *proportion*, which states the equality of two ratios. We say, for example, that A is to B as C is to D, and write down the proportionality as:

$$\frac{a}{b} = \frac{c}{d}$$

In practice we find, for instance, that 25 is to 100 as 1 is to 4:

$$\frac{25}{100} = \frac{1}{4}$$

and are by no means surprised that an American calls 25 cents 'a quarter.'

We are getting ready now to 'home in' on the mysterious proportion called phi. Although we need four quantities to compute a proportionality, we can often manage to use only three terms—simply by repeating one of them:

$$\frac{a}{b} = \frac{b}{c}$$

For example, 2 is to 4 as 4 is to 8: the middle term is shared. In words, maybe: 'John is half his father's weight, and the youngster is half John's weight.' This works perfectly well, *if* it happens to be true.

Now there is a special case, and only one, in which the equality of two ratios that states a proportion can be expressed using only *two* terms. Obviously it happens when the middle term is shared, and the fourth term is a function of the original two terms. Thus:

$$\frac{a}{b} = \frac{b}{a+b}$$

Or, in the verbal example, the father happens to weigh as much as John and the youngster combined. Let us try to show this, using sample weights. Suppose that father weighs 200 lb; so John has half his weight, that is, 100 lb, and the youngster is half that again, namely 50 lb. So far, so good, as to the halving criterion. But, just a minute, 200 does not equal 100 plus 50, which is only 150 lb.

Think about this until you realize that the two-term proportionality has a *unique* ratio of b to a—and that it cannot be a half. It is in fact the mysterious phi. Now phi will always have the same value, if the equation is to work, whatever sets of numbers are involved. Then let us calculate the value of phi, which the high-school student can do—assuming s/he can remember the formula for solving a quadratic equation. Here goes:

$$\frac{a}{b} = \frac{b}{a+b}$$

$$\frac{a(a+b)}{a} = \frac{b^2}{a}$$

$$\frac{(a+b)}{a} = \frac{b^2}{a^2}$$

$$1 + \frac{b}{a} = \left(\frac{b}{a}\right)^2$$

Since

$$\frac{b}{a} = \phi$$

$$\phi^2 - \phi - 1 = 0$$

Solving this quadratic:

$$\phi^2 = \frac{+1 \pm \sqrt{1+4}}{2}$$

which, in the positive case, is

$$\frac{1 + \sqrt{5}}{2} = 1.618034$$

Try this with some numbers. Suppose that the youngster weighs 100 lb. Then John will weigh (roughly) 162 lb; and father will weigh 162×1.62 which is (roughly) 262 lb. This time the equation works, since John and the youngster together also weigh 262 lb. If the family sounds overweight, then halve all the numbers. Father is 131 lb, John is 81 lb, and the baby is 50 lb. The two ratios are still calculated as phi, while $81 + 50 = 131$ as required.

What has this to do with our model, the syntegral icosahedron? We shall find out, but to do so we must develop a spatial insight. Most people are not accustomed to thinking about three-dimensional constructions; it is important to move our thinking along from the abstract ratios that denote proportionality to the filling of space itself. The connecting link is the expanding series that results from continuing the phi relationships typified by father, John, and the youngster. If we start from an origin 0 and add a unit, the series begins 0, 1—and the next term is also 1, since the two terms are added to find it. By the same rule, the next term is 2; then comes 3, followed by 5. We are generating the famous Fibonacci series, which progresses thus: 0, 1, 1, 2, 3, 5, 8, 13, 21, 34, 55, 89 ... The series is unique, and also startling, in that it is both additive and geometric at the same time. Each term is the sum of the previous two terms, and their proportionality rapidly converges on phi; 8/5 is already 1.6, which is close to phi, while 89/55 equals 1.61818, and that is very close indeed.

It is this dual property that makes the Fibonacci series famous, because it well describes biological growth patterns. So-called 'gnomonic' growth preserves the organism's characteristic shape by maintaining phi proportionality for every unit addition of time. The growth of living things is not a matter of abstract proportion: those organisms are actually filling three-dimensional space after all. As will be shown, this kind of growth tends toward the formation of spirals: we see them in sunflowers and fir cones and also in shells. The nautilus shell is a well-known example.

We approach the space-filling version of the series by looking for the phi proportionality in two dimensions—where it appears as a rectangle. The larger side is phi times the shorter side. The ancient Greeks found this shape aesthetically pleasing; it moved into architecture; medieval artists named it the Golden Rectangle. This area is not only satisfying to the eye: it has the same sort of recursive power as that observed in the linear series. That is because it consists of a square plus a residual rectangle, which is itself Golden. The original and the included rectangle are similar rectangles. And the smaller rectangle may be similarly divided, and so on, *ad infinitum*. Consider Figure 11.1, which gives us directly

$$\frac{x+1}{x} = \frac{x}{1}$$

and by cross-multiplying we go straight to a familiar quadratic equation:

$$x^2 - x - 1 = 0$$

which we already know has the positive root of $1/2(1 + \sqrt{5})$, namely phi.

The continuation of this process yields a diagram such as Figure 11.2, in which four iterations of the golden recursion are carried through.

The spiral growth pattern is implicit in Figure 11.3. Just as the Fibonacci series rapidly converges on the phi proportionality, the spiral shown is asymptotic

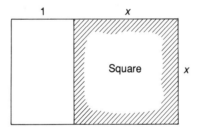

Figure 11.1   The Golden Rectangle

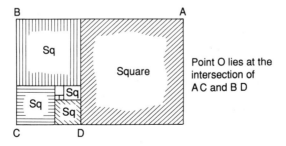

Figure 11.2   Recursions of the Golden Rectangle

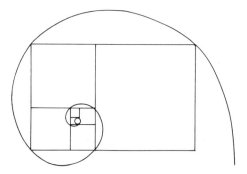

Figure 11.3   Approximative logarithmic spiral

to a logarithmic spiral with characteristic ratio and quadrantal pulsation phi. The following phi proportions that lie on diagonals are also interesting:

$$\frac{AB}{BC} = \phi = \frac{OA}{OB} = \frac{OC}{OD}$$

Incidently, since the shrinking process at the centre of the diagram could go on indefinitely, we may recognize a condensation point which is the 'origin' of the spiral. Its coordinates are

$$\frac{\phi}{\phi + \dfrac{1}{\phi}} \quad \text{and} \quad \frac{1}{\phi + \dfrac{1}{\phi}}$$

We begin to see how space is filled with reflections of the algebraic number that we educed from a consideration of proportionality using the minimal number of terms. That insight was due to Plato himself; it was Sir Theodore Cook who named the proportion phi. Now make the step from the two-dimensional diagram to the simplest three-dimensional version. It is easy enough to conceive of the recursive diagram that uses rectangles as being a drawing of a set of boxes shown in plan. The boxes could be of uniform thickness, like tiles; or the golden section could be brought into the third dimension also.

That was behind a thoroughly practical proposal that I submitted to the Post Office in Britain just 30 years ago. I had noticed how higgledy-piggledy the parcel sorting operation was: people packed their parcels in the most remarkable shapes; stacking them and transporting them was a nightmare, and economically inefficient. So I proposed to the responsible Minister (his name was Tony Benn, in his first ministerial appointment in the office then called

Postmaster General) that the Post Office should sell prefabricated boxes of recursive Golden Section to the public. These could be stacked and transported conveniently on pallets. He liked the idea, and many others that I included in a reform package advanced for the Department.

Alas, his civil servants liked none of the proposals. This was not how things were done. In a democratic society, people must be free to pack parcels however they wished. And so forth. When, some 20 years later, the Post Office began to sell prefabricated parcel boxes, their proportions were not golden at all. Filius Bonacci received no credit, and the sorters and transporters no benefit. The same is apparently the case in France also.

Anecdotes aside, we have now come to appreciate phi proportionality in three-dimensional space. The developing discussion moves from the *description* of space in this way to the *generation* of a three-dimensional space that is intrinsically golden. Take three Golden Rectangles of exactly the same size, and intersect them orthogonally and symmetrically in thin air. The result is as shown in Figure 11.4.

As can be seen, there are 12 corners to this total figure; and because it is regular, all the distances between neighbouring corners mark 12 equally distributed points on the sphere that encloses the diagram. And, if all 30 of the dashed lines are put in place, then we have the icosahedron. This is a surprise. The model that was originally chosen for its convenience in describing a 'democratic' societary structure, using numbers for infosets and teams that looked appropriate, turns out to be a fundamental structure, with a potency derived from a minimalist logic of relations.

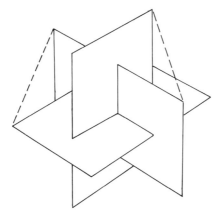

Figure 11.4   Symmetric display of orthogonal Golden Rectangles

Now look at Figure 11.4 end-on, so that it presents itself as shown in Figure 11.5; eight of the corners are visible.

Considering only the corner (= vertex) ringed, we draw the five icosahedral edges it subtends, and discover a regular pentagon lying on a plane (Figure 11.6). The edges of the pentagon are all of unit length. In three-dimensions, the lines OA, OB, OC, OD, and OE are also of unit length. They are not so in the diagram because the vertex O is raised above the pentagonal plane, which is itself foreshortened: AB is further from the eye than point D. Then consider the pentagon on its own, and draw 'diameters' from A to D, and from C to E, to intersect at point X, as shown in Figure 11.7.

Consider the identical isoceles triangles ADE and CDE. Then,

$$\angle DAE = \angle ADE = \angle DCE = \angle CED$$

Therefore, $\triangle ADE$ and $\triangle DEX$ are congruent (two equal angles). Also, $\triangle EAX$ and $\triangle ADB$ are congruent ($AE \parallel BD$ and $AB \parallel CE$), whence, $AE = AX$ (because $AD = BD$). From the similarity of triangles, the unit length of the edges of the pentagon, and the equality of AE and AX, it follows that

$$\frac{ED}{XD} = \frac{AD}{ED}$$

$$\frac{1}{AD - 1} = \frac{AD}{1}$$

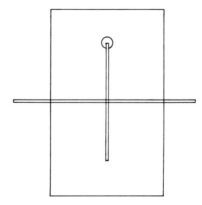

Figure 11.5   End view of orthogonal Golden Rectangles

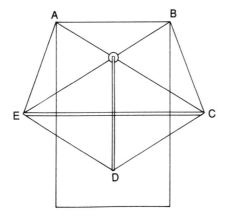

Figure 11.6   Disclosing the pentagon

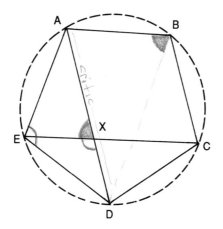

Figure 11.7   The pentagonal diameter

Then

$$AD(AD - 1) = 1$$

$$AD^2 - AD - 1 = 0$$

This is the familiar quadratic equation again:

$$AD = \frac{1}{2}(1 + \sqrt{5}) = \phi$$

Obviously, AD (the line joining 'neighbouring' vertices as long ago defined) is an internal brace—a 'critic' trajectory in the dynamic structure. AC, BD, BE and CE are also braces. They are all phi proportional to the unit icosahedron—a polyhedron in which all the edges are taken as 1.

Chapter One said, 'There are, astonishingly enough, only three quantities that measure the physical extension of the icosahedron.' That, of course, referred to the length of the edge, the length of the polar axis, and the length of the brace—the 'critic' relation. The axis is not of direct concern, having no structural role. Hence in a unit icosahedron, the *only* significant measure is phi. It is the characteristic number of this whole construction-in-space.

A CALL TO EXPERIMENT

Experience shows that understanding what the icosahedral space is really like is greatly enhanced by building a model for oneself. It is much easier to do this than one might think. The kind of equipment that the Infoset needs to run a Syntegration is necessarily elaborate. It needs to be painted 12 different colours and to have its 30 internal braces in place. But simply to investigate the basic structure and to come to grips with phi proportionality needs little enough equipment: it is the physical act of assembly that helps.

Components may be purchased at any supermarket and many corner stores. Thirty sticks are needed for the edges, and these usually come in a choice of three sizes. The smallest sticks are sold as toothpicks, and the longest as skewers for kebabs; in between is the cocktail stick for spearing olives and cherries. The 12 vertices are gum-drops: these usually come in two sizes, and sometimes three, to match the sticks.

It certainly bears out the earlier contention that people are ill at ease in three-dimensional space, although they inhabit it, to see what happens next. Even having followed explanations of the kind given here, most people cannot construct an icosahedron without help. The clue to progress is to be found in the recent demonstration of the planar pentagon.

Make a pentagon, flat on the table, by sticking five sticks into five gum-drops. Make the angles slightly greater than a right-angle: the elasticity of the gum-drop will soon accommodate to the correct angle of 108°. The unit will become stable, in fact, when the five radial spokes are put in. The easiest method is to take a sixth gum-drop and insert five sticks into it at equal intervals, pointing slightly down, so that the result stands up like a five-legged spider. When the other ends of the sticks are inserted in the vertices of the pentagon, a stable structure appears. It would be stable anyway, if fabricated accurately; but the tension in the gum drops resulting from all those sloppy angles works in the client's favour. The result is a polar cap of an icosahedron, which has half its vertices already in place. Start again, and make a second polar cap. All 12 gum-drops and 20 sticks have been used: there are just 10 sticks left over.

Hold the two polar caps facing each other, like a pair of cymbals, and rotate them. The position needed is where each of the caps is the inverse shape of the other. That is, if one cap has a side on the base and an apex at the top, then the other should be placed as in Figure 11.7—standing on a point. The missing 10 edges then stitch the two polar caps together in a zig-zag pattern. Two of the new sticks go into each pentagonal vertex, which is already provided with three of its sticks, making five in all.

At a Syntegration, it is a good practical tip to distribute a kit of gum-drops and sticks (bagged-up overnight) to each participant. Let the group discover its general 3-D ineptitude before guiding the experiment through. The gasps of delight when the structures actually come together attest to the magical quality of this form—enhanced no doubt by permission to eat the extra gum-drops provided with the kit ...

It is difficult to wire-in the internal braces, given the ephemeral nature of the gum-drop medium, but it is a key part of the experience to grasp the essential character of phi proportionality. Longer sticks may be provided to examine the internal structure. In particular, the participant should discover the orthogonal system of Golden Rectangles with which we began. Since the model will probably be standing on one of its 20 faces, the pattern of rectangles will be twisted at an angle in relation to the walls and floor of the room, and it is not easy to recognize. It is helpful to rock the model on to one edge, when one orthogonal set will be found parallel to the walls and floor.

There is, moreover, more than one set of orthogonally oriented Golden Rectangles, and that is confusing. The clue is that every pair of parallel edges (of which there are no less than 15) subtends a Golden Rectangle, since the ends of each pair are connected by an internal brace whose measure is phi. Hence there are five different orthogonal sets. They may be found by rotating the model relative to the ground around the pentagon (hence the five sets) of a polar cap. However, that is hardly necessary. It soon becomes clear that the whole icosahedral space is defined by intersecting Golden Rectangles, which is to say that it is an interpenetration of phi-ness.

As we know, the 12 corners of the rectangles are vertices of the icosahedron, and they lie on a sphere. There are an infinite number of ways to position this construction, but always buried inside are representations of the other four Platonic solids. One in particular is the central space delineated by the crossing internal braces. As we know, each vertex subtends a pentagon. When its internal braces cross, a smaller, inverted, pentagon is formed (Figure 11.8). Given that there are twelve vertices, twelve such pentagons are formed inside, constructing between them a twelve-sided figure whose faces are regular pentagons. It is a regular dodecahedron.

From the beginning (see Chapter One), it had been clear that for our purposes the internal space could be invaded in search of tensegrity, whereas a geodesic dome could not afford to clutter its space and had to seek tensegrity in its outer skin. But strength comes from elastic tension, and not from brittle rigidity. This was the main reason for not inserting the six polar axes as structural members. The destruction of the internal space by using the polar axes yields an icosahedron consisting of 20 identical tetrahedra all radiating from the sphere's centre, and is inimical to the tensegrity notion as developed in geodesics.

The central dodecahedron thus became inviolate in my mind; and because for years I had been using these forms as mandalas in meditation, it acquired the private name of the 'sacred space.' There is something special about it—and its centre, which is also the centre of the sphere. The intention was not to use this private name publicly, but no satisfactory alternative presents itself. Physicists named the fundamental constituent of hadrons the quark after James Joyce, and had already termed two of its six aspects as 'strange' and

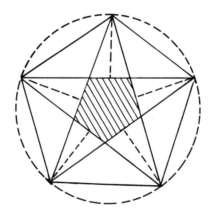

Figure 11.8   The internal pentagon

'charmed.' If they can get away with that, then let me keep my mystical term. By the same token, I shall add that the sacred space 'breathes' with the cosmos through invisibly fine tubes connecting the centre of each dodecahedral face to its orthogonal vertex. The bridge from this mystical to the normal description lies in Aristotle's pneuma, the chi of Chinese medicine, and ends up (quite safely) with the segments of polar axes which subtend the dodecahedron—marked with dashed lines in Figure 11.8.

The objective of this chapter has been to explain the structural nature of the icosahedron, and also to discuss it in ways that should lead to an easy familiarity with its inner workings. To illustrate the point, I go back to the end of Chapter Two and the two diagrams that show how teams of players are formed, and how the critics are appointed. These two 'clocks' define (correctly) the social relationships involved. At the time, which was in preparation for the first experiments at Manchester, I thought of the clocks as planar 'projections' of the icosahedron. But they are really entailment charts rather than projections, and this is why they did not serve at all well when used as the basis for allocating topics and collecting votes. The spatial relationships within the icosahedron are not reflected (except for the team polarities) at all.

As soon as my colleague Dr Don Burrill heard about the practical difficulties, namely that there were cognitive problems with the clocks, he gave me proper geometrical projections analogous to the circular projections of the Earth's surface, centred at the north pole. He pointed out that how the icosahedron is depicted in a plane space depends upon the viewpoint from which it is made.

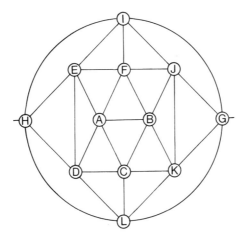

Figure 11.9   Edge-centred planar projection of an icosahedral surface

An individual is represented by an edge. So we may have an edge-centred projection of the icosahedron in which the individual yellow–red, for instance, has pride of place. On this diagram yellow–red appears as A–B (Figure 11.9).

Then note also that we need no fewer than 30 orientations of this chart, one for each player, to display to each player his/her own 'central' role. This is just as it should be, in that it emphasizes the democratic symmetry of the syntegration.

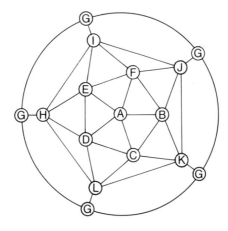

Figure 11.10 Pole-centred planar projection of an icosahedral surface

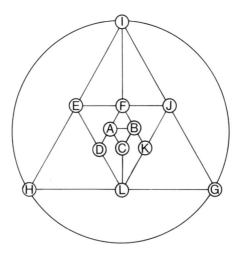

Figure 11.11 Face-centred planar projection of an icosahedral surface

From the standpoint of the *team*, and in this case Team A, a pole centred projection is needed, which looks as shown in Figure 11.10. Naturally this emphasizes the pentagonal aspect of the total structure, because each team has five members. In pursuit of democratic symmetry, in this case we need 12 copies of the chart, focusing on each team in turn as central to affairs.

This leaves the third option: a face-centred projection, which looks as shown in Figure 11.11, where the face-in-focus is ABC. As Don said, he included this projection for the sake of completeness. None of those concerned with the development of Syntegrity had yet discovered a useful meaning or particular significance for a face—the triad formed by two members of a team with someone else who is actually defined as belonging to each of the alternate teams of the other two (but see subsequent thinking recorded in Part Five, Surplus Six). The arrangement looks as if it might be significant at a deep level; it has to be noted that many Indian mandalas reflect this configuration. This time, obviously, 20 charts would be needed to focus on each of the faces in turn.

In each of these projections we are concerned only with edges and vertices. The internal braces do not appear, and indeed the basic phi-ness of the icosahedron tends to be obscured. There is no convenient substitute for three-dimensional space, after all, which is why it is so helpful to play with gum-drop models. Walking around *inside* the model is a different experience again ...

Chapter Twelve

THE DYNAMICS OF
ICOSAHEDRAL SPACE

The account of icosahedral space given in the previous chapter refers to a structure that is static, although if we think of the model as both spinning and tumbling in thin air it defines a 'sphere of phi-ness' that is not an inappropriate image for the hum of activity and the buzz of communication that are generated by a real-life syntegration. The protocols in use effectively engender the hum and the buzz. Is that really the basis of the 'reverberation' that was noticed in the experiments and discussed descriptively in Part One? If so, it is not surprising that infosets become aware of their corporate identity: syntegration provides a thorough social mixing after all.

It is in this sense, which people often refer to as 'team spirit,' or '*esprit de corps*,' and Maeterlinck invoked with his 'spirit of the hive,' that the term 'group consciousness' occasions no surprise. The idea that a team, and in our case an infoset, represents a whole that is greater than the sum of its parts is familiar, and is reflected in demotic usage: 'I like to run a happy ship' and 'the old school tie prevails once again' are British examples. In the United States, the continual presidential exhortations to 'my fellow Americans' embody a notion of group consciousness that might well be derived from the official motto '*e pluribus unum*,' which people perhaps do not read as they pass round dollar bills. Even a crowd of people, assembling fortuitously, may acquire an intent, and through that an identity, as Elias Canetti brilliantly showed (Canetti, 1962).

Very well, people are mutually aware: that is, they are aware of each other as members of a social group that has identity. In a syntegration, especially, this mutual awareness is uppermost in the mind of each participant—the protocols insistently remind him/her that the group has a common goal. Moreover, a syntegration seeks something better than a set of twelve statements to which everyone has assented (perhaps with some reluctance). It seeks to create an integral statement that is more than a list of aphorisms or separable intentions (compare, for example, the ten commandments or the fourteen points of Deming; neither of these is indivisible). Syntegration is a portmanteau word for *synergistic* integrity, after all.

The term 'group consciousness' will be restricted to the meaning discussed here, as it seems to conform to accepted usage. Then the reverberation of ideas would be a label for the humming and buzzing experienced over time by a static set of relationships made dynamic through the operation of protocols. But the implied question at the start was, is that really all? What other basis for reverberation might there be?

I think that there is a dynamic implicit in the icosahedral model that pre-exists the hum-and-buzz activity. In the last chapter, a term describing the internal brace as 'a critic *trajectory*' was disingenuously dropped by way of preparation. A relationship between two points may be marked by an arrow to show that it is directional; and a continuum of directional relationships defines a pathway. To further the discussion of reverberation, let us trace a remarkable pathway through the icosahedral space. It is difficult to disentangle, because it wanders through all three dimensions, and occupies four separate planes. The reader would surely find it a help to look at a gum-drop model as s/he follows the prescribed route, but those with good visualization capacity may manage without it.

Stand the model on one of its vertices, and tilt it slightly away from you. Spin the model on its point until another vertex is close to your eye; call it A. Adjust the tilt a little so that A's polar vertex, called B, lies directly behind and is obscured by A. Concentrate on the two pentagonal polar caps that subtend A and B. Each lies on a plane, of course, and the two planes are parallel. The nearer pentagon has its apex up high; the more distant is inverted, and is actually balanced on its apex, which is part of the icosahedral vertex that is standing on the ground. Call that vertex C.

We now find that an edge of the nearer pentagon (the A polar cap) cuts in half each of the vertices of the further pentagon (the B polar cap) as it traverses in front of it. The result is shown below, Figure 12.1.

This diagram is geometrically speaking exact, because we are dealing with regular pentagons on parallel planes. Looking at the three-dimensional model with human eyes, however, the intersections do not seem completely perfect unless the head is moved very slightly to follow the line of sight; this is due to the optical effect called parallax.

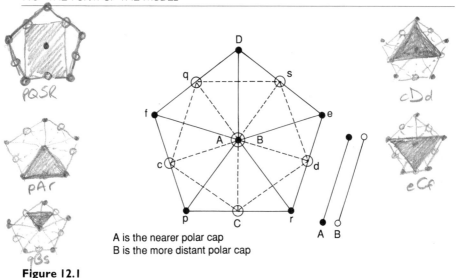

A is the nearer polar cap
B is the more distant polar cap

Figure 12.1

Consider the unmarked lines pq and rs, and note that each of these demarcates an internal brace in three-dimensional space. Its correct measure is therefore phi, although the distance of p from q and r from s on the diagram is less than phi—the effect this time is due to foreshortening. In three-dimensional space, however, pqsr is a golden rectangle.

Here is another point of interest. As you look down on the specially aligned model, you will discover four *vertical* (that is, relative to the floor and walls) planes. The nearest is defined by the triangle pAr, and the most distant by the inverted triangle qBs. Each of these is built of icosahedral edges, so the sides are of unit length. In between lie the vertical triangles cDd and eCf. Each of these is built of internal braces, with sides of length phi. They are inverted in relation to each other.

The dynamic pathway it is proposed to reveal is to be found in half of the infoset. Ten people are eliminated by clearing out the internal apparatus of the diagram: that is to say, the vertices A and B vanish, together with the radial edges representing the A and B teams. It might be recalled from Chapter One, when we discussed the invariant factor 2 in Euler's equation, that Buckminster Fuller saw it as the need to 'neutralize' a pair of poles in accounting for 'spinnability': we have now done just that by taking out A and B. This leaves only the structures that define the juxtaposition of the two polar pentagons themselves. The third team chosen for elimination is team C, radiating from the pivotal vertex C, on which the model was actually standing. One of Team C's members has already left, because s/he was a member of Team B, so we have removed in all 14 people. Without vertex C, the model is left standing on a pentagonal plane (although two arms of the pentagon itself are missing, since they were members of the eliminated team B). Nine vertices are left, and 16 of the 30 infosetters. Let us hasten to note that by revolving the model, a different set of 16 people would be considered, and so on. All our considerations lead to fully symmetric results.

The diagram is now redrawn to show the nine retained vertices (Figure 12.2). Three of the four vertical planes enumerated earlier have lost their embodiments: only the phi-edged triangle we knew as cDd remains, hanging from the apex of the model, as shown. The nine vertices now appear as points and are numbered clockwise. The figure is drawn as regular to emphasize that the matters to be discussed do not depend upon the orientation of the diagram: any two adjacent points will serve as the 'base.' There is, moreover, something to be gained in drawing attention to the three-dimensionality of the original model (of which this is a plane projection) through a hint of perspective that has to do with parallax again. Notably, the shrinking of the base pr on the old figure to the distance between points 4 and 5 in the new figure reflects the inattention that visual acuity seems to allot to the foot of the diagram; the parallel which used to be qs is now at the forefront of much 'busy-ness.' This pr base appears optically shorter than its counterpart, with the result that the parallel lines pq (5–8) and rs (4–1) appear to diverge. Of course, the entire diagram is slightly distorted, since the distance between any two points is a ninth of the circumference, instead of a tenth. However, these optical adjustments by no means interfere with any of the formal properties under discussion.

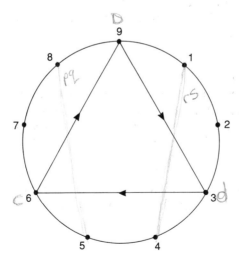

Figure 12.2

It was said that a series of directional relationships denotes a dynamic pathway. If the series returns to the starting point, then the pathway has the significant property that it is closed. The shortest symmetrical closed pathway to be found in the figure is an equilateral triangle, and the one illustrated is generated by the simplest algorithm—the so called 'rule of three.' Any message travelling around this loop could fairly be described as 'reverberating,' since it would go on circulating indefinitely if it had enough energy to propagate it. Certainly we can imagine a little booster to amplify the signal at points 3, 6 and 9 without compromising either the dynamic logic of the figure or the semantic content of the message. And as far as syntegration is concerned, this particular pathway is already specified in our model since each of the three lines is actually a phi-space.

We might make a closed loop out of the remaining points too; some possibilities are shown below in Figure 12.3.

All three figures have closed dynamic pathways that could be expected to convey reverberating messages. Observe the basic topological properties that all such figures have (necessarily) in common: there are six paths composing the closed dynamic pathway, and each point is subtended by two paths. However, these examples do not correspond to the icosahedral model as constructed, in which the internal paths are all braces of measure phi. The question arises of whether a closed phi pathway exists—to be defined by a unique rule, rather than an arbitrary heuristic. We seek an algorithm, and a famous one already exists. Let us find it by considering the unit whole of the circle as already analysed, and dividing that unit by a number.

For example, one divided by two yields the decimal five, and one divided by five yields the decimal two. Neither answer proposes a single path, still less an algorithmic pathway, although one divided by four does: the decimal suggests moving from two to five—but the pathway does not extend beyond that path. One divided by eight offers a second step: the decimal reads one, two, five— and stops. A third, a sixth, and a ninth (the very numbers used before) all denote oscillations: their decimals simply recur at a single point. It is only the fraction of sevenths that generates a closed path. Moreover, it is one that takes up all the available numbers in conforming to the topological necessities already remarked.

The decimal version of one seventh is 0.14285714285714 ...; that is to say, that the string of numbers repeats itself after six digits: 0.142857. Let us trace this algorithmic pathway on the nine-point circle, on which the continuous triangular loop 3,6,9 is already traced, as shown below in Figure 12.4.

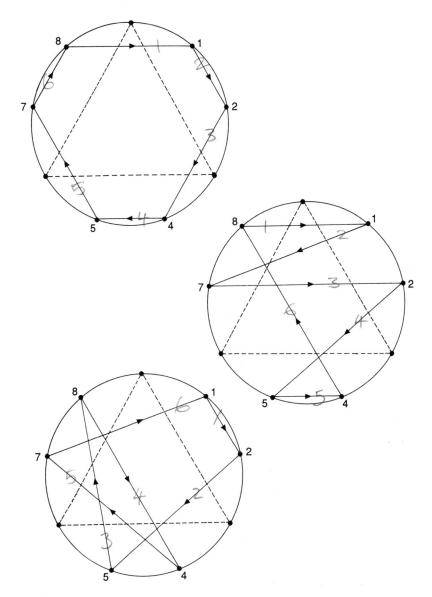

Figure 12.3

Adhering to the nomenclature that called this an algorithmic pathway that is closed and therefore continuous, and recalling that only the denominator seven generates such a route, another astonishing feature of the process may be noted, that is, it makes no difference what digit is used as the numerator— so long as it is not seven itself!

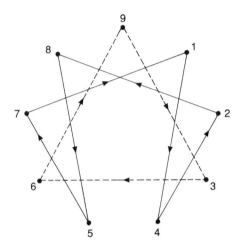

Figure 12.4

Consider:

$$\begin{aligned}
\text{one seventh} &= 0.142857 && (1...)\\
\text{two sevenths} &= 0.285714 && (2...)\\
\text{three sevenths} &= 0.428571 && (4...)\\
\text{four sevenths} &= 0.571428 && (5...)\\
\text{five sevenths} &= 0.714285 && (7...)\\
\text{six sevenths} &= 0.857142 && (8...)
\end{aligned}$$

The algorithmic pathway is always the same, since it is continuous: all that changes as the numerator changes is the entry point into the loop.

As has already been said, this diagram is already well known: it has been credited with a mystical significance for a very long time. Its name is the enneagram (*ennea* is Greek for nine).

This book is a story and an illumination rather than a text book, and the account of the enneagram that follows is a personal account. Thorough research into the history of this diagram would be interesting, but not significant to current purposes. What may be significant is the widespread interest it has commanded, and the serendipitous route by which it entered the invention of team syntegrity.

I first heard about the enneagram in conversations during the 1960s with the English mystic John Bennett. His book on the subject (Bennett, 1983) did not appear until the 1980s, but he had surely been influenced much earlier by Ouspensky, whose work (Ouspensky, 1949) was already well known to seekers after esoteric knowledge. Ouspensky attributed the diagram to Gurdjieff, and makes these curious remarks: 'The diagram is peculiar to this teaching. It is found nowhere else. When it was first given by G. he observed that several things in this system could be found in other ancient systems of esoteric teaching, but not the Enneagram.' Ouspensky was lecturing in 1944. He went on to say that Gurdjieff referred to the triangle as the Law of Three (representing three forces, active, passive, and neutralizing), and to the decimal as the Law of Seven (relating to the order of manifestation, and represented by the tonic sol-fa, where doh stands at the apical point 9—which of course belongs not to the sevenths division, but to the threefold division).

From 1971 to 1973 I worked for President Salvador Allende in Chile (Beer, 1981). In Santiago there was a mystical mission known as Arica, after the Northern Chilean town on the border with Peru where the group had its base. A Buddhist monk resident with the mission presented me with an elaborate triple stage mandala, made of coloured felts and threads, which he described as a personal communication from him to me based on what he had known of me 'for ever.' It is a hanging, some six feet high. In the topmost stage, I at once recognized the enneagram. It was not until later that I discovered (Ichazo, 1976) that the founder of Arica, Oscar Ichazo, was actively teaching how to 'break the tyranny of the ego' (as he put it) by using multiple mystical representations of the enneagram. And it appeared that the diagram—Ichazo calls it an enneagon—belonged to the Sufi mystical tradition, which is why I called the attribution to an invention by Gurdjieff 'curious.' It seems that the reference 'peculiar to this teaching' could not refer merely to Gurdjieff himself, but to his own sources. Bennett traces the doctrine about self-renewal back 4500 years to Mesopotamia, and goes forward via Babylon to the ancient Greeks. A so-called enneagram turns up in a book called *Arithmologia* by a Jesuit priest, Athanasius Kircher, published in Rome in 1665. This was differently composed, through three equilateral triangles, but seems to have figured in the generation of Gurdjieff's thinking.

Ichazo had used (different) interpretations of the enneagram to analyse fixations, traps, ideas, passions, and virtues—each in a ninefold categorization. As further commentary on the diagram came casually my way, I read enneagrammatic analysis of the human soul, of the process of cooking a meal, of the profession of marketing, and of the Lord's Prayer. In particular, an explicitly Catholic expatiation (Beesing *et al.*, 1984) was published in 1984 by a Jesuit priest, a Dominican nun, and another priest, which identifies nine personality types, and uses the enneagrammatic structure to throw light on their spiritual and emotional behaviour. As to origins, these authors say, 'the Enneagram has a long but shrouded history. It is reputed to have originated in Afghanistan almost 2000 years ago, perhaps in the early years of Christian influence in Persia, and then thought to have infiltrated into Moslem circles after that religion invaded central Asia and the subcontinent of India. Until the present century it remained strictly an oral tradition known only to Sufi masters who would reveal to an individual disciple only the part of the Enneagram pertaining to that person's personality type.' They go on to acknowledge the role of Ichazo, and say that he was taught the Sufi tradition in La Paz, Bolivia, by 'a man whose name he pledged not to reveal.'

Now Sufism is an Islamic tradition, and the Prophet was not born until AD 570. The Vedas, however, are the most ancient Sanskrit scriptures, and are generally regarded as dating from 1000 to 4000 BC. 'Veda' is the Sanskrit word for 'knowledge,' and the Indian culture had plenty of that. In particular, it seems that Indian number theoreticians knew about the recurring seventh. According to Keith Critchlow (Critchlow, 1979), who is drawing on work dealing with vedic mathematics by Jagadguru Shankaracharya, new insights were obtained by meditation and visualization. As to methodology, numbers were associated with letters, 'not in order to conceal knowledge but in order to facilitate the recording of their arguments.' Whether the cycles of numbers aided the memory in reciting the vedic sutras, as he suggests, or the numbers were recalled through remembering the verses, as I suspect, may not be a pertinent question, since the 'wholeness' constantly preached by vedantic philosophy might have seen the *identity* of the number system and the sutra insights as (what would be called) the True Realization. However this may be, Jagadguru uses the numerological vedic system to demonstrate the affinity between the numbers nine and seven. Having divided one by seven to obtain the 0.142857 sequence, he finds a recurring sequence of remainders generated by the division: 3, 2, 6, 4, 5, 1. He provides methods whereby the enneagrammatic sequence can be projected from the remainders. He also notes that the two halves of the sequence, namely 142 and 857, when added together give the answer 999—which means that either half can be discovered by subtracting the other half from this total. As to the triangle, we note that if one third is represented as 0.333 recurring, and two thirds as 0.666 recurring, then a whole of three thirds is represented as 0.999 recurring.

The ancient Indian culture, working from visualization rather than reckoning, and the use of mandalas for transmitting elaborate but not ratiocinative information, remains mysterious to Western science. That it is real is underwritten by the extraordinary history (Kanigel, 1991) of Srinivasa Ramanujan, a poor boy born in a small town outside Madras in 1887. He was unschooled, and was dead at 32, but he became known as 'the one superlatively great mathematician whom India has produced in the last 1000 years.' Befriended by the pre-eminent British mathematician of his day, G. H. Hardy, who brought him to Cambridge, Ramanujan worked by vedic visualization. He said: 'An equation has no meaning for me unless it expresses a thought of God.' This is not the kind of language most favoured in our Western seats of learning; still less would be the suggestion that the remark enshrines a tautology, although Plato might have thought so.

The meaning behind these last paragraphs surely has to do with the nature of consciousness: we shall return to the topic soon. Meanwhile, I had been using the enneagram in meditations ever since receiving my personal mandala from the Buddhist monk in Chile, and it came to my aid in a strange way. As early as 1956 I had begun to wonder if it would be possible to give a rendition of the Requiem Mass with paint and canvas. It was strange that so many musical settings have been composed, but no pictorial version seemed to be known. Because of my Eastern studies and yogic practice, I conceived the idea of making a ring of paintings that would act as a mandala, when the viewer stood in the centre of the circle and allowed the whole group of paintings to impinge upon whatever personal sensibilities s/he brought into the interaction. The exact formulation of the plan was elusive, precisely because it posed the problem of informational overload. There are $n(n-1)$ directional relationships between n paintings, and 10 (or sometimes more) figured in the project. To receive 90 complicated vibrational messages at the centre of the Requiem mandala would be highly confusing, especially to the man who would be doing the painting! How traditional Eastern mandalas absorb their own variety became a key question. The answer seemed to be by large-scale repetition of *similar* visual images, where 'information' resides in juxtaposition and complicated variation. But the Requiem paintings that were being formulated over those 30 years were not at all similar ...

At some point during the 1980s the conceptualizing of possible paintings crossed with meditational experience with the enneagram. The idea was born that by marking an enneagram on the floor of the room, and mounting nine (rather than ten) pictures at the points of the star, visual attention could be drawn to 18 of the 72 directional reverberations. And instead of standing still at the centre, the viewer could walk round the exhibit following the algorithmic pathways of the triangle and the sevenfold sequence. To cut the story (Beer, 1993) short, the project was undertaken in the execution of ten paintings (the nine, plus an entrance painting) between 1987 and 1989. Nine of the ten canvasses are each 5 by 3.5 feet in size; the other is the *De Profundis*: it is 7 feet high and 4.5 feet wide. The work was first exhibited in 1992 in the Metropolitan Cathedral of Christ the King in the Catholic Archdiocese of Liverpool and returned there in 1993.

In the interim, as recounted in Part One, the Syntegrity project became highly active, the main experiments were conducted, and I acquired a new colleague,

Joe Truss. It was a surprise to us both to discover, early on, a mutual interest in the enneagram. Indeed, Joe had actually founded a business based on a complicated enneagrammatic model. We talked a lot about it, as did all the collaborators in the icosahedral geometry involved in syntegration. Boris Freesman, for example, who had uncovered the Freesman Exclusion during the Toronto experiment, came through with the news that any numerator divided by seven would generate the enneagrammatic sequence—as reported earlier in this chapter: a fact at that time unknown to the group. But it was Joe Truss who kept worrying away at the idea that the enneagram had something to do with the icosahedron. He thought that there must be some kind of mathematical mapping connecting the two, but says that he did not expect to discover the diagram itself.

The reader already knows that it is there because the chapter began smoothly enough by exposing it. But it is a matter of great interest that in the whole literature to which reference has already been made, the enneagram occurs as a *plane figure*. Nowhere had there been the slightest hint that a three-dimensional manifestation existed. Even when I knew that he was looking for a mapping, it seemed to me that, even if nine enneagrammatically related vertices could be discovered, Truss would simply have displayed a geometric curiosity of no particular importance. No wonder the search took so long, given that the diagram was discovered spread across four vertical planes; and as so often happens, the discovery was almost accidental. Joe was rolling a model across the floor, when he suddenly saw it; as we know, chance favours the prepared mind. Moreover, he had the greatest difficulty in finding it again. The rolling model was landing on a face each time, and the aspect changes depending on the orientation of spin. As I have presented the result, the model is balanced on a vertex to bring another vertex to the fore.

Turn now to the question of importance. Joe came to my house late at night to show me his discovery, and he was very excited. Well, all such moments are exciting. But I was unprepared that he should say, 'Do you see what this means? The icosahedron is the actual *origin* of the enneagram, and the ancients knew it. Could it not be possible that the plane figure was coded esoteric knowledge?' Obviously (now!) it could ...

Secondly of importance: it had taken such a lot of finding and it took so much subsequent locating to demonstrate to others, that the three-dimensional enneagram seemed to be like one small shrimp locked in an ice cube. It was not until much effort had gone into generalizing the algorithm that I realized that the enneagram is ubiquitously present. Consider: if it can be detected when the icosahedron stands on one vertex, it must be detectable when the model stands on any vertex. Moreover, if it is present when *these* two poles are aligned, it must be present when *any* two poles are aligned. Thus it comes about that points 4 and 5 on the enneagram refer to *any* side of the icosahedron—which therefore enfolds *30* three-dimensional, four-planar, enneagrams. Importance? It was with a certain amount of frisson that I reported in the last chapter that the icosahedral model conceived as a spinning sphere could be regarded as 'an interpenetration of phi-ness.' But phi is simply a one-dimensional length, even when used to demarcate the orthogonal configuration of three golden rectangles. That the spinning sphere is an interpenetration of three-dimensional four-plane enneagrams is (as they say) something else.

Joe had another report to make and it concerned the strange importance of the number seven. He quoted Arthur Young (Young, 1991) who was in turn quoting his mentor Oswald Vebler. Seven is the largest number that can be interconnected in subsets of three; each pair of subsets shares one element, but not more than one. More than seven elements cannot be connected. Mathematically, one can achieve seven triangles from seven points, but if eight points are attempted, it breaks up. 'In other words,' says Young, 'if you tried to make the universe out of eight principles, it would split up into two groups.'

Next Young realized that seven colours are required to make a map on the surface of a torus in order that all bordering countries can be distinguished by differences in colour. (The famous 'four colour problem' handles this for a plane surface or a spherical surface alone.) Young then explained how the two different circularities of the torus make it possible to have separateness and connectedness in the universe at the same time. A fence around a person cuts him/her off on one surface, but leaves that person connected with the outside by putting a core through the sphere on which s/he stands.

So, 'a speculative question,' wrote Joe Truss to me: 'Are the polar opposites (of the icosahedron) connected not by a line but by a hole creating a three-dimensional torus?' Yes indeed: I already had six of them interconnecting through the dodecahedral sacred space mentioned at the end of the last chapter. Thanks to Joe Truss, I now understood why. It is for 'breathing.'

Thus we return to the opening discussion in this chapter about the nature of group consciousness. It could be summarized by a definition with the restrictive meaning: the mutual awareness of members of a social group of each other and of the group's identity. Such a group consciousness clearly resides in the minds of the group members. However, because of the experience with syntegration, and because of the present inquiry into the form of the model, I wish to erect a stronger hypothesis. It is that there is such an entity as a *group* mind that operates at a different level from group consciousness as defined.

It would operate, if it exists, as a self-conscious entity. The difficulty with this concept is that such a mind could not be independent of the mentation of the members of the group, but would transcend their individual abilities.

Now it is all very well to talk about mentation, which is to say *mental* activity, but (whatever else this may be) it is certainly a function of brains—which are discrete physical entities. Thus the concept of a group with a mind seems to imply that the group has a brain, which would entail the creation of shared channels of information—having very high variety. It is at least possible that the multiple enneagrammatic structure, reverberating as it does, provides a complex of linkages to constitute such a 'corporate brain' that would then give rise to its own consciousness. At any rate, and in order to discuss the matter at all, we have to distinguish this new idea from the accepted idea of group consciousness. It needs a name for ease of reference, a name that relates self-awareness to the infoset (as defined, and as syntegrationally organized). No appropriate terminology exists, and that is revealing: this is an idea new to the culture. In fact, the Oxford English Dictionary devotes no less than 24 pages to defining the word SET, but nowhere comes forward with an adjectival form, which we need to qualify 'consciousness.' With apology for the neologism, then, the word 'infosettic' is proposed as the adjectival form of infoset, which is the portmanteau word for information set as used throughout this book. (This adjectival ending is preferred over the alternatives -ous, -ary, and -al after considering the philological aspects, but mainly for the sake of euphony.)

The hypothesis that there is such a thing as an infosettic consciousness is, at least in principle, falsifiable, as required by Popperian methods of science. If it exists it should make the infoset more competent than its component member consciousness, or even the group consciousness defined. Experiments have yet to be designed, and will be difficult to conduct; all there is so far is empirically based suspicion which suggests the formulation of an hypothesis for which there is so far no scientific support. But at least some (very) dead wood may be cleared away.

Throughout my own philosophical life of 50 years the epistemological problems implicit in this discussion have been perfectly evident. At the start, there was frequent reference (no longer fashionable) to the 'mind–body problem' in which philosophy became enmeshed by continental rationalism, as it was known. Descartes, Spinoza, and Leibniz set the scene for a dualism that could not be assuaged, because no forces are demonstrated to exist whereby mental states impinge directly on physical substance (telekinesis), or indeed the reverse (torture and sex are both mediated by the nervous system). Thus I was familiar as a student in 1943 with the quip, 'What is mind?—no matter. What is matter?—never mind.' But as usually happens with dysfunctional dichotomies, the solution is to dissolve the categories themselves.

Beginning with research in neurocybernetics in the 1950s, I became convinced that information may flow between discrete locations in the absence of 'connecting wires' as a result of inferential processes that can be shared. Here is a perfectly straightforward example. A mile-long stretch of straight roadway runs down a hillside at the foot of which is a narrow one-lane bridge across a stream that courses down the valley. Another similar roadway runs down the opposite hillside towards the same bridge. Two cars travelling in opposite directions crest each of the hills simultaneously, and travel down towards the bridge. Each driver can see the other, but they cannot communicate in the ordinary 'connecting wire' sense. But communicate they do; and one car eventually gives way to the other in crossing the bridge. It seems that messages travel back and forth between the drivers continuously—by inferences drawn from their relative speeds. In the extreme case, the more timid driver sees the more aggressive accelerate rapidly, and lets him win the race. But with more casual drivers the likelihood is that there is a continuous adjustment of speed by both parties and courtesy determines the outcome.

Is it too much to suggest that there is a shared consciousness operating here, in the absence of wires? 'Come,' some will say, 'they are looking at each other—there are pathways of light, photons even, transporting visual images; there is no mystery.' Of course there is no mystery. There is no mystery about infosettic communication either. The point in both cases is simply whether it is convenient to abandon the body–mind dichotomy and to talk about a shared consciousness instead. Shared illusion is the basis of all human epistemology in any case. These matters are discussed in greater detail in the speculative Part Four.

Chapter Thirteen

SELF-REFERENCE IN ICOSAHEDRAL SPACE

It seems to be common ground among those (and certainly the cyberneticians) who have considered the matter that consciousness has to do with self-reference: the entity that we call conscious is aware of itself. Closure in the sense recently discussed seems to be a prerequisite. The ancients had the symbol *ouroboros*, the snake eating its own tail, to epitomize closure; the alchemists used the symbol of a dragon rather than a snake—and sometimes deployed a pair of dragons, each eating the other's tail, which emphasizes that distinct parts may figure in holistic closure. But closure, although evidently necessary to consciousness, is equally clearly not sufficient. Otherwise a fastened padlock or a clasped necklace would be self-aware. Two further concepts already encountered in this book are fundamental to the development of this chapter. They are recursion and iteration: both were already involved, for example, in the generation of the approximative logarithmic spiral in Figure 11.3. It is necessary to think about them more elaborately, and to make rather difficult ideas more accessible I resort once again to recounting a personal experience.

The summer before my 17th birthday (1943) was spent in Croydon Public Library, near London, studying the *Principia Mathematica* of Russell and Whitehead. I was due to enter university in the autumn to read philosophy and psychology, and the problem of consciousness was high on the hit list. But I was coming from mathematics, and at once confronted in the *Principia* a symbol I had never seen before. It was Russell's assertion sign ⊢:, meaning 'it is asserted that.' What is the difference between saying a given proposition and saying you assert the proposition? It sounded like a claim that the speaker is aware of himself giving utterance.

Over the next few years I developed a new symbolic logic that recognized a hierarchy of assertions that was sharply distinguished from any hierarchy of languages which were supposed to be necessary to handle problems of paradox (typified by the statement 'this is a lie,' which if true is false, and if false is true). I wrote, 'In *Meaning and Truth* Russell says: the arguments for the necessity of a hierarchy of languages are overwhelming, and I shall henceforth assume their validity ... (then, in his footnote) they are derived from the paradoxes.' My counter argued that it is perfectly possible to say, within one's own initial language, that the proposition one is entertaining as true is actually false. All language is actually subjective, and no higher order language exists *sui generis* in which propositions declared in the speaker's own language could be questioned. The following argument is abstracted from Chapter Eleven of a massive book called *Panencleisis* written over a period of nearly 10 years. (The title was an early recognition of the holistic philosophy; there are three volumes written in longhand; no attempt was ever made to publish it.)

'An expression is proposed that would run like this:

There is	:	$* -$
(which is being entertained in my mind)	:	$m -$
(as a true notion)	:	$F: m -$
(which denies)	:	$[F]$
(which is being entertained in my mind)	:	$m -$
(as a true notion)	.:	$F: m -$
(which denies)	:	$[F]$
.		.
.		.
.		.
.		.
.		.
.		.
a proposition	:	p

The expression becomes:

$$* - \{m - [F: m - ([F]: \{m - [F: m - ([F]: \{m - [F: m([F]...p$$

It is possible, then, to have a continued qualification of p by a recurring set of symbols, so that p itself can never be expressed.'

Because the expression offers 'a protracted predicate which can never acquire a subject,' the expression cannot result in a paradox. Nothing, in fact, is being said. Only there is a state of mind reflecting on its own activity. That quotation summarizes my conclusions at the time—some 40 years ago.

Although I had the presumption as a teenager to disagree with Russell (*in absentia*!), and also argued that Wittgenstein was right when the two philosophers disagreed with each other, I was still in awe of him. Thus there is detectable relief in another passage that says of the *Principia*, 'it is essentially tautologous; and, as Russell himself has always insisted, the logical formulae of which it consists *state* nothing.' So what was the wonderful work all about? Obviously, it was about mentation itself: the *Principia*'s author was aware of himself having nothing to say, demonstrating this by writing three volumes to prove it. And we may now note that the argument was recursive and iterative, even if closure was no more than putative. It has exactly the quality that this book calls 'reverberative.'

During the 1950s I went on to construct a set-theoretic model of the brain (Beer, 1962). This revealed a physical correlate of the closure that is a precondition of consciousness. It conceived of the brain as an organ concerned essentially with devising a homeostatic balance between events happening in the sensory and the motor cortex. This is a very different model from the popular model in which the organism uses its brain as a kind of computer to work out how to interact with the outside or 'real world.' According to this popular model, events in the 'real world' are sensed, albeit imperfectly, by the body's sensory organs; inputs are used for cerebral computation; and the brain tells its owner 'what to do.' But neurocybernetics had discovered a more useful depiction. The brain is actually responding to its own states: closure, recursive iteration, reverberation—these are basic characteristics of neurophysiological activity. Warren McCulloch (who was my mentor) was among the first to understand this: to come to terms with his insights, it is valuable to browse among his collected works (McCulloch, 1989). Probably the most frequently cited pioneer paper to offer scientific demonstration of the revised model is 'What the Frog's Eye Tells the Frog's Brain' (Letvin *et al.*, 1959), of which McCulloch was the senior author. The junior author was the great Chilean biologist and cybernetician Humberto Maturana. He went on to write a biology of cognition (Maturana and Varela, 1980) of great profundity, and more recently, with his collaborator Francisco Varela, he has written a book (Maturana and Varela, 1987) that expounds the new epistemology in popular terms.

In support of the insight that the brain is dealing with the homeostasis of its own internal states may be cited the neurophysiological fact that there are 10^5 times as many internal receptors as external receptors in the body. So say what one will about the nature of the 'reality out there,' and how it impinges on awareness, the brain is necessarily preoccupied with internal inputs and is *neurologically closed*. Moreover, as Ross Ashby used to say, the brain has no brain inside to guide it. The key point all this seeks to disclose is that awareness is best described as self-awareness; that consciousness is a reflection of its own activity. The neurophysiological facts and an epistemology properly based on cognitive psychology give point, then, to the early philosophical speculation with the nested, recursive symbolism quoted at the start. This disputed that a paradoxical proposition could ever be uttered: then there was no need to erect a Russellian hierarchy of languages to explain it. By the same token, is it possible to utter *any* unequivocal propositions, or were the processes of ratiocination actually concerned with the awareness of the propositions being under consideration? It weighed heavily with me that Goedel's Theorem showed how formal languages were in the last resort 'undecidable' (Nagel and Newman, 1958).

Now please meet Professor Heinz von Foerster, physicist and magician, and one of the founders of cybernetics. At an early meeting with him, probably in 1960 at the latest, he wrote on a napkin: THIS SENTENCE HAS _____ LETTERS, and he asked me to fill in the number. I counted 22 letters, and was about to write the words in when the trap became apparent. Soon I discovered 'the answer' and nearly fell into that trap too. Why should my answer be unique? In fact, there are two numbers that serve; the point is that looking for them makes one realize that a process is involved in which each possible answer has to take account of *itself*. Heinz went on from there, and developed a theory of recursive functions as part of his philosophy of science called Constructivism (Siegel, 1986).

Here is one version of his argument. In mathematics it is familiar to nominate operators that act on variables, and to define a variable in terms of the outcome of an operation—just as we say that 64 is the result of the operation called 'squaring' on the variable 8. In recursive number theory, to go further, the number 8 is defined as the result of adding one to the number 7; to define 7 add one to the number 6; and so on. Let us apply this procedure. Start with a variable called x, and define the next number in the series as the result of performing an operation Op on it, thus:

$$x_1 = \mathrm{Op}\,(x_0)$$
$$x_2 = \mathrm{Op}\,(x_1)$$

and so on, for instance:

$$x_4 = \mathrm{Op}\,(x_3)$$

We may, however, substitute for x in the second equation, because it was defined in the first. This yields a new definition of x_2:

$$x_2 = \text{Op } (\text{op}(x_0))$$

and continuing:

$$x_3 = \text{Op}(\text{Op}(\text{Op}(x_0)))$$
$$x_4 = \text{Op}(\text{Op}(\text{Op}(\text{Op}(x_0))))$$

At this stage, von Foerster observes that the formulation emphasizes a *process* rather than the 'thing' that was x_0. It is at once clear how this bears on our earlier discussion when he puts the algebra into human terms: a sensorimotor competence gets confused with its object. His example will stand much consideration: when a child is learning to sound a toy trumpet, the trumpet itself is not a constant. What, we may wonder, is the trumpet's ontological status? If it is best described as an infinitely long series of operations, and if we are aware of the operations rather than any thing, it is easier to understand the basis of George Berkeley's 'subjective idealism,' the argument that we do not 'know' an objective reality, but only the contents of our own minds— which influenced Western philosophy so greatly for 250 years. Certainly we can see that when Dr Johnson scorned Berkeley by tripping on a stone, he was not displaying much intellectual refinement. And if Berkeley, being a bishop, felt like justifying the physical existence of things that were not at the time the subject of anyone's mental process by saying that they were contemplated in the mind of God, he was in good cybernetic order—so long as his interlocutors were not atheists.

Returning to von Foerster, we find him writing out a recursive series that is actually infinitely long. It runs:

$$x(\infty) = \text{Op}(\text{Op}(\text{Op}(\text{Op}(\text{Op}(\text{Op}(\ldots$$

and says that it can never reach x, and therefore might be thought to produce nothing. This seems to be just the puzzle with which this chapter started. But Heinz has more to say, and it is best to quote him directly (with his emphasis):

'Contemplate this (that is, the above) expression

(i) the *independent variable* x_0, the *primary argument*, has disappeared;

(ii) since $x(\infty)$ expresses an indefinite recursion of the operator Op on to operators Op, any indefinite recursion *within* that expression can be replaced by $x(\infty)$. So:

$$x(\infty) = \mathrm{Op(:Op(:Op(...}$$

$$
\begin{array}{ll}
: \; : & \rule{3cm}{0.4pt} \; x_{(\infty)} \; \rule{4cm}{0.4pt}\!\!\!\rightarrow \\
: & \rule{3cm}{0.4pt} \; x_{(\infty)} \; \rule{3cm}{0.4pt}\!\!\!\rightarrow
\end{array}
$$

So an infinite concatenation of operators on operators can be replaced by the simple $x(\infty)$. Hence, we could replace the infinite concatenation of operators within one operator by $x\infty$, thus transforming an infinite expression into a finite expression, whereby $x\infty$ is the result of an operation on $x\infty$. Hence

$$x(\infty) = \mathrm{Op}(x\infty)'$$

This discourse surely sounds as if it must be circular, as we say pejoratively. But it *has* to be circular, once logical closure is understood! The snake eats its own tail. It is more to the point to ask what are the conclusions of this continuation of the argument. This is critical:

'Certain values can be plugged into this equation, and thus solve it. It produces a self-value, similar to the value of "This sentence has _____ letters."'

That is: certain *stable* values emerge from infinitely recursive computations. They produce themselves.

As was said earlier, there are two solutions to the equation about letters, so that this kind of 'circularity' is not after all vacuous. Moreover, the notion that physical things are the stable states of chaotic processes, is not altogether at variance with modern physics.

The German mathematician, David Hilbert, known eponymously for the vector space that he defined some 100 years ago, coined mathematical terms starting with the prefix *eigen*, which is German for *self*, to handle self-reference as we begin to understand it here. Thus we may speak of eigen-functions, for example, and eigenvectors, and eigenvalues, where the functions, vectors, and values take their usual meanings, but in a self-referential domain. Let us see first of all what this means in practice. Choose any number (I pick 93 out of the air), and take its square root—let us say to two places of decimals. Here is the process, the performance of a recursive square-rooting machine:

$$93.00 \rightarrow 9.64 \rightarrow 3.11 \rightarrow 1.76 \rightarrow 1.33 \rightarrow 1.15 \rightarrow 1.07 \rightarrow 1.04 \rightarrow 1.02$$
$$\rightarrow 1.01 \rightarrow 1.00 \rightarrow 1.00$$

The series converges on 1.00, and is clearly going to stay there. Since the same thing happens regardless of the number chosen for the start, there must be something special about the process. It is that it reaches an equilibrium. Remember what happened with the von Foerster Op series. The integer one, 1.00, is in fact the eigenvalue of *the operation of a square root*. And the initial value disappears. Now, however, we are not left with nothing, but with a stable value that characterizes what is going on. It bears a lot of thought to consider that the eigenvalue is a better measure of 'reality' than the apparently real measure that began the process, or the toy trumpet of the example that *seems* to end it. Even more dramatically, Heinz von Foerster says (Foerster, 1977), 'In cognition and management it is the "reality" that is computed away by recursion.' Earlier in the book, the epistemological problem of universals in classical philosophy was mentioned, and these enquiries seem to bear upon it. I can think of redness independently of some thing that is red—or consider that I can. Is this redness the analogue of the eigenvalue of successive red-thing experiences? And is a 'successful company' the analogue of the eigenvalue of a long series of annual operations called 'publishing the balance sheet'?

In each respective case, cognition and management, the 'reality' of red this-and-thats and of the actual profit figures has indeed been 'computed away by recursion'—in favour of something that transcends the content of the denumerable set which underlies it. Perhaps this is also the explanation for the infosettic consciousness that was hypothesized as transcending the totality of member consciousness in a syntegration. In which case there are interesting questions to contemplate about the eigenvalues of the syntegral icosahedron, and we shall turn to those matters shortly.

Before doing so, however, and because of the journey we previously followed into space as distinct from linear series that may converge on eigenvalues, it may be useful to appreciate them in a wider context. Consider the diagram shown below, which derives from an example provided by Hugh Campbell (Campbell, 1968).

Starting with a familiar rectangle such as abcd, a certain linear transformation T is performed that has the effect of squashing it—let us say to the shape a'b'c'd'. The eigenvectors that define abcd are Oe and Oc. Under the transformation, vector Oc' becomes a scaler multiple of Oc, and vector Oe'

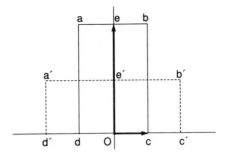

becomes a scaler multiple of Oe. Then the ratios of the determinants

$$\frac{|\,Oc'\,|}{|\,Oc\,|} \quad \text{and} \quad \frac{|\,Oe'\,|}{|\,Oe\,|}$$

are the eigenvalues under the prescribed transformation. The example is here only to let us see visually, rather than via the background matrix algebra, that this particular transformation has a *self-hood* that is invariant—however the squashing is done—because particular T-based equilibrial ratios are preserved. Perhaps the alternative terms for eigenvalues as characteristic or latent roods aids the visual impression of invariance in 2-D space. (Campbell himself prefers to use the term 'characteristic' for the vectors and values, remarking that *eigen* is the German word for *characteristic*. But we shall adhere to the translation 'self,' as being stronger, and to the German word as being unique in a way that the ordinary usage for 'characteristic' is not.)

It is the time for the final personal anecdote in the story-line behind these developments, as having some psychological interest. At some time during the 1960s I had a deep discussion with von Foerster. This is a note made on my return home to Britain. It is not likely to be misremembered, because it is still pinned to the window frame in front of the desk in the cottage in Ceredigion:

SELF-CONSCIOUSNESS

A number λ is an eigenvalue of a kernel $k(x, t)$
iff *e* function $y(x) \not\equiv 0$
such that

$$y(x) = \lambda \int_a^b k(x, t)y(t)\, dt$$

... λ is an ultimate terminal
$\therefore$ computes itself.

The opening statement is pure scene setting; but I think that the final two lines are directly quoted from Heinz. The wording became lapidary in effect. All the time that the syntegral icosahedron was in gestation, those lines were in the air ... it was a long time before the conscious connection through the notion of reverberation was made, and the idea was born that the model might in some sense be the map of a synergistic self-aware collegiate.

THE GRAPH-THEORETIC APPROACH

'Map' is a good word to use because, in mathematical terms, this model is a graph. When this whole invention was first presented to colleagues in the faculty of the European Business Management School of the University of Wales at Swansea, Dr Assad Jalali proposed to investigate it graph-theoretically. He devised an account of what he called my 'playful' graphs—because of the team element in what might be viewed as a management game (Jalali, 1993).

The properties of the syntegral icosahedral graph are expressed in terms of its components: edges (e), vertices (n), and valency, the number of edges subtended by each vertex, (k), by which it is fully connected.

First of all, the connected graph requires that the number of edges joined at each vertex is the same: then the graph is *k-regular*, and this implies that $kn = 2e$. In our own case, then, both sides are computed at 60.

However, the non-hierarchical structure of the graph corresponds to something much stronger than regularity, namely *symmetry*. In graph-theoretic terms, *automorphism* is entailed by this symmetry. The mathematical word, which means literally 'having the form of itself,' is pleasing to our developing insight into the nature of self-referential systems.

Jalali went straight on to include the critic role, the internal brace, in the graphical model. The implied equation is $n(n-2) = 4e$, and in our case, both sides are computed as 120.

Comparing the two equations, the third emerges: $n = 2(k+1)$, and the computed value is 12. However, what matters is not that the values validate the equations for the special case, but that the equations generalize the graph. It is shown that any graph conforming to the syntegral logic is determined by

$$kn = 2e \tag{13.1}$$

$$n(n - 2) = 4e \tag{13.2}$$

$$n = 2(k + 1) \tag{13.3}$$

It could be, after all, that the syntegration logic is not limited to the icosahedral graph that engendered it. There are higher dimensions of polyhedra, named polytopes, some of which might satisfy the threefold criteria. It is surely intellectually irksome, and tiresome in practice, to restrict syntegrations to 30-member infosets. An embedded enneagram has only 16 members, as elucidated in the last chapter; but that has only some of the properties of the full-scale graph.

With this encouraging thought, let us continue to explore the mathematical underpinnings. The graph is *transitive*, which means in the first place that any edge is replaceable by any other, and exhibits *opposition*, in that its vertices are arranged in pairs of poles. Thirdly comes the measure of distance, different from the golden phi value of distance, that counts the number of steps it takes to move from vertex to vertex. So the distance between adjacent vertices is measured as one. It is because all 30 such distances are of the same length that the graph is automorphic. The two-step distance has the value of phi, of course. The distance between the polar opposites is three, meaning that it takes three moves along edges to reach the opposite pole. The *diameter* of the graph is measured in terms of this number of moves, so that we speak of this graph as having diameter three. And that is to expose a stronger transitivity than that affecting merely edges. The automorphism of a square, for example, involves the mirror images of the triangles into which the square is divided by its diagonal. Even so, the square has a diameter of two, because it takes two steps to get from one corner to its opposite corner along the edges. The mathematician declares that the first non-trivial graph of our sort has diameter three (as has the icosahedron itself). Finally in this elaboration, we see from the polarity of our graph that its automorphism is *involutive*: the operation that moves distance three, applied twice, returns to itself. Moreover, the pole has maximum remoteness in the association scheme.

Summing up: the syntegral graph is symmetric, connected, of diameter 3, and exhibits involutive isomorphism around all six polar axes. Numerical values obey the three equations already cited.

Jalali went through the list by valency. Paraphrasing:

$k = 2$:   We have the hexagon: six players and six teams: perfect symmetric properties. But it has only two players per team, and therefore not many 'closure' properties—despite being closed—because it is only two-dimensional.

$k = 3$:   We have the cube. This represents a game with twelve players and eight teams. But there are only three players per team.

$k = 4$:   We have a rather unfamiliar graph with twenty edges and ten vertices: unfamiliar indeed.

$k = 5$:   This gives the icosahedron from which we started.

The 'Jalali List' is most interesting. The syntegral graph conditions evinced by the icosahedral model are not met by most of the Platonic Solids with which we started in Chapter One. The tetrahedron, octahedron, and dodecahedron are out. Note especially that the octahedron has diameter two, not three, and therefore attracts the label trivial. With hindsight, it is possible to connect this fact with the experience in California (Chapter Five), where the behaviour of the participants was atypical of icosahedral syntegrations: it seems that there may not have been sufficient psychosocial separation in the mathematical space provided.

Next, there is the discovery of the valency-4 figure that Jalali described casually as 'unfamiliar.' It was wholly new to me! The figure has eight triangular faces and four square faces, and therefore looks irregular. According to the graph-theoretic prescription, however, it is k-regular as required—and it also meets the other mathematical criteria. The logic has not specified that the *faces* should be transitive. Four of the polar axes are of the same physical length, being diagonals of the central cube, but the fifth is longer. Thus the physical model can be oriented in a number of different ways relative to floor and walls. Yet the figure still exhibits involutive automorphism about its polar axes. Then, perhaps, the infoset participant will not accept that s/he is involved in a fully democratic (as defined) space, even though s/he can be shown the mathematical demonstration that, in terms of relationships, it is so. On the other hand, to be pragmatic, the numbers work out conveniently. Twenty people discuss ten topics in teams of four. [Four critics are available per team under existing protocols (that is, the target team stands at distance two).] The possibilities here are surely worthy of thorough examination.

Even so, the mathematical investigation already suggests that there is something very special about the syntegral icosahedron—so much that it might be considered the first term in a possible series of syntegral graphs among the higher dimensions of polyhedra, the polytopes. Jalali has pointed to Paley graphs, in which the number of edges (and therefore the size of the infoset) is defined by the valency k times one more than itself [that is to say, $e = k(k + 1)$] for any integer n times four. The first integer is $n = 1$. Valency $k = 4n + 1 = 5$. Then the number of edges at $k(k + 1) = 5 \times 6 = 30$. This is the icosahedron. The series advances as follows:

Term n	$k = 4n + 1$	$e = k(k + 1)$		
1	4 + 1	5 × 6	=	30
2	8 + 1	9 × 10	=	90
3	12 + 1	13 × 14	=	182
4	16 + 1	17 × 18	=	306

and so on. The last regular polytope has 600 vertices, which would have 299 members per team and involve 90 000 people. There is also a relevant non-Paley graph, connected with projective geometries, with $35 \times 36 = 1260$ edges. Whether useful protocols could be developed for such large infosets is a matter for conjecture. Remember that the valency k gives the size of each topic team, and that number rapidly gets out of hand. By the seventh term in the Jalali series, and using 812 people, $k = (4 \times 7) + 1 = 29$ team members, so each of the 12 teams could operate as an icosahedral syntegration. So far, we have talked about aggregates of icosahedra, in which a hypericosahedron is defined as an icosahedron of which each member (edge) has previously undergone a syntegration on the same topic. Looking at the situation as a reduction of a Paley graph would have the same practical protocol, but instead of saying that $30 \times 30 = 900$ people had been engaged to produce second-stage results, we should point to a connected syntegral graph with $29 \times 30 = 870$ (edges) people, whose teams consisted of 12 icosahedra.

It is an open question as to how large numbers can best be dealt with: an epidemiology for the spread of syntegral icosahedra in global society is needed. It could be postulated on a viral model of discrete breeding units, or looked at as some vast molecule (compare buckminsterfullerene) or a polypeptide chain. All that it is necessary to establish here, from the perspective of world governance, is that new global networks of appropriate scale can in principle and should in practice be developed.

Now, however, we should return to the basic icosahedral syntegration on the understanding that this is happening over time within a populated (by people!) eigenspace. We fully understand that the *information* that will finally condense into the 12 Consolidated Statements of Importance is buzzing and humming around the eigenspace continually from first to last. A 'snapshot' of this immensely complicated interpersonal interaction is, however, obtained at the conclusion of each iteration.

When the syntegration begins, no information has passed. The eigenspace is described by its eigenvectors (recall the Hugh Campbell exercise with rectangles) which resolve into an underlying eigenvalue of the operation of the syntegral graph. This, like the square root operation, can be shown to have an underlying eigenvalue of 1.00. However, because of the population of people who are graphical *associates*, there are other eigenvalues: plus and minus one divided by the square root of five. The negative value does not interest us: attention then focuses on the eigenvalue $1/\sqrt{5}$. The reappearance among all the ones and twos of the square root of five is what strategists used to call a 'surprise free scenario.' To understand exactly how it arises, however, the matrix algebra of the graph-theoretic treatment of association schemes with opposition (see Part Five, Surplus One) has to be tackled. Otherwise, take the value on trust.

Because we are dealing with an informational process, it is best to consider what happens by starting from one particular vertex (although the same is true of all) which is determined by 12 eigenvectors. As soon as the syntegration starts, the information generated there begins to *spread*. After only one iteration, that information is divided between ten of the remaining vertices via members and critics, and something will immediately be known at the polar opposite vertex, because Aggregated Statements of Importance are then published. Now there is no means of knowing how much information has arrived where: it is spreading by a stochastic process that can be discussed only in terms of probability theory. Since the process is symmetric, the probabilities are evenly spread, and after a number of iterations will tend to equality. That is, the information will be evenly distributed everywhere—precisely by the process that we have been calling reverberation. This paragraph defines just such a process as mathematical statisticians call *ergodic*. Over time, and independently of the initial position from which it starts, the process finds a limiting form. The square root operation is ergodic, and so is that of the syntegral graph.

Once syntegration starts, then, from the standpoint of the original vertex chosen, other eigenvalues arise within the eigenspace, and these are responsible for pushing information outwards towards an equal spread, towards informational homogeneity—which the infosetter calls the process of Outcome Resolve. And the same kind of process, though not the same set of transitional probabilities, applies to each vertex.

Thanks to the ergodic property, then, and the structural symmetry of the graph, the eigenvectors are constantly changing value (as with the Campbell rectangles), but the eigenvalue is a scale constant. The speed of the process of entropy that evens out the information depends upon the size of the eigenvalue: its absolute value for homogeneity is the *minimum* to which reverberation can take it.

Iteration can now be understood in terms of ergodicity, as the number of episodes of syntegration that are needed to approximate the eigenvalue to its minimal value. The function that defines the entropy of information is

$$y = \left(\frac{1}{\sqrt{5}}\right)^n$$

where n is the number of iterations. So, after the first iteration, for $n = 1$, the eigenvalue has its original measure, which is 0.45. After the second iteration, the function is squared, and it becomes 0.20 (these results are taken to only two places of decimals). The whole graph of the function is shown in Figure 13.1.

Obviously this function is asymptotic: entropy steadily increases, but will never reach zero. However, after six iterations, information in the network is

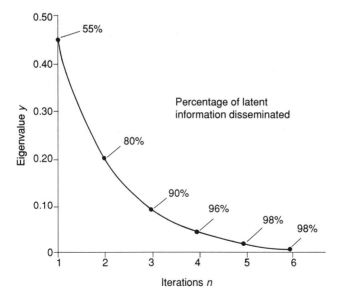

Figure 13.1 Syntegrity iterations. Eigenvalue $y = 1/\sqrt{5}$ for n iterations

99% homogeneous. This is measured by the fall in the eigenvalue to a minimum. The latent energy of the informational system has almost been used up.

From an information-theoretic standpoint, this assumes adequate channel capacity in the communications system, and requisite variety in transduction between individuals. It follows that the scheduling protocol for a syntegration is of vital importance: the capacity of the syntegral graph to resolve the outcome through homogeneous insight must not be compromised by shortages of time or facilitation. Evidently, this warning is especially relevant for any computerized, networked syntegration, and much research is needed to establish appropriate 'electronic protocol.'

In the meantime, a mathematical result of high importance has been established in the curve just exhibited. We should like to know the optimal number of iterations that a syntegration needs. One episode has only 55% resolving power; two episodes takes us to 80% of the ideal, which is not too bad. With three episodes, the Outcome Resolve is 90% effective. Hence the question arises, given the cost in time, of whether further iterations are justified. Working backwards from the virtual perfection of six iterations, it is surely impracticable to make another episodic investment after five, merely to achieve a 1% improvement. Even four iterations reach 96% effectiveness; surely that is a reasonable cut-off point to use. Maybe 90% is enough ...

Consult the empirical findings. After three iterations, about half of the people questioned considered that it would be worthwhile (if time were available) to iterate again. It seems that this is the equilibrial answer in most people's (averaged) expectations. But there is a non-mathematical reason for staying with three episodes. There is no allowance within the equations for sheer empathy among participants. The mathematical model considers only the formal properties of the syntegral graph. The experiments showed that participants luxuriate in the potency of the technique: the psycho-social process verges on the euphoric. There is experimental reason to think, therefore, that syntegration is more efficient than the model predicts. Three iterations are enough.

EPILOGUE

Chapter Fourteen

THE CONCEPT OF RECURSIVE CONSCIOUSNESS

ANOTHER STORY BEGINS

Warren McCulloch was nearly 30 years older than I, and I was about that age when we first met. It soon became obvious that I had closely recapitulated his early intellectual life, although his training had been formal whereas I was largely self-taught. In my teens I had set down this statement: 'There is only one mystery: why or how is there anything?' It seemed clear to me that if this mystery could be solved, the universe would necessarily follow, in all its complexity. But soon another clause was added: 'And whence comes this question?' Small wonder that (see Chapter Thirteen) I was soon worrying about Russell's assertion sign, and am still worrying today over the nature of consciousness. Warren responded with his own story: how, 30 years before me, he had proposed to his tutor, a Quaker philosopher: 'There is just one question I would like to answer. What is a number that a man may know it, and a man, that he may know a number?' We suspected, I think, that our two questions were much the same question. At any rate, I was happy to share in his delight in the Quaker's reply, and also to accept it for myself: 'Friend, thee will be busy as long as thee lives.'

Warren finally wrote an address under the heading of this question (McCulloch, 1960) and sent me the script. Typically, he ranges over the history of philosophy, delves into his own work on probabilistic logic, and ends with a formidable equation. It includes the Quaker story, of course, explaining that 'all impersonal questions arise from personal reasons and are best understood from their histories,' and denying that his stories are due to reaching 'what Oliver Wendell Holmes would call our anecdotage.' He told the Quaker story again in an article published posthumously, 5 years after his death, thus making a special impact on me. It was called 'Recollections of the Many

Sources of Cybernetics' (McCulloch, 1974), which is again anecdotal and autobiographic, and is offered with similar justification. In this paper McCulloch confesses that it took him from 1920 to 1964 to learn how to count the spirals in a pine cone properly, because of confusions between left- and right-hand sets of spirals. He finally resolved matters by painting one set green and the other set red. I recalled his concern with this problem when writing Chapter Eleven, in which I lightly bestowed the information that a pine cone's spirals follow the Fibonacci Series! Warren was very taken with the fact that nature knew how to do this, whereas it had taken him so long to master the trick.

In following my mentor's example in the use of anecdote, I consider that I have special justification in this chapter. First, I must acknowledge intellectual debts to him which are difficult to make precise. His publications record *post facto* intellectual adventures that I shared through the osmosis of friendship, and especially through extremely elaborate conversations that often involved violent disagreements. But, as he has written, we must learn 'to fight fair in our shirtsleeves.' Second, my purpose now is to convey personal insights that have scientific bases the interpretation of which is disputable, in a sense in which the main book's report of research and mathematical analysis is not disputable. This essay is kept separate from the exposition of team syntegrity itself because of this. Nor can a synoptic treatment of current theories of consciousness be attempted here.

Such theories come from many directions, and all deserve study. Let me mention especially the approach from cognitive science (Varela *et al.*, 1991), from computer science (Winograd and Flores, 1986), from mathematical logic (Devlin, 1991), from mathematical physics (Penrose, 1989), from philosophy (McGinn, 1991), and from quantum physics (Zohar, 1991). Each of these books is recent, but they pay little heed to either the neurocybernetics or its associated epistemology on which consciousness (whatever it is) depends. This is a loss in each case, and a severe loss in the last two works cited. Perhaps the original cybernetic work is too old to be respectable, or maybe it is too young and original to have been assimilated yet.

Fortunately, however, there is another recent book that sets out the whole story as I would have the subject approached. Its authors represent respectively anthropology, psychology and cognitive science, and psychiatry (Laughlin *et al.*, 1990). It is highly recommended.

Having made these obeisances and explanations, I proceed on my idiosyncratic path.

THE CENTRAL IMPORTANCE OF RECURSIVITY

The principle of recursion has been invoked throughout this book. Loosely expressed, it looks at systems embedded within each other, like so many Russian dolls, each of which has a unique identity, despite the embedment. Now the dolls are not physically connected beyond their mere embedment, and mostly we confront embedments where there are other physical connections than that. Although such arrangements involve various sorts of dependence, they do not necessarily imply hierarchical dependence in the command–obedience sense, nor compromise the integrity of the included identity. A capacitor in a radio, a piston in an engine, a rabbit in a wood, and a star in a galaxy are all examples of embedded identities. But the question of relationships is not a trivial one. Hegel's axiom of internal relations reminds us that the relations by which terms are related are an integral part of the terms they relate. Already we are speaking about terms rather than things themselves; and even the physical Russian doll Q cannot be itself if it is not both larger than the P it contains and smaller than the R that contains it.

As embodied in the Viable System Model, the principle of recursion asserts that all viable systems contain, and are contained in, viable systems. This is by no means loosely expressed: it is rigorously determined by the Law of Cohesion in VSM theory. In this, however, recursion entails that *all* systems that are contained are themselves viable. This is like pointing out that one Russian doll could be entombed with a toy mouse, and another with a pebble. The recursivity of the dolls has nothing to do with the presence or absence of associated mice and pebbles. As a result, it is easy to propose an embedment of recursions that leads to a non-viable system. That says nothing about the principle, so long as there are other recursive embedments that do continue the chain of viable systems.

Critics of the VSM habitually fall into this logical trap. They point in triumph at an included system within a viable system that is manifestly not viable, as if its mere existence invalidated the principle of recursion. Those who have studied the VSM well know that its origins lay in my early attempts (1950s) to model the human nervous system mathematically. People are so accustomed to defending their own integrity as individuals in a spirit of ego-attachment that they are reluctant to imagine that the embedment of viable systems that entails their own selves from their families, forbears and so on back, does not stop finally and conclusively with ME. This ME includes a hat. So is my hat supposed to be viable in itself? Ha ha.

After I had written *Brain of the Firm* (Beer, 1972) and *The Heart of Enterprise* (Beer, 1979), my distinguished colleague Professor John F. Morris speculated that I might next write *The Big Toe of Business*. His thoughtful article and the joke were well taken; but many others have missed the point. There is no reason why a toe should be a viable system and capable therefore of independent existence. That is because although it is a recognizable and included entity, it does not comply with the VSMs criteria of viability. It is not a System One. It so happens that I am writing these words in hospital while awaiting the amputation of a toe, and I expect to confirm the hypothesis. The circumstance says more for Jung's views on Synchronicity than for my devotion to science. (PS. Hypothesis confirmed: toe maintains identity in labelled bottle, but is strictly non-viable.)

The ME that I set out to investigate is not the irreducible armour-plated ego, who struts on the world stage even when sitting down, but a community of cells. These cells are highly differentiated (despite the commonality of their DNA component); they are self-organizing; they are self-sustaining; they are often but not always self-reproducing. They are eukaryote cells, having a nucleus bound by a membrane that contains the genetic blueprint; and naturally it was exciting when (some 20 years ago) a colleague, Dr Richard Foss, showed me how the VSM mapped on to the eukaryote cell. So this was the ultimate viable system, and the differentiation process showed how groups of cells collaborated to form organs—precisely because they share the appropriate information: they are (by our definitions) infosettic. Moreover, they are organized into embedments of viable systems.

Given that my cybernetic focus of attention was the regulation of the whole body effected by the nervous system, the VSM embedments moved down from the whole-body recursion (with its Systems Five, Four, Three lodged in the brain itself, and its Two and Three Star represented by the sympathetic and parasympathetic autonomic systems) to neural assemblages (betokening Systems One) such as those regulating the solar plexus, or functions such as respiration, or modalities such as sleep, sex, and the fight/flight response. But if the ultimate viable system is the cell, in the case of the nervous system we are talking about neurons—all ten thousand million of them, organized into recursive communities of infosettic character, and all in being (although not yet fully organized) by the 18th week of gestation of the human being.

THE NEURON, REDUNDANCY, AND DISBELIEF

How do we see the neuron itself? Or, to share in this history as revelatory, how did we see the neuron? In the 1950s, I knew for sure that neuronal transfers must entail at the least an input transducer, a switch, a (minimally) one-shot memory, an output transducer, and an amplifier to boost the transmitted signal. From the engineering standpoint, an artefact could use a solenoid as a switch (transistors existed, but were grossly unreliable). I built such an electro-mechanical device, which was nearly the size of a shoebox, and recall a euphoric conversation with Heinz von Foerster in which we realized that an electromechanical brain consisting of ten billion shoeboxes would cover the English county of Yorkshire. A little later (1956), however, I had a Feranti Pegasus computer, one of the very first to be marketed, and could install the logical equivalent of the electro-mechanical neuron—programming McCulloch–Pitts neural networks out of such individuals. The computer itself used valves (vacuum tubes in US parlance) as switches, so at least the mechanical had left the electro-mechanical system, and things were faster. The Pegasus was programmed in machine language to undertake this kind of research; it was possibly the most expensive space heater ever invented.

It was already clear, however, that neurons were more than switches of this kind, even though they certainly switched. The startling fact is that tens of thousands of dendrites impinge on the soma of any single neuron—some offering excitation and some inhibition. Thus the concept of the neuron as a 'majority organ' was derived. The axon was supposed to fire if the former numbered more than the latter. But the biochemistry is so complicated and the biophysics so minuscule that the proposed digital machine looked more and more like an analogue machine. John von Neumann did many of the sums in the 1950s (Beer, 1959), but the truly seminal paper had been published, incredibly enough in 1943 (McCulloch and Pitts, 1943). It was the first of Warren's papers that I ever read, and was entitled 'A logical calculus of the ideas immanent in nervous activity.'

It is often forgotten by those invoking McCulloch–Pitts neural networks that they were founded not only on Walter Pitts's brilliant mathematical analysis, but on Warren's meticulous empirical experimentation. For instance, this paper revealed that the period of latent addition, during which a neuron may respond to impulses crossing from thousands of neighbouring synapses, lasts for less than one quarter of a millisecond. The concern here is no more than to show that some subtleties of the brain have been understood for half a century to the point that makes some contemporary writing (in Artificial Intelligence, for instance) look absurd. We are often confronted with metaphors picturing the brain as a computerized telephone exchange. And now that we have left solenoids behind, and vacuum tubes, and are finally into solid-state technology, it is all too easy to think of the brain as a network of chips which are, after all, networks of a different recursion themselves. But if you give a glass of wine to a computer you will not change any firing thresholds, and neurocybernetics was dealing with that problem all those years ago. Incidentally, it is more than 20 years since I wrote in *Brain of the*

Firm (Beer, 1972), 'the transfer function of a neuron is an eighth-order non-linear differential equation, in which all the variables are subject to subtle changes on the microsecond scale.' I had this from McCulloch, of course, but did not say so. I was in those days too embarrassed to record that when I had asked him if 'eighth-order' was significant he said, 'Of course it is, you idiot. I couldn't get more than eight electrodes into a single Purkinje cell.' Science is made like this—imperfectly, yes, but also under the constant need to be rediscovered (as will be illustrated shortly).

Such was the neuron that I contemplated in the 1950s. It was immensely complicated, even though logics based on simplifications of this complexity were yielding plausible results, particularly as to reliability. It was better thought about as analogue rather than digital, better viewed as probabilistic rather than deterministic. As a result, concatenations of unreliable neuronal components could be made to generate arbitrarily reliable outcomes thanks to redundant probabilistic logics.

The nervous system protects itself against the shocking unreliability of its component neurons by composing them into redundant networks: the brain may well be redundant in the order of 20 000 to 1. This is necessary because the firing threshold of a neuron changes under all manner of circumstances: that single glass of wine, for example, will affect millions of neurons arbitrarily distributed over the cortex—and in any case it is estimated that 100 000 neurons simply burn out every day. This situation and its practical solution is extensively discussed in Chapter Fourteen of *Brain of the Firm* (Beer, 1972).

So far, so good: we were able to automate a mill rolling steel rods, in Rotherham, Yorkshire, which never once suffered a breakdown or made any sort of error, and despite invited sabotage, as long ago as 1958. People came from all over the world to see it; but in Bristol in 1993 it was still impossible to convince engineers of the cybernetic facts that underwrite critical safety systems. It comes down to this: how could increasing the number of unreliable components possibly improve the reliability of the whole? The idea is patently absurd. But I should like to push the orthodox objector off a cliff, and catch him/her in a rotten net with an alarming 30% chance that it would break. I should, however, provide a succession of a hundred rotten nets on the way down, and not much fear a charge of murder ...

In the meantime, in a consulting role, I made several attempts to convince NASA that the concept of 'zero defect' was unscientific and impractical. Specifically: by increasing the regulatory payload by a factor of three, protection through redundant logics would increase reliability 1000-fold. But the whole focus of attention at NASA was the huge cost in dollars of accelerating every gram of payload to escape velocity: they were not about to 'waste' dollars on redundant hardware. After the success of Apollo Thirteen, and despite some tragedy, the whole Apollo programme had to be acknowledged as a triumph with congratulations and unfeigned joy. But the notion of 'zero defect' itself remains implausible 25 years later. Experience in 1993 has been gravely flawed.

Once more in this chapter, Synchronicity attains to high visibility. Yesterday (as I write) the billion-dollar Mars Observer spacecraft disappeared, doomed (NASA has announced) 'by a broken transistor in a small but crucial clock.' So much for the neurocybernetics of the 1950s. But consider this reaction quoted in today's newspaper from the Director of Aerospace and Science Policy for the American Institute of Aeronautics and Astronautics: 'This is a real management and image problem for Martin-Marietta' (the owners). Quite so; and equivalently placed officials are making equivalent diagnoses for equally fatal diseases in education, and in health, not to mention the economy itself. 'We are not getting our message through to the public,' those responsible say. The message is perfectly clear, sadly enough. It is not that we need to work harder and pay more for ineffectual policies, but that the policies themselves need to be changed. This means existing paradigms have to change first, and that any new discovery has to be made repeatedly for perhaps half a century before it seeps into Establishment consciousness.

HOMEOSTASIS AND ULTRASTABILITY

One of the experiences that had great impact on my thinking about the neuron was viewing short pieces of a film (it might have been Roger Sperry who made and screened it) showing a neuronal synapse actually firing: it brought home the fact that we are dealing with a *living* system. It was not as though I lacked respect for the tiny beast—with its intricate neuronal logic manipulating complicated mathematical functions, with its evident capacity to compute in stochastic processes, with its biochemistry that involves packets of transmitter substance containing only 10 000 molecules crossing a synaptic cleft that is only 1/50 000th of a millimetre wide (see Beer, 1972, for more details). No: what made it all come alive was the way the machinery physically moved. When the axon fired, the nerve processes jerked away from the soma of the neuron, much enlarging the synaptic cleft, and thereby making it that much more difficult to cross. They recoiled as if shocked through the net effect of the electrical discharges. Obviously the neuron would need time to recover before it could fire again. I knew this to be true: the 'refractory period' was perfectly well documented. But to witness a physically lively response was somehow different from knowing the consequential scientific facts. Here was a switch that manifestly responded to its own activity. It had an identity that recognized an environment, and it changed its own physical structure depending on what was going on. It was *learning* in some sense. And if the individual neuron was alive and learning, what could be expected of concatenations of neurons at other levels of recursion? We were a long way from the solenoid in the shoebox now ...

Life: its biological purpose seemed to be survival—Darwin had taught us that much. Nineteenth century intellect was dominated by the science–theology debate about purpose; but (whatever the theological outcome) the survival of the fittest became accepted scientific fact in one form or another, and whatever the recursion—since the survival of the species was contingent on the survival of the propagating individual. In the middle of the century came notification of the key mechanism that could sustain life towards survival: Claude Bernard's homeostasis, as it was later called by Walter Cannon in his famous work (Cannon, 1929). The early cyberneticians knew all about this, and they knew much more after Ross Ashby had meticulously investigated the process. Indeed, he 'designed a brain' around this one fundamental concept (Ashby, 1952). My friendship with him began soon afterwards and influenced me greatly. In particular, this extraordinary intellect constantly generated extravagantly imaginative ideas—and then enquired into them with a surgical precision that could be infuriatingly pernickety. He died in 1972.

Some readers will find this perfunctory account of 100 years' worth of biology nugatory, especially as much more has happened in neurocybernetics during the last 20 years. The story to be explained, however, has again needed its proper context, because that last 20 years have also witnessed the vitiation of the most important of Ashby's ideas about survival worthiness. It is called ultrastability. And it was directly implicated in the invention discussed in the next section.

Homeostasis means (literally, from the Greek roots) staying the same— stationary. Thus the basic idea is that when some critical variable becomes disturbed by environmental perturbation, a 'homeostatic' mechanism will return it to its equilibrial state. The notion is supported in particular by the secondary notion of error-controlled negative feedback: deviation from the norm is to be detected, and changes made in the inputs to the system to effect the required result. A perfect example of a homeostat thus conceived is a room thermostat. We set the temperature we prefer, and the fuel supply is adjusted to keep the thermometer steady. This already proposes a variety of technological problems, as anyone who owns a thermostat knows. Maybe it is wrongly positioned; maybe it is insensitive; maybe it is over-sensitive, and starts to 'hunt'—to oscillate. But the technology to handle such problems is well understood, even if the householder finds it too costly to buy. The biological version, however, is at once more challenging. No-one has discovered a thermostat in a Briton preset to 98.4 °F, or in an American for some reason differently set to 98.6 °F. The body obviously regulates itself—and without actual thermometers—to stay within fairly close limits of temperature regardless of extreme outside variations. If it does not succeed, it dies. This not only illustrates why survival-worthiness has appeared to be the outstanding biological criterion: it establishes that the body can recognize its own physiological limits of performance. They do not have to be pre-set.

The power of this idea was immediately transferable to social systems and in particular to managerial situations. Who said that return on investment 'ought to be' $x\%$? Who said that costs must be cut 'across the board' by $y\%$? Both the phrases in quotes are entirely unphysiological—they are not generated by internal criteria of limit, but are imposed by authority. They are approximations to the real needs of the system, and these in turn are variable within it. I pressed this objection, and the cybernetic solutions suggested by biological homeostasis, very strongly during the 1950s (Beer, 1959, especially), and with considerable practical success.

There was, however, much criticism on the following lines. Maybe biological systems are primarily concerned to survive, said the managerial critics; but management is not concerned with stasis, with keeping still, it is concerned with progress: more output, cheaper production, and so forth—with higher profits.

And so operational research became preoccupied with maximization, assuming that managers knew exactly what to maximize, and over what term. This unjustified assumption led to much difficulty. For example, managers who were screaming for maximum pay-off in the minimum time were surprised to be told to sell the assets and split the proceeds. That was not, they said testily, what they meant. Management scientists proceeded to offer more subtle approaches: 'satisficing' replaced maximizing, for instance; but this begins to look like promoting stasis again ... Never mind, perhaps; whatever the powers-that-be may say, they are overwhelmingly in favour of the status quo when the societary chips are down, because they have all manner of investment in it—and much to lose by change.

Echoes of these long-standing arguments still reverberate, long after the debate missed the key cybernetic point and went rushing forward into the dogmatism that bedevils the managerial scene today. This point was that biological homeostasis is not, after all, concerned with absolute stasis in any case. It is a learning system that evolves heuristically. If the homeostat fixes its own physiological limits as a result of its experience, then as its experience evolves over time, its handling of its own criteria of survival will evolve to accommodate that experience. All biological homeostats are learning systems. Of course it is as absurd to complain that no 'learning circuit' has been found as it would be to contend that the body cannot actually regulate its temperature because it contains no encapsulated thermometer. Both capabilities, included in the concept of *physiological* limits, are functions of the behaviour of the viable system at every level of recursion. It must be that the homeostat itself evolves through self-organizing ability—if the organism is to survive. Then the critics' complaint that using survival-worthiness as a criterion results in a stasis that makes survival impossible is paradoxical in the extreme.

A device that seeks equilibrium in the face of expected perturbation, that is perturbation already familiar from experience, is capable of stability. But a device that can adapt to unexpected perturbation, insofar as the new perturbation is outside the range of familiar experience, is capable of *ultrastability*. This was Ashby's major discovery about homeostasis, and it is not generally understood or even known.

Here is a simple mechanical image to illustrate this vitally important distinction. We have a machine tool robot residing in a building that is known to be a fire hazard. Therefore, we fit the robot with an engine, and equip it with a thermometer. If the temperature rises to a dangerous level, the doors open automatically, the engine is switched on, and the machine tool robot trundles out of the endangered building. This system is a homeostat that can maintain equilibrium in the face of anticipated disturbance: it exhibits stability. Now consider a machine tool robot that resides in a normal building in which fire hazards are unexceptional The robot has an engine but no thermometer. Unfortunately, the building becomes a raging inferno. The machine tool robot melts. But suppose instead that a cybernetician has installed a test program inside the machine tool robot that continuously undertakes complex tasks and verifies its own satisfactory performance. Fire breaks out, and the temperature rises. The robot does not know this: it has no heat sensors and it cannot smell the smoke. But it begins to get wrong answers to its test programs—as it would if there were an earthquake or if an unauthorized person began to interfere with its programming. Such a machine is ultrastable. It is designed on the model of a biological homeostat.

THE ALGEDONODE

Starting again from the primary level of the neuron, we need to conceive of an heuristic switch. The shoebox logic still applies (input and output transduction, switching device, one-shot storage, transmission amplifier) as necessary—but it is certainly not sufficient. Nor can it be made sufficient by analytic means: that is, no algorithm can be specified to adapt to unknown inputs directly. The algorithm the neuron contains must specify the *homeostatic heuristic* that yields an ultrastable outcome. The neuron must be organized to respond to its own environment, and then to fire according to a set of probabilities. Suppose the outcome of an initially random firing is favourable to the neuron's performance (which means successful adaptation to the neuronal environment), then the probability of firing within this pattern of inputs will be reinforced; if not, the probability of firing will be diminished.

However, as we have seen, such a decision system is utilitarian: there is no rationale, no theory about unknowns, no attempt to explain. There is only the rule: reinforce success, extinguish failure. And the means for doing this is to modify the probabilities of firing versus not firing, according to experience gained in performing successfully within the closed neuronal environment, through positive or negative regulatory feedback. It was natural, particularly in the scientific milieu of the 1950s and 1960s, to use behavioural labels to describe this neuron. It can be thought of as a reward and punishment system; it can be thought of as responding to pain and pleasure. Thus I called this model neuron *algedonic* (*algos* = pain, *hedos* = pleasure), and dubbed it an algedonode. The first one was built out of a roulette wheel, to supply the random element in the heuristic design, and the sensorium consisted of brass plates acting as electrical contacts mounted on a wooden insulator. Activity was monitored by a pair of lights, red and green. Figure 14.1 demonstrates how it works. Note that the four slides shown on the left represent only one slide, but illustrate four of its possible alternative settings about to be described.

Spinning the wheel represents the creation of a neuronal environment. The probabilities shown in Figure 14.1 at Case One are set so that there is an equal chance of the outcome being red or green. Say that green is lit, representing a 'successful' result. Then the wooden strip moves down one place, so that contact X, which rested on brass plate A, now rests on brass plate B. That is Case Two. Then, at the next spin of the wheel, the chance that the outcome will be 'successful' has risen to 60 : 40. And so on. Hence the algedonics work by collecting contacts on to plate B in rewarding the green light; and, oddly enough, exactly the same thing happens if the algedonode is punished for showing a red light. That is because the computation is zero-sum: if we subtract contacts from plate A we automatically add them to plate B.

This algedonode adapts rapidly, of course, but an interesting provision has to be added. A mechanical stop on the sliding wooden panel operates to prevent

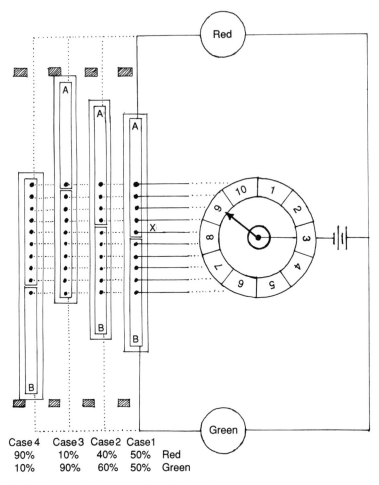

Figure 14.1 Schematic diagram of an algedonode

all the contacts from arriving on either plate A or plate B, as we see in Cases Three and Four. At least one contact must remain on either plate. Were this not so, the algedonode would become fully conditioned, and no longer capable of learning if circumstances changed. It is impossible to reinforce a response that can no longer occur. That means to say that if the definition of 'successful' ceases to be appropriate, the algedonode must be able to register the other criterion. This provision is the very essence of biological homeostasis and the secret of ultrastability.

The single algedonode so far described, like the single neuron, takes a single binary decision. Both the nervous system and managerial societies do, however, make more elaborate decisions, which I simulated as a pattern of eight binary outputs. The complex algedonode competent to generate this pattern of red and green lights was arranged as an interconnected array of 32 elements. Eight columns selected the pattern of eight lights, and each of the four rows received a separate environmental input from its own roulette wheel. Decisions taken algedonically by each row were used to halve the probabilities of the row in the next rank—culminating in the fourth row's decision to halve the probabilities attaching to the lighting of each red or green light by switching on one of the two. Then, of course, the algedonic responses embodied in the slide mechanisms were used to make the whole unit learn whatever eightfold response might be appropriate. Neurophysiologically, the machine was conceived as a model of a concatenation of cells such as a ganglion, a network of neurons constituting a subsidiary nerve centre. Managerially speaking, it modelled four 'ranks' of management reaching a complex decision, but coping *independently* with the issues pertinent to each rank at the same time. Thus the ganglionic algedonode is 'successful' in two separate dimensions: it is ultrastable at each level of management; it is ultrastable with respect to the corporate outcome. The whole machine is described in detail in *Brain of the Firm* (Beer, 1972), Chapter Five. Note that a device of this comparative simplicity is able to recognize and reinforce 256 different output patterns. Evidently this design is not constrained by the actual numbers used. There could be a 100 contacts instead of 10. Moreover, the slides do not have to move in discrete and equal steps. If we had a large, unspecified number of contacts, and if the slide moved in randomly spaced increments, the representation would be much closer to the neurophysiological fact.

We are left with the problem of suspiciously teleological language. The word 'successful' was placed in quotation marks because it implies a purpose; and if the purpose is to survive, then *which* embedded system (the individual neuron, the ganglion, the brain, the person, the family, the species) is the cynosure of survival, and over what *period* (this event, this week, this lifetime, this generation) is the survival-worthiness to be accounted? Above all, who or what is making these teleological judgements? Logical closure is the hallmark of viable systems. The closure includes the environment. In the case of the algedonode, it is the environment that attributes value to redness and greenness: the neuron *qua* switch responds to that value. But this statement simply pushes the dilemma one stage back. It seems that the value is imported from outside—in which case there seems to be a hierarchy after all. Not so: there is a nesting, a set of embedments; but these help to determine environments—they are not necessarily autocratic, although they may be so in the limiting case. That simply means that if anyone's environment includes someone with a gun who is saying, 'hands up,' then the survival motive prescribes obedience. It cannot be inferred from this single event that we are living in a fascist state. The problems of embedments and their particular values are more complicated than this.

HEURISTIC HIERARCHY VERSUS HETERARCHY

Consider the following set of embedments. It is chosen from the social rather than the neurophysiological domain, because this makes it easier to discuss in terms of reward. But the neurophysiological argument is the same, *mutatis mutandis*.

The algedonode *qua switch* has no preference between the colours that constitute its output. But its environment includes someone who holds an aesthetic preference for red, and therefore facilitates activity when the red light is lit. The likelihood that the outcome will be red begins to rise. But this aesthetic milieu is embedded in a financial milieu in which green light is worth four times as much money as red light. A financial wizard proposes to the aesthete that (despite his personal preference for red) he should begin to reinforce the green outcome. 'I shall split the proceeds with you' gloats the financial wizard. The aesthete does not understand this language at all: he has no interest in money. The financial wizard therefore manipulates the situation so that the aesthete finds life uncomfortable. Hooligans bang on his doors and break his windows—except, he notices, when the green light happens to be shining ... He finds it best to facilitate green outputs after all. Naturally, the financial wizard pockets all the proceeds herself.

'The desire for food,' explains a gourmand who has read Maslow to a gourmet who has not, 'is stronger than you think. Here's a bet. You see this financial workaholic striving like mad to make the green light shine? I have offered her all the food she can eat, free, for six months to let us have a nice burst of red.' But the gourmand was mistaken. The financial wizard lived on snacks and diet powder, and was interested only in her bank account. So the gourmand, to win his bet, had to unload all his stocks into her specialized market segment, and the red frequency began to increase. However, a philosopher, interested in the ethics of the betting confraternity ... You will not wish me to continue.

Each subsystem 'speaks its own language,' which is not comprehended by the embedded subsystem. The primary switch in the social example is as far removed from those ethical considerations that subtly influence its environmental closure as the neuron is removed from the cerebral cortex. The environment that partakes of the closure of the algedonode is highly complicated, and it cannot be analysed because the embedments that are relevant from event to neuronal event are not unique or reproducible. They are anastomotic: that means that they branch out in every direction so that relevant embedments cannot be isolated or even traced. No-one can say by what route through a river delta a cupful of water arrived in the ocean ...

These experiments in algedonics disclose the distinction between systemic embedment and hierarchic organization to the full. Hierarchy means government by priests: it is a central fact of sacerdotal organization that every level of authority commands all of the levels lower down. The pope has authority over the parishioner in addition to the bishop and the priest. Other social organizations have followed suit. The general has authority over the enlisted soldier in addition to the colonel and the sergeant. The office boy had better not make cheeky remarks to the corporation president when he passes in the corridor either ...

Viable systems are not of this kind in the biological domain, and in particular the neurophysiological domain. According to the Viable System Model, which is also organized as a set of embedments, social systems should not be conceived of hierarchically either—despite the church and the army and the corporation. So if nests of embedments are not hierarchical in this sense of transitive command, what other adjective can be applied? The antithesis to hierarchy, government by priests, is sometimes said to be heterarchy—which means (O.E.D.) 'the rule of an alien.' *Hetero* means other or different; and the regulatory systems of different levels of embedment are indeed alien to each other as the example illustrated. 'They do not speak the same language.'

Many years before the invention of the algedonic computer, McCulloch had investigated (McCulloch, 1945; 1989, volume 2, pp. 467–471) the logic of a fascinating problem in values. It seems to happen, yet how is it possible, that situations occur where A is preferred to B, B to C, but C is preferred to A. This, he proved, meant that hierarchies of values do not exist. He proceeded mathematically. A hierarchy of values entails that values are magnitudes of some kind, and to maintain consistency of preference the irreducible nervous net computing them would have to map on a plane. He showed that this topological mapping is impossible without crossing over from one neural circuit to another non-adjacent circuit, thereby (in effect) leaving the plane surface. And this betrays the principles of magnitude. In his summary, he says, 'the apparent inconsistency of preference is shown to indicate consistency of *an order too high* to permit construction of a scale of values.' Those are my italics: the whole argument seems to bear significantly on the concept of consciousness, for I argue that consciousness involves the heterarchical (in this precise sense) transcendence of embedment. 'Experimental aesthetics, economics, and conditioned reflexology have produced instances in which, under constant conditions, preference was circular. One such instance would have been sufficient basis for categorical denial of the subsumption that values were magnitudes of any one kind. Thus, for values there can be no common scale.' So McCulloch, in 1945: value structures are heterarchic, and not hierarchic (as defined).

I have not used this terminology myself and shall not do so again, partly because its introduction into the literature has not seemed very helpful: the putative antithesis between hierarchy and heterarchy lacks precision. Michael Arbib, an eminent authority, for example, commenting on the cited McCulloch paper goes so far as to refer to heterarchy in the sense of 'a structure which might be thought of as hierarchical, but shouldn't be' (Arbib, 1989). What is really going on is that hierarchies may display autonomy at each level of rank within an overall scheme that generates a collaborative outcome—exactly as happens in the algedonode. Hence I have taken the view that hierarchies do not have to be based on the sacerdotal model, but may involve autonomous embedments. This position is consonant with the previously expressed view that a homeostat is not committed to unadaptive behaviour. Then just as a biological-type homeostat answers to a criterion of ultrastability, so a biological-type hierarchy is fundamentally heuristic.

ULTRASTABLE HOMEOSTASIS VERSUS HETEROSTASIS

Coming closer to today from the algedonode of the 1950s and 1960s, when I was first speaking of the *heuristic* neuron, the 1980s have disclosed the *hedonistic* neuron (Klopf, 1982). Here is another adjective that implies searching, and this one specifies that the search is for pleasure. Klopf's emphasis on the neuron as reactive and goal-seeking is well taken, his mathematical models are disarming in their exclusion of the emotive and somewhat anthropomorphic language of his text, and his claim that a proper view of the neuron has implications for social systems takes a leap in which I happily join him. But he makes his whole approach dependent on his distinction between homeostasis and (this time not heterarchy but) heterostasis.

Having adopted the classical view of homeostasis as unadaptive, Klopf is able to reject the view of cyberneticians (Ross Ashby and J.Z. Young are mentioned) that homeostasis is central to living behaviour, which he says is a secondary goal to the primary goal of heterostasis: 'An organism will be said to be in a condition of heterostasis with respect to a specific internal variable when that variable has been maximized.' The hedonistic heterostatic neuron is seeking to maximize pleasure; so we have this breathtaking utterance: 'There is a straightforward way of classifying neuronal states into two categories, these being the states of depolarization and hyperpolarization. Given the evident excitatory nature of pleasure and the inhibitory nature of pain, the following equivalences suggest themselves for the neuron:

Depolarization $\equiv$ pleasure

Hyperpolarization $\equiv$ pain

One implication of these equivalences is that a neuron will seek to obtain excitation and to avoid inhibition.' The book cited is based on these early allegations: surely the non-metaphorical identifications itemized and high-lighted above have led us to a simplistic teleology.

In the algedonic usage, the words pain and pleasure, *algos* and *hedos*, are acknowledged to be metaphorical, a way of avoiding any pretence that the rationale of the neuron's transfer function is understood. They are simply labels for negative and positive feedback in the neuron's interaction with its environment. In the algedonic usage, the neuron adjusts probabilistically to an environment that challenges its adaptation capability in unexpected ways, and this adjustment could certainly not be achieved by maximizing a single variable—if only because the process entails a fixed goal. These are the keys to the heuristic neuron, the hierarchic ganglion with local autonomy, and the ultrastable homeostat. And these are the concepts on which the theory of recursive consciousness shall rely. I do not know why both the terms that I shall in future exclude, heterarchy and heterostasis, should begin with the same prefix meaning 'other,' since the reasons for their introduction were completely *hetero* as between themselves. But they are both misleading in my opinion. This is said not by way of assault on alternative approaches, but to explain that the exclusion of notions that are pervasive in the literature is not an oversight.

The principles that I have been seeking to make clear are vital to this approach to consciousness, since the argument has already been established (in Chapter Thirteen) that 'consciousness is a reflection of its own activity.' If so, there must be an agreement on what that activity is. The neuron, if it is indeed well modelled by the algedonode, does precisely reflect its own activity. The settings in the electro-mechanical version (both simple and ganglionic, please note) are at all times Markovian representations of experience in the algedonode. That is, these settings fully determine the conditional probability distribution for future events—because they enshrine its whole history.

The exception would seem to be pathological. An algedonode in a trapped state (that is, one whose condition passes from A to B to C to D to A to B to C to D to A, and so on indefinitely) would at all times enshrine only the internal history of its oscillatory cycle; thus its propensity to oscillate would not be reflected in the conditional probability distribution of the moment. No such situation arose in any of the algedonic experiments; however, such a potential pathology is worth noting, particularly at the level of social systems in which it might well be endemic.

EMBEDMENTS AND THE TOKENS OF CONSCIOUSNESS: INDIVIDUAL

The brain deals with the ultrastable homeostasis of its own internal states; and the basic characteristics of neurophysiological activity to this end are logical closure, recursive iteration, and reverberation that computes the eigenvalues of its own processes. So argues Part Three of this book. Chapter Thirteen, in particular, argues that consciousness is a reflection of its own activity in just this sense. Armed with these criteria, we may seek these tokens of consciousness within the embedments of the system that demarcate the purview of human experience.

Recursive embedments are not objectively given, however. We choose them, by recognizing processes that have special meaning for us, because they give meaning to our own human experience. *Structure is attention to process.* The structure of embedments now advanced is my choice, and the terms that are chosen to denote the embedded systems need the support of the connotations provided for them in this chapter. Thus it is the validity of the processes that are discussed as creating the architecture of consciousness that is truly in question, not whether the processes that are the structure have been given the best (still less the 'correct') available names.

Human experience recognizes the physical existence of 'myself' as a body with limbs and organs. With a little sophistication in description it recognizes the community of cells, all sharing a common genetic blueprint, which exhaustively constitute that body. Insofar as awareness is to be considered, it recognizes in particular the nervous system and its basic viable unit, the neuron. The heuristic neuron is thus chosen as the first embedment, as modelled here by the algedonode.

The second embedment is the concatenation of cells called a ganglion that forms a subsidiary nerve centre. In this, many neurons with their nerve processes, axons and dendrites, are embodied in a framework of dense fibro-elastic connective tissue. This is modified here by the multiple algedonode that constitutes a heuristic algedonic hierarchy, to which a whole section has already been devoted.

The third embedment, however, involves a new kind of machinery. It is based on the concept of reliability through redundancy (see this chapter) and the possibility of potential command (see Chapter Ten). No longer is the concatenation of neurons to be regarded as an organized collection of denumerable neurons, forming a tumescence (swelling) of nervous tissue that is structurally coherent in its performance. This third-level concatenation has a location, but is to be defined by the recruitment of neural information based on its relevance to a particular set of tasks. Then 'command,' the process of regulatory decisions, is potential in whatever concatenation of cells shares the needful information at any given time. It is this self-organizing property that raises the potential for ultrastability to a level recognizably different from algedonic homeostasis at the second level, and superior to it because of its greater flexibility of informational structure.

In the terminology of this book, we have encountered at the third embedment an *infoset*. Its model is the Staffordian graph, and its task is syntegration. Note the word model. It is not suggested that only 30 neurons participate, or that they are arranged in icosahedral patterns any more than the model of the algedonode requires the nervous system to be made out of strips of wood and brass. But the mathematical characteristics elucidated in Part Three are the architectonic of the third embedment. This concatenation of neurons is recognized as an information set precisely because it relies on a flow of relevant information, constantly changing, within its structural purlieu, in order to take coherent decisions. Now I have been accustomed to discussing the redundancy of potential command as a feature of the brain itself. But in considering this architectonic of embedments, the question arises of whether so powerful a tool of reliable computing does not occur at a neurophysiologically lower level—in the autonomic nervous system that pervades the body. Every logical expectation points to this likelihood. The techniques of potential command are self-organizing properties of nervous networks themselves: why should the cerebrum have copyright in them?

Considering the nervous nets that are infosets as defined by a shared purpose in the body, we encounter the concatenation very appropriately called a *plexus*. Most people have heard of the solar plexus (sometimes with rueful reason) because it is large and powerful in effect: it is a plexus, a concatenation, within the sympathetic nervous system. But it may be a surprise to learn that there are a great many more of these plexus networks (a physiological text to hand lists 34 nervous plexuses; this discounts plexuses of blood vessels). What they have in common is dedication to a special purpose: complex regulation of the particular organs in their locale—in the classical neurophysiological language. Or, to put the point in the language of this book, they are devices attaining to ultrastability through heuristic homeostasis with their immediate environments. The neurons involved share purpose and information: they are infosets.

The fourth embedment is surely the brain itself: that is, the cerebrum, to exclude the 'old' brain (the pons, medulla, and cerebellum), which is the part of the autonomic nervous system that lies within the skull. Since the criterion of human experience was adopted at the outset, it is not highly contentious to say that the cerebrum is generally regarded as the seat of human consciousness —or, at the very least, that it is indispensable to consciousness incarnate.

No sooner is the association made between consciousness, to the nature of which this enquiry is dedicated, and the fourth embedment, than the obvious question arises: what about the first three levels of embedment? All three exhibit the tokens of consciousness, as I have called the conclusions so far. Is the heuristic neuron, the algedonic hierarchy, or the ultrastable plexus conscious in itself? The average westerner is likely to answer, 'no.' But how does s/he know? S/he is likely to have identified consciousness with the brain in advance. Suppose that a degree of consciousness is attached to the first three recursions: it is natural that all this emerges into human *recognition* precisely at that level of recursion, the fourth, in which the human personage recognizes itself to *be* that integral human.

This is infosettic consciousness of which we speak; but the infoset was first hypothesized at the third embedment, the level of plexus. Presumably only the infoset plexus could be aware of its own infosettic consciousness, if such exists: the fourth level does not speak language three ... But the architectonics of the theory do not preclude the consciousness at level four *of the existence* of infosettic consciousness at level three. This is a subtle contention, and not susceptible to scientific proof. The choice of processes to embody structure was, however, made contingent on human (not typically Western) experience from the start of this section. Judging from reported Eastern experience, human awareness of infosettic consciousness in the first three embedments is possible.

Let us specifically consider the third (plexus) embedment from an Eastern perspective. It is not implausible to identify the six 'spiritual centres' which the yogi calls chakras with plexus activity in the body. The solar plexus and the cardiac plexus especially coincide with the third (Manipuraka) and fourth (Anahata) chakras. The others might well involve more than one plexus. The first is the basal chakra (Muladhara); the second (Svadhishthana) is associated with the genitals; and the fifth chakra (Vishuddhi) is at the throat. The sixth chakra (Ajna) is in the head itself: the yogi identifies all the chakras as centres of consciousness, but points to Ajna as central to them all. Then the human being's awareness of whole selfhood may be located there in yogic terms. But knowledge *of the existence* of infosettic consciousness within the other five chakras is possible to the initiate, as I attest from yogic experience myself.

Ajna, known familiarly in the West as the 'third eye,' is depicted between the eyes on the exterior of the body. But the chakras lie within, on the plane of the spinal cord. It has been remarked that the most prominent structure deep in the brain at the level of Ajna is the pineal gland. This organ, part of the endocrine system, was proposed as the seat of the soul as long ago as as the time of Descartes. It was a much more recent discovery that the pineal, deep-seated as it is in the brain substance, is none the less photosensitive: a third eye indeed ... But the concatenation of neurons that I regard as corresponding to Ajna is the reticular formation of the brain stem. Physiologically this is not known as a plexus; but the structure fits the criteria that have been advanced both as cybernetic devices and as tokens of consciousness.

In the set-theoretic brain model (Beer, 1962) frequently referenced here, I wrote that the ascending reticular formation comprised the mechanism for closure of the whole thalamo-cortical system, and called the assemblage 'a subtle conditioning mechanism.' Having hypothesized and mathematically described the existence of an 'Ashbean Ultrastable Machine' in the midbrain as an integrator of the sensory and motor cortexes at the thalamic level, I nominated the reticular formation as alerting the reward function deriving from internal homeostatic processes. Then all these interactions in the centre of the brain constituted the master algedonode, as the term was later. At the time I wrote, 'The process of conditioning becomes a homeostatic struggle for dominance between an organized and a random response at the thalamic level, which will eventually be settled by an equilibrium which perfectly measures the relevance of the conditioning to the general experience of the organism.' Both McCulloch and Ashby were members of the small group to whom I presented this model in Urbana in 1960, the former being the foremost authority on the reticular formation, and the latter having discovered homeostatic ultrastability in the first place. Neither demurred at these speculations. Although I was not at that time publicly mentioning such matters, my own yogic experience had already convinced me that this neural concatenation involving thalamic activity in ultrastable homeostatic correspondence with the ascending reticular formation could in fact be identified with Ajna. I had taught myself to be conscious of its activity.

May I now return briefly but significantly to Dr Harry Klopf, whose hedonistic neuron (Klopf, 1982) was discussed earlier. His concept of heterostasis was criticized, and indeed rejected; but areas of enthusiastic agreement were also noted. He writes on page 53: 'it is hypothesized that the midbrain and thalamic reticular formation is the seat of the mental experiences of which we are aware.' Now this contention is based on much empirical neurophysiological evidence gathered in the last decade; and it seems that there is now fairly general agreement among neuroscientists that consciousness has a location. This of course refers to what this theory is calling the fourth embedment.

EMBEDMENTS AND THE TOKENS OF CONSCIOUSNESS: SOCIETARY

Conceptual dichotomies have bedevilled human thinking, and have persistently been overthrown in the process of enhanced understanding. Because it is at root interdisciplinary, the science of cybernetics over the last half century has played a noble part in reaching toward the Hegelian synthesis that hides behind the contradiction of thesis and antithesis. The dissolution of the mind–body problem has already been mentioned; and it was Norbert Wiener himself who propagated the definition of cybernetics as involving regulation 'in the animal and the machine'—thereby denying the entrenched dichotomy that so long existed between the animate and inanimate systems. Both are subject to many of the same laws that involve informational transfer. Such methodological considerations were mooted in Chapter Twelve, when it was suggested that a 'group mind' might exist as an entity, as distinct from the consensual sharing that is often and conversationally referred to as 'group consciousness.' The difference between these two concepts can be specified: the more familiar idea accepts the dichotomy that the culture has erected between the individual and the social group, while the notion of a group mind straddles the divide.

The ideas advanced in Part Three tentatively, out of scientific rectitude, are embraced freely in this essay. It must be evident that the theory of recursive consciousness puts group mind forward as the fifth embedment of consciousness, simply because the neighbourhood infoset displays the usual tokens of consciousness. Then the division of this portion of the essay into Individual and Societary is a last concession, made for ease of reference, to a classical dichotomy that it explicitly as well as implicitly rejects.

The neighbourhood infoset, so called because its members are in intimate personal interaction, is the subject of the book's first nine chapters. There is no need to expatiate further here. The sixth embedment, consisting of the hyperset of neighbourhood infosets, has the hypericosahedron as its basic model: this was discussed in Chapter Ten. When the neighbourhood concept, enhanced as it is by the hyperset extension, retreats from the logistical complications of large-scale personal contiguity into the technosphere, it becomes the seventh embedment: the technospheric infoset.

These three embedments, it should be noted, have points in common with embedments one, two and three. The fifth embedment is a unit, as was the original algedonode, although its individuality has a social rather than a personal significance. The hyperset, which is the sixth embedment, compares with the hierarchy of algedonodes at the second embedment, insofar as it embraces a collection of (societary, in this case) individuals that are unit infosets. Again there is a heuristic amalgam seeking ultrastable homeostasis. And just as the plexus of the third embedment constitutes a dedicated subsystem dealing with local areas of concern, so the technospheric infoset is conceived as deploying its self-organizing identity out of concern for specific issues of global significance. Outstandingly identified at embedment seven are environmental groups using the technosphere to cross national boundaries in the protection of the atmosphere, for example, or the preservation of energy resources, or the movements for population control or peace.

The three societary embedments under discussion are as identifiable as the first three embedments disclosed in the individual human being. There is a vast operational distinction between the two sets. Those embodied in the individual work very well; the societary threesome work hardly at all. It might be productive to examine the reasons for this, which are blatantly obvious in the context of this theory.

Embedment seven is not a total novelty: it is just that the technosphere itself has only recently come into existence in electronic guise. Its attempts at self-regulation through its bulletin board and so on are gauche in the extreme. Now the electronic technology has replaced a technology of scholarship that lasted for centuries, and was anything but gauche. It shared the language of Latin; and despite the sacerdotal tyrannies exercised in the political sphere, and the relatively small numbers involved, it developed a markedly liberal infosettic consciousness. The interaction between the Pope and Newton and the younger Voltaire, for example, creates a vivid image of a technospheric infoset, and probably similar images based on earlier technologies could be conjured long before the eighteenth century. There was the language of courtly love, for example, expressed in French during the eleventh to thirteenth centuries, not to mention the yet earlier technospheric infosets of the Roman Empire ...

All such images of the seventh embedment, teasingly evocative as they may be, need to be viewed in the perspective of societary development: population explosion; exponential interaction of individuals, tribes and nations; economic exploitation; and so on (see Beer, 1975). It comes to this: the role of the eighth embedment, which is consciousness at the level of global governance, has totally changed. The technology has emerged that updates the scholarly Latin and the courtly French, but there is no cerebrum. And the brain-like capacities which would make the eighth embedment comparable to the fourth embedment in the individual are therefore missing. We are stuck with the woeful inadequacy of the United Nations. The Romans did better than that. But all of this was touched on before in Chapter Ten; and the objective now is not to redesign the world, but to recognize the infosettic principles on which the vision of a conscious Gaia can be based. Maybe Gaia is conscious already, but we humans are no more sensitive to this eighth embedment than we are to the first, the algedonic. All our conditioning about consciousness is focused on the fourth embedment, where the almighty ego resides.

The lessons to be learned are really to do with the pathology of the whole system: if the proposed description of consciousness is taken as given, the failures are seen to depend on faults in the machinery that embodies consciousness as defined in each embedment. Outstandingly, this relates to the eighth embedment: and the route to enhancement is suggested in the descriptions of the sixth and seventh, based on the infosettic consciousness of the fifth.

My own analysis of societary defects and managerial shortcomings, together with my best prescriptions for remedial action, are spread over the whole corpus of my work. There is one particular issue, however, worth putting into focus here as it concerns a question of consciousness at the seventh embedment—that of the technological infoset. It concerns professionalism. A profession is a technological infoset par excellence: it shares an awareness of the world among its membership in infosettic consciousness.

The claim is that this infosettic consciousness is defective, because it is in the nature of a profession to adhere to a stereotype that is necessarily out of date. Some professions, and medicine is a good example, are ostensibly up-to-date because they follow their technological noses with all the vigour provided by the interests that foster and propel the technologies involved. But the stereotypes of health care that are served are not properly re-examined; and the infosettic consciousness is stuck—stuck in its own historical mud and with the bills for escalating costs. What it comes down to is that the models that underlie the infosettic consciousness, which are very central to the shared information and purpose that any infoset upholds, gradually become surrogates for social reality. An address entitled 'The surrogate world we manage' (Beer, 1973) looks carefully at how the process works.

But there are other professions, and politics is a good example, in which there is zero technological innovation to promote even ostensible improvement. The politician is managing a surrogate of the world inhabited by his/her constituents, and increasingly they are noticing the fact that their world is nothing much like the politicians' world. There are curious results. Instead of discovering the technology of cybernetics, which offers a science of regulation, to redesign the governmental process and machine, the politician has embraced the technology that metabolizes politics as a *profession*: television. Politics is feeding its heuristic homeostat on the equivalent of anabolic steroids: adaptation moves more and more quickly—but not on to ultrastability, because the drugs denature the learning mechanism. We witness an infosettic consciousness among politicians that is zany because its societary homeostats have been thrown into uncontrolled oscillation.

Thirdly in this list of brief illustrations of the pathology of embedment seven comes the profession on which, after television, the politician most relies: economics. The Robinson Crusoe economy, on which the infosettic consciousness of economics is ultimately based, is a surrogate world indeed. There is no need to write a diatribe here about the abysmal failure of economic consciousness to comprehend: its internecine disagreements lead to contradictory prescriptions—and when applied, none of them is effective. What ought to gain attention is the impregnability of the profession itself, and the political dependence it has created. In particular, the short-term consciousness of the political infoset just criticized requires economic support and justification that operates in short cycles. Thus the recession of the 1990s in the West, which the cybernetician is bound to recognize as betokening a fundamental shift of the economic power between blocs that are pushing and shoving and sliding over each other like so many tectonic plates, has to be perceived and interpreted as a temporary effect.

The profession filters its information so as to recognize any short-term cycle. The possibility (see earlier) that any such cycles are trapped states cannot enter infosettic consciousness because its models are politically driven surrogates. The possibility that any such cycles belong to a larger and more far-reaching envelope curve of a different order of magnitude is likewise discarded. Witness the contradiction between an Establishment technospheric economic infoset (typified by Samuelson, say) advocating the interpretations and nostrums of the short-term consciousness, and the findings of Systems Dynamics (led by Forrester) which operate in the long-term conscious. The former expects recovery from the recession of the early 1990s within months, and the latter in years. Speaking from a more general cybernetic perspective than the economic infosettic consciousness allows, I observed the tectonic movement of power from the First World to the Pacific Rim; and now the further shift to mainland China is predictable. Within the cyberset of infosettic consciousness, the eighth embedment, the expectation for the United States in particular is that it will be lucky to survive at all in any recognizable form.

But these speculations are here only to illustrate the general point about the pathologies of infosettic consciousness. '*Tempora mutanur nos et mutamur in illis*' used to be a dependable Latin tag, reliable in its sonorous antiquity: 'Times change and we change with them.' Don't you believe it. We are failing to expand societary infosettic consciousness, and the surrogate world is all we understand.

TRANSCENDENCE

Please recall the arguments of Chapter Thirteen on the nature of self-reference, whence came eventually the definition of consciousness as a process that computes itself, that transforms into its own eigenvalue. 'It weighed heavily with me that Goedel's Theorem showed how formal languages were in the last resort "undecidable."' The solutions then derived involved the transformation of what is undecidable into a different kind of statement—different because it is expressed in a different language that is inaccessible to anyone trapped in the original Goedelian sentence. The principle of transformation, so described, was central to the epistemology of embedments: remember the different classes of players in the wood-and-brass algedonic experiments.

Next please review the arguments of this chapter about McCulloch-style heterarchies, and in particular the dilemma of circular preference. Warren was quoted: 'the apparent inconsistency of preference is shown to indicate consistency of *an order too high* to permit construction of a scale of values' (and those are still my italics). He needed a third dimension to escape from the closure of the circuitry mapped on the plane—a transformation indeed.

In fact, the word transformation as used in the two paragraphs above is somehow not strong enough. After all, linguistic translation is typical of transformation—one noun, for instance, being directly displaced by its other-language equivalent. Both of the examples refer to transformations more powerful than this replacement of one word or state by another: they both deal in the resolution of logical breakdown. This is the reason for using the word transcendence. It betokens escape from the logical trap and the resolution of inconsistency.

Not only remote, impersonal logics are concerned, however. Consider the vivid remark (Vickers, 1970) of Sir Geoffrey Vickers: '*the trap is a function of the nature of the trapped.*' Such indeed is the human predicament. And people find, as a result, that they cannot argue their way out of the trap, because their rationality is conditioned to the trap's own premises. They cannot take an intuitive leap out of the trap because the walls are perceived as too high. Most people, it has to be said, are not even aware of their trapped predicament. People who become aware of it need to transcend their own natures, to expand consciousness so that a transcendent nature is revealed behind the self image that s/he has agreed to accept. This is a spiritual process because it means looking beyond the material and social world out of which traps are invariably constructed.

According to this theory of recursive consciousness, each embedment contains its own definition of proximate transcendence: it is that the consciousness that is operational at any one level may aspire to the consciousness of the level in which it is embedded. This is one step away—hence the qualification proximate. The notion is conveyed in Figure 14.2 by the short arrows.

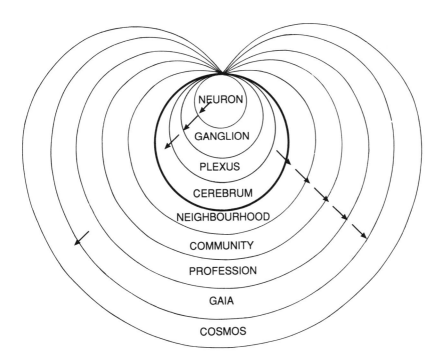

Figure 14.2 Theory of recursive consciousness. Note: each of the terms carries the connotations heuristic, algedonic, ultrastable, and infosettic, all as defined in the text

The diagram in Figure 14.2 is so drawn, however, that the transcendence beyond the proximate transcendence—that is, to the level of the next higher embedment—*is also proximate*. There is one single point from which a single step will move consciousness into any other level of consciousness. I take this topology to depict the realm of human experience known as the mystical. Many scholarly people do not wish to countenance the existence of any such realm. For those who are willing to entertain the concept, however, it is important to see how the theory of recursive consciousness can readily embrace it.

There are many mystical traditions, and it seems likely that the recursive infosettic model together with the diagram's topology could contain, and be illuminated by, any one of them. Because of my familiarity with the yogic tradition, and because the foundations of a neurophysiological version have already been laid in this chapter, and finally because what I shall say is veridical through subjective experience, the essay returns to the chakras.

The yogic chakras are spiritual centres that this theory allots to the third embedment. This is the level at which infosettic consciousness is taken to emerge with a meaning close to that accepted in ordinary conversation— although taking this set of locations as themselves harbouring that consciousness is not so accepted. Six chakras were listed and named, and five were associated with neural plexuses. The sixth, called Ajna, was associated with a particular concatenation of neural nets in the.centre of the cerebrum. There is another chakra in the catalogue. Thus some authorities refer to 'the seven chakras,' but there is good reason to treat the seventh as a class on its own.

The name of this chakra is Sahashara: it is known as the crown chakra, because it is located on the top of the head. Chakra is the Sanskrit word for wheel, and the six chakras may be visualized as spinning. Freely spinning chakra wheels should be excellent images of well functioning ultrastable homeostats; and the adept may be thought of as trained to notice malfunction as the sputtering of a spinning firework that has jammed. In this etymological usage, Sahashara is called the thousand-spoked wheel. In poetic usage, in which each chakra is visualized as a lotus blossom with a unique number of petals (Ajna has two), Sahashara is called the thousand-petalled lotus. Spiritual energy is depicted as the serpent-power called Kundalini, residing in the basal chakra, Muladhara, and under certain complicated conditions this power uncoils and rises through the other chakras. Energy may be concentrated via Kundalini in any of the chakras: that is why it was possible to speak of consciousness *of the existence of* infosettic consciousness, as awareness of directed energy concentrated in any of these locations.

The adept may be visualized as concentrating energy in one of the six chakras, and projecting it from the body into the outside environment. whence it may return to the internal energetic system—probably via the basal chakra. This is the image of a homeostat, firmly based in the neurophysiological realm, completing closure through the mystical realm. This is because the energy, although travelling outside the body through physical substance, is not detectable by the measuring instruments of physics. The word mystical is used by default—and none the worse for that. It is a common usage, though often denied by the user. Maximum power in the circuit that returns via Muladhara (the basal chakra) can be visualized as generated from the third chakra, Manipuraka. Maximum distance from that same basal chakra gives closure through Ajna—the very centre of consciousness itself. Recapitulating: if these images aid in understanding half-cognized experience, so be it; if they appear alien to experience, please treat them as adding roundness to the recursive model.

The seventh chakra, Sahashara, is unique in the following way. Energy released through the crown may be taken as the image of transcendence from the body altogether. Sahashara lies beyond the embedment of popular consciousness in the brain: then what does this transcendence mean?

The diagram shows a final closure of the system of consciousness beyond the eighth embedment—*ipso facto*, then, in proximate transcendence to *all* embedments. The fourth attracts special attention, because it is demarcated by the envelope of the physical body. The eighth attracts special attention because it is demarcated by global consciousness. Let us call the final closure *cosmic* consciousness. The theory of recursive infosettic consciousness is complete.

In Jungian language, the adept in transcendent experience is suspended timelessly at the boundary of the plenum and the void (Jung, 1967). In Teilhardian language, maybe the diagram at its singularity denotes the Omega Point (Teilhard de Chardin, 1959). Many such parallels could be drawn. For the yogi, the identification of all the embedments, and particularly his/her own selfhood embodied at the fourth embedment, with the cosmos conceived as universal consciousness, is expressed by the mantra Tat Tvam Asi: 'That You Are.' These are the last three words of a quotation from one of the ancient Vedic scriptures, the Chhandogya Upanishad, expressing the cosmic identification:

That subtle essence
which is the Self of this entire world,
That is the Real,
That is the Self,
That You Are.

Tat Tvam Asi: तत्त्वमसि : That You Are.

PART FIVE

COLLABORATORS' SURPLUS

INTRODUCTION

Dr Assad Jalali begins this set of important contributions with the details of the mathematical investigation that he undertook and to which the main text refers. It is pleasing to see the basic geometric ideas behind the model advanced with both rigour and elegance, and this exposition will certainly be preferred to my own in Chapter Thirteen by any reader equipped to come to grips with it.

In marked contrast to this scientific language, *Joe Truss* and his own collaborative team of *Chris Cullen* and *Wendy Walsh* provide the simplest and most direct statement of the latest protocol for running a syntegration. It describes the activity in the very terms used by Dr Jalali when his own investigation began. He called the basic model a 'playful' graph, because he conceived of syntegration as a 'game.' Here, then, is the game plan, together with the rules of the game—although it is a serious game indeed that we play.

We have seen in Chapter Eight just how vexed are the questions of allocation of topics to vertices and players to roles. So bridging the gap between the alarmingly recondite Surplus One and the disarmingly straightforward Surplus Two comes the practical use of mathematics to aid the syntegration in actual process rather than its understanding. This is the algorithm devised by Josephine Hancock—a first attempt, as described in the text, to find a scientific way of translating the preferences of participants into infosettic action. I mentioned in Chapter One the fascinating letter written to Senator Titius Aristo by Pliny the Younger about a prisoner who, if guilty, could be sentenced to death or to exile—showing how much it matters whether one decides on the guilt or the fate first. This has long stood as proxy for the problem of *ordered decision* in my own mind, which is a very general problem in management. One with which I was faced personally, for example, had to do with choosing a whole zoo of mainframe computers. Should one choose the type by main characteristics and then the nationality of the manufacturer—or vice versa? Obviously this was a political decision of a heavy sort. Then does one allocate topics to vertices, before considering individual roles at all, or try to make the toptic/vertex assignment a function of role preference? Surplus Three shows how the task was actually approached as an integral decision, which may well need to be partitioned in one of several possible ways. This is why I referred to Jo as Pliny the Later.

Both facilitators who write next are professionals in that field, and both have been concerned with syntegrations. Their chapters are labelled 'perspectives': the extent to which their windows open on to different views of the same thing is fascinating. *Alan Pearson* concentrates on the process *qua* itself, while *Dr David Beatty* is concerned with the mapping of social interaction on to the icosahedral space. They are both much interested in the extent to which the facilitator should intervene in events. Both would agree that it is vital to preserve the facilitator's credibility: but where does amiable lubrication of the process wheels turn into what may look like *dirigisme*? In my own terminology, *any* degree of facilitation is absorbing infosettic variety; the debate is about form and appearance as much as about process technique. The hexadic reduction, after all, must be a massive variety attenuator—or it has not worked. But Surplus Four and Surplus Five do indeed provide their own perspectives on all of this.

On his return in Surplus Six, *Joe Truss* has his own view to state on this matter. But his main objective is to talk about his realization of the operational meaning of the icosahedral 'face,' the ubiquitous equilateral triangle, as offering an approach to developmental planning in its most practical form. This new set of discoveries, briefly expounded in Surplus Six, is so exciting that I urge him to write his own book about it. It is best that he now takes off by himself, using Chapter Nine as his springboard.

Dr Allenna Leonard completes the Collaborators' Surplus with number Seven, which is a concise explanation of the Viable System Model (VSM), for those who have not met it, as an aid to their understanding of some of the portions of my text that invoke it. At least, that is all I asked her for; but as usual she responds with creative insight by means of an illustrative example devised to bring out features of the VSM that are commonly misunderstood. So Part Five ends as it began, with elegance, though of a different sort.

THE COLLABORATORS

David J.F. Beatty has a doctorate and a consultancy practice. He is an adjunct faculty member in the Department of Adult Education, Ontario Institute for Studies in Education, Toronto, Canada. A Director of Team Syntegrity Inc., he is currently developing Business Builder, a syntegrity system for launching small business start-ups.

Josephine Hancock had her schooling in Britain and Bahrain, taking her honours degree in Management Science at the European Business Management School, University College Swansea. She is currently a research student there, specializing in managerial cybernetics, and will shortly submit her doctoral thesis on aspects of syntegration.

Assad Jalali holds BSc and MEng in Electrical Engineering from Tehran University, MSc in Mathematics from Birmingham, and DPhil in Mathematical Logic from Oxford University. He has done postdoctoral research in the universities of Oxford, Birmingham, and Edinburgh, and had headed the Department of Basic Sciences of the Engineering Faculty of Tehran University for 2 years. He is currently a lecturer and the co-ordinator of quantitative research in the European Business Management School, University College Swansea.

Allenna Leonard, having a Masters degree in Administration and a doctorate in Regulation, has worked in organizational cybernetics for 10 years as consultant, teacher, trainer, and writer. She is a Director of Team Syntegrity Inc. in Toronto, but works internationally.

Alan Pearson is President of the Stafford Beer Foundation and a Director of Team Syntegrity Inc. Having taken his degree in commerce in England he moved to Canada, where he followed a distinguished career in the Canadian Public Service for 15 years. As president of Alan Pearson Associates Inc., he has been practising as an independent corporate-planning consultant for over a decade.

Joe Truss, with a Masters degree in Business Administration, has worked in both the arts and business for over 25 years as an entrepreneur, manager, trainer, and consultant. He is the President of Team Syntegrity Inc. and the Founder of the MetaMatrix Learning Network.

REVERBERATING NETWORKS
Modelling information propagation in syntegration by spectral analysis
Assad Jalali

INTRODUCTION

In the autumn of 1990, Professor Stafford Beer gave a series of seminars in the University of Swansea, Wales, in which he introduced his 'team syntegrity.'

The structural basis of the syntegrity is the regular icosahedron. The participants or the team members in the syntegrity are represented by the edges of the icosahedron. The vertices represent statements or propositions advocated by the members. The distances between vertices, in a sense, represent the degree of dissimilarity or difference between the corresponding statements. In particular, any two antipodal vertices are supposed to represent two opposite statements.

In devising 'team syntegrity,' a crucial element in Beer's thinking has been to postulate a geometric substructure or *site* totally immune to any consideration of hierarchy among the participating members. This requires a high degree of *symmetry* from the site of the game.

The second important element in this quest has been the desideratum of allowing for 'grades of difference' between statements. In particular, the sites are expected to provide for the possibility of opposition between statements. These considerations, the author believes, have been the main reason for the choice of the icosahedron. The latter provides for a symmetric network of communication between the participants in order to discuss and modify the statements efficiently.

If it is true that the essence of 'team syntegrity' lies in the way the statements are related to one another and also to the participants, then it is also true that the Euclidean metric properties are of no direct relevance to the syntegrity. It follows, therefore, that what is essential are the *graph*-theoretic properties of *sites* rather than their (Euclidean) metric properties.

Led by the foregoing logic, the author tried to isolate those graph-theoretic properties of the icosahedron which are 'essential' to the syntegrity, and subsequently to investigate the class of graphs which are characterized by these properties.

This investigation has resulted in the identification of the *sites* as the class of connected graphs of diameter 3 which are distance transitive and admit an internal involution. This class is closely related to *the strongly regular graphs, association schemes with opposition*, and the rank 3 groups. The results of these studies, which already partially, but privately, have been communicated, will appear in Jalali, 1993. In that report it is argued that the *association schemes with opposition* are the most appropriate sites for the implementation of generalizations of Beer's syntegrity. The 'icosahedral site' is the first member of a combinatorially very rich chain of mathematical objects.

An extremely effective tool for understanding and constructing association schemes is the spectral analysis of the algebras of these schemes. The eigen-structures of these algebras are also central to the analysis of the process of propagation through the site of the information generated at vertices.

From a practical viewpoint also it is exceedingly important to know about the mechanism and speed of the flow of information in the site of the syntegrity. Therefore, our interest in the aforementioned spectral analysis is not prompted solely by theoretical considerations. In fact, our objective in preparing this chapter is exclusively practical, and we hope that those who are interested in implementing Beer's syntegrity will find it useful.

In this chapter we present a complete and self-contained spectral analysis of the 'icosahedral site,' and investigate alternative ways of modelling the flow of information in it. We have deliberately avoided any reference to the association algebra of the icosahedron. Our proofs are all direct and elementary.

The relatively small size of the icosahedron has made such a direct approach feasible without, we hope, making it too cumbersome.

We would like, finally, to stress the importance of Beer's conceptual contribution by devising his syntegrity and thereby introducing the notion of *symmetry* in Organizational Studies. This notion has played (and continues to play) a most crucial role in the development of modern physics.

The finite relatives of some mathematical objects of immense importance to the modern physicist—such as *simple Lie groups*—are ubiquitous in the study of the association schemes. The author believes that this phenomenon is not purely accidental, and ventures to suggest that the concept of *symmetry* may prove to be, in the future, as fruitful in Organizational Studies as it has been in the physical sciences.

FROM PENTAGON TO ISCOSAHEDRON

Let G be the graph of the icosahedron. We label the nodes of this graph as follows: we choose, arbitrarily, a node and call it the top, and denote it by $\top$. The *opposite node* is called the bottom and is denoted by $\perp$. We next consider the nodes which are adjacent to $\top$. This, as a subgraph of G, is a *Pentagon* and we denote it by H. We then choose, again arbitrarily, a node of H and call it 0. We next choose a direction of rotation, yet again arbitrarily, and label the nodes of Pentagon, following 0 in the direction we have chosen, $1, 2, 3$, and 4 consecutively. We label the opposites of the nodes $0, 1, 2, 3$, and 4 by $\tilde{0}, \tilde{1}, \tilde{2}, \tilde{3}$, and $\tilde{4}$, respectively. These are all distinct (as opposition is an involution) and constitute a subgraph $\tilde{H}$ of G. Clearly $\tilde{H}$ is the set of nodes adjacent to $\perp$. $H \cap \tilde{H} = \phi$, as otherwise the *graph distance* between $\perp$ and $\top$ would be no more than 2. The nodes adjacent to 0 are $\top, 1, 4$ and two more nodes. $\perp, \tilde{0}, \tilde{1}$, and $\tilde{4}$ cannot be among the two, hence these should be, of necessity, nodes $\tilde{2}$ and $\tilde{3}$. The same argument can be applied to other nodes. Figure S1.1 summarizes adjacency.

Now let matrix A be the matrix of adjacency (the *incidence matrix*) of the pentagon H:

$$A = \begin{array}{c} \\ 0 \\ 1 \\ 2 \\ 3 \\ 4 \end{array} \begin{array}{c} \begin{array}{ccccc} 0 & 1 & 2 & 3 & 4 \end{array} \\ \left(\begin{array}{ccccc} 0 & 1 & 0 & 0 & 1 \\ 1 & 0 & 1 & 0 & 0 \\ 0 & 1 & 0 & 1 & 0 \\ 0 & 0 & 1 & 0 & 1 \\ 1 & 0 & 0 & 1 & 0 \end{array}\right) \end{array}$$

A is also the incidence matrix of $\tilde{H}$ (or more precisely that of $\tilde{0}, \tilde{1}, \tilde{2}, \tilde{3}$, and $\tilde{4}$).

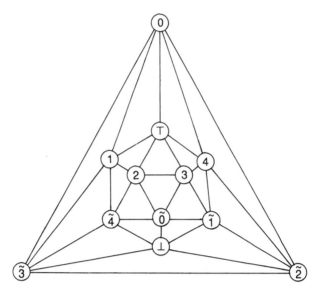

Figure SI.I A planar representation of the icosahedral graph with labels

Let M be the incidence matrix of the icosahedron with the following ordering of the nodes: $\top$; $0, 1, 2, 3, 4$; $\tilde{0}, \tilde{1}, \tilde{2}, \tilde{3}, \tilde{4}$; $\perp$. Then,

$$M = \begin{pmatrix} 0 & \mathbf{e}^* & \mathbf{0}^* & 0 \\ \mathbf{e} & A & B & \mathbf{0} \\ \mathbf{0} & B & A & \mathbf{e} \\ 0 & \mathbf{0}^* & \mathbf{e}^* & 0 \end{pmatrix} \qquad (S1.1)$$

where $\mathbf{e}$ is a 5-vector of ones and $\mathbf{0}$ a 5-vector of zeros; $*$ is the sign of matrix transposition. The matrix B is the matrix of cross-incidence between H and $\tilde{H}$. It is clear that $A + B + I_5 = J_5$, where I_5 is the 5×5 unit matrix and J_5 is a 5×5 matrix whose entries are all ones. Hence,

$$B = J_5 - I_5 - A \qquad (S1.2)$$

THE EIGENVALUES AND EIGENVECTORS OF A

The matrical equation $A\mathbf{v} = \lambda \mathbf{v}$ can be written as $v_{i+1} - \lambda v_i + v_{i-1} = 0$, $i = 0, 1, \ldots, 5$; with the convention that $v_{-1} = v_4$. The v_is are the components of an eigenvector of A corresponding to λ. In the above equation we can assume that i varies over all integers with the understanding that $v_{i+5} = v_i$ for all i. This latter *difference* equation has the following general solution:

$$v_i = \sum_{j=0}^{4} a_j \cos \frac{2ij\pi}{5} + \sum_{j=0}^{4} b_j \sin \frac{2ij\pi}{5}$$

If we now substitute from this equation into our original equation, we have

$$\sum_{j=0}^{4} \left[\left(a_j \cos \frac{2ij\pi}{5} + b_j \sin \frac{2ij\pi}{5} \right) \left(2\cos \frac{2j\pi}{5} - \lambda \right) \right] = 0$$

for all i. Adding together the left-hand sides of the above for $i = 0, 1, 2, \ldots, 4$, and noting that

$$\sum_{i=0}^{4} \cos \frac{2ij\pi}{5} = -1 \quad \text{and} \quad \sum_{i=0}^{4} \sin \frac{2ij\pi}{5} = 0$$

we obtain

$$\boxed{\lambda = 2\cos \frac{2j\pi}{5}} \qquad j = 0, 1, 2, 3, 4$$

Note that $2\cos(2\pi/5) = 2\cos(8\pi/5) = (\sqrt{5} - 1)/2$ and $2\cos(4\pi/5) = 2\cos(6\pi/5) = -(1 + \sqrt{5})/2$.

Note also that $(1 + \sqrt{5})/2$ is the so-called *golden ratio*, which we denote by g. The eigenvalues of A, therefore, are 2 (simple), g^{-1} (double), and $-g$ (double).

It is now easy to see that the normalized eigenvectors of A have the following form:

$$\left(\frac{1}{5}\right)^{1/2} \begin{pmatrix} 1 \\ 1 \\ 1 \\ 1 \\ 1 \end{pmatrix} \quad \text{for } \lambda = 2;$$

$$\left(\frac{2}{5}\right)^{1/2}\begin{pmatrix} 1 \\ \cos\dfrac{2\pi}{5} \\ \cos\dfrac{4\pi}{5} \\ \cos\dfrac{4\pi}{5} \\ \cos\dfrac{6\pi}{5} \end{pmatrix} \quad\text{and}\quad \left(\frac{2}{5}\right)^{1/2}\begin{pmatrix} 0 \\ \sin\dfrac{2\pi}{5} \\ \sin\dfrac{4\pi}{5} \\ -\sin\dfrac{4\pi}{5} \\ -\sin\dfrac{2\pi}{5} \end{pmatrix} \quad\text{for } \lambda = g^{-1};$$

$$\left(\frac{2}{5}\right)^{1/2}\begin{pmatrix} 1 \\ \cos\dfrac{4\pi}{5} \\ \cos\dfrac{2\pi}{5} \\ \cos\dfrac{2\pi}{5} \\ \cos\dfrac{4\pi}{5} \end{pmatrix} \quad\text{and}\quad \left(\frac{2}{5}\right)^{1/2}\begin{pmatrix} 0 \\ \sin\dfrac{4\pi}{5} \\ -\sin\dfrac{2\pi}{5} \\ \sin\dfrac{2\pi}{5} \\ -\sin\dfrac{4\pi}{5} \end{pmatrix} \quad\text{for } \lambda = -g$$

We denote these eigenvectors, respectively, by $t_0, t_1, t_2, t_3,$ and t_4, and also denote by T the matrix $(t_0, t_1, t_2, t_3, t_4)$. Hence,

$$A = T \wedge T^{-1} \tag{S1.3}$$

The matrix $\wedge$ is the diagonal matrix: $Diag(1, g^{-1}, g^{-1}, -g, -g)$.

The matrix T is the matrix of the *finite Fourier transform* for $n = 5$. Using equation S1.3, or the *Cayley–Hamilton equation* $A^3 - A^2 - 3A + 2I_5 = 0$, we can obtain higher powers of A. The eigenvalues g^{-1} and $(-g)$ suggest the involvement of the *Fibonacci sequence* in the expression of different powers of A.

We denote the terms of the Fibonacci sequence by φ_n. Hence

$$\varphi_{n+2} = \varphi_{n+1} + \varphi_n \text{ subject to the initial values } \varphi_0 = 0;\ \varphi_0 = 1 \tag{S1.4}$$

We also define another (non-conventional) Fibonacci sequence ψ_n as follows:

$$\psi_{n+2} = \psi_{n+1} + \psi_n \text{ subject to the initial values } \psi_0 = 2; \ \psi_1 = 1 \quad (S1.4')$$

Now we can compute powers of A very conveniently in terms of the notation just introduced:

$$\boxed{A^n = (-1)^{n+1}\varphi_n A + (-1)^n \varphi_{n-1} I_5 + 1/5(2^n - (-1)^{n-1}\psi_{n-1})J_5} \quad (S1.5)$$

φ_n and ψ_n can be recursively computed from equation S1.4. They also have the following explicit expressions:

$$\varphi_n = \frac{1}{\sqrt{5}} (g^n - (-g)^{-n}) \quad \text{and} \quad \psi_n = g^n + (-g)^{-n}$$

Note that

$$\psi_n = \varphi_{n+1} + \varphi_{n-1} \quad (S1.6)$$

In the table below values of φ_n and ψ_n are given for $0 \leqslant n \leqslant 12$.

n	0	1	2	3	4	5	6	7	8	9	10	11	12
φ_n	0	1	1	2	3	5	8	13	21	34	55	89	144
ψ_n	2	1	3	4	7	11	18	29	47	76	123	199	322

GEOMETRIC DIVERSION

The appearance of the 'golden ratio' in the expressions of the eigenvalues of A is not accidental. In order to see more clearly the 'reason' for the appearance of the 'golden ratio' we refer to its definition in Chapter Eleven. According to this definition, the 'golden ratio' is the ratio of the length of the diagonal of a regular (Euclidean) Pentagon to the length of the Pentagon's edge.

In the following we present a geometric method for solving the matrical equation $A\mathbf{v} = \lambda\mathbf{v}$, and thereby express the solutions in terms of the 'golden ratio' as defined above.

Let 0, 1, 2, 3, and 4 be labels for the consecutive vertices of a regular Pentagon in the Euclidean space (Figure S1.2). Let ω be the centre of the Pentagon, and $\mathbf{v}_i$ be the planar vectors $\overrightarrow{\omega i}$, $i = 0, 1, ..., 4$. It is clear that $\mathbf{v}_{i-1} + \mathbf{v}_{i+1}$ is proportional to $\mathbf{v}_i$ and that the constant of proportionality does not depend on i. Hence $\mathbf{v}_{i-1} + \mathbf{v}_{i+1} = \lambda \mathbf{v}_i$, for $i = 0, 1, ..., 4$. Let $\overrightarrow{\omega 0} + \overrightarrow{\omega 2} = \overrightarrow{\omega \alpha}$. Then, as $\overline{2\alpha} = \overline{2\omega}$, and $\angle \alpha \omega 2 = \angle 032 = 72°$, the two isosceles triangles $\alpha \omega 2$ and 032 are similar and, therefore,

$$\frac{\overline{\omega \alpha}}{\overline{\omega 0}} = \frac{\overline{23}}{\overline{02}}$$

The left-hand side of this equality is λ, as $\overline{\omega 0} = \overline{\omega 1}$, and the right-hand side, by definition, is g^{-1}. Hence $\lambda = g^{-1}$. As our $\mathbf{v}_i$s are planar, the eigenspace corresponding to the eigenvalue g^{-1} is two-dimensional.

Next, let $\mathbf{v}_i = \overrightarrow{\omega(2.i)}$, $i = 0, 1, ..., 4$, where the multiplication is modulus 5. More explicitly, $\mathbf{v}_0 = \overrightarrow{\omega 0}$; $\mathbf{v}_1 = \overrightarrow{\omega 2}$; $\mathbf{v}_2 = \overrightarrow{\omega 4}$, and so forth. These new $\mathbf{v}_i$s also satisfy equations $\mathbf{v}_{i-1} + \mathbf{v}_{i+1} = \lambda \mathbf{v}_i$, for all $i + 0, 1, ..., 4$, and for a constant λ independent of i (see Figure S1.3).

Let $i = 1$ and $\overrightarrow{\omega \beta} = \overrightarrow{\omega 0} + \overrightarrow{\omega 4}$. It is easy to see that the two isosceles triangles 012 and $\beta 0 \omega$ are similar and, therefore,

$$\frac{\overline{\omega \beta}}{\overline{\omega 4}} = \frac{\overline{20}}{\overline{21}}$$

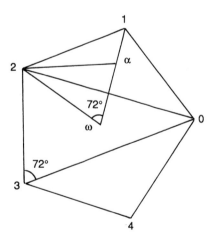

Figure S1.2

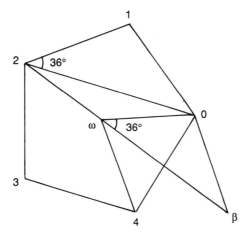

Figure S1.3

As $\overrightarrow{\omega 2}$ is in the opposite direction to $\overrightarrow{\omega\beta}$, $\overrightarrow{\omega\beta} = -g\overrightarrow{\omega 2}$. Hence this time $\lambda = -g$. Again, as our vectors are planar, the eigenspace corresponding to the eigenvalue $-g$ is two-dimensional.

Setting $\mathbf{v}_i = \overrightarrow{\omega(\beta.i)}$ or $\mathbf{v}_i = \overrightarrow{\omega(4.i)}$ does not result in new eigenvalues. If we set $\mathbf{v}_i = \overrightarrow{\omega(5.i)}$, $i = 0, 1, \ldots, 4$, then $\mathbf{v}_{i-1} + \mathbf{v}_{i+1} = 2\mathbf{v}_i$. Hence this time $\lambda = 2$. As all $\mathbf{v}_i$s are identical, the eigenspace corresponding to the eigenvalue 2 is one-dimensional. This completes the geometrical derivation of the eigenvalues of A.

THE EIGENVALUES AND EIGENVECTORS OF M

Let $\mathbf{w}$ be an eigenvector of M. We partition $\mathbf{w}$ according to the partitioning of M in equation S1.1 as follows:

$$\mathbf{w} = \begin{pmatrix} a \\ \mathbf{u} \\ \mathbf{v} \\ b \end{pmatrix} \tag{S1.7}$$

Then the equation $\mathbf{Mw} = \lambda\mathbf{w}$ can be written thus:

$$\begin{cases} \mathbf{e}^*\mathbf{u} = \lambda a \\ a\mathbf{e} + A\mathbf{u} + B\mathbf{v} = \lambda\mathbf{u} \\ B\mathbf{u} + A\mathbf{v} + b\mathbf{e} = \lambda\mathbf{v} \\ \mathbf{e}^*\mathbf{v} = \lambda b \end{cases} \tag{S1.8}$$

Substituting in equation S1.8 for B from equation S1.2, and noting that $J_5\mathbf{v} = (\mathbf{e}^*\mathbf{v})\mathbf{e} = \lambda b\mathbf{e}$, and $J_5\mathbf{u} = (\mathbf{e}^*\mathbf{u})\mathbf{e} = \lambda a\mathbf{e}$ we obtain

$$\begin{cases} (a + \lambda b)\mathbf{e} + (A - \lambda I_5)\mathbf{u} = (A + I_5)\mathbf{v} \\ (\lambda a + b)\mathbf{e} + (A - \lambda I_5)\mathbf{v} = (A + I_5)\mathbf{u} \end{cases} \tag{S1.8'}$$

On adding together the above equations we obtain

$$(1 + \lambda)(a + b)\mathbf{e} = (1 + \lambda)(\mathbf{u} + \mathbf{v}) \tag{S1.8''}$$

We distinguish the following two cases:

$$\lambda = -1 \quad \text{and} \quad \lambda \neq -1$$

Case 1. $\lambda = -1$. In this case the first of equations S1.8' will reduce to

$$(a - b)\mathbf{e} = (A + I_5)(\mathbf{v} - \mathbf{u})$$

Multiplying both sides by $\mathbf{e}^*$ and noting that $\mathbf{e}^*(A + I_5) = 3\mathbf{e}^*$, $\mathbf{e}^*\mathbf{u} = -a$, and $\mathbf{e}^*\mathbf{v} = -b$, we obtain

$$5(a - b) = 3(-b + a)$$

Therefore, $a = b$, and as $A + I_5$ is non-singular, $\mathbf{v} = \mathbf{u}$.

The above argument shows that $\lambda = -1$ is a fivefold eigenvalue of M. For basic eigenvectors corresponding to $\lambda = -1$, we choose $\mathbf{u}$ to take (vector) values $(1/\sqrt{2})\mathbf{t}_i$, $i = 1, \ldots, 4$.

Clearly $\mathbf{e}^*\mathbf{t}_i = 0$ for $i = 1, \ldots, 4$, and therefore the corresponding a is zero.

Next, we set $\mathbf{u} = (1/\sqrt{12})\mathbf{t}_0 = (1/\sqrt{60})\mathbf{e}$. The a $(= b)$ corresponding to this vector is $-\mathbf{e}^*\mathbf{u} = -5/\sqrt{60}$. Hence the five eigenvectors corresponding to $\lambda = -1$ are as follows:

$$\mathbf{w}_0 := \frac{1}{\sqrt{60}} \begin{pmatrix} -5 \\ \mathbf{e} \\ \mathbf{e} \\ -5 \end{pmatrix}, \quad \mathbf{w}_i := \frac{1}{\sqrt{2}} \begin{pmatrix} 0 \\ \mathbf{t}_i \\ \mathbf{t}_i \\ 0 \end{pmatrix} \quad i = 1, 2, 3, 4 \tag{S1.9}$$

Case 2. $\lambda \neq -1$. In this case equation S1.8″ reduces to $(a + b)\mathbf{e} = \mathbf{u} + \mathbf{v}$. We eliminate $\mathbf{v}$ between this equation and equation S1.8′ to obtain

$$(a + \lambda b)\mathbf{e} + (A - \lambda I_5)\mathbf{u} = (a + b)(A + I_5)\mathbf{e} - (A + I_5)\mathbf{u}$$

or

$$(2a + (3 - \lambda)b)\mathbf{e} = (2A - (\lambda - 1)I_5)\mathbf{u} \qquad (S1.8''')$$

If $\mathbf{u} = \mathbf{e}$, then $\mathbf{v} = (a + b - 1)\mathbf{e}$ and $2a + (3 - \lambda)b = 5 - \lambda$.

Further, $\mathbf{e}^*\mathbf{u} = \lambda a = 5$ and $\mathbf{e}^*\mathbf{v} = 5(a + b - 1) = \lambda b$. These three equations have three sets of solutions, as follows:

$$\begin{cases} a = 1 \\ b = 1 \\ \lambda = 5 \\ \mathbf{u} = \mathbf{e} \\ \mathbf{v} = \mathbf{e} \end{cases} \qquad \begin{cases} a = \sqrt{5} \\ b = -\sqrt{5} \\ \lambda = \sqrt{5} \\ \mathbf{u} = \mathbf{e} \\ \mathbf{v} = -\mathbf{e} \end{cases} \qquad \begin{cases} a = -\sqrt{5} \\ b = \sqrt{5} \\ \lambda = -\sqrt{5} \\ \mathbf{u} = \mathbf{e} \\ \mathbf{v} = -\mathbf{e} \end{cases}$$

Next we assume that $\mathbf{u} \neq \mathbf{e}$. In view of equation S1.8‴, then $2a + (3 - \lambda)b = 0$, and $\mathbf{u}$ must be an eigenvector corresponding to the zero eigenvalue of $(2A - (\lambda - 1)I_5)$. The eigenvalues of the latter matrix are $2\mu - (\lambda - 1)$, where $\mu = 2$, g^{-1}, or $-g$.

Hence we have

$$\begin{cases} \lambda = 5 \\ \mathbf{u} = \mathbf{e} \end{cases} \text{(which we had earlier)}$$

$$\begin{cases} \lambda = 2g^{-1} = \sqrt{5} \\ \mathbf{u} = \mathbf{t}_1 \quad \text{and} \quad \mathbf{t}_2 \end{cases}$$

and

$$\begin{cases} \lambda = -2g + 1 = -\sqrt{5} \\ \mathbf{u} = \mathbf{t}_3 \quad \text{and} \quad \mathbf{u} = \mathbf{t}_4 \end{cases}$$

This completes our search for the eigenvalues and eigenvectors of M. The remaining eigenvectors are as follows:

$$\mathbf{W}_5 := \frac{1}{\sqrt{12}} \begin{pmatrix} 1 \\ e \\ e \\ 1 \end{pmatrix}$$

is the eigenvector corresponding to $\lambda = 1$;

$$\mathbf{W}_6 := \frac{1}{2\sqrt{5}} \begin{pmatrix} \sqrt{5} \\ e \\ -e \\ -\sqrt{5} \end{pmatrix} \quad \text{and} \quad \mathbf{W}_{6+i} := \begin{pmatrix} 0 \\ t_i \\ -t_i \\ 0 \end{pmatrix}, \quad i = 1, 2$$

are a basis for the eigenspace corresponding to $\lambda = 2g^{-1} + 1 = \sqrt{5}$; and

$$\mathbf{W}_{6+i} := \begin{pmatrix} 0 \\ t_i \\ -t_i \\ 0 \end{pmatrix}, \quad i = 3, 4 \quad \text{and} \quad \mathbf{W}_{11} := \frac{1}{2\sqrt{5}} \begin{pmatrix} -\sqrt{5} \\ e \\ -e \\ -\sqrt{5} \end{pmatrix}$$

constitute a basis for the eigenspace corresponding to $\lambda = -2g + 1 = -\sqrt{5}$.

If we set $\mathbf{W} = (\mathbf{w}_0, \mathbf{w}_1, \ldots, \mathbf{w}_{11})$, then

$$M = WDW^{-1} \tag{S1.10}$$

where D is the diagonal matrix:

$$\text{Diag}(-1 \ (5 \text{ times}), \ 1, 2g^{-1} + 1 \ (3 \text{ times}), \ -2g + 1 \ (3 \text{ times}))$$

Different powers of M can now easily be obtained either by equation S1.10 or by using the minimal polynomial of M, namely

$$M^4 - 4M^3 - 10M^2 + 20M + 25I_{12} = 0 \tag{S1.11}$$

If we set $I_{12} = I$, $J_{12} = J$ and denote by I^r a matrix whose entries are all zero except those on the north-east to south-west main diagonal which are all ones, then the powers of M can be expressed thus:

$$M^n = (-1)^n \left(\frac{I + I^r}{2} - \frac{J}{12} \right) + \frac{5^n}{12} J + \frac{(\sqrt{5})^n}{2\sqrt{5}} \left[M - \frac{J}{2} + gI - g^{-1}I^r \right]$$

$$+ \frac{(-\sqrt{5})^n}{2\sqrt{5}} \left[\frac{J}{2} - M + g^{-1}I - gI^r \right] \tag{S1.12}$$

FLOW OF IDEAS AND RANDOM WALK ON ICOSAHEDRON

The edges of our icosahedron represent the participants in Beer's syntegrity, and vertices represent the group of five incidental edges and, therefore, the corresponding team of five participants all discussing and modifying a 'changing proposition.' It is at these teams (i.e. vertices) that new ideas germinate and changes appear, and it is through the medium of the participants (edges) that changed ideas are disseminated from one team to a neighbouring team.

There are at least two possible ways of modelling this propagation of new information. In the first approach information is viewed as *indivisible units* which reside at any point of time at a unique vertex. These units, however, *episodically* or *continuously* (with respect to time) are transferred with a certain probability to an adjacent vertex (team of participants). Hence the information generated at a vertex in an episode of time, may be found, after the passage of some episodes at any other vertex (or even at its birthplace) with a certain probability. The pattern of change in these probabilities, as time goes by, is of interest. Owing to the *ergodicity* of the structure of the icosahedron and its *symmetry*, as we shall see, in the 'long' run a state of equilibrium will prevail in which these probabilities all tend to 1/12. The *speed of convergence* towards the equilibrium state is the measure of how *transpiring* our system is.

The second way in which the transfer of information can be viewed is to consider units of information as (infinitely) *divisible*. In this model a constant *proportion* of the information residing at each vertex, episodically or continuously, is transferred to the adjacent vertices and is divided amongst them equally.

The above two conceptually distinct approaches, from a formal–mathematical point of view, are equivalent. The probabilistic approach, however, provides us with a richer conceptual framework. Therefore, we follow this approach with the recognition of the fact that the results we obtain can be translated from the *language of probability* to that of *proportions*.

While holding to the probabilistic view point, we treat the passage of time, first as episodic and then as continuous.

EPISODIC TIME

In this case the model depicting the flow of information is a Markov Chain with 12 states. We assume that in each episode, any unit of information present at a vertex is transferred to an adjacent vertex with probability p ($0 < p \leqslant 1/5$), and remains where it is with probability $1 - 5p$.

The One Episode Transition Probability Matrix of the Markov Chain denoted by $\mathscr{P}$ here has the following expression in terms of M:

$$\mathscr{P} = (1 - 5p)I + pM \tag{S1.13}$$

The n-episode transition probability matrix of our chain is indeed $\mathscr{P}^n$. Equation S1.12 provides us with means of obtaining all such matrices. In fact,

$$\mathscr{P}^n = (1 - 6p)^n \left(\frac{I + I^r}{2} - \frac{J}{12} \right) + \frac{J}{12} + \frac{(1 + \sqrt{5}p - 5p)^n}{2\sqrt{5}}$$

$$\times \left[M - \frac{J}{2} + gI - g^{-1}I^r \right] + \frac{(1 - \sqrt{5}p - 5p)^n}{2\sqrt{5}} \left[\frac{J}{2} - M + g^{-1}I - gI^r \right] \tag{S1.14}$$

If the information of interest is generated at the starting episode (this is purely conventional) at a given vertex (vertex T, say), then our initial state-probability vector has zero for all its components except the one corresponding to T, which is 1. After n episodes, however, the components of state-probability vector are $(\mathscr{P}^n)_{Tj}$, where j varies over all the labels.

It is evident from equation S1.14 that the above probabilities depend only on the graph distance between the vertices T and j. The distance takes the values 0, 1, 2, and 3. Hence for every n we need to know only four probabilities. This important fact is at the heart of the relationship between our graph and the *association algebras* we mentioned in the Introduction.

The four sequences of probabilities are as follows:

$$\begin{cases} (\mathscr{P}^n)_{\delta = 0} = \frac{1}{12} + \left\{ \frac{5}{12} (1 - 6p)^n + \frac{1}{4} \left[(1 + \sqrt{5}p - 5p)^n + (1 - \sqrt{5}p - 5p)^n \right] \right\} \\[2mm] (\mathscr{P}^n)_{\delta = 1} = \frac{1}{12} + \left\{ -\frac{1}{12} (1 - 6p)^n + \frac{1}{4\sqrt{5}} \left[(1 + \sqrt{5}p - 5p)^n - (1 - \sqrt{5}p - 5p)^n \right] \right\} \\[2mm] \hfill (\text{S1.15}) \\[2mm] (\mathscr{P}^n)_{\delta = 2} = \frac{1}{12} + \left\{ -\frac{1}{12} (1 - 6p)^n - \frac{1}{4\sqrt{5}} \left[(1 + \sqrt{5}p - 5p)^n - (1 - \sqrt{5}p - 5p)^n \right] \right\} \\[2mm] (\mathscr{P}^n)_{\delta = 2} = \frac{1}{12} + \left\{ \frac{5}{12} (1 - 6p)^n - \frac{1}{4} \left[(1 + \sqrt{5}p - 5p)^n + (1 - \sqrt{5}p - 5p)^n \right] \right\} \end{cases}$$

where δ represents the graph distance.

A most reasonable choice for p is the value $1/6$. In the language of *proportions*, this value corresponds to the case when a unit of information generated at a vertex in any episode will be shared, in the next episode, among all the vertices which are incident to at least one of the edges incident to the original vertex.

For $p = 1/6$, equations S1.15 simplify to the following:

$$\begin{cases} (\mathscr{P}^n)_{\delta=0} = \dfrac{1}{12} + \dfrac{\psi_n}{4 \times 3^n} & (\mathscr{P}^n)_{\delta=1} = \dfrac{1}{12} + \dfrac{\varphi_n}{4 \times 3^n} \\[3mm] (\mathscr{P}^n)_{\delta=2} = \dfrac{1}{12} - \dfrac{\varphi_n}{4 \times 3^n} & (\mathscr{P}^n)_{\delta=3} = \dfrac{1}{12} - \dfrac{\psi_n}{4 \times 3^n} \end{cases} \tag{S1.16}$$

for $n \geq 1$.

The Fibonacci sequences φ_n and ψ_n have been introduced earlier. It is clear from the above probabilities that our Markov chain is geometrically ergodic. For large n, $\varphi_n \sim g^n/\sqrt{5}$ and $\psi_n \sim g^n$. Hence our probabilities approach the equilibrium state with the geometric regression rate of $g/3 = 1/1.8541$, for large n. For general n, the deviations of the above probabilities from $1/12$ are equal to $\psi_n/4 \times 3^n$ and $\varphi_n/4 \times 3^n$.

The table below provides the values of these deviations for $n = 1, \ldots, 12$.

n	1	2	3	4	5	6
$\psi_n/4 \times 3^n$	0.083	0.083	0.037	0.022	0.011	6.17×10^{-3}
$\varphi_n/4 \times 3^n$	0.083	0.0278	0.0185	9.26×10^{-3}	5.14×10^{-3}	2.74×10^{-3}

n	7	8	9	10	11	12
$\psi_n/4 \times 3^n$	3.31×10^{-3}	1.79×10^{-3}	9.65×10^{-4}	5.21×10^{-4}	2.81×10^{-4}	1.51×10^{-4}
$\varphi_n/4 \times 3^n$	1.49×10^{-3}	8.00×10^{-4}	4.32×10^{-4}	2.33×10^{-4}	1.26×10^{-4}	6.78×10^{-5}

By examining equations S1.15, one can see easily that the p which leads to the fastest rate of convergence is $1/5$. This corresponds to the case where vertices discharge at every episode all their information to the neighbouring ones. In the language of *probabilities* this case corresponds to a *symmetric random walk over the graph of icosahedron.* For $\lambda = 1/5$, equations S1.15 reduce to the following:

If $n = 2m$:

$$(\mathscr{P}^n)_{\delta=0} = \frac{1}{12} + \left\{\frac{1}{12 \times 5^{n-1}} + \frac{1}{2 \times 5^m}\right\};$$

$$(\mathscr{P}^n)_{\delta=1} = \frac{1}{12} - \frac{1}{12 \times 5^n} = (\mathscr{P}^n)_{\delta=2};$$

$$(\mathscr{P}^n)_{\delta=3} = \frac{1}{12} + \left\{\frac{1}{12 \times 5^{n-1}} + \frac{1}{2 \times 5^m}\right\}$$

If $n = 2m + 1$: (S1.17)

$$(\mathscr{P}^n)_{\delta=0} = \frac{1}{12} - \frac{1}{12 \times 5^{n-1}} = (\mathscr{P}^n)_{\delta=3};$$

$$(\mathscr{P}^n)_{\delta=1} = \frac{1}{12} + \left\{\frac{1}{12 \times 5^n} + \frac{1}{2 \times 5^{m+1}}\right\};$$

$$(\mathscr{P}^n)_{\delta=2} = \frac{1}{12} + \left\{\frac{1}{12 \times 5^n} - \frac{1}{2 \times 5^{m+1}}\right\}$$

As is evident from these equations, although we have achieved a faster rate of convergence, the deviations are now an oscillating function of n. The maximum deviation in even episodes is

$$\frac{1}{12 \times 5^{n-1}} + \frac{1}{2 \times (\sqrt{5})^n}$$

and in odd episodes is

$$\frac{1}{12 \times 5^n} + \frac{1}{2 \times \sqrt{5} \times (\sqrt{5})^n}$$

For large n, the first term can be ignored and the deviation is proportional to

$$\left(\frac{1}{\sqrt{5}}\right)^n \sim \left(\frac{1}{2.236}\right)^n$$

Hence our chain is, as expected, geometrically ergodic with regression rate of $1/2.236$.

The oscillation in deviation we mentioned is a result of the complete lack of memory in our model when $p = 1/5$. This seems, to some extent, unrealistic, and therefore in our opinion the model with $p = 1/6$ is preferable.

CONTINUOUS TIME

In this case we are dealing with a 12-state Markov Process. The transition probability matrix after time t is equal to $\mathscr{P}(t) = \exp(\nu t Q)$, where the matrix Q is related to the matrix M as follows:

$$Q = -I + \frac{1}{5} M \qquad (S1.18)$$

By using once again equations S1.12 we can obtain $\mathscr{P}(t)$:

$$\mathscr{P}(t) = \exp(-6\nu t/5)\left(\frac{I + I^r}{2} - \frac{J}{12}\right) + \frac{1}{12}J + \frac{1}{2\sqrt{5}} \exp(-2\nu t/\sqrt{5})$$

$$\times \left[M - \frac{J}{2} + gI - g^{-1}I^r\right] + \frac{1}{2\sqrt{5}} \exp(-2g\nu t/\sqrt{5})\left[\frac{J}{2} - M + g^{-1}I - g^{-1}I^r\right]$$

$$(S1.19)$$

Again, the determining probabilities are the following:

$$\begin{cases} (\mathscr{P}(t))_{\delta = 0} = \frac{1}{12} + \left\{\frac{5}{12} \exp(-6\nu t/5) + 1/2 \exp(-\nu t)\cosh\frac{\nu t}{\sqrt{5}}\right\} \\[3mm] (\mathscr{P}(t))_{\delta = 1} = \frac{1}{12} + \left\{-\frac{1}{12} \exp(-6\nu t/5) + \frac{1}{2\sqrt{5}} \exp(-\nu t)\sinh\frac{\nu t}{\sqrt{5}}\right\} \\[3mm] (\mathscr{P}(t))_{\delta = 2} = \frac{1}{12} + \left\{-\frac{1}{12} \exp(-6\nu t/5) - \frac{1}{2\sqrt{5}} \exp(-\nu t)\sinh\frac{\nu t}{\sqrt{5}}\right\} \\[3mm] (\mathscr{P}(t))_{\delta = 0} = \frac{1}{12} + \left\{\frac{5}{12} \exp(-6\nu t/5) - 1/2 \exp(-\nu t)\cosh\frac{\nu t}{\sqrt{5}}\right\} \end{cases} \quad (S1.20)$$

where ν represents the speed of dissemination of information.

The process is obviously ergodic. The graphs of the above probabilities with respect to $\tau = \nu t$, the internal time of the network, are plotted in Figure S1.4.

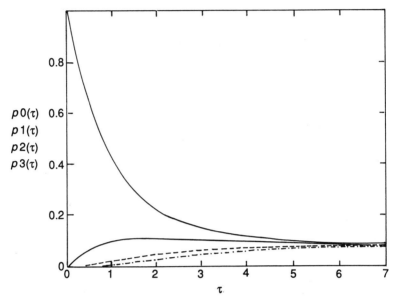

Figure SI.4   The levels of existing information, after (an internal time) period of τ, at the distances $\delta = 0, 1, 2, 3$ from the point of germination of the information

As can be seen, despite many analogies, the episodic time model exhibits more richness and variety, and as, in our view, it is also more realistic, it is preferable to the continuous time model.

$$\tau: = 0, 0.1, ..., 7.0$$

$$p0(\tau): = \left(\frac{1}{12} + \frac{5}{12} \exp\left(-\frac{6}{5}\tau\right)\right) + \frac{1}{2} \exp(-\tau)\cosh\left(\frac{\tau}{\sqrt{5}}\right)$$

$$p1(\tau): = \left(\frac{1}{12} - \frac{1}{12} \exp\left(-\frac{6}{5}\tau\right)\right) + \frac{1}{2\sqrt{5}} \exp(-\tau)\sinh\left(\frac{\tau}{\sqrt{5}}\right)$$

$$p2(\tau): = \left(\frac{1}{12} - \frac{1}{12} \exp\left(-\frac{6}{5}\tau\right)\right) - \frac{1}{2\sqrt{5}} \exp(-\tau)\sinh\left(\frac{\tau}{\sqrt{5}}\right)$$

$$p3(\tau): = \left(\frac{1}{12} + \frac{5}{12} \exp\left(-\frac{6}{5}\tau\right)\right) - \frac{1}{2} \exp(-\tau)\cosh\left(\frac{\tau}{\sqrt{5}}\right)$$

FROM PROTOTYPE TO PROTOCOL
Design for doing
Joe Truss

The chapters in Part One of this book relate the development of Team Syntegrity through its experiments in application and research in theory. As more and more insights emerge from ongoing research and application, expanding both the opportunities to apply Team Syntegrity and the understanding of why the underlying structure of the icosahedron provides such a rich and powerful model for group process, it is necessary to stop now and again simply to describe the current state of affairs.

The purpose of this chapter is to provide a description of a Syntegration as it would take place today. It supplants the description developed at the start, as given in Chapter Two. This description outlines the various stages of a Syntegration when used by a group of people to explore a question of significance to the group. The group could be members of an organization seeking to initiate a strategic planning process, or a group of concerned citizens tied together only by their mutual interest in a significant issue.

Syntegration as outlined in these pages does not include either the goal setting process described later in *About Face* (Surplus Six), which is an extension of the basic protocol, or the electronic support that can be provided for the Hexadic Reduction and Topic Auction phases of the basic protocol which is explained in *Elective Selection* (Surplus Three). The intent here is simply to give the reader an opportunity to understand the basic process as it has evolved through the experiments and research described in detail in earlier chapters of this book.

INTRODUCTION

In order to simplify what may appear to be a complex process, Syntegration is presented in this chapter as a 'game,' in which there are 'players, a game board, locations on the board, activities, tools and supplies.' Like all games, there are instructions and rules needed in order to play. In the following pages, the 'stages' of the game are summarized in order to provide the reader with an understanding of the flow of the process.

At the end of this chapter is a sample schedule showing how the stages of the game can be mapped out over 5 days.

The definitions and illustrations on the next few pages clarify terminology relating to both Syntegration and its underlying structure, the Icosahedron.

ILLUSTRATIONS AND DEFINITIONS

Team Syntegrity	A proprietary technology developed by Stafford Beer whereby 30 people come together to explore a subject of interest to the group. The Team Syntegrity technology uses the form of the Icosahedron as the basis for organising and scheduling the activities and discussions of 30 people around 12 major topics.
Syntegration	An event in which the Team Syntegrity protocol is applied.
Syntegrating	The act of playing in a Syntegration.
Icosahedron	One of the five regular polyhedra that has 20 triangular faces, 30 struts, and 12 vertices (Figure S2.1).
Vertices	The nodes which connect five struts, shown by the black circles in Figure S2.1.
Struts	The edges of the Icosahedron, shown by the 30 shaded parts in Figure S2.1.

Faces	The 20 triangular shapes surrounded by three vertices.
Players	The 30 people actively involved in the Syntegration.
Lead Facilitator	The facilitator who sponsors the Syntegration, creates the opening question, invites facilitators, players and helpers to participate, and co-ordinates the playing of the game.
Facilitators	The people who facilitate the Syntegration game.
Helpers	The people who support the facilitators.
Game Board	The facility used as the site for the Syntegration.
Location	Rooms where particular activities take place.
Stages	The four major components of the Syntegration process, referred to as *Opening*, *Importance Filter* (includes Generating Statements of Importance; Problem Jostle; Hexadic Reduction; Topic Auction), *Outcome Resolve*, and *Closing*.

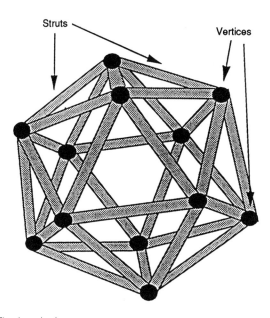

Struts

Vertices

Figure S2.1 The Icosahedron

Activities	Tasks that players do during each stage of the Syntegration.
Visual Applause	A means of allowing participants to attach sticker dots to statements to 'display' their support.
Tools	Equipment that is needed for the Syntegration.
Supplies	Supplies that are needed for the Syntegration.

TEAM SYNTEGRITY AND THE ICOSAHEDRON

EXTERNAL CONNECTIONS (FIGURE S2.2)

Each vertex of the Icosahedron corresponds to one of the 12 topics for discussion, and is assigned a colour as shown. The colour of the vertex becomes the colour that identifies one team and one topic. The members that belong to one team are represented by the five struts that connect to one vertex.

The role of each player in the Syntegration is defined by one of the 30 struts. Each strut is divided into two, and coloured to correspond to the two connecting vertices. For example, the strut connecting the Red and Gold vertices would be coloured Red–Gold, red from the red vertex to the middle of the strut, and gold from there to the gold vertex.

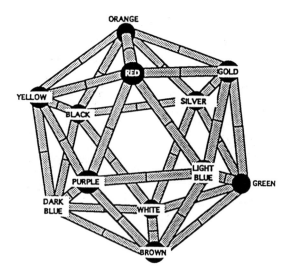

Figure S2.2   The external Syntegrity Icosahedron

The Red team, then, consists first of 5 team members as defined by the 5 struts connecting to the red vertex: Red–Gold, Red–Light Blue, Red–Purple, Red–Yellow, and Red–Orange struts. In addition, each member of the Red team is also a member of another team.

INTERNAL CONNECTIONS (FIGURE S2.3)

Each internal line connecting two vertices inside the Icosahedron defines a second role for each player—the role of critic for a team. The Red team, for example, consists not only of the five members indicated above, but includes five critics: Black–Silver, Black–Dark Blue, Green–Silver, Green–Brown, and Brown–Dark Blue.

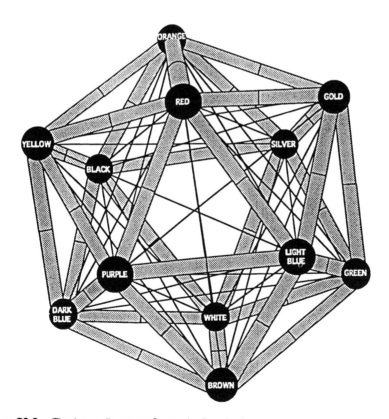

Figure S2.3 The internally strung Syntegrity Icosahedron

Table S2.1   Configurations of teams and their players

TOPIC MEETING	TEAM MEMBER	CRITIC OF:	and:	TEAM MEMBER	CRITIC OF:	and:	TOPIC MEETING
RED TEAM TOPIC:	Red–Orange	Green	Dark Blue	White–Brown	Gold	Yellow	WHITE TEAM TOPIC:
	Red–Gold	Black	Brown	White–Dark Blue	Orange	Light Blue	
	Red–Light Blue	Silver	Dark Blue	White–Black	Gold	Purple	
	Red–Yellow	Silver	Brown	White–Green	Orange	Purple	
	Red–Purple	Black	Green	White–Silver	Light Blue	Yellow	
BLACK TEAM TOPIC:	Black–Orange	Green	Purple	Light Blue–Brown	Silver	Yellow	LIGHT BLUE TEAM TOPIC:
	Black–Silver	Red	Brown	Light Blue–Purple	Orange	White	
	Black–White	Gold	Purple	Light Blue–Red	Silver	Dark Blue	
	Black–Yellow	Gold	Brown	Light Blue–Gold	White	Yellow	
	Black–Dark Blue	Red	Green	Light Blue–Green	Orange	Dark Blue	
ORANGE TEAM TOPIC:	Orange–Gold	White	Purple	Brown–Dark Blue	Red	Silver	BROWN TEAM TOPIC:
	Orange–Silver	Light Blue	Dark Blue	Brown–Purple	Black	Gold	
	Orange–Yellow	White	Light Blue	Brown–Green	Red	Black	
	Orange–Red	Green	Dark Blue	Brown–White	Gold	Yellow	
	Orange–Black	Green	Purple	Brown–Light Blue	Silver	Yellow	

GREEN TEAM TOPIC:

Green–Gold	Black	Purple	Yellow–Dark Blue	Silver	Light Blue
Green–Silver	Red	Dark Blue	Yellow–Purple	Gold	White
Green–White	Orange	Purple	Yellow–Red	Silver	Brown
Green–Light Blue	Orange	Dark Blue	Yellow–Black	Gold	Brown
Green–Brown	Red	Black	Yellow–Orange	White	Light blue

GOLD TEAM TOPIC:

Gold–Silver	Brown	Yellow	Dark Blue–Purple	Orange	Green
Gold–Light Blue	White	Yellow	Dark Blue–Black	Red	Green
Gold–Red	Black	Brown	Dark Blue–White	Orange	Light Blue
Gold–Orange	White	Purple	Dark Blue–Brown	Red	Silver
Gold–Green	Black	Purple	Dark Blue–Yellow	Silver	Light Blue

SILVER TEAM TOPIC:

Silver–White	Light Blue	Yellow	Purple–Red	Black	Green
Silver–Black	Red	Brown	Purple–Light Blue	Orange	White
Silver–Orange	Light Blue	Dark Blue	Purple–Brown	Black	Gold
Silver–Green	Red	Dark Blue	Purple–Yellow	Gold	White
Silver–Gold	Brown	Yellow	Purple–Dark Blue	Orange	Green

YELLOW TEAM TOPIC:

DARK BLUE TEAM TOPIC:

PURPLE TEAM TOPIC:

Each team has five members, defined by the five struts that connect one vertex, and five critics, defined by the internal connections. Correspondingly, each player is a member of two teams and a critic of two teams.

Polar opposites are the two vertices that are farthest away from each other.

The pairs of polar opposites are the following:

Red and White
Black and Light Blue
Orange and Brown
Green and Yellow
Gold and Dark Blue
Silver and Purple

Table S2.1 shows the configurations of all 12 teams, and identifies the players that make up each team.

GAME TERMINOLOGY

Many of the activities that form part of the game have special names, whose meaning will not be fully clear until the process is understood. Below is a list of these terms, and a short definition.

Opening Question	A question posed to the group of 30 people, which forms the basis for the discussions and exploration over the 3 days. An opening question might be: 'What are the most important issues for planning that our organization is likely to face over the upcoming 5 years?' The opening question establishes the context for the Syntegration, and therefore must be carefully crafted.
Statement of Importance	A sentence of not more than 10 words that is meaningful to a player in relation to the opening question. [Note: as the game is played, Statements of Importance (SIs) become 'Aggregated,' then 'Consolidated,' and then 'Final.']

Problem Jostle	Refers to an activity that involves negotiation and discussion of initial SIs in order to arrive at Aggregated Statements of Importance (ASIs).
Hexadic Reduction	Refers to an activity that involves reducing Aggregated Statements of Importance to arrive at 12 Consolidated Statements of Importance (CSIs).
Topic Auction	Refers to an activity in which players determine which CSIs or topics they will discuss with other players during the team meetings.
Outcome Resolve	Three iterations of team meetings, involving members and critics, in which a topic is discussed for a specified time period, and a statement is written reflecting the best thinking of the team on the topic. The 'Reverberation' created by repetition of meetings is central to Syntegrity.
Polar Reverberation Meetings	A meeting involving three pairs of players. Each pair consists of two players corresponding to polar opposite struts. The three pairs have the relationship defined by the orthogonal golden rectangles that symmetrically intersect the Icosahedron.
Plenary Session	A meeting of the whole group, including facilitators, helpers, and players.

OBJECTIVES OF THE GAME

Syntegration is a collaborative rather than a competitive game. The objective of the game is for 30 people to create Final Statements of Importance (FSIs) which become answers to the opening question. The game is over when there are 12 FSIs, corresponding to the 12 topic areas identified by the 30 people, that represent the best possible thinking (within the specified time constraints) of the team members and critics in relation to the opening question.

How people arrive at these statements is as important as what the final statements are. Therefore, the Team Syntegrity protocol defines the way the game needs to be played.

THE TEAM SYNTEGRITY PROTOCOL FOR SYNTEGRATION

SETTING UP THE GAME

Roles and Responsibilities

The people involved in a Syntegration include a Lead Facilitator, Facilitators, Players, and Helpers.

Lead Facilitators are sponsors for a Syntegration game. They are responsible for the creation of the opening question and inviting all others to play. Their role includes preparing people for their roles as facilitators, players, and helpers. They co-ordinate the arrangements for the game board, for tools and supplies needed, and ensure that facilitators understand all the rules and instructions for the game. Lead Facilitators also have some responsibilities relating to the completion of the game.

Facilitators are responsible for the integrity of the Syntegration process. Their role is to help players understand what is involved during each stage of the game, and to communicate the instructions and rules needed at each stage. Facilitators may act as scribes, recording information for players at points in the process. Facilitators are discouraged from offering comments relating to content or subject matter, unless specifically invited to do so. Their role is to manage the process of Syntegration.

Players are the 30 people responsible for answering the opening question. They are the active participants in the discussions during which the 12 topics are identified and the statements created. Their role is to be creative thinkers in exploring the opening question and its implications. Players play three roles at various times throughout the 3 days, that of team member, team critic, and observer.

Helpers are people who support the facilitators, arrange for refreshments, record and transcribe information, and provide supplies needed by players throughout the 5 days.

The Game Board

The game board, or facility, needs to accommodate up to 40 people. Several locations are needed, including:

- The Main Room—a large room in which all players can gather with facilitators and helpers to receive instructions and information

- Meetings Rooms A and B—two rooms large enough for at least 10 players to hold team meetings

- The Play Room—a lounge area for snacks and refreshments with space for players to socialize when resting from the game

- The Work Room—a space where administrative tasks can take place

Figure S2.4 provides an example of how the game board might be set up.

Tools and Supplies

Tools and supplies are listed in Chapter Two. They include such things as tables, chairs, overhead projector, easel stands, computer or typewriter, paper, pens, file cards, stick-on memo notes ('Post-it notes'), circle stickers ('dots'), tape, and push pins.

PLAYING THE GAME

The Six Stages

Opening (3–4 hours)

- Registration

- Introduction, which includes:

  - Meeting other players

  - Constructing an Icosahedron

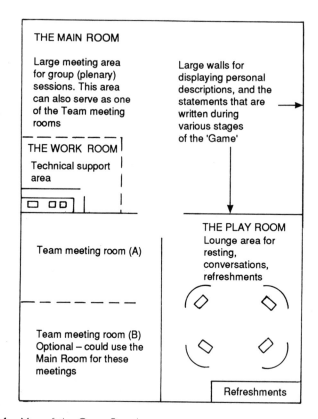

THE MAIN ROOM

Large meeting area for group (plenary) sessions. This area can also serve as one of the Team meeting rooms

Large walls for displaying personal descriptions, and the statements that are written during various stages of the 'Game'

THE WORK ROOM

Technical support area

Team meeting room (A)

THE PLAY ROOM
Lounge area for resting, conversations, refreshments

Team meeting room (B) Optional – could use the Main Room for these meetings

Refreshments

Figure S2.4. Map of the Game Board

The Importance Filter (8–9 hours)

- Generating Statements of Importance

- Problem Jostle

- Hexadic Reduction

- Topic Auction

Outcome Resolve (24 hours)

Outcome Resolve Iteration 1

- Plenary Session

- Twelve team meetings

- Polar reverberation meetings (optional)

- 'Visual Applause'

Outcome Resolve Iteration 2

- Twelve team meetings

- Polar reverberation meetings (optional)

- 'Visual Applause'

Outcome Resolve Iteration 3

- Twelve team meetings

- 'Visual Applause' (optional)

Closing (3–4 hours)

- Final plenary session

In addition to the plenary sessions listed above, each of the 5 days should begin and end with a plenary session. In some cases, the plenary session at the beginning of the day can replace the need for one of the sessions that initiate a stage of the game.

DETAILED DESCRIPTIONS OF EACH STAGE

Plenary Sessions

Plenary sessions, whether at the beginning of a stage of the game, or at the beginning or end of each day, are intended to provide information and answer questions players may have. Facilitators will describe what happens next in the game, and deal with any issues involving the large group. Plenary sessions take place in the Main Room.

Opening

During the Opening, people become acquainted, learn about the game, and create one or more Statements of Importance (SIs) which evolve the 'playing field' for subsequent discussions. The Opening ends when the SIs have been organized, transcribed from file cards to a typed list, and distributed for review to the players.

Registration

In addition to welcoming players and handing out the materials and name tags to players as they arrive, Registration is designed for people to meet one another and enjoy refreshments. In cases where people do not know each other, players write personal descriptions and post them on the wall of the Play Room.

Introduction

During the Introductory Plenary Session, facilitators welcome players and outline the expectations for the 5 days. Some 'icebreaker' activities are usually included to create more opportunities for players to meet one another. Information is provided to players about the Icosahedron. Players are given an opportunity to build their own Icosahedron model using toothpicks and gum-drops, much as described in the main text.

Importance Filter

The goal of the Importance Filter is to arrive at the 12 topics that will be discussed by the 12 teams, and to configure the 12 teams by identifying the five members and five critics for each team. This stage ends when every player knows the two teams of which he/she is a member and the two teams of which he/she is a critic, in addition to the topics that will be discussed by each team.

Generating Statements of Importance

Players are given file cards and asked to write one or more Statements of Importance (SIs) based on the Opening Question. These SIs are posted and reviewed by all players. Facilitators and players work together to bring some organization to these statements by grouping like SIs together. The statements are transcribed and distributed to all players.

Problem Jostle

During the Problem Jostle, it is very important that everyone can see everyone else, hence the need for a large open room and the use of flags and poles with flip charts and writing paper that can be seen easily from all parts of the room.

The Problem Jostle is designed to explore the initial Statements of Importance, and clarify and refine specific SIs or groups of SIs. Players solicit support from other players for statements they believe to be important to understanding and answering the opening question.

Any player can select any Statement of Importance that they wish to be a topic for consideration during the game. Players actively solicit support from other players. Their goal is to obtain a minimum of five signatures on their statement, reflecting the agreement of other players that this statement should be considered.

Once there are five signatures, the statement becomes an Aggregated Statement of Importance (ASI) and is posted on the wall for review by all players.

Hexadic Reduction

The Hexadic Reduction is a two-part process. The first part involves reviewing all the ASIs that have been posted on the wall, and grouping similar or over-lapping ASIs together. Part two allows players to indicate their level of support for the statements by placing one or more circle stickers ('dots') on each statement they wish to support. Players are encouraged to place their 'dots' strategically in order to ensure that the topics of most interest to the group are selected as topics. The 12 ASIs with the largest number of 'dots' become Consolidated Statements of Importance (CSIs), or the 12 topics that will be explored by the 12 teams during the Outcome Resolves. Once the 12 CSIs are identified, Facilitators assign each CSI or topic to a coloured vertex of the Icosahedron model.

Topic Auction

The purpose of the Topic Auction is to connect each player to their unique role as defined by one of the 30 struts of the Icosahedron. The Topic Auction ends when each player knows the two teams of which he/she is a member, and the two teams of which he/she is a critic. Once all roles have been assigned, coloured team badges are distributed to players in preparation for the Outcome Resolves.

Outcome Resolve

The goal of the Outcome Resolve is to create Final Statements of Importance (FSIs) for each of the 12 CSIs or topics. Evolving these statements takes three iterations of meetings, Outcome Resolve Iterations 1, 2, and 3.

Outcome Resolve Iteration I

Twelve Team Meetings. Each topic team meets for about 40 min during which the team explores the topic and evolves a statement that reflects the implications of the topic with respect to the opening question. Two teams meet simultaneously, followed by two more teams, until all 12 teams have met. Given that each team consists of five team members and five critics, this means that 20 players are involved in team meetings at any one time. The remaining 10 players are encouraged to act as observers and sit in on one of the team meetings.

During each team meeting, generally the five team members spend time exploring the issue or topic, then ask for input and ideas from the critics.

Because each player is actively involved in four different team meetings, two as team member and two as team critic, they naturally begin to share information as they move from one team meeting to the next. In addition, while in the role of observer, players have the opportunity to listen to the dialogue in two other team meetings, and carry this information with them into their team meetings. It is this sharing of information that creates reverberation in the system. In order to maximize reverberation, when in the observer role, players are encouraged to plan opportunities to talk with any players that they do not meet in the course of the scheduled team meetings.

Polar Reverberation Meetings (optional). Because of how the internal connections or critic lines are established in the Icosahedron, there is, for each player, a player that they will never meet unless they make special arrangements outside the team meetings. This is due to the fact that each player has a polar opposite player, and owing to the nature of the team meeting schedule there is no way for these polar opposite players to meet. Consequently, in order to enhance further the effect of reverberation, polar opposite team meetings can be scheduled to take place after Outcome Resolve Iteration 1 and Iteration 2.

A polar reverberation meeting involves six players, three pairs of polar opposite struts or edges. The three pairs are related through the golden rectangles that intersect the Icosahedron orthogonally. There are five such sets of golden rectangles making up the 30 edges of the Icosahedron. Figure S2.5 shows one set of six struts.

During a polar reverberation meeting, each player takes about 5 min to brief the other five players about their topic and how their statement is evolving. This is an information sharing session. All 30 players meet in five groups of six simultaneously. Each group of six players represent all 12 topics creating five different views of the entire Syntegration as it progresses.

'Visual Applause.' Once all topic team statements have been reviewed by players, players are given the opportunity to reflect how they feel the statements are developing. Players place one or more 'dots' on those statements they feel they can support. In addition, to ensure that their ideas will be considered by the team working on the topic, players are encouraged to attach comments (or even graffiti) using 'Post-it' notes.

Outcome Resolve Iteration 2

Outcome Resolve Iteration 2 is virtually the same as Outcome Resolve Iteration 1. Teams meet again to revise their statements, taking into account the level of support the statement received as reflected by the number of 'dots,' the comments of other players, and the evolution of their own thinking resulting from participating in and observing other team meetings.

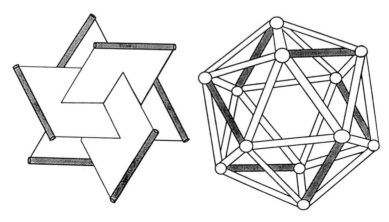

Figure S2.5 The six struts of a set of orthogonal golden rectangles within the icosahedron. Note how each strut touches two of the twelve vertices of the icosahedron

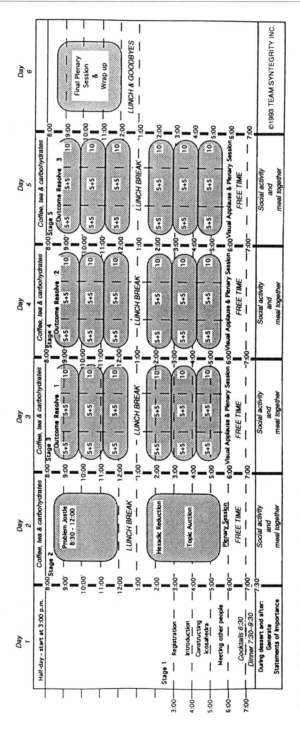

Figure S2.6. Sample Syntegration schedule

The 12 team meetings are followed again by Polar Reverberation Meetings (optional) and 'Visual Applause.'

Outcome Resolve Iteration 3

The final set of 12 team meetings is similar to the previous Outcome Resolve Iterations. However, this is the last opportunity for teams to revise their statements. Following the team meetings with 'Visual Applause' is optional, though appropriate if the Syntegration is to be followed up with other activities designed to move to setting goals or action planning.

Closing

The goal of the Closing is to review the final results of the Syntegration and provide an opportunity for players to reflect on their experiences during the 5 days.

Completing the Game

Once the game is over, the Lead Facilitator needs to ensure that copies of the following documentation are provided to all players and others involved in the Syntegration:

- All initial Statements of Importance

- All Aggregated Statements of Importance

- All Consolidated Statements of Importance

- All Final Statements of Importance

A sample Syntegration schedule is shown in Figure S2.6.

ACKNOWLEDGEMENTS

This chapter was the result of a truly collaborative team effort. Its clear presentation and logical layout are mostly due to Wendy Walsh and Christine Cullen, who managed to turn what was becoming a complicated, hard to follow manual into an elegant, user-friendly guide.

PLINY THE LATER
Elective selection
Josephine Hancock

The call to experiment in Chapter Eight describes how to build an icosahedron out of toothpicks and gum-drops. If you indeed answered this call you may have been surprised at how strong the completed structure is, considering the construction materials. This phenomenon is due to synergy, where the strength of the whole is more than the sum of strengths of its component parts. An icosahedron derives its strength from the combined effect of two types of force. The first of these is compression, which occurs in pockets at the nodes. The second force, that of tension, exerts itself continuously throughout the whole structure. It is the combined effect of compression and tension that enforces the integrity of the whole, hence the term syntegrity.

In the human terms of syntegrity, compression appears as the 'togetherness' and co-operative aspects that convert five individuals into a team, whereas the tensile forces represent the conflict necessary for debate. There are two special sets of tensile connections within the icosahedron that are important to the Team Syntegrity protocol. The first of these is well documented in Chapter One, where Stafford explains how the central space of the icosahedron is interlaced by the next but one vertex connections that signify the critical roles. Later chapters set out the duties and responsibilities of the critics to ensure cohesion and to promote reverberation.

The nature of the second set of tensile connections is, however, less explicit. These are the six pairs of polar axes about which the icosahedron can be made to spin. A polar axis has as its ends the two teams that appear opposite one another on the icosahedral model and therefore meet simultaneously in separate rooms during the Outcome Resolve. Each meeting consists of five team members and five critics, so that during any one session, ten infoset members are excluded from the activities of another ten.

An infoset member's two specific roles are determined by their team membership due to the Freesman and Adjacency exclusions. There are, however, no such rules or principles to determine the arrangement of polar opposite teams so how may we decide upon the best arrangement?

If we take the term polar opposite in its literal sense then, as in a tug of war, the two teams could be thought of as pulling in opposite directions and therefore topics with opposing viewpoints could be placed on a polar axis. Unfortunately, in practice it is unlikely to be possible to discern six pairs of axes where the polar teams display strictly opposing views. Many of the topics may be completely unrelated, leaving no criteria for deciding upon the arrangement. Another criticism of this technique is that an opposing viewpoint has a high correlation (albeit negative) with its antagonist and yet the two teams will never meet to air their differences. Alternatively, we could hang any criteria at all and simply arrange the polar teams at random, but can we be sure that this will not change the final outcome? What effect, for instance, might it have upon reverberation?

Chapter Seven describes a technique called Hexadic Reduction, which reduces the unknown number of Aggregated Statements of Importance (ASIs) generated by the Problem Jostle to six pairs of polar opposites using the principles underlying George Kelly's Personal Construct Theory. Kelly's method was originally carried out upon individuals and the data, once collated, showed that in general those people considered 'normal' had different priorities in the way in which they classified the world than those subjects who were considered mentally ill.

Data are worth nothing if one cannot generalize from them. The problem with Hexadic Reduction, however, is that it tries to construct a Kelly grid from 30 minds simultaneously, drawing the object for classification randomly out of the bag. The only mechanism for arriving at consensus is who can shout the loudest, which is clearly non-democratic and therefore perverts the ethos on which the Syntegrity approach is based.

The method is not all bad, however. It is an attempt to extract from the infoset information about what they regard as valuable by looking at the possible ways of distinguishing between the topics on offer. The problems arise when we move away from the context of one person's opinion and into the realm of an infoset. An infoset is a 30-person culture, albeit a temporary one, where each person plays his or her own role whilst simultaneously personifying the ethos of the whole infoset.

It was whilst thinking about this duality that I hit upon an idea that would solve the allocation of topics to nodes indirectly without ever having to ask the question of which topic should appear opposite another. Before explaining the method in detail I should like to outline the logic by which it was arrived at and, in particular, why the need arose for a two-stage process.

At the end of the Problem Jostle the infoset will have produced an unknown number of statements. Each of these statements represents the beginnings of discussion topics, but only 12 of them may go on to the Outcome Resolve stage and become fully fledged teams. The protocol must therefore provide a mechanism to:

1. decide upon the 12 topics that will become teams,

2. assign these teams to the coloured nodes of the icosahedron,

3. assign each of the 30 infoset members to a coloured strut of the icosahedron,

before the Outcome Resolve phase can take place.

Putting this into the context of the duality identified above, problem 1 affects the whole infoset and must therefore be decided by the whole. Problem 3, on the other hand, affects only individuals, whilst problem 2 affects both the whole infoset and individual members of it.

The duality of the problem lies in the fact that the solution of team to node assignment is intrinsically linked to the assignment of infoset members to struts. This statement is non-trivial and takes some considering. If we first decide upon the allocation of topics to nodes we necessarily create a set of 30 possible struts from which the infoset may choose for their individual team roles. A different team–node allocation would provide a different set of 30 struts.

We have already said that we do not know what criteria to use for team to node allocation, but we can, however, extract from the infoset individual preferences regarding the roles they wish to play. These data could then be used to decide which struts are needed, the creation of which would simultaneously solve the allocation of topics to nodes.

This is the approach I have used and the rest of the chapter details the workings of the algorithm to carry out the allocation process. The method, named Elective Selection, is split into two parts. The first part (the Topic Election) finds a solution to problem 1 by asking infoset members to detail their topic preferences and then aggregates the data to arrive at the consensus choice. Part two of the algorithm solves problems 2 and 3 simultaneously, again using each individual's team membership preferences. However, the same data set may not be used for both parts because the infoset's preferences for struts will depend upon which 12 topics are on offer.

The need for two stages of preference collection is not new. Pliny the Younger records a similar situation in a letter to Aristos where the outcome of a trial would have varied considerably had the senators decided upon the nature of the punishment before they had decided upon the guilt or innocence of the accused. Thankfully, our situation is not one of life or death.

THE PROCESS OF ELECTIVE SELECTION

STEP ONE: TOPIC ELECTION

The methodology begins at the end of the Problem Jostle stage when the infoset will have produced an unknown number (n) of Aggregated Statements of Importance (ASIs), which represent the embryonic topics proposed as teams for the Outcome Resolve stage of the syntegration. Each team is represented by a node on the icosahedron so that n must be contracted to 12 before the Outcome Resolve can commence.

The number of ASIs can be initially reduced by asking the infoset to study all of the topics and to suggest possible elisions. The originators of the suggested topics are then invited to discuss the possibility of combining their topics. If an agreement can be reached a new unified ASI will replace the originals. When all such elisions have been exhausted, overlap and duplication will hopefully have been removed and n will have reached its lower limit.

The problem on our hands is now essentially one of variety attenuation and a mechanism for extricating 12 ASIs from n is needed. In deciding what that mechanism ought to be, it is important to note that the infoset has a vested interest in the content of the ASIs, but the facilitators do not. The protocol should therefore provide a mechanism that allows the infoset to promote its self-organizing properties, and not a method whereby variety is suppressed by facilitators' intervention.

The simplest way of achieving this is to hold an election as no detailed explanation is required and everyone is familiar with the instrumentality, so that there is no question of a 'black box' mechanism at work manipulating the outcome. There are several ways in which the voting process could be carried out, but after experimental consideration I have opted for allocating 100 votes to each infoset member, which has the added bonus that associations with percentages make the arithmetic easier.

To begin the election, a time should be agreed by which all votes must be received at the 'polling stations' manned by facilitators. An infoset member is not required to place all of his/her votes in one go, thus allowing people to hang back and observe the unfolding scenario in order to place their votes tactically. As yet there are no rules regarding how votes should be allocated such as upper and lower limits on the number of votes cast on one particular ASI or on the number of ASIs voted for. Further experimentation will no doubt indicate whether or not any such constraints are necessary.

The logistics of the Topic Election are handled by a suite of computer programs driven by the following menu:

1. Input a member's vote.

2. Display voting totals for all ASIs.

3. Query member's voting record.

4. Display whole vote matrix.

5. Display members with votes still to cast.

6. Calculate the 12 most popular ASIs.

Each infoset member must be allocated a number from 1 to 30 and each ASI a number from 1 to n, before votes can be input through option 1 above. The member number corresponds to a row of the vote matrix and the ASI number to a column. The number of votes cast by a member x for a topic y can then be placed in cell X, Y. Option 2 then displays the voting totals to date for all ASIs by summing down the columns. These figures should be periodically updated by facilitators on large boards so that the infoset can see the current state of affairs. Ideally LCDs, linked directly to the computer, should be used so that vote totals can be updated in real time.

Option 3 of the menu extracts a single row from the matrix to remind individual infoset members of the votes that they have so far placed. To reduce the number of queries of this kind, the infoset should be issued with forms on which to keep track of their own votes. Towards the end of the alloted voting time, option 5 can be used in order to chase up those members who still have votes left to cast. When all 30 members have allocated all of their votes, option 6 will calculate the 12 ASIs that will become teams for the Outcome Resolve, by simply summing all of the votes and taking the top 12 totals.

STEP TWO: TOPIC AUCTION

This stage of the Syntegrity protocol is the most complex in terms of variety handling, because it involves the solution of two interlocking problems. The first of these is the arrangement of ASIs around the nodes of the icosahedron, and the second is the allocation of infoset members to struts of the icosahedron. This situation is exceptional in that the solution of the first problem reduces the number of possible solutions of the second. In other words, if the topics are first allocated to nodes then Joe Bloggs cannot be a member of both team 4 and team 11 if these teams are not adjacent, the strut does not exist, and the option has therefore been removed. The importance of this point lies in the problem already discussed, of having no suitable criteria for identifying polar opposites, or even for that matter team adjacencies. This being the case, we have no means to justify a team allocation that allows 30 strut options but removes any other possibilities.

The actual number of possibilities in this scenario is startling; indeed, it would take our fastest computers several centuries to enumerate all solutions completely. There are, in fact, almost four million ways of allocating topics to nodes and for each one of these solutions there are 30 factorial ways of allocating infoset members to the created struts:

$$11 \quad \times \quad \frac{10!}{5!5!} \quad \times \quad \frac{5!}{10} \quad \times \quad 5!$$

$$\downarrow \qquad\qquad \downarrow \qquad\qquad \downarrow \qquad\qquad \downarrow$$

| Fix 1st node then 11 ways of choosing polar opposite | $^{10}C_5$ ways of choosing the 5 polar teams | 5! ways of ordering the 5 teams but ÷ 10 to account for symmetry | 5! ways of ordering the last 5 teams |

$$= \frac{11!}{10} = 3\,991\,680$$

For each one of these team arrangements, the infoset may be allocated to struts in 30! ways.

So how are we to handle all of this variety? Well, if we tackle the problem from a different angle and attempt, instead, to allocate infoset members to their preferred team roles, then the allocation of topics to nodes will necessarily be solved simultaneously.

What is required, then, is an algorithm that will maximize the satisfaction of all 30 infoset members. That satisfaction can be based on the votes given by each infoset member to each of his/her preferred topics, so that if Joe Bloggs is allocated his desired membership of teams 4 and 11, the voting total of the strut is the sum of the votes he gave to topic 4 and to topic 11, but here's the crunch: the voting total of one particular allocation of topics to nodes, and people to struts, is then the sum of the voting totals for all 30 struts, but this cannot be calculated until after a solution has been found! In view of this, what we need is an algorithm to find a starting solution and then a hill-climbing heuristic that will improve the starting solution by swapping infoset members, and possibly even topics, until little more improvement can be made to the voting total.

This starting solution could be chosen at random, but in view of the enormous variety involved, I set about devising and programming an algorithm to find a good starting solution, which could then be converged more quickly to a near-optimal solution by the hill-climbing heuristics.

THE ALGORITHM

From the Topic Election we know which twelve ASIs will go through to form the teams of the Outcome Resolve, and as these are the only topics that we are now interested in we must ask the infoset to express their preferences in terms of possible team membership for the 12 remaining teams. This can be done by using the same suite of programs as in the Topic Election, but the created data matrix will now have only 12 columns.

For the sake of simplicity the syntegrity protocol has assigned colours to the nodes of the icosahedron so that the teams can be referred to by their colour names and infoset members by their two team colours, such as 'Mr Black–White.' We need then to assign two team colours to each infoset member by identifying their preferred strut and, in so doing, discover which ASIs will become which team colours. The colours and their adjacencies are fixed as defined in Chapter Two and Figure S3.1 illustrates their

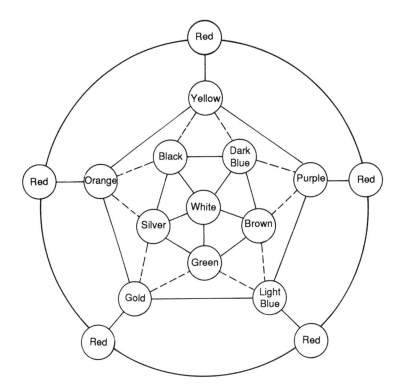

Figure S3.1 Dashed lines are zig-zagged connecting struts between Red and White polar caps

connections using the pole-centre planar projection of an icosahedral space from Chapter Eight.

In order to explain how the algorithm works, let us code our 30 infoset members 1 to 30 and our ASIs A to L. The first step of the algorithm is then to sum down the columns of the data matrix to find the vote total for each ASI and then to fix the least popular of the 12 as the first team. The logic behind starting with the least popular team is that fewer people are interested in discussing this topic, so it is sensible to assign its five members whilst we may choose from all 30 rather than later when those voting highest for it may have been allocated elsewhere. Assume in our case that the least popular ASI is D; owing to symmetry it is unimportant which colour we start from, but as it is at the centre of Figure S3.1, let us call it the White team.

By scanning column D, we may select the five highest votes, the rows these appear in are then the White team members, let us say 10, 19, 11, 4, and 8.

As the White team now has its full complement of five members, we may remove column D from the matrix.

We now need to know which ASIs will form the second teams of the five White team members. Taking each member in turn we scan their row and locate the column containing their highest vote, and this then becomes their second team assignment. Let us say that in our case, member 10 is assigned to J, 19 to H, 11 to B, 4 to F, and 8 to L. Figure S3.2 shows this situation.

We cannot as yet assign colours to J, H, B, F, or L because although we know from Figure S3.1 that White is connected to Dark Blue, Brown, Green, Silver, and Black, we cannot glean the mapping of ASIs to colours without the pentagon connecting struts which define the order in which teams surround White.

To ascertain this ordering, we need to find from the remaining 25 unassigned members the five who will be the struts that make up the pentagon surrounding the White team. Taking J, the first ASI in our list, we can scan the column to locate the row containing the highest vote and assign this person, say 14, to team J. Scanning row 14 we may now find the highest vote that this person gave to the four ASIs H, B, F, or L; this then becomes their second team defining the end of their strut, let us say B. We may now remove person 14 from the matrix as he/she has been allocated to his/her two team assignments.

Now taking topic B we scan the column to find from the remaining 24 people the row with the highest vote, say 7, and assign this person to team B. Finding the highest vote person 7 gave to the three remaining teams of H, F and L gives us the second team assignment for person 7. Again, as row 7's assignment has been completed we must remove him/her from the matrix.

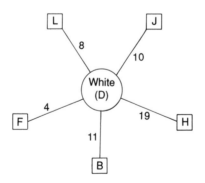

Figure S3.2

This process is repeated until we have a chain linking all five teams, and the last team connects with the first to complete the pentagon. Let us assume that our result has given us the 'pentagonal cap' shown in Figure S3.3.

This means that the ordered chain is F–J–B–L–H; however, we do not know whether this chain should circle White clockwise or anticlockwise. In other words, if we call F Dark Blue, then I could either be Black or Brown. This is important as it will define the connections with White's polar opposite cap surrounding the Red team. The colour assignments must then be left until we have decided how best to join the two pentagonal caps surrounding White and Red.

In order to find the Red team's pentagonal cap we must repeat the procedure thus far, starting with the least popular of the six remaining ASIs and assigning this to Red. Let us assume that Figure S3.4 shows this result.

Having found the two pentagonal caps encircling the polar opposite teams of White and Red, we have assigned 20 of the 30 infoset members to their two team topics. All that remains is to join the two ordered chains of J–B–L–H–F and A–I–C–E–K with the zig-zagged struts that will complete the icosahedron. Taking the first topic in the white chain, J, scan its column for the row with the highest vote, let us say 28, then assign them to the J team. Then scan the votes given by person 28 for the five teams in the Red chain for the highest, say A, and make this their second team assignment. Now remove person 28 from the matrix.

Looking at Figure S3.1, we can see that the White pentagonal cap is the small pentagon in the centre, and that the Red pentagonal cap is shown by the larger pentagon surrounding it. The dashed star depicts the ten struts connecting the

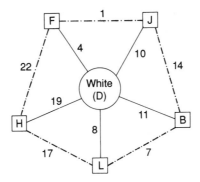

Figure S3.3   Dot-dashed line, pentagonal cap

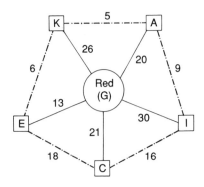

Figure S3.4 Dot-dashed line, pentagonal cap

Red and White polar caps. From this we can see that if J is connected to A, then A in turn connects back to either B or F, because the team at the end of the strut from A must also connect to J.

From the nine remaining people, select the one who has voted the most for team A, say person 2, and assign him/her to A. Next, compare person 2's votes for B and for F taking the highest (F) to be 2's second team assignment. Now remove person 2 from the matrix. We now have eight people remaining from which we select the highest voter for topic F, say person 29, and assign him/her to team F.

In deciding which other team person 29 will take part, we again only have a choice between two, K or I, because it must also connect with A. Supposing that with our imaginary data the chosen team is K, we now have the situation depicted in Figure S3.5.

Having assigned these three struts, we know how the Red and White chains slot together and so the remaining seven struts are given. K must connect to H because F is connected to J and H. Likewise, H must then connect back to E because K is connected to A and E. The five remaining struts are then E–L,

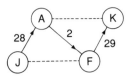

Figure S3.5.

L–C, C–B, B–I, and then I back to J to complete the circle. All that now remains is to assign the final seven infoset members to these struts.

We can no longer apply the technique used throughout the algorithm, of taking the first team finding the highest voter for it and then choosing the topic he/she voted highest for from those remaining to be their second team, because both teams for the remaining seven struts have now been defined, and they are no longer optional. Instead, for all remaining people we find their voting values for each of the last seven struts and then allocate them to the highest. For example, if person 24 placed 10 votes on topic K and 15 on topic H, the strut K–H has for him/her a voting value of 25. If by the same token member 24 has voting values for H–E of 10, E–L of 5, L–C of 0, C–B of 0, B–I of 30 and I–J of 5, then he/she will be allocated to strut B–I.

This then completes the allocation of infoset members to teams, and in the process gives us all team adjacencies, but we still have 10 teams without colours. Now that we know, however, that the Red and White pentagonal chains fit together, it does not matter how we assign the colours as long as they follow a similar chain. In other words, as Dark Blue is connected to Purple, which is connected to Brown, which is connected to Light Blue...; if we call J Dark Blue, then A is Purple, F is Brown, K is Light Blue, and so on. Equally, we could call J Silver, in which case A would be Orange, F Black, and K Yellow.

This completes the algorithm as it stands; hill-climbing heuristics have yet to be devised and the performance of several alternative algorithms compared. This research will be the subject of my Doctoral Thesis which is due for publication at the end of 1994 by the University College of Swansea.

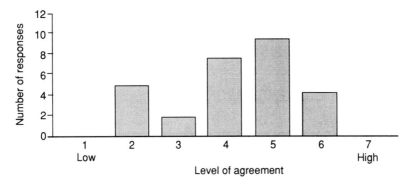

Figure S3.6   Did the Elective Selection stage work? Data from a syntegrity event held in London, February 1993

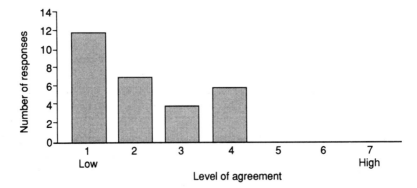

Figure S3.7   How successful was the Kelly-style reduction? Data from a syntegrity event held at Tylney Hall, March 1992

The Elective Selection algorithm outlined in this chapter was first tested at a syntegrity event held in London in February 1993. Despite various hardware problems, the programs were made to run and produced an allocation that was acceptable to all 30 infoset members. At the end of this event questionnaires were completed by participating members and the resulting data are displayed in the histogram in Figure S3.6. The relative success of this method can be seen by comparing this histogram with that constructed from data collected at a syntegrity event held at Tylney Hall in March 1992, where a non-rigorous Kelly-style approach was used for the Hexadic Reduction (Figure S3.7).

YOU DRIVE FOR SHOW BUT YOU PUTT FOR DOUGH
A facilitator's perspective
Alan Pearson

INTRODUCTION

The hypothesis embodied in this book may perhaps be stated as follows. By following the Team Syntegrity protocol, a set of 30 people who accept to be members with equal status of a group to discuss some subject matter requiring action will create a robust structure of mutually acceptable ideas on that subject matter (under 12 headings) and a robust structure of relationships among themselves with respect to action on such subject matter.

The above formulation makes fewer assumptions about the dedication of the participants than does the book, because facilitators would be unwise to overestimate the enthusiasm or commitment of participants at the outset of a syntegration.

Pragmatists may well balk at the arbitrary constraints of Team Syntegrity: 30 participants, 12 Topics. They may be disinclined to submit themselves to the elegant exigencies of the icosahedron.

PURPOSE

Every syntegration needs an authentic pretext. Someone must be able legitimately to convene the syntegration. Participants must be willing to accept that the invitation is worth accepting.

Why are we here? What is all this for? What are you/we trying to accomplish? These are questions for the host to answer.

For example, it may be that the boss has decided to consult his or her top subordinates, or most promising young turks, or most demanding clients, or whatever, on the future of the enterprise, the design of the product, or whatever. There is an infinity of possible authentic pretexts. The point is that each syntegration must have one. And it must be clear. And it must be credible. For, once it is stated, it becomes the pole star—the ultimate guide to the unfolding process of the syntegration.

If the pretext is 'Let's get a bunch of decent people together to discuss the world,' the outcome is likely to be just discussion (its quality being limited by the capability of the participants).

If the pretext is 'Let's get some of our fast-track managers and professionals together with our top echelon of management to map out the future of this corporation a decade from now,' the outcome will be a picture of the future painted by those who will make it happen (its quality, too, being limited by the capability of the participants).

Whatever the pretext, the purpose of a syntegration is what it does, no doubt. The host, however, ought to have an *a priori* purpose, which may with luck turn out to be shared by the participants. Such a purpose could be articulated in any one of various forms, depending on the level of specificity sought.

At its most general, a purpose might be stated as 'to develop a shared vision of the future,' which would tend toward a passive forecast. A more pro-active formulation might be 'to develop a shared vision of success.' 'To develop a set of shared values' would be a relatively passive purpose, whereas 'to develop a set of shared policies' would be a relatively pro-active one. The most pro-active formulation of a purpose would perhaps be 'to agree on concerted action.'

Each formulation poses a different challenge to the facilitators. To define a shared vision of the future, one may settle for what Neuro-Linguistic Programming calls 'fat' words—general terms concealing unresolved ambiguity. But to define a course of concerted action requires 'thin' words—specific, accurate, unmistakable. Naturally, the latter is a much more exacting facilitation challenge than the former.

PARTICIPANTS

The term 'infoset' may be adequate to identify qualifications for participation in the formal model. However, the facilitation challenge is greatly affected by the terms on which participants are recruited. There are at least five, not mutually exclusive, criteria for participation in a syntegration: affinity, entitlement, role, capability, accountability.

If one wanted merely a warm and enthusiastic discussion, one would settle for affinity: 'If you are interested in the subject matter, come along.' If one wanted to avoid accusations of exclusivity, one might have to accept the entitlement criterion: 'This is a meeting of the Board and Jack, though he thinks this is all nonsense, is a board-member too.' If one considered it unwise not to involve all relevant players one would impose the role criterion: 'It is foolish to create a vision of the future of this hospital without involving representatives of the physicians.' If one were aiming to generate a top-level corporate strategic plan, one might wish to set a capability criterion: 'Jack may be the general manager of the widgets division, but he's not very bright, having got his job as a result of being a cousin of the previous owner, and is now close to retirement.' If one wanted the plan to stick, one might require an accountability criterion: 'There's no point in producing a strategic plan unless the person responsible for new product development is involved.'

In descending order of potential unwillingness to engage wholeheartedly in a syntegration, these criteria might be listed as follows.

1. Entitlement: 'You've got to include me but I don't have to cooperate.'

2. Accountability: 'I can fulfil my accountability any way I choose, and collaborating with the rest of you in this boondoggle does not appeal to me.'

3. Capability: 'You may need me for my smarts but I'm too elevated and too busy to mix in.'

4. Role: 'You need a physician, like me. How fortunate that I enjoy engaging in stimulating group processes.'

5. Affinity: 'This is an absolutely crucial issue. I'd travel half-way round the world to get in on a serious discussion of it.'

Beyond Dispute is written on the assumption that participants want to play. The definition of 'infoset' implies that. However, in practice, particular syntegrations will need to be designed to accommodate more or less unwilling or at least deeply sceptical participants. Enthusiasts will collaborate to make the process work. Cynics will not lift a finger to save it, and indeed may happily sabotage it.

Host, organizer, and facilitators must therefore work together to ensure that all the participants develop a sufficiently constructive attitude toward Team Syntegrity.

Working relations take many forms. For some people, raw power is a last resort. For others, it is the first. Team Syntegrity seeks to minimize the room for arbitrariness and to undercut capricious decision-making. This may not be of much comfort to some leaders. Them it probably cannot help. But for leaders—responsible authorities—who want the best-informed decisions out of their organizations and who want maximum voluntary commitment to the enterprise from its members—for them Team Syntegrity can be a cybernetic breakthrough, making the organizational whole far greater than the sum of its parts.

Except in explicitly democratic institutions, responsible authorities must be able to reject simplistic democracy. Authority, as legitimate power, enjoys legitimate prerogatives which can overrule the will of the majority. Whose organization is it anyway? Owners form an association to pursue objects that benefit clients/customers/members. In the limit, they may dissolve the organization if it is led, or allowed to be dragged, away from those objects. Widely shared enthusiasm is not the same as the dictatorship of the majority.

Perfect democracy empowers equally the incompetent, the ignorant, the evil, the foolish, and the stupid, along with the decent.

Although Team Syntegrity is designed as a non-hierarchical procedure, its product and impact must always be set in the context of the host or sponsor, and the roles of the participants in the world beyond the syntegration. In practice, fortunately, it always will be so, in the sense that every participant leaves with the prerogatives he or she arrived with. They will undoubtedly leave changed, and therefore likely to exercise those prerogatives differently than before. But they are not coerced by the views of others into acting later against their own better judgement.

It is true that Team Syntegrity provides no opportunity for a formal authority to impose views on participants; it is non-hierarchical. Equally, however, it provides no opportunity for the will of the majority to force conformity on the minority; in this sense, it is not democratic either.

PROLOGUE

From a facilitator's viewpoint, therefore, Team Syntegrity is initially a challenge in participant orientation. In order to focus participants' minds on substantive discussion and strategic decision-making, they need to be relieved of doubt and uncertainty with respect to procedure and logistics.

Team Syntegrity is unavoidably a complex logistical puzzle for the uninitiated. Considerable effort is therefore required to assure the participants that the syntegration will follow a sensible and comprehensible course, and that the process does indeed liberate rather than constrain them.

Beyond the challenge of simple traffic management, facilitators need to understand in what way Team Syntegrity may usefully be thought of as a self-organizing process, and to what extent active facilitation is required to make the most of the time available.

Some of the participant-orientation questions can be pre-empted by clear and simple set-up statements, at the beginning of the syntegration, and at the beginning of each phase. Some can be dealt with in Question and Answer sessions at set-up time. Others will only be answered in the experience of the syntegration itself.

A very great deal, however, depends upon the set-up statements: the prologue.

Why are we here? What is all this for? What are you/we trying to accomplish? These are questions to which the host must have direct and authentic answers.

What is going to happen? is a question that the facilitators must answer, convincingly, from the outset.

Each of the phases of a syntegration presents its own questions from the participant-orientation perspective.

The Problem Jostle: What kind of SIs are being solicited? What for? What happens to my ideas? How can I prevent other people's stupid ideas from taking over? Why are the 12 Topics that result from the Hexadic Reduction the right 12 to be discussed? I expect the Topics to be interesting, but what is the payoff to all this talk?

Perhaps the key characteristic of a Statement of Importance is less that it be innovative than that it be a *factor*. I remember from my time as an officer-cadet nearly 35 years ago the form of the Military Appreciation, in which one was required to identify Factors affecting the Aim. Whenever one was inclined to put forward a factor, one asked the question, So what? If one could not come up with an answer, one had not identified a factor. So, it seems to me that an SI must not just seem important, it must pass the 'So what?' test of relevance. (Facilitators would merely explain the test, participants would administer it for themselves.)

The Topic Auction: Why have the CSIs been allocated to particular vertices of the icosahedron? How do I get to be a player on Topics that I care about? How do I get to critique on Topics that seem to me potentially dangerous? Who can I trust to shape the discussions in which I cannot participate?

The Topic Auction has consistently proved to be an awkward moment in the process of syntegration. Perhaps if participants were each given a sticker bearing their own name they could be confronted with a model of the icosahedron, with a Topic name arbitrarily attached to each vertex, and be left to negotiate with each other to attach their names to particular struts. At least the participants would be implicated in the compromises necessary to resolve conflicts among individual preferences.

The Outcome Resolve: Why are there three iterations? How are they different from each other? What is the final product supposed to be?

The entire process of a syntegration: Why is it so shapeless? Why do they want 3–5 days of my valuable time for that? Why can it not be made to seem more efficient/more economical/less time consuming?

PROCESS

Beyond Dispute lays out the information-theoretic assumptions behind the reverberations generated by a syntegration: adequate channel capacity, and requisite variety in transduction between individuals. Thus, it argues, there must be no shortage of time or facilitation. Whether there will be a shortage of either must in the final analysis depend to a great degree on the scope, or variety, of the universe of discourse.

The participants and the facilitators together must continuously judge the balancing of variety between time and scope, within the imposed constraints of the syntegration. Since, in any particular syntegration, time, channel capacity, and transduction variety are largely predetermined, it is the scope of the subject matter that must be cut to fit, in terms of depth, specificity, ambiguity, etc. For any given time allocation, participants must judge how superficial, general, or unclear, they will allow themselves to be. Skilful facilitation will help participants to maximize the degree of shared meaning in spite of this inevitable compromise.

Shared meaning depends upon clarity of semantics and of logic, and mutually understood primitive terms (in the philosophical sense, i.e. elemental terms that must remain undefined). It requires a high degree of talent and skill in a facilitator, in the first place to spot inconsistencies, and then to enable a group to reach transparent clarity, at all three levels.

Channel capacity is a function of the following: usable time (and the efficiency of its use); available media of expression (text, diagrams, models, etc., in the 3-line Statements of Importance (SIs), 8-line Aggregated SIs (ASIs), 20-line Composite SIs (CSIs), and in the one-page products of the various iterations of the Outcome Resolve); and role functions (idea maker, advocate, discussion leader, as 'team member' and 'critic' in 10-person discussions, along with synthesizer as 'observer,' and voter as generic 'participant').

Skilled facilitators can enhance the media of expression available to participants. They can also attempt to raise the efficiency of usable time by engaging in active clarification and setting a high-energy pace. The trade-off may, however, be to put contemplative, repressed, shy, or reticent participants at a disadvantage, and thus to fail to bring out their potential contributions.

Requisite variety of transduction depends on clarity and unambiguousness of discussion (which facilitators can do something about). However, it also depends on the intelligence or conceptual capacity of the participants. In particular, if the capacity of the listener to make distinctions is cruder than that of the speaker, the subtlety of the speaker's point will be unavoidably lost. That is what can often lower consensus to the level of the highest common factor (not, strictly speaking, the lowest common denominator) and lobotomize the group.

When the purpose of the conversation is to gain authorization for action, rather than mutual comprehension, this is not necessarily a fatal flaw. For the leading thinkers can impress the others into silent though willing acquiescence. However, the aim of Team Syntegrity is to reach a profound degree of shared meaning. To pursue such an aim requires deliberate consideration of the participants' qualities in terms of matched, or at least minimum, conceptual capacity, and perhaps subject-matter knowledge. Otherwise, transduction might not have requisite variety.

Some facilitators will be tempted to work on relaxing the common constraint—that the quality of the output is always limited by the capability of the participants—by coaching, teaching, or making substantive suggestions. In my opinion, this is a perversion of the facilitator's role.

I am strongly of the opinion that if there is any question that the participants, themselves, together lack the necessary capability, then efforts must be made to enrich the group of participants, not to give facilitators licence to 'improve' the product. Indeed, only participants are entitled to a judgement about the intrinsic quality of the product (though it is a responsibility of the facilitator to ensure that participants face the issue of quality and set their own standards).

In particular, it would be inappropriate for facilitators independently to elide SIs into ASIs or into one another, or otherwise play with the intellectual product of the participants, under the illusion that the facilitators 'understand.' Rather, the facilitator's role is to induce the participants to perform those functions to their own satisfaction.

All this puts an unavoidable burden on the host, and on the designers of the syntegration, to qualify participants. This is perhaps a blow to naïve wishes about 'democracy' in Team Syntegrity. However, reverberation can only enhance shared meaning if the participants are all capable of grasping meaning at roughly the same level. To follow the engineering parallel: what do you need to know about the material (participants), in order to predict the strength of the resulting tensegrity structure (Outcome)?

Beyond Dispute seems to presume that a team and its critics need no orientation to the purpose and or meaning of the three iterations of the Outcome Resolve. It is as if reverberation is expected to be its own reward. This view seems to derive from treating the agenda as merely the categories of discussion (Topics).

If I understand the Latin correctly, however, agenda is a list of doings not just sayings. In other words, it is talk about action. Team Syntegrity, as described, is unclear about the connection between discussion and action. Alternatively, it implies a necessary and direct connection between the two. As a result, it leaves that connection entirely in the hands of the participants. If they are an activist bunch, they might come up with a plan. If not, talk will do.

I earn my pay helping well motivated people turn discussion into action. It is a widely necessary service. Good people often find it excruciatingly difficult to turn that trick for themselves, to formulate their deeply felt concerns into a problem to be solved—a cause for action, and to express their wish to resolve the problem in terms that define—and guide—future action.

As a corporate-planning consultant, therefore (and in spite of the pure cybernetic argument), I am inclined to consider treating reverberation as its own reward to risk a serious waste of potential focus. I would argue that the risk of arbitrarily curtailing variety by *offering* a direction is far outweighed by the risk of having participants drift to the end of their syntegration having achieved a degree of mutual understanding but no basis for action.

To adapt the golfing adage: 'You discuss for show, but you decide for dough.'

Various authorities have modelled the process of planning. One might take Boulding's (1956) 'image' along with Miller, Galanter and Pribram's (1960) 'plan'; or Bandler and Grinder's (1979) Neuro-Linguistic-Programming 'reframing' sequence; or Burke's (1969) pentad of dramatism: 'act–scene–agent–agency–purpose,' which leads to the deduction of 'let us' from 'we must,' which in turn derives from 'it is.'

I find Burke's (1969) 'let us ← we must ← it is' sequence very powerful. Interpreted in this light, the first iteration of the Outcome Resolve could be concerned with 'it is': specifying the state of affairs that requires action. The second iteration could then focus on 'we must': constructing the vision of a future to be accomplished. Thus, the third iteration could be devoted to 'let us': developing a joint strategy for realizing the vision. This approach would re-work what is essentially the same material from three progressively more action-oriented points of view—nudging reverberation along.

To offer this progression would not be to impose it. Participants in a syntegration will discuss whatever they wish, with or without the 'approval' of the facilitator (as long as the facilitator behaves competently); for it is the participants' syntegration, not the facilitators'.

CONCLUSION

The strength of Team Syntegrity is in the process, not in the subject-matter expertise of the facilitators. Their job is to lubricate that process, to remove all structural and procedural barriers to a full and clear exchange of views among the participants. Please note that I use the term 'full and clear,' not the cliché 'full and frank.' 'Frank' is dependent on the strategic choices of the participants; for a syntegration is a working discussion not a psychotherapy group. Intimacy is not an objective, though in fortuitous circumstances it might be a by-product.

However, a *clear* exchange on the issues is an important responsibility of the facilitators. After all, there are many possible reasons for a lack of clarity in a discussion, for example: semantic confusion (probably the most frequent cause); logical confusion; emotional involvement; and substantive indeterminacy or uncertainty. It is up to the facilitator, in the last analysis, to expose semantic and logical confusion, to mitigate the dysfunctional effects of emotional involvement, and to bring to the surface instances where the participants must admit to themselves, 'We simply do not know.'

ONE MAN'S SIGNAL IS ANOTHER MAN'S NOISE
Another facilitator's perspective
David Beatty

NOISE: 'a meaningless jumble of signals.

Noise, as the name implies, is worthless—and often counterproductive, because it is mistaken for information. However, what is "meaningless" to one person may convey meaning to another.

N.B. It follows that it is worth suspecting noise of being data in disguise.' (Beer, 1979, p. 282).

A Professor at Arizona State University teaches a course in Ignorance to 4th year medical students. She argues that doctors need to be experts in acknowledging when they don't know and moving on to finding out what they need to know. Perhaps many of us in management consulting could profit from a similar humility.

Syntegrity is comparable to a number of organization development tools—search conferences, strategic planning events, action learning, learning systems, etc. I have been involved in them all. Syntegrity calls to us as a new paradigm. It feels like false inquiry to explore the human dynamics of syntegrity in terms of a traditional taxonomy, importing the noise of inappropriate conventions.

Reframing ignorance as curiosity and replacing certainty with speculation, I shall look at the human dynamics in a syntegration, inquiring into the facilitation and research questions implied in converting a physical model into a human experience. There will be a fair amount of noise on the way—but at least it will be new noise.

I have been a participant in one Syntegration, facilitator for two, and a co-conspirator in Team Syntegrity Inc. for 3 years. I have been part of the syntegrity conversation since 1985 when Stafford Beer convened his Experiments in Applied Epistemology with the McLuhan Centre at the University of Toronto. Exploring syntegrity has been as rich a journey for me as was my crossover to a systemic universe when I encountered the Viable System Model in 1976.

The design signal is now loud and clear. However, getting the humans into the model (and vice versa) is still a noisy process. Part of this noisiness is the uncertainty that attends any newly forming group, particularly one nominating itself for a significantly different process. Another part is the societal context in which such new events are defined (e.g. an experiment; a strategic planning event; a search conference). The more basic question is the suitability of the language of syntegrity for use in physical and consciousness universes. Can the precision of physical tensegrity be transferred to the human dynamic of syntegrity?

PERSON AS STRUT AND STRING

What does it mean to state that the individual 'connects' the two groups in which s/he is in active connection? How does the (phi distant) string experience differ from struthood? In what sense is the icosahedron, as it flows through the vertices, embedded in individual consciousness, and/or in group statements? Does the person come as a straight strut or is s/he a stochastic element which gradually gets straightened into place as the shape takes hold? Or as one participant put it, 'I don't know whether to strut my stuff or stuff my strut!'

If we are using the analogy of a 'meaning space' that is shimmering into existence through interpersonal communication, the construction space is in individual minds in relationship with each other (bodies, too, as expressed by the spontaneous dancing that has emerged in several syntegrations). Individuals are both weavers of the icosahedron and elements of the weave as their own mindsets take form. Several levels are co-producing each other.

In addition to the 'redundancy of potential command' there is an immanent redundancy of identity—that is, there are many channels (processes) where what is coursing through the architectonic may suddenly coalesce into an event, a pattern, a personal initiative that marks the identity of the experience —in individuals, in the mutual awareness, in the coalesced statements (any of these would qualify as 'information').

Each participant is a golden rectangle composed of two active champion roles (strut) and two critic roles (string). This gives her direct experience of one third of the shape (assuming equal listening power in both roles). She has access to all other groups through the presence in these four groups of members with direct access to the rest of the groups. Thus, for example, member Red–Orange has:

1. her own total (intrapersonal) experience of four vertices per iteration— Red, Orange, Green, and Dark Blue;

2. interpersonal access to all the other groups through the connectivity of membership of other members of these groups. Red–Orange can hear about groups Purple, Black, White, Brown and Yellow as Critic of Dark Blue.

Information can flow through each mind from any vertex of the shape. Note that this can only happen by the second Iteration since the shape has not been totally formed until after the first. From that point on, it is possible to imagine a stochastic process of signal/noise reverberation occurring in each individual until they 'get it'—what ever identity 'it' eventually forms. The chaotic buzz and interaction of the icosahedron shape sets up an optimal landscape for crystallizing 'identity' in an unpredictable form.

After the first iteration, this 'shape' is in existence whether the person is in meeting or not. 'Fallow' time can thus be considered part of shape time.

A high-quality human icosahedron depends on the attention and skills the participants bring to their multiple functions.

a. Intrapersonal: individuals anticipate, observe, interpret, act, reflect, adjust, filter, amplify the events in terms of their own world view, and · shift that world view in the light of what they encounter.

b. Interpersonal: they must send and receive communication that is salient to topics (vertices), and that brings relevant information from other vertices. They must serve in different roles for each other—critic, colleague, leader, cheerleader, debating opponent, foil, etc.

c. Each person, in addition to being a strut is one of five connectors in a vertex. As such, s/he acts as agent for that perspective, as co-creator of its identity (statements and norms), as emissary to other groups, and as agent for other groups—at least the one other in which s/he is active.

d. They must participate in and take responsibility for the community results. They write and read statements; they vote on offerings; they show up on time; they care about the outcomes; they look for the emerging integrity.

The more strongly each of these recursions tunes in to the design signal ('what a syntegration is all about'), the stronger will be the positive feedback loops, and the more dramatic the reverberation.

Thus, the inside dynamic of a strut is the information coalescing and reverberating in minds, parallel to the energy that courses through the tensile physical fabric.

The external form is behaviour—the extent to which the individual communicates (transduces) ideas, moods, data between the groups to which s/he belongs.

What are the conditions necessary to ensure sufficient 'take' of struthood? Independent variables that affect syntegration success could include:

Intrapersonal: Strength of commitment to infoset; 'buy-in' to the syntegrity protocol: accuracy of understanding of role expectations; strength of interest in assigned behavioural patterns, e.g. frequency of communication; use of 'fallow' time; saliency of conflict and its resolution.

Small Group: Task/maintenance tradeoffs; critic communications; air time; leadership styles; norms.

Inter-Group: Group identification; inter-group cooperation; bulletin board functions; dot voting.

Total Community: Meta-communication; participant-facilitators; participants-in-total-session; purpose of syntegration.

These are only some of the variables relevant to the dynamic. One could also inquire into syntegrations from information-processing viewpoints, from anthropological, from organizational, and from cybernetic disciplines.

One hopes that other researchers catch this signal of theoretical richness and operational replicability—great publications and fast theses!

IDENTITY (SELF-AWARENESS)

The icosahedron is a fascinating shape—enneagrams, golden rectangles, phi-ness, the symmetrical spin, balance, etc. What began as an operational research question—what structure can we find as an antidote to a virulent organizational disease?—has turned into a magical template.

Facilitators and participants agree that there is something unique happening in this shape. Cynics can write this off as the halo effect of a temporary culture, or as a charisma effect, or to a reporting bias of any good snake oil salesman. No need to take a course in ignorance!

The physical characteristics of flexibility, strength, and permutability are a function of the shape. The communication phenomena of redundancy, inter-connectivity, and recursiveness are the human counterparts. Success of syntegration is expressed in terms of 'identity.' What might we observe to indicate that 'identity' is occurring?

1. Identity is the group culture—feeling, trust, respect, animation, etc., shared by those who build the experience together. This occurs at individual, interpersonal, small group, and community levels. Again, these recursions are connected by positive feedback loops—as one improves, the others improve.

2. Identity is the collected statements and what they identify as the kernel of the spin and buzz of the icosahedron in play. This information deposit is the intersect of what individuals have considered worthy to transmit, transduce, and transform. It is the unique intelligence capture of this cosmological thinker toy.

3. Identity is the comprehension, commitment, change, etc., taken in by and carried away with the individual.

4. Identity is the shared follow-up action of the event—the 'aha' of con-verging on a direction/solution which members agree to pursue together after the experience.

Each of these outcomes may qualify as the shape 'popping into existence' in participant consciousness. Intriguing vistas open up for qualitative research. It may be that the participants themselves are the most appropriate researchers on this question, and inviting their attention to a self-reflection task may be an excellent way to induce shape consciousness.

From the view of facilitating shape identity, objectives include (a) to enable each player to develop icoshahedron (infosettic) consciousness; (b) to encourage a finely tuned communication system to emerge and resonate; (c) to detect and deflect noise in and between participants; and (d) to be alert to the grains of identity that are building, and amplify these signals.

We shall return in a later section to the question of where the facilitators are in the physical space.

CONTEXT: IS TIME SPACE?

The icosahedron whirls in three-dimensional space, standing out beautifully and clearly as a structure. (A stringed icosahedron on display is extremely helpful during a syntegration.) But syntegrations occur within a myriad of situations, mind sets, and systems. Participants' perspectives are cluttered with expectations on what this is all about, embedded styles and capabilities, a lifetime of politics, hierarchy, etc. Rather than spinning in an empty space, the shape has to emerge out of a gooey fudge.

This signal/noise concern is a very real one in launching a syntegration. The explanation of syntegrity is to some degree perceived as mumbo-jumbo—be it marvellous or maddening. People are ignorant of syntegrity processes, but they do have an ingrained repertoire of ways of behaving in small and large groups. An ambiguous, new group situation, where egos are lured out into the open (Problem Jostle) launches some interesting scripts! In fact, the goal of the lead-up to the Outcome Resolves is to do just that—to get ideas that have not been beaten to death already, to light the passions of conviction and purpose, to locate the most powerful coordinates for catapulting a new identity into existence. The potency of the initial mixture is critical, but it also unleashes a variety of volatile encounters.

There are also a number of 'gravitational drags' on the creation of the structure—low commitment, low understanding, 'real world' demands, long-winded explanations, wordsmithing traps, late attendance, personal styles, etc. People try to convert syntegrity to a framework they know how to manage, to a script where they can play their favourite part.

The building of the shape is a journey in creating community. In addition to variables of purpose, perception, and attitude, there are issues of skills. (Do participants know how to release their creativity? Do they know how to critique ideas? Are they articulate about principles, values? Are they effective listeners? Do they know how to give and receive constructive feedback, build effective groups, handle conflict?, etc.)

Given the purposive attention and the number of skills required to get on the syntegration wavelength, there is a steep learning curve that has to be climbed to make it to a high-performing zone. Individuals, or groups, doing more than one syntegration could certainly capitalize on this learning.

Our initial task has been to create the mechanics of the protocol. The measurement of participant reactions has been encouragingly high, indicating success in holding a valued conference event (the implicit comparison for most members). But our ambitions are greater. Finding the setting wherein rhythms of personal, group, and community can begin to pulse through the structure with less interference will open up a wider vista of human effectiveness. This social invention responds to our desperate need for a non-hierarchial organizing and regulating system. The immense amount of work done on the theoretical and operational fronts now opens up the world of applied epistemology and social invention.

From a social intervention point of view, the ideal conditions in which to ferment a high-quality shared state of mind via the icosahedron would be:

1. a purpose that matters to the individuals and which is linked to subsequent action (infoset conditions);

2. an orientation phase that builds a desire to use syntegrity to build community together (knowledge of method);

3. time to learn how to operate effectively in a syntegration setting, and time to unlearn dysfunctional approaches (skills);

4. sufficient time for groups and the community to reflect on the process (action learning);

5. an opportunity for the participants to take control from the facilitators (ownership).

WHAT IS AT THE CENTRE OF THE ICOSAHEDRON?

The open space in the centre of the communication shape holds emerging meaning. It is perhaps here that the synergy and recursiveness of the structure in human dimensions create the identity we do not know how to label.

Initially, at the centre of the emerging shape is the question that focuses the attention of the infoset (e.g. what will be the major issues for human resource development in the next 15 years?). Around it are configured 12 powerful statements on which to launch the resolves. These are to be creative, arguable points of attack which at least five people have indicated are worthy of candidacy, and that have survived a reduction process. The task of the groups is to elaborate and communicate the agreements they can reach over the next 2 days (3 meetings in each vertex group).

A 'shape' is invoked, operationalized, as the machine for operating on this central question. When the syntegration is over, there is a set of statements that captures the agreements generated from each of the vertices. A 'universe of discourse' has been created, and crystallized into these 12 overlapping points of view.

The initial tests have not yet researched the semantics of these outcomes. Is there a pattern, or family of information patterns, produced by icosahedral organization? Does this shape produce better problem-solving, consensus-building, creative integration, etc.? How would we define original? How do we describe the shared semantic space implied in integrity? How has the tension (difference) surfaced and evolved in statements? What is the correspondence between written statements and personal belief and commitment?

Again, the call is out to communication researchers—each syntegration tracks all statement generation from original individual Statements of Importance through to the third iteration group statements.

In this content dimension we also encounter another channel in which the signal/noise dynamic is in play. Many of us are not used to defining, critiquing, or recognizing high-quality statements. Potency loses ground to politeness. Seeds of wisdom face the pruning urges of wordsmiths. A sudden gust of critic comment sweeps across the ground of agreement in every meeting.

Participants need to be clear on the purpose of statement generation. Are the statements to be agreed by all at the end? Is it a spin-off report of where the group's energy was at, or is it a sales tool to convince others to follow along? Do they represent mandates for action by the members? Groups have tough choices to make in how to use their time wisely in regard to content, and the relationships that enable exploration of values, novelty, and difference. The agenda is overflowing. Is the statement the equivalent of the colour—namely just a topic title to draw five people together? What kind of 'meaning' distances are implied by contiguity and polarity of topics?

Syntegrations are often finished before the statements have been mined for convergence/divergence. Statements have not yet had the benefit of follow-up utility.

Examination of the statement trail and final statement patterns should reveal valuable insight into the thinking and influence processes in non-hierarchic groups.

WHERE ARE THE FACILITATORS IN THE MODEL?

Among the virtues of the icosahedron are its self-organizing and democratic attributes. Who are these 3–5 persons 'facilitating' the process and where do they appear in the physical model?

a. They are the guardians of the protocol. They champion the structure, give leadership to the protocol and print out the product of the interactions. However, in this universe the raw material may reject the rules.

b. They are the attractors (recruiting, motivating, describing, launching). Disparate energies coalesce into the shape under their guidance. They stand in the centre of the space, conjure it into existence, answer ongoing questions about the process, and hope to disappear into thin air.

c. They survey the epigenetic landscape in which positive interactions are encouraged, and destructive tendencies curbed (informal conversations, large group meetings, bulletin board comments, etc.). They produce a force field in which the nascent shape can take hold—through encouraging participation, averting blow-ups that shatter the framework, drawing participants' attention to reverberation effects, keeping the outside world at bay, etc.

Techniques for each of these functions could be described, but more important is the highlighting of the underlying dilemma. The facilitators are often important personalities in the community, and they have the perception/skill to make significant swings in outcome. They are the champions (or the agents of those) who called the participants into attendance. And yet the distinguishing claims of syntegration are its egalitarian and self-organizing structures. How hazy or highlighted should the lines of facilitator communication be?

This dilemma is accentuated by time compression. Learning a new protocol, meeting the ideas and personalities of 29 others, becoming committed to the results—these processes are complex. It offends the professional know-how of many of us to stand on the sidelines and watch groups flounder. What is the minimum critical design of the facilitator role?

The urge is to invent the 'moves' required to enable syntegration to succeed as a 'training' or 'conference' event. Alan Pearson's contribution is a good example of a 'focus-driven' approach to this challenge: by specifying the questions for each round, one hopes to concentrate the group energy/intelligence on the essence of what makes statements significant. The facilitator in each group coaches the group to squeeze the most out of its interactions. The professional skill is to do this with minimum denaturing of participant experience or expression.

At the alternative end of the continuum, *laissez-faire* advocates count on the residential situation, interpersonal attraction/friction, pressure to accomplish, uncertainty, to ignite a 'breakthrough' where the syntegration achieves its unique identity. The syntegrity landscape is rich enough to elicit value from low-intensity experiences, and to dampen explosive intensities. The facilitators are a safety net to keep the 'noise' of arousal within bounds in the early stages, and to shepherd players back into the shape to confront their questions.

Another expression of these two approaches is the use of a manual which participants use to self-organize—as in the World Citizen Projects—or the creation of an advance training process to teach participants relevant skills for syntegration (e.g. creative problem-solving; feedback skills; statement creation/critique techniques).

In each of these five aspects of the shape, I have compared an icosahedron of physical and human components. The message is that this structure is a unique organization, and we ought to experience and investigate it as such. In moving from one paradigm to another, the loudest interference comes from the old signal. The importance of the Infoset is not just one of shared purpose, but also a willingness to tune in to a new process. We may find that we are not only ignorant, but profoundly so—and that would be a blessing! What the mind is blind to, the eye cannot see.

ABOUT FACE
A turn for better planning
Joe Truss

INTRODUCTION

When Team Syntegrity was first invented by Stafford Beer, it was seen as a means of addressing and strengthening the links between the internal and immediate management functions of the enterprise and the external and future management functions of the enterprise, called the Three–Four Homeostat in the Viable System Model (VSM). An explanation of this model follows in Surplus Seven, where Allenna Leonard writes in support of the references to the VSM here, as also to those made in Chapters 14 and 9. In the latter chapter, and referring to System Three as Operations and System Four as Development, these two functions were shown to require massive interaction to maintain a balance between investment for the future and maintenance of the day-to-day business. Both of these functions are prerequisites of organizational viability and the activity between them is the most vulnerable underbelly of the enterprise.

Jo Hancock, one of the collaborators involved in development and research relating to Team Syntegrity was the first to ask, 'So, I understand that the vertices of the Icosahedron correspond to the 12 topics, and the struts to the 30 people, but what about the faces?' At the time, there was no answer to this question.

Another question that remained unanswered related to how the Syntegration protocol could by expanded into a full planning application.

Over subsequent years of exploration, development, and application of Team Syntegrity, the richness and power of the underlying Icosahedral model and the supporting protocol have become more apparent, revealing many opportunities to expand the original protocol to include goal setting, tactical planning, and organizational scheduling.

The purpose of this chapter is to explain how Team Syntegrity supports a complete planning process. In doing so, Hancock's question, 'What is a face?,' will be answered and the expanded applicability of Team Syntegrity to the Viable System Model will be adumbrated.

WHAT IS STRATEGIC PLANNING?

There are two broad interpretations of the term 'strategy' when applied to organizational planning. In one definition, strategy encompasses the whole panorama of organizational planning and decision-making activities, including establishing mission and vision, and setting objectives and goals. In this case, strategy is inclusive of both means and ends. In the other definition, it is the objective that is paramount. It is based on mission and vision, and achieved through various strategies which refer to specific plans and decisions. In this case, strategy is the means to achieve ends that lie outside the strategy itself. For the purposes of this chapter, when we refer to strategy or strategic planning, it will be with reference to Chapter Nine, which offers a lexicon of planning based on the underlying constantly changing flow of information in the organization. These four modes of planning are Normative, Developmental, Strategic, and Tactical. We can simplify our explanation without doing harm to the purpose of this chapter by eliding the Normative, Developmental, and Strategic modes into the one term—strategic. This also seems to be supported by the popular usage where the distinctions of Normative and Developmental are rarely used.

When an organization undertakes to do strategic planning, it does so within some context that it itself defines. This context cannot possibly contain everything that is relevant to the organization, and therefore only a subset is used. This subset becomes the planning 'space' for the organization. Although this space cannot be known precisely, it establishes the general boundaries of constraints and opportunities for the purpose of planning.

If the planning space is too constrained, the result can be 'the buggy-whip syndrome,' which means that the organization performs efficiently, but with a focus on output that is no longer relevant to its context. If, on the other hand the space is set too loosely, the organization may lose its focus or even its identity. It is analogous to the classic battle of organizing for efficiency versus organizing for adaptability. The key is to achieve a balance of both. Here

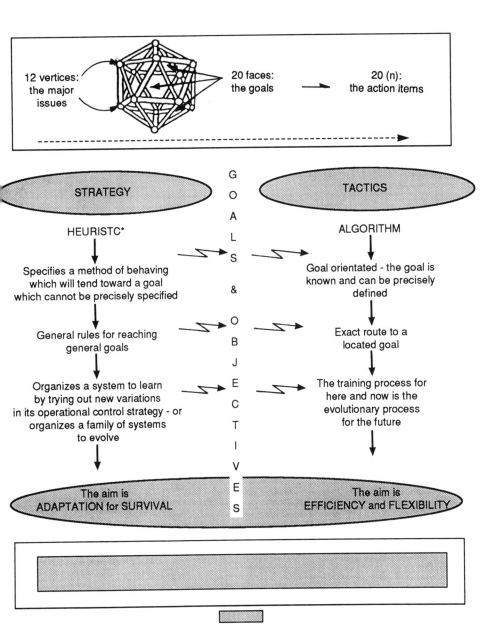

Figure S6.1 Team Syntegrity—platform for planning. *Heuristic techniques are determined within a framework specifying the mode, the limits, and the criteria of search. Adapted from definitions of heuristics and algorithms in Beer (1972)

again we see an example of the importance of System Three–System Four homeostasis.

Figure S6.1 reflects in graphic form the alignment of strategy with *heuristic* techniques, the aim being adaptation for survival, and the alignment of tactics with algorithms, the aim being efficiency and flexibility. Think of strategy as the 'rules of thumb' that define possible options. Tactics, on the other hand, are *algorithms*, and can only be identified in relation to a known and precisely defined goal. Tactics, then, are procedures for delivering a chosen option.

Strategic planning involves moving from establishing options and general rules, to setting and defining specific goals and objectives. It also means keeping informed about implementation of tactics. The options and general rules establish the heuristic space. The known goals and objectives that are precisely defined establish the tactical range.

Tactics, the procedures and specific actions, are related to strategy through their connection to specific goals and objectives. Creation of algorithms to implement tactics should be the role of those responsible for the activities defined by the tactical plan and not those who defined it. This does not exclude anyone from involvement with both activities. What it says is that the person or group that is held accountable for the outcome should be given responsibility for determining the action. This is what empowerment means. Control resides in the strategic activities and particularly in the setting of goals and objectives, and in continuously knowing what is going on with the actions that are designed to deliver those goals and objectives.

The aim of creating this planning landscape is to (i) evolve a robust planning space (ii) translate the opportunity and constraint boundaries of this heuristic space into specific goals and objectives, and (iii) empower those directly involved in the day-to-day operations to develop the procedures to deliver specific actions to achieve the set goals and objectives.

BEYOND SEARCH: THE STRATEGIC PLANNING APPLICATION

When the Syntegration protocol as described in Surplus Two is used by an organization for the purposes of strategic planning, the 12 Final Statements of Importance (FSIs) which are created during the final Iteration of the Outcome Resolve become the platform for planning.

These 12 FSIs that evolve represent the 12 most important issues or critical success factors and can be considered as 'boundaries' established by the organization to define and limit the heuristic space for strategic planning. The process of arriving at these FSIs creates the heuristic space within which planning can be done. This space is not only made up of information, but also of relationships.

In Surplus Four, Alan Pearson's approach from the point of view of facilitation of a syntegration suggests the use of the second and third iterations of the Outcome Resolve to move closer to articulating action items relating to the 12 issues. This might be particularly applicable where the syntegration participants are not from the same organization or group, and where they need to arrive at some specific actionable decisions. In this case, however, the syntegration should be held over 5 days to allow meetings of the Outcome Resolve to last 60–75 min each, rather than the 40 min allowed in a 3-day event. On the other hand, this approach would clearly prevent a fuller exploration of the issues and might hamper the effect of reverberation in the evolution of the heuristic space. In the case of an organization, given that all subsequent planning activities will be affected by the foundation which evolves from the shared understanding achieved during syntegration, they would be advised to use the time to explore the issues fully. Further, the protocol described below achieves a high degree of alignment and interdependence between strategy and tactics and displaces the need to use any of the search phase time for defining actions.

Once the heuristic space for strategic planning has been created by the evolution of 12 FSIs, the process for setting specific goals can begin.

ABOUT FACES AND GOALS: TURNING TO PLANNING

Each face of the Syntegrity Icosahedron has a particular dynamic created by the three topic/vertices that surround it. These three topic/vertices represent three specific FSIs. This triadic set of FSIs has a dynamic relationship to the other nine FSIs. There are 20 such triadic sets of FSIs, which is the number of permutations of the 12 vertices and 30 struts that form the 20 faces of the icosahedron.

What, then, are these faces?

The faces of the Syntegrity Icosahedron are *goal-specifier generators*.

Each face is made up of a unique combination of the three colours of the surrounding vertices as shown in Figure S6.2a. Adjacent faces share the two colours of the strut separating the faces from each other (see Figure S6.2b). Thus, the 12 colours are distributed over the 20 faces in combinations of three colours each, with adjacent faces sharing two of these three colours. Each colour is represented in five faces.

The three surrounding vertices are connected by three struts. Figure S6.2a and b shows the relationship between the struts and the faces. Each of the three struts connecting the three vertices that surround a face defines a person/role in the Planning Syntegration. People in these three roles have helped to create, as members of their topic/vertex teams, the FSIs that now drive the specification of a goal.

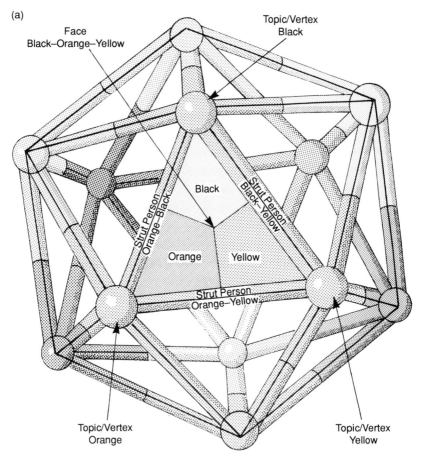

Figure S6.2 Illustrations of the faces of the Syntegrity Icosahedron

These 3 Faces are joined by struts
Black–Orange, Orange–Yellow and Yellow–Black
to Face Black– Orange–Yellow. This shows how
the Face/Goal Black–Orange–Yellow will have in
common 2 issues (colours) with each of these 3
adjoining Face/Goals

(b)

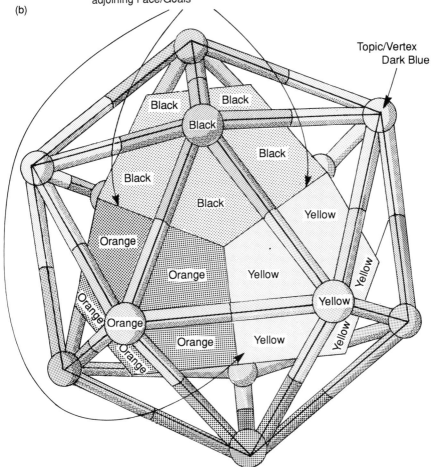

Topic/Vertex
Dark Blue

Black–Yellow strut which connects Black Topic/Vertex
and Yellow Topic/Vertex, is one side of
Black–Yellow–Orange Face and one side of
Black–Yellow–Dark Blue Face

Figure S6.2 (Continued)

For example, in a Syntegration where the Black topic is *Reduce Costs*, the Yellow topic is *Increase Quality*, and the Orange topic is *Expand Market share* (by referring to Figure S6.2, the colour connections described below can be traced):

- The Black, Yellow and Orange vertices form a face where the struts/ people Black−Yellow, Yellow−Orange, and Black−Orange connect.

- Person Black−Yellow has helped formulate the Black and Yellow FSIs.

- Person Yellow−Orange has helped formulate the Yellow and Orange FSIs.

- Person Black−Orange has helped formulate the Black and Orange FSIs.

Person Black−Yellow was a team member on Yellow Topic with person Yellow−Orange, and was a team member on Black Topic with person Black−Orange, but was not a member of Orange Topic. However, Yellow−Orange and Black−Orange were both members of Orange Topic. This set of relationships interlinking this group of three people is similar for every person/strut in every face.

- Together, these three people, Black−Yellow, Yellow−Orange and Black−Orange, specify a goal that meets the opportunity/constraints set by the three surrounding vertices or FSIs. In our example, this means that the goal will be related to the three topics of *Reduce Costs*, *Increase Quality*, and *Expand Market share*.

- In addition, Black−Yellow not only participates in developing the goal that corresponds to the face surrounded by the Black, Yellow, and Orange vertices, but also participates in developing the goal that corresponds to the face surrounded by the Black, Yellow, and Dark Blue vertices. Likewise, each of Yellow−Orange and Black−Orange also participate in developing one other goal based on the third colour in their adjoining faces.

In this way, each tripartite team generates specifications for one high-level goal. There will be 20 such goals. Each one is different, but has evolved and been tested by the 'push and pull' of the three important issues surrounding each face. In addition, because each of the three people involved in developing one goal is also involved in developing another (the adjacent faces), each goal shares two issues with each of its three adjacent faces (see Figure S6.2b). No goal is developed in isolation from other goals. All are connected.

The result is the development of 20 interconnected, directional goals which are created to serve the '12 most important issues' or topics for the organization as identified by the 30 people. Since the 12 vertices correspond to these 12 topics, this becomes the richest intermingling that can take place among topics while also ensuring complete systemic equality. That is, each topic has an exactly equal opportunity to influence the entire system.

Similarly, this systemic equality is mirrored in the relationships and roles of the people involved, as the 30 participants all share the same number of interconnections to the whole. Please note that equality does not mean limiting the contribution of any role, person, or topic. It does mean providing equal opportunity for contribution to all.

The planning system that evolves exhibits the qualities of redundancy, reverberation, and robustness. Redundancy is a measure of how many links can be broken before the system will collapse; reverberation refers to the ability of information to move through the system, without the direct contact of all participants to each other and to all topics; robustness refers to the ability of the system to be sustained under pressure and react to change.

As the information in the system approaches maximum distribution throughout the system (as the eigenvalue of the Syntegrity Icosahedron approaches 1), each face of the Syntegrity Icosahedron can be thought of as a dynamic plane that reflects the interactions of its three surrounding vertices and their relationships to other parts and the Icosahedral whole. A face can therefore also be described as a ' systemically informed dynamic decision plane.'

SETTING GOALS

Establishing a goal involves a meeting between people representing each of the three struts surrounding a face. Generally, this involves a meeting of three people. Sufficient time needs to be allocated to ensure the members can reach a goal that meets the opportunity/constraints of the three topics.

The maximum number of people who can meet at one time is 24 , making 8 teams of 3 members each. (Since each person is a member of two face-groups, all of the face-meetings cannot take place at once. Only 8 of the 20 faces have struts that are not shared with adjacent faces, resulting in the maximum of 8 meetings with 24 people.)

There are many ways of scheduling team meetings to ensure the most effective use of time while ensuring a continuation of reverberation through the system. To reduce variety it makes sense to limit to three the number of active participants in the decision making process which converges on a specific goal. It also seems reasonable to encourage inactive participants to observe these meetings and so add to the reverberation.

FROM GOALS TO ACTIONS AND BEYOND

Once these 20 general goals have been established, they form the basis for setting more specific goals and objectives and for tactical planning. It could take any number of actual action items, or algorithms, to accomplish the goals and objectives.

Activities are in progress to develop further the theory and practice of the goal-setting process in a variety of contexts, and to explore the implications of the organizational scheduling system that evolves from using Team Syntegrity for strategic planning applications. Developments include computer software for conducting electronic Syntegrations and for scheduling member, team, and group activities and accountabilities.

It is known that the 20 faces and 12 vertices of an icosahedron correspond to the 20 vertices and 12 faces of an embedded dodecahedron. Inside the embedded dodecahedron is another icosahedron whose 20 faces correspond to the dodecahedron's 20 vertices and whose 12 vertices correspond to the dodecahedron's 12 faces. Inside this icosahedron lies another dodecahedron, and so on indefinitely. While the faces and vertices of the icosahedron and the dodecahedron change into each other, the number of struts in each remains the same at 30. By looking through any one face of the outer icosahedron along a straight line to the centre, one is provided a view of triangles contracting into points and expanding into smaller triangles lined up one inside the other in an endless series. Imagining all 20 faces simultaneously going through this transformation reveals a perfectly symmetrical reduction of regular polyhedral space within regular polyhedral space with each level encapsulating the next through regular structural relationships. There are endless recursions of equilateral triangles and pentagons, held in equilibration by an underlying regularity of form maintained by the constant number of struts. The pattern that arises from the relationship between 20 and 12 (Euler's Theorem: $V + F = E + 2$, explained in Chapter One) is that the 30 struts are held in a state of perpendicularity at each level of recursion. Each level has a fractal self-similarity of shape and structure surrounded and configured by the level before it and surrounding and configuring the level after it like a set of embedded Russian dolls. Unlike the dolls, however, as you plunge inwards to the point at the very centre, it recedes to infinity.

This infinitely recursive correspondence of vertices, faces, and edges has far-reaching implications for continuous organizational planning and scheduling and for ensuring ongoing alignment of actions, goals and strategy.

Teams can be organized easily around respective activities, and scheduling becomes much simpler to manage. It is possible to track every activity defined within the system by team and team member, through multiple recursions, and *the entire system is based on 12 colours.*

An organization adopting the Syntegrity architecture will organize 12 teams according to the 12 colours. The 30 multiple roles which correspond to the 30 struts and the 20 general goals which correspond to the 20 faces will create a sustainable connection between the 12 issues or critical success factors and people or roles. The result is that each critical success factor, goal, and activity generated by this planning system can be easily scheduled, carried out, and accounted for by interconnected work teams. Because of the interconnections and interdependences that arise from the Syntegrity structure, changes to any factor, goal, or activity that can affect other parts of the system, initiated and/or managed at the 'local' level by the accountable team can also trigger an assessment of the implications of this change to the overall system and other affected teams.

To use an analogy, imagine a lake where the water has been separated into many pools through the use of breakwater barriers. Although water is able to flow freely from pool to pool through passageways created in these barriers, large waves cannot pass through without breaking up. This maintains an overall state of relative calm in the lake. Even when there is a lot of wave activity in individual pools, waves cannot come together and grow into a tidal wave large enough to swamp the entire system.

CONNECTING MICRO TO META: FROM PLANNING AND SCHEDULING TO STRUCTURAL DESIGN

This planning system can be implemented in parallel, *without requiring changes to existing organizational structures.* Functional reporting, span of control, and other aspects of organizational structure do not have to change to accommodate this form of organizational planning and organizational scheduling.

However, as organizations try to move away from a structure of hierarchical bureaucracy, which remains the dominant organizational form today, they will continue to move towards more participative structures. To do so, they will have to solve the problem of proliferating complexity resulting from reduced centralization. Rather than the two-dimensional matrix-type organizational structure, which is proving to be too complex for large organizations, a three-dimensional system that closes in on itself offers the requisite interconnections without unmanageable complexity. The Syntegrity Icosahedron may well provide a viable architecture for the design of such three-dimensional organizational systems.

The discovery of C_{60}, the new form of carbon known as buckminsterfullerene, is expected to revolutionize materials science and has engendered great excitement in the fields of chemistry, physics, and mathematics (discussed earlier in the book).

This soccer ball-shaped molecule has elaborate symmetries based on the icosahedron. The connection of this shape to so many diverse fields and applications, and our own present understanding of Team Syntegrity makes it tempting to suggest that the icosahedron offers a new model for the structural design of organizations.

Only time will tell if Team Syntegrity proves to be the viable model for the new 'molecular organization.'

SUMMARY

Moving from the 12 FSIs which define the organization's heuristic space for planning to setting the 20 organizational goals relating to the 12 FSIs establishes a planning and scheduling system which has the qualities of redundancy, reverberation, and robustness.

The people involved in establishing each goal understand how the three topics evolved into the FSIs which inform and constrain the development of their goal. The same people have also been directly involved in crafting three other FSIs, and indirectly involved in evolving all 12 FSIs.

The reverberation set in motion during the initial Syntegration continues into the goal-setting process. The system has sufficient redundancy and robustness to survive attrition and sufficient reverberation to accept and inform new members.

The control inherent in the creation of the heuristic space for planning, and in the development of interconnected, informed goals, makes empowerment at the level of tactical planning and operations possible.

Without control, empowerment will continue to be unacceptable to those who are held accountable for the results of others, namely, managers at all levels of the organization. Without empowerment, Ashby's Law of Requisite Variety will continue to ensure that we fail to convert 'people power' into organizational accomplishment.

Although Team Syntegrity can be applied in the context of any existing organizational structure, it is itself a model for the evolution of a new kind of organizational structure. Just as the carbon molecules synthesized in poly-hedral form are affectionately called 'Buckyballs,' perhaps the molecular organization of the future synthesized in Syntegrity Icosahedral form will be affectionately called 'Staffyspheres.' Then, as Beer has often said, it will be truly 'easier done than said.'

THE VERY MODEL OF A MODERN SYSTEM-GENERAL
How the viable system model actually works
Allenna Leonard

We have been looking at freer, non-hierarchial patterns of planning and discovery. But other structures are also necessary to the running of things, and they do not necessarily import authoritarian styles. One of these is Stafford Beer's Viable System Model. It, like the syntegrity process, is pre-eminently a means of handling variety. The VSM is a recursive model, that is, each successive unit is nested within the next larger one. Each model may proceed up and down organizational levels from the small group to any one of the several structures in which it is embedded. This is a logical structure which need not be attached to any traditional structure of management, or be limited to the description of legal entities. Indeed, because of the way the model seeks the optimum balance between the vertical and horizontal control of variety, its users tend toward prescribing the largest amount of autonomy consistent with maintaining the integrity of the whole.

Still, the Viable System Model does *look* hierarchical in the way the bare bones picture sits on the two-dimensional page. In order to get around this impression, I have sometimes drawn the model sideways, with the environment, including customers and suppliers, in the dominant position. This is, of course, where they should be if the organization is seriously committed to continuous improvement, customized production, self-directed work units, or any of the other systemic modes of activity. But, as its shape makes it difficult to depict within the proportions of the standard page or flip chart, vertical versions of the model are easier to handle.

To indicate the use of the model outside traditional structures, let us begin the description of the VSM with an emerging non-hierarchical group. It is a prerequisite of a Viable System Model that there be a viable system to be modelled—that is, a system with an identity and a purpose which is, in principle, capable of surviving its appointed time, whether definite or indefinite. The initiators may have either a short- or a long-term purpose in mind; the identity may be more or less fluid; but an identifiable purpose must be there if the organization is to have any possibility of coherent action.

LET'S HAVE A PARTY!

In many North American communities there is a tradition of holding 'street fairs' or 'block parties' in the summer. This is a good example of a self-organizing group which operates within a short time frame and a loose structure. If it is to be a 'viable system,' and succeed in holding its party, this small group will have to fulfil the same general criteria as will a large organization, albeit much more modestly.

Our group's identity and purpose emerge when various individuals get together, decide to have a party and explore the sort of party they want to have. Do they want to break even or raise some money for charity? Focus on the arts or activities for small children? Run for an afternoon or all weekend? Try out offerings for the County Fair at the end of the summer? These are the sorts of decision the organizers will make based on their preferences, their resources, and the characteristics of their community. Plans will be made for a theme, publicity, some music or other entertainment, games, food and drink, and an opportunity for local associations and craft people to display and sell their goods.

So far so good. The group can sit around someone's kitchen table, decide what needs to be done and parcel out the jobs. They set a date and work backward from there to schedule the required notifications and activities. They decide how much space is needed for refreshments, merchandise stalls, and information tables and allocate sites for them. Somebody arranges to see about a permit to close the street, necessary insurance, rules or licenses for serving refreshments, power for lights and sound systems, publicity, and the other details. When the event occurs, each member of the group has a clear picture of what everyone is supposed to be doing and is able to substitute when required. Maybe one or more of the organizers will, in the event, assume another role and play in a band or sell crafts. After it is over, the stalls are taken down, the litter swept up, and the street returns to normal until the next summer.

The point of this example is that our group of neighbours planned a fairly high variety project and the several sorts of management support required fell into place. First, each particular activity needed to be identified and arranged. Next, these activities had to be made to work smoothly together. Then some decisions were taken about how to operate the whole as a single structure. The project needed a purpose or identity (in this case a summer celebration on Maple Street), a planning phase, and finally a standard by which it could be judged to have succeeded or not. It began slowly, became intense during the event and clean up, and then proceeded to the wind down: payments, returns of rented equipment, thank-you notes, etc.

These are all the management tasks that appear in the Viable System Model in Systems Five (identity and purpose), Four (planning), Three (overall management of the event), Two (smoothing out glitches and oscillations), and One (managing the actual operations themselves). Now, around the kitchen table, there were no bosses and no employees. Everyone knew each other and each other's circumstances and constraints. Someone is home with children during the day: there's the contact phone. Someone has a van: there's the transport. Someone has a computer with a graphics package and will print the notices. Someone else works at City Hall and will see to the permits ... Some individuals might have more say than others but the differential would, for the most part, be based on either having more time available or the experience of having done it before.

The appropriate division of labour fell out of the individuals' shared knowledge of one another. In a small group, this sort of arrangement certainly works. When the group outgrows the kitchen table, however, it works less and less well until the efforts needed to communicate overwhelm the activities and everyone becomes frustrated by the proliferating variety. This is when many growing community organizations begin to think they need officers and committees even when their values and the commitment of their volunteers are strongly linked to democracy and full participation.

The amount of attention which must be paid to organizational structure increases with increasing size and scope of the organization just as the importance of the physical structure of a building increases with increasing size and weight of the loads it must support. Organizations typically add managers and bureaucrats to maintain a complex structure but their efficiency and effectiveness are often more comparable to those of the flying buttress than to reinforced concrete—to say nothing of the geodesic dome.

Also, organizations are dynamic. To survive, they have capabilities to perceive their circumstances accurately, to respond, and to adapt to change. Even the street fair, with a lead time of 2–3 months, may have to adapt to unexpected weather or other local events. Most organizations, even the smallest, are embedded in larger or more comprehensive ones. The street fair is embedded in its community and its traditions. It may also be an organization that will send crafts and entertainment to a larger event, say the County or State Fair.

THE VSM AND THE LARGE ORGANIZATION

Few organizations are as simple and straightforward as a neighborhood committee. Most are faced with an overabundance of variety, and need to break down the complexity to manageable proportions. The VSM is a very helpful tool in this task. It especially helps to distinguish between external and internal customers, to sort out the internal services, and to indicate where inconsistencies are buried inside overlapping management domains.

SYSTEM ONE

One way to begin is to look at the exchange between the organization and its external customers. What does this organization make or do? It is these activities that all the management functions exist to support. They are the reason it exists; not the staff functions, however prestigious they may be. The next step is to look at how these activities or operations can best be grouped together and how one should be distinguished from another. There are probably 100 different distinctions that would make sense for the full population of organizations and probably a dozen or so that would be worth looking at for any single one. Take the journalist's basic set of questions: who? what? when? where? how much? The answer to 'who?' might be the customer, the user, the group or sort of employees, the distributor, the licensor, the supplier, the creditor, the regulator ... When doing a VSM to diagnose or design an organization, only a handful of the possible distinctions will be relevant to any particular observer. Some reflection is required to make a selection and to see what relationships will be most fruitful to examine. One of the most instructive exercises may be to try out several and see what priorities or connections are implied by each. It is also helpful to examine the communications between the organization and its environment to see if they are consistent and equal to the situation, e.g. is the variety on one side matched by variety on the other?

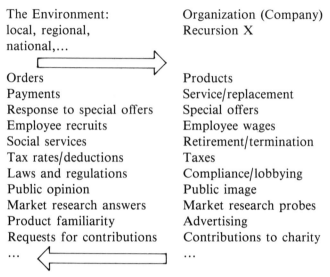

The Environment: Organization (Company)
local, regional,   Recursion X
national,...

Orders   Products
Payments   Service/replacement
Response to special offers   Special offers
Employee recruits   Employee wages
Social services   Retirement/termination
Tax rates/deductions   Taxes
Laws and regulations   Compliance/lobbying
Public opinion   Public image
Market research answers   Market research probes
Product familiarity   Advertising
Requests for contributions   Contributions to charity
  ...   ...

The best way to begin exploring their relationships is to experiment with different layouts by looking at what goods, services, resources, or information flow among them, then to look at their connections to their environments. How do they define their relevant environments? How do they send goods, services, and information to them? How are their messages amplified so that they reach their intended targets? How do they collect resources and information back from their environments? How do they filter the information they want from all that is available? If the pattern begins to change, how soon is it apparent?

Finally, look at how each operation is managed to produce the goods, the services, and the information. This management cannot know every detail of the operation and its environmental links even if the managers and the producers are the same individuals. If an operation is efficient, more time and energy must go into production than into management. Only a limited amount of the information about the operation can be selected by the management for its attention and only a limited amount can be communicated by management to the operations. The best balance will change with time and circumstance. These relationships among operations and with their management and their environments define the System One units.

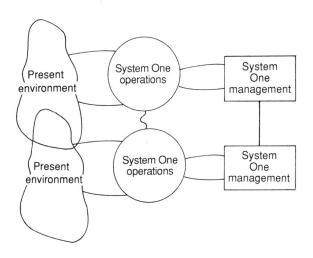

If there were nothing to be gained or lost from the fact that the System One units are part of a larger whole, there would be no need for additional management functions. But they are part of a whole and that means a different set of criteria and specialized functions apply. They are the Systems Two through Five.

SYSTEM TWO

System Two is a specialized management function that keeps the System One activities in balance. It damps the oscillations that inevitably occur when two or more operations routinely call on common resources or services. System Two may be manifested in schedules for maintenance, order processing, personnel forms, accounting procedures, safety regulations, and the like which, are not executive decisions but practices agreed to be necessary to operate smoothly and avoid glitches.

SYSTEM THREE

System Three takes up the management work when there are executive decisions to be made from the broader perspective of the whole. Whenever there
is a group of activities to be managed rather than only one, the fact of their
being a whole changes the equations. What would be the best option for a
single part may be less effective or even detrimental when the part is one of
several. It is the job of System Three to provide coherence and to look for
synergy. It cannot substitute effectively for System One management and delve
into the details because it does not have as much information about any one
operation as its own management. Specific functions such as the legal
department, management accounting, union negotiations, and production and
sales management are part of System Three.

System Three speaks to the System One activities with two voices. By far the
dominant mode should be the two-way communications of resource
bargaining, suggestion and counter suggestion, and coaching. There is also a
command mode used to communicate decisions taken on behalf of the whole
and to convey information, such as legal and contract compliance requirements, which are not subject to alteration.

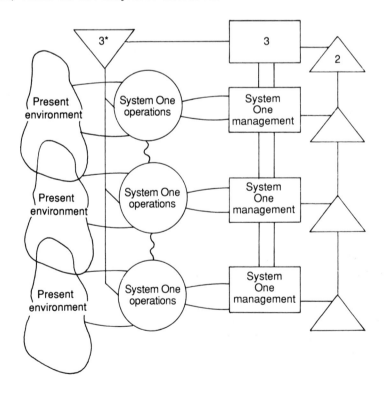

There is one exception to System Three's exclusion from the details of running the System One activities. That is when concentration on a specific aspect of the System One activities is required in order to monitor or assess it on behalf of the whole. This is called a System Three Star. It communicates on an audit channel. The yearly or close-out financial report will surely be one of its functions, but so will the special quality inspection and the review of vehicle leasing arrangements. The key is that these queries are discrete and sporadic, undertaken to make specific decisions, not fishing expeditions.

Systems Two and Three support the enterprise in its day-to-day, internal workings. When an organization is part of a mature and stable sector, these account for most of the management support required. When such conditions do not apply—and they apply to fewer and fewer organizations these days—a substantial focus on the future is necessary to remain a viable system.

SYSTEM FOUR

The future is the focus of the work undertaken by System Four. It maintains probes into the environment to watch for trends and events that will have an impact on the organization. Some of these make predictions that are highly speculative; others such as those looking at demographic change or implications of new technology may issue their predictions with a probability approaching certainty. Market research, R&D, and simulations are examples. System Four also undertakes activities that will affect the relationship between the organization and its environment in the future, such as planning, public relations, lobbying, training, and recruitment. Systems Three and Four must have many avenues of communication with one another to make sure that they are in synch.

SYSTEM FIVE

Closure is provided by the functions of System Five: maintaining the identity of the whole and monitoring the balance between present and future driven efforts. System Five, which is assuredly not limited to upper echelon staff, is where the 'corporate culture' and its vision and values are embodied. It is a System Five role to be reflective and to keep checking out the answers to perennial questions such as, 'what counts as success?'

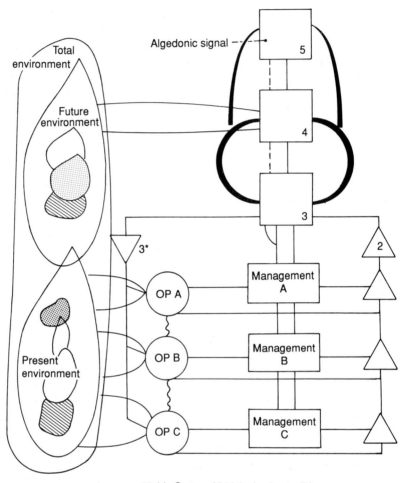

Viable System Model: simple rendition

When the five systems of the Viable System Model have been described for an organization, it is worthwhile to look also to the next level in which the organization is embedded and to the Three, Four, and Five subsystems embedded in each of their System One units. A full-scale rendering of a VSM for a large company, non-profit organization, or government jurisdiction could yield hundreds of particular models. It is a daunting task, but perhaps less so than trying to sort out the complexities of entities employing tens if not hundreds of thousands of people to assure that their values and procedures are aligned.

The Viable System Model brings into focus the functions and communications channels which are ubiquitous in living organizations. Beer developed them from the commonalities he observed between the human nervous system and the organizations people formed to make products and perform services, and checked them against many other kinds of viable system. Others have extended the range of the model into fields as varied as botany and beekeeping and used it to analyse the relationships found in language and families. So, the VSM is not an 'exclusive' model with respect to the entities to which it can be applied. Whatever survives over its appointed term is, after all, a viable system. Nor is it exclusive with respect to coexistence with quantitative measures or with other systemic management methods. In fact, it functions very well as an umbrella model in which to co-ordinate efforts prompted by other systems-based models, such as Activity Based Costing, Systems Dynamics simulations or Total Quality Management. Any organization operating in a complex environment needs to be able to utilize different viewpoints, although they may come with varying degrees of precision and specification, to allow a good look at the big picture. And that is a very important picture to see.

The VSM can be used in connection with syntegrations in two basic ways.

In the first instance, the VSM may provide the overall organizational context within which a syntegration is conceived. Chapter Nine has already discussed the most likely usage—using a syntegration to balance the Three–Four homeostat. But it is as well to remember that the VSM consists of a myriad of interlocking homeostats, and the syntegration protocol could in principle be used to help integrate any subset of antithetic protagonists. These applications, it is noted, derive from the interior organizational dynamics of the VSM. And even when details are not to be elaborated, the common vocabulary of VSM provides ways of discussing organizational affairs which avoid many of the pitfalls of turf conflicts. In any actual syntegration, these common concepts may save valuable time for a fuller discussion of the opening question.

In the second instance, the organization should be thought of as drawing itself together into its System Four focus. In that capacity, it ventures out into the environment to recruit a diverse group of stakeholders. These then form an Infoset competent to engage in a syntegration on a question important to the organization's future. Such a syntegration should be interdisciplinary; educators, social anthropologists, lawyers, engineers, customers, even, perhaps, competitors, might be included. Moving back within the organization, syntegrations could be held with members of System Three, Four, or Five at different levels of recursion to achieve maximum understanding and alignment around organizational goals. Now we are back inside the organization, and dealing with a special case of the first instance applications. The new thinking might provoke a special challenge within System One, calling for a syntegration along the horizontal axis. Again, a Three-Star exploration could make use of syntegration to pursue a quality initiative or to take stock following a merger or divestiture.

Here is a final thought about syntegrations that involve the whole organization as conceived through the VSM. They might be appropriate activities to mark beginnings, midpoints, and ends of temporary organizations such as government task forces, or, indeed, whole administrations.

REFERENCES

Arbib, Michael (1989), A note on 'A heterarchy of values determined by the topology of nervous nets,' in *Collected Works of Warren S. McCulloch*, Intersystems Publications, Salinas, CA, Vol. 2, p. 473.

Ashby, W. Ross (1952), *Design for a Brain*, Chapman and Hall, London.

Bandler, Richard, and Grinder, John (1979), *Frogs into Princes*, Real People Press, Moab, UT, p. 160.

Bavelas, Alex (1952), Communication patterns in problem groups, in *Cybernetics: Transactions of the Eighth Conference, 1951*, Josiah Macy Jr Foundation, New York.

Beer, Stafford (1956), The impact of cybernetics on the concept of industrial organization, in *Proceedings of the First International Congress on Cybernetics, Namur, 1956*.

Beer, Stafford (1959), *Cybernetics and Management*, English Universities Press, London.

Beer, Stafford (1962), Toward the cybernetic factory, in *Principles of Self-Organization*, Eds von Foerster and Zopf, Pergamon Press, New York; see also Beer (1994).

Beer, Stafford (1969), The aborting corporate plan, in *Perspectives of Planning*, OECD, Paris.

Beer, Stafford (1975), Homo Gubernator, Address to the Fifth Annual Conference of the Pierre Teilhard de Chardin Association (1970), in Beer, Stafford, *Platform for Change*, Wiley, Chichester, New York, pp. 20–37.

Beer, Stafford (1972), *Brain of the Firm*, 1st edn, Allen Lane, The Penguin Press, London.

Beer, Stafford (1973), The surrogate world we manage, Presidential Address to the Society for General Systems Research (1971), *Behavioral Science*, **17**, No. 3.

Beer, Stafford (1975), *Platform for Change*, Wiley, Chichester, New York.

Beer, Stafford (1979), *The Heart of Enterprise*, Wiley, Chichester, New York.

Beer, Stafford (1980), Conferences: a call to experiment, *Transnational Associations*, **32**, 94–97.

Beer, Stafford (1981), *Brain of the Firm*, 2nd edn (with five new chapters), Wiley, Chichester, New York.

Beer, Stafford (1985), *Diagnosing the System for Organizations*, Wiley, Chichester, New York.

Beer, Stafford (1989), The viable system model: its provenance, development, methodology and pathology, in *The Viable System Model*, Eds Espejo and Harnden, Wiley, Chichester, New York.

Beer, Stafford (1990), On suicidal rabbits: a relativity of systems, *Systems Practice*, **3**, No. 2, 115–124.

Beer, Stafford (1993), Requiem, *Kybernetes*, **22**(6), 105–108.

Beer, Stafford (1994), in *How Many Grapes Went into the Wine: Stafford Beer On The Art and Science of Holistic Management*, Eds Harnden and Leonard, Wiley, Chichester, New York.

Benjafield, J., and Adams-Webber, J. (1979), The golden section hypothesis, *Journal of Psychology*, **70**, 517–518.

Beesing, Maria, *et al.* (1984), *The Enneagram*, Dimension Books, New Jersey.

Bennett, John G. (1983), *Enneagram Studies*, Samuel Weisner, Maine.

Boulding, Kenneth (1956), *The Image*. University of Michigan Press, Ann Arbor (cited in Miller, George A., Galanter, Eugene, and Pribram, Karl H., *Plans and the Structure of Behavior*, Holt, Rinehart and Winston, 1960, pp. 1–4).

Burke, Kenneth, *A Grammar of Motives*, University of California Press, Berkeley, CA, pp. xv, 336–337.

Campbell, Hugh G. (1968), *Matrices with Applications*, Meredith, New York.

Canetti, Elias (1962), *Crowds and Power*, Victor Gollancz, London.

Cannon, Walter (1929), Organization for physiological homeostasis, *Physiological Review*, **9**, 399–431.

Cleveland, Harlan (1991), Message from the president, in *World Academy of Arts and Sciences News*, July.

Critchlow, Keith (1979), *Time Stands Still*, Gordon Fraser, London.

Davis, Garry (1992), *Passport to Freedom*, Seven Locks Press, Washington, DC.

Devlin, Keith (1991), *Logic and Information*, Cambridge University Press, Cambridge.

Edmondson, Amy C. (1987), *A Fuller Explanation: The Synergetic Geometry of R. Buckminster Fuller*, Brickhauser, Boston.

Espejo, Raul, and Harnden, Roger, Eds (1989), *The Viable System Model*, Wiley, Chichester, New York.

Foerster, Heinz von (1977), The curious behavior of complex systems: Lessons from biology, in *Futures Research*.

Fuller, R. Buckminster (1979), *Synergetics: the Geometry of Thinking*, Macmillan, New York.

Ichazo, Oscar (1976), *The Human Process of Enlightenment and Freedom*, Arica Institute, New York.

Jacobs, Jane (1984), *Cities and the Wealth of Nations*, Random House, New York.

Jalali, Assad (1993), Association schemes with opposition, in *European Business Management School Technical Report*, University of Wales, Swansea.

Judge, Anthony J. N. (1980), Metaconferencing, *Transnational Associations*, **32**, No. 10, 411–420.

Jung, Carl (1967), *Septum Sermones ad Mortuos*, Steward and Watkins, London.

Kanigel, Robert (1991), *The Man Who Knew Infinity*, Washington Square Press, New York.

Kelly, George (1955), *A Theory of Personal Constructs*, Norton, New York.

Klopf, A. Harry (1982), *The Hedonistic Neuron: A Theory of Memory, Learning, and Intelligence*, Hemisphere Publishing, New York.

Laughlin, Charles D., Jr, *et al.* (1990), *Brain, Symbol and Experience: Toward a Neurophenomenology of Human Consciousness*, Shambala New Science Library, Boston.

Leonard, Allenna (1987), *Broadcast Regulation: A Comparison of Perspectives*, PhD Thesis, University of Maryland, College Park, Ann Arbor, University Microfilms.

Letvin, J.Y., *et al.* (1959), What the frog's eye tells the frog's brain, *Proceedings of the IRE*, **47**, No. 11; see also McCulloch (1989), *Collected Works*, Vol. 4, pp. 1161–1172.

Maturana, Humberto R., and Varela, Francisco J. (1980), *Autopoiesis and Cognition*, Riedel, Dortrecht.

Maturana, Humberto R., and Varela, Francisco J. (1987), *The Tree of Knowledge*, Shambala, Boston.

McCulloch, Warren S., and Pitts, Walter (1943), A logical calculus of the ideas immanent in nervous activity, *Bulletin of Mathematical Biophysics*, **5**; see also McCulloch (1989), *Collected Works*, Vol. 1, pp. 343–361.

McCulloch, Warren S. (1945) A heterarchy of values determined by the topology of nervous nets. *Bulletin of Mathematical Biophysics* 7.

McCulloch, Warren S. (1960), What is a number that a man may know it, and a man, that he may know a number?, Alfred Korzybski Memorial Lecture, *General Semantics Bulletin*, Nos 26–27, 7–18; see also McCulloch (1989), *Collected Works*, Vol. 4, pp. 1225–1242.

McCulloch, Warren S. (1974), Recollections of the many sources of cybernetics, *ASC Forum*, Vol. VI, No. 2, pp. 5–16; see also McCulloch (1989), *Collected Works*, Vol. 1, pp. 21–49.

McCulloch, Warren S. (1989), *Collected Works*, Four Volumes, Ed Rook McCulloch, Intersystems Publications, Salinas, CA.

McGinn, Colin (1991), *The Problem of Consciousness*, Blackwell, Oxford.

Merril, Judith (1969), *Daughters of the Earth*, Doubleday, New York.

Miller, George A. (1967), The magical number seven, plus or minus two: some limits on our capacity for processing information, in *The Psychology of Communication*, Basic Books, New York.

Nagel, Ernst, and Newman, James R. (1958), *Goedel's Proof*, New York University Press, New York.

Ouspensky, P. D. (1949), *In Search of the Miraculous*, Harcourt Brace Jovanovitch, Florida.

Penrose, Roger (1989), *The Emperor's New Mind*, Viking, New York.

Schecter, David (1993), Beer's 'Team Tensegrity' and the challenge of democractic management, in *Organizational Fitness*, Campus Verlag, Frankfurt, New York.

Schwaninger, Markus and Espejo, Raúl (1993), *Organizational Fitness*, Campus Verlag, Frankfurt, New York.

Siegel, Lynn (1986), *The Dream of Reality: Heinz von Foerster's Constructivism*, Norton, New York.

Teilhard de Chardin, Pierre (1959), *The Phenomenon of Man*, Harper & Row, New York.

US Congress, House Subcommittee on Inter-American Affairs of the Committee on Foreign Affairs (1975), *United States and Chile During the Allende Years*, US Government Printing Office, Washington, DC.

Varela, Francisco, *et al.* (1991), *The Embodied Mind*, MIT Press, Cambridge, MA.

Vickers, Geoffrey (1970), *Freedom in a Rocking Boat*, Allen Lane, The Penguin Press, London.

Wiener, Norbert (1948), *Cybernetics*, Wiley, New York.

Wiener, Norbert (1954), *The Human Use of Human Beings*, Doubleday, New York.

Winograd, Terry, and Flores, Fernando (1986), *Understanding Computers and Cognition*, Ablex Publishing, Norwood, NJ.

Young, Arthur (1991), The theory of process, excerpted from an article by Gail Bernice Holland in *The Quest*, Autumn.

Zohar, Danah (1991), *The Quantum Self*, Flamingo Harper-Collins, London.

INDEX

Index compiled by Annette Musker